D1595836

AMERICAN FATHERHOOD

American Fatherhood

A History

Jürgen Martschukat

Translated from the German by Petra Goedde

NEW YORK UNIVERSITY PRESS

New York

NEW YORK UNIVERSITY PRESS
New York
www.nyupress.org

Originally published as "*Die Ordnung des Sozialen: Väter und Familien in der ameri-kanischen Geschichte seit 1770*" by Campus Verlag, 2013. The translation of this work was funded by Geisteswissenschaften International—Translation Funding for Humanities and Social Sciences from Germany, a joint initiative of the Fritz Thyssen Foundation, the German Federal Foreign Office, the collecting society VG WORT and the Börsenverein des Deutschen Buchhandels (German Publisher & Booksellers Association).

References to Internet websites (URLs) were accurate at the time of writing. Neither the author nor New York University Press is responsible for URLs that may have expired or changed since the manuscript was prepared.

Library of Congress Cataloging-in-Publication Data
Names: Martschukat, Jürgen, author. | Goedde, Petra, 1964–   translator.
Title: American fatherhood: a history / Jürgen Martschukat; translated from the German by Petra Goedde.
Other titles: Ordnung des Sozialen. English
Description: New York : New York University Press, 2019. |
Includes bibliographical references and index.
Identifiers: LCCN 2019012349 | ISBN 9781479892273 (cl: alk. paper)
Subjects: LCSH: Fathers—United States—History. | Families—United States—History. | Fathers—United States—Psychology. | Work and family—United States—Psychology. | Racism—United States—Psychological aspects.
Classification: LCC HQ1090.3 .M3713 2019 | DDC 306.874/2—dc23
LC record available at https://lccn.loc.gov/2019012349

New York University Press books are printed on acid-free paper, and their binding materials are chosen for strength and durability. We strive to use environmentally responsible suppliers and materials to the greatest extent possible in publishing our books.

Manufactured in the United States of America

10 9 8 7 6 5 4 3 2 1

Also available as an ebook

I dedicate this book to Algis, Carolina, and Paula

CONTENTS

Introduction

This book explores the significance of families in American history, with an emphasis on the meanings, practices, and politics of fatherhood. It moves chronologically through American history from the revolution to the present and shows how American society has been organized through families. In pursuing this aim, I do not presuppose a specific family type, such as the nuclear family, as the "natural" foundation of American society. Instead I ask how the concept of the nuclear family was endowed with such overwhelming importance, even though living arrangements and family formations have been highly diverse throughout American history. Rather than portraying a certain type of family as "natural" and as a foundation of American society, I explore the richness of family formations and understand society as a multifarious and constantly changing assemblage with families as nodal points, connecting individuals in myriad ways into a malleable social order. The term "social order" is not meant to invoke order as opposed to chaos, but refers to a set of relations, institutions, values, and practices that maintain and enforce certain patterns of relating and behaving.[1]

Families are neither homogenous nor unvarying, and neither is society. Sociologist Bruno Latour has described society—or, as Latour says, "the social"—as a trail of historically variable "associations between heterogeneous elements."[2] These elements merge into a social order through the family as a medium that comes in all kinds of forms and shapes. Thus, the family is of crucial importance for the government of societies. The government of liberal societies in particular, as I detail in the first chapter, is not limited to making and implementing political decisions but involves the management of people and things by all kinds of means and on multiple levels in order to lead them to a suitable end. Thus, good government requires the creation of opportunities and shaping the patterns of thought and behavior that are deemed beneficial for a society and its wealth and productivity. Families, as the following chapters argue, are most important for liberal government because they interconnect individuals and society. Families are like switchboards for who participates in what ways in the social arena, for who occupies which position, for who can claim which rights for themselves, for who gains access to what resources and fulfills which tasks. These positions, rights, claims, and obligations are negotiated *in* families as well as *through* families. The position taken by individuals *in* families and *of* diverse family formations in society shapes their relationship to themselves and to others; it regulates their participation in society and history.[3]

In recent decades, historians have shown how our chances for participation in society depend on the definition of our sex, the color of our skin, where we come from, how old we are, what we believe in, how much money we make, or whom we desire and are in love with. The power of categories such as gender, race, ethnicity, age, religion, wealth and class, and sexual orientation evolves in the lives of individuals through family relations—not exclusively, but considerably. It is within and through family relations that the power of categories unfolds in the shaping of one's identity, of one's relations with others, and of one's place in society.[4]

This is a book about the diversity of the family in American history and how, at the same time, a certain kind of family—the nuclear family—operated as a powerful regulatory ideal. Since the late eighteenth century, the nuclear family of children and parents with specific gender roles evolved into the centerpiece of American society (even though as a sociological concept the nuclear family was not invented before the mid-twentieth century).[5] This very specific type of family formation was long praised as the ideal and even the "natural" breeding ground for the creation of well-working citizens of a liberal society. The space and position people could claim in society and their access to its resources depended largely on how close their actual living arrangements matched the ideal of the nuclear family, and whether they were even deemed capable of living according to this ideal at all—for instance, depending on their race or sexual preference.

As a regulatory ideal, the family with a working father, a stay-at-home mother, and children has been remarkably solid over the past two centuries, and part of its power derived from the fact that it was long considered the one living arrangement that most closely matched human beings' "natural" inclinations. However, the invocation of the nuclear family as natural and deeply rooted in American history very much represents the invention of a tradition, and, as Stephanie Coontz has argued, those who actually lived in nuclear families were hardly ever in the majority.[6] The stubborn persistence of the nuclear family ideal is thus countered by the diversity of real life in the American past and present. People came together and separated again, sometimes forever, sometimes temporarily; they were single parents or widowed, sought communal living arrangements or other forms of social organization, lived with same-sex partners or stayed solo, to name just a few of many more options. How common certain living arrangements were very much depended on the specific period and configuration of American history, for instance if people were on the move or not, if they lived enslaved or in freedom, in war or in peace, and so on. Tensions between the imagined ideal of the nuclear family and the lived reality of family formations are at the center of my book. The characters I spotlight in the pages to follow are central figures in the dominant narrative of American history, yet few lived in a nuclear family constellation.

This is a broad subject that barely fits between the covers of a single book, so I have narrowed my focus to the father and explore fatherhood in its diverse forms, functions, and relations in the family, society, and history. In a book that explores how individuals, families, and society are intertwined, the father takes a special position. A father was expected to govern himself and his family, in the sense of to support, to provide for, and to conduct other family members. A father who lived up to these ideals and demands represented the ideal citizen of a well-working liberal republic. This ideal of the citizen-father responded to and at the same time generated expectations addressed to men and family formations; it shaped hegemonies and contributed to the marginalization of women and those men who were not willing or able to live up the ideal or who were not considered to be able to do so from the very beginning.

The following twelve chapters offer varieties and different forms of the "father": father figures, fictional fathers, political fathers, fathers as ideal types, as well as flesh-and-blood fathers. As fathers exist only in relation to others, I always portray them in their interactions with other men (fathers and non-fathers), women and children, people of different color and different faith, indigenous and immigrant, and many others. Some chapters are told through the eyes of non-fathers—a bachelor, daughters, mothers. I show how a particular type of father and a particular form of family reigned supreme in American history and society, while many different types of fathers and family formations existed. American society makes a multilayered dynamic space in which associations, hegemony, and marginalization are constantly called into question and reconfigured.[7]

The first chapter covers the American Revolution and the founding of the republic. It also develops the conceptual basis for the remainder of the book and thus is the only chapter that is not structured around a central character. Rather, by drawing on the political discourse of the revolution and Early Republic, it develops the principles of governing in a liberal republic and also exposes their imbalances. The second chapter approaches the nuclear family in the Early Republic through the countermodel of the religiously and sexually utopian Oneida Community. The third chapter looks at fatherhood from the perspective of an enslaved father, whose slave narrative portrays him as struggling to live up to the demands of nuclear family fatherhood. The fourth chapter covers westward expansion through the life of a girl. Motherless, she made the trek with her father, but spent large stretches of the journey separated from him. The fifth chapter also revolves around separation, that of a Confederate soldier from his wife and children during the Civil War. Chapters 6 and 7 lead us into urban America at the turn of the twentieth century. One deals with the bachelor as prototypical non-father, the YMCA, and the emerging sexual sciences, the other with immigrant families and the life of a young Jewish woman from Poland in New York City's Lower East Side. Chapter 8 explores how a certain vision of the Native American father became a model for white, middle-class, modern fathers in early twentieth-century America, who were considered as not living up to their paternal role. Chapter 9 covers the Great Depression and asks what happens to families and society when fathers fail as breadwinners. The tenth chapter analyzes how, after World War II, a fictional father from a novel and Hollywood movie, the "Man in the Gray Flannel Suit," managed to epitomize sociological and popular wartime discourses. The character both affirmed and challenged the dominant model of the nuclear family. Chapters 11 and 12 take the liberation movements as their point of departure and follow the recent debates about African American fatherhood and gay marriage. Chapter 11 takes the perspective of a hardworking but disillusioned African American father in the Watts neighborhood of Los Angeles in the 1970s, chapter 12 that of a lesbian couple in San Francisco in the twenty-first century.

My sources for this history include personal letters, autobiographies, and other writings, sociological and other studies, films and interviews, to profile a diverse group of individuals from the revolution to the twenty-first century, from New England to New York, the Midwest, California, and the Deep South. My hope in this book is to show, through close observation and synthetic overview, the multiplicity of fatherhood and its role in shaping American history and society.

1

Fathers and the New Republic, 1770–1840

We have been told that our Struggle has loosened the bands
of Government every where. That Children and Apprentices
were disobedient—that schools and Colleges were grown
turbulent—that Indians slighted their Guardians and Negroes grew insolent to their Masters.
—Letter from John to Abigail Adams, April 14, 1776

The American Revolution tested a central tenet of Enlightenment
thinking, namely that human beings were born free and should govern
themselves. However, creating a liberal society of free people required
more than "just" simply a new constitution and a new system of laws. It
required new forms of governing that led people to learn how to handle
their freedom and how to govern themselves. The physician, philosopher, and politician Benjamin Rush expressed this demand most directly
when he stressed that the political revolution also had to include "a revolution in our principles, opinions, and manners." Besides new political
institutions, the new republic needed new rules, conventions, and living
conditions, which animated people to lead a responsible, productive,
moderate, virtuous, "republican" life. Looking back on this period from
the vantage point of 1818, John Adams identified this transformation of
the American people—their principles, their sentiments and affections,
their political, social, moral, and religious characters, and their sense of
themselves—as the "real American revolution."[1]

With self-government being the new liberal paradigm, the ascribed
potential for self-government became a major force in establishing differences in society.[2] Liberal governing was said to work best when coercion was kept at a minimum and the governed had as little awareness as
possible of being governed. Ideally people would draw the "best" conclusions and come to the "best" decisions by themselves, based on their
civic competence and understanding. The physician, reformer, and au-

thor William Alcott perfectly summarized this concept and sentiment by speaking to husbands and fathers as supreme governors in particular and by advising them that "the art of bearing rule, in the family circle, if not elsewhere, is to govern as if we governed not."[3]

Thus, in order to comprehend the meaning and practice of government in liberalism, it does not suffice to examine the formal authority of the state and its instruments; rather, we need to replace "the history of domination with the historical analysis of procedures of governmentality," as claimed by Michel Foucault.[4] This means taking a closer look at the multiple levels and forms of governing, from the state and its administration to the level of the family and the individual and their interconnections. Therefore, "liberal" refers to more than a political system of representative government, constitution, and the division of power, meant to protect individual liberty. "Liberal" also means a social and political practice and reason that governs through freedom and by generating political subjects who are acknowledged as using their liberties in a particular, responsible manner. In this vein, historian Carroll Smith-Rosenberg has called for an analysis of the American Revolution and Early Republic that shifts the focus "from the writing of a new constitution to the *constitution* of new political subjects."[5]

Families became an important lever in this project because they were seen as the site where self-government was taught, and at the same time a person's living arrangement was taken as reflecting a person's ability for self-government. The family became the fulcrum of the practices and rationalities of liberal governing, and its ideal shape seemed the two-generation family with parents and children. In this configuration of individuals, family, and society, "the father" was considered as of crucial importance because he was seen as the person most able to govern himself and others and to even serve as the best example of self-government. Therefore, a history of families and fatherhood is always a political history, not necessarily of institutional politics, but of how society is organized and governed through the family, how this connects to the inclusion and exclusion of people, how social, economic, and other differentiations gain shape through family norms, practices, and related institutions.[6]

Governing through the Family

The letters of Abigail and John Adams in late March and April 1776 indicate that the Founding Fathers considered the break with colonial rule and the capacity for self-government a male domain. In what is perhaps the best known passage in Abigail's letters, she tested her husband's commitment to freedom by admonishing him to "remember the ladies" and to not forget that men were "naturally tyrannical." Therefore, Abigail maintained, the new constitution needed to include constraints on men's exercise of power. In his answer John ridiculed his wife's claim, and their exchange of letters signals the ensuing conflict over active participation in the new liberal order. It also shows his understanding of political freedom and self-determination as predominantly male.[7]

Revolutionaries likened their struggle for independence to the transition from boy to man, which served to present their emancipation from the patriarchal sovereignty of the British Crown as self-evident and as male. According to historian Jay Fliegelman, this was the core motive of the revolution: "We look to manhood—our muscles swell out with youthful vigour" and "the day of independent manhood is at hand."[8] Thomas Paine, one of the leading revolutionary thinkers, proposed to answer the doubtful question of whether independence was really in the interest of the American people with its obverse: "Is it in the interest of a man to be a boy all his life?"[9]

The revolution was presented as a fight against patriarchal tyranny as well as a male coming of age. In late eighteenth-century America, despotic fathers were seen as a legitimate cause for rebellion for a young nation and young men alike. Concepts of fatherhood and parental government had for some time been undergoing a transformation. Puritan despots, who demanded complete submission and saw themselves as being endowed with authority and sovereignty directly from God, were no longer considered good fathers. Rather, good fathers were exemplary, leading a model life, acting prudently and responsibly, working on self-improvement and fulfilling their duties toward themselves and others.[10] This shift from patriarchal autocrat to model leader of the family over the course of the eighteenth century interacted with the shaping of affective individualism and the consolidation of a colonial society that ran their businesses increasingly independent from the Crown.[11] Thus, as submission to parental authority became less self-evident, so did submission to the British Crown, and they both overlapped in revolutionary America. Americans looked on King George III as a despotic and historically anachronistic father figure who tried to reassert his authority over his unruly offspring in the aftermath of the French and Indian War by taking away liberties they had come to enjoy. Time had run out on this patriarchal model of governing.

Given this rhetoric and historic change, at first glance, it seems rather confusing that revolutionary leaders themselves would turn to paternal metaphors when referring to their leadership role, such as "fathers of the republic" or "Founding Fathers." However, in contrast to the British king, they were careful to liken their type of government to that of a good republican father who had the privilege of taking the lead in family and society because of his own ability and competence. To be sure, this does not mean that good leadership was insignificant for puritan patriarchy, and neither that old patriarchal structures did completely disappear. Their traces persist today.

The two competing models of fatherhood played prominent roles in the political discourse of the revolutionary era. For instance, when in 1787 the Pennsylvania delegates were asked to ratify the new constitution, they worried that the new American president could govern in a patriarchal and despotic manner. James Wilson, who represented Pennsylvania at the Constitutional Convention and would later become one of the first Supreme Court justices of the United States, eased his fellow citizens' fears by emphasizing that the future president would act not as a despot but as a caring and responsible father figure, which embodied autonomy and political rationality, core concepts of the revolution and the new American republic.[12] Freedom and independence would no longer be constrained by sovereign patriarchal power but be fostered and stabilized by paternal leadership and government. Fathers thus again assumed a hegemonic position in society and politics, but this time built on different expectations.

Central to this new notion of government, and the relation between individuals, family, and society, was the concept of the contract. Relationships between governors and the governed, between parents and children, between husbands and wives came to rest less on the principle of authoritarian rule but more on the foundation of reciprocal contracts.[13] This was true not only for the understanding of the republican body politic. Expositions on republican marriages emulated the theory of the social contract, claiming that through marriage women voluntarily transferred their rights to their husbands, because of the latter's superior leadership qualities as well as their ability to protect the family. Acceptance of the alleged greater competency of husbands and fathers mirrored the acceptance of male republican leaders as "political father figures."[14]

This leads to several conclusions. First, this outright contradiction, namely the claim of a free society while at the same time women's lack of rights within marriage ("coverture"), is made conceivable by a model of marriage as a contract between two parties.[15] This idea of a contract not only presupposed women's voluntary obedience to male leadership, but even interpreted it as female fulfillment of the pursuit of happiness.[16] A greater leadership capability among men came to be seen as an expression of a natural disposition.

A second conclusion concerns the relationship between family, society, and the state. During the colonial period families were seen as miniature versions of and model units for the state. Yet in a liberal republic they became pivotal as the fulcrum through which to govern, hone leadership skills, and shape as well as regulate the social order. The family rose to the means through which to organize society.[17]

Families became switchboards for installing individuals in various positions and functions, both within the family and within society, depending on gender, age, and other factors. For instance, different positions of fathers and children, of sons and daughters in society were orchestrated through the family. Another example was that different living arrangements elicited different measures of recognition, depending on age, sexual preference, religious orientation, ethnicity, or race, and this had a major impact on a person's chances to participate at society.

The loving, caring family with a breadwinning father, a homemaking mother, and several children became, in the decades after the revolution, the regulatory ideal at the core of American society. At this point it is important to bear in mind that it was conceptualized as white and middle class, but that it had powerful effects on all Americans. It was precisely this and no other family configuration that was perceived as the best locus for shaping republican citizens and subjects. Its hegemonic status soon was hard to contest because it became so closely intertwined with the power structures in American society, shaped by race, class, gender, sex, ethnicity, and religion. This kind of family formation was assumed to be the best place to experience and teach competence, virtue, morality, self-control, and autonomy, all values of greatest importance for the republic. Therefore, families were seen as the foundation of the republic, as John Adams noted in his diary in 1778, a claim that politicians would repeat endlessly over the centuries.[18]

Civic engagement, cooperation, responsibility, but also the ability to yield, were seen as important for the family man as for the republican. It is no coincidence that the most influential theorists of the social contract, John Locke and Jean-Jacques Rousseau, also wrote treatises about education.[19] The political dimension of education points to the permeability of the boundaries between private and public spheres. Even though the private sphere of home and child rearing was considered as female and the public sphere of politics and profession as male, rearing good republicans was a decidedly political task that women took on as "republican mothers."[20] Still, just as the public sphere was not exclusively male, the family was more than a maternal empire.[21] The "republican mother" stood beside the "republican father," who was seen as possessing the necessary competence and self-control to guide the family.[22] Just as the American president was expected to guide the nation and carry out his political responsibilities "with paternal care and affection," so too was the family father expected to show his responsibility toward his family in a caring manner, preferably with such subtlety that other family members considered their decisions and actions as the fruits of their own reflections and competencies rather than the result of good external guidance.[23] Advice manuals, which were becoming more and more popular, declared that the governed would take real pride in their own virtue only when they believed that they acted virtuously out of their own free will. An authoritarian patriarch at home was considered to be as damaging to his family as a political tyrant was to the republic.[24]

In addition, the functions of fathers inside and outside the family were inextricably intertwined. Historian Robert Griswold called bread-winning "the great organizing principle of men's lives" in modern society. True as this might be, women always took on paid work as well, and breadwinning also encompassed more than providing for the family in material ways.[25] Securing the well-being of a family was the best proof of a man's ability for self-guidance as well as of his personal and political responsibility. The ability to care for a family signaled more than anything else manly and civic maturity. By the same token, the respect men received as citizens was often directly connected to the way in which they positioned themselves within the family. Success at work for the greatest benefit of his family was seen as a sign of a man's success as a father, which in turn secured his power in the family and society.[26]

This new kind of paternal hegemony rested on concepts of manliness, which became increasingly powerful over the years. The ability for self-guidance and to act responsibly became at once foundation and expression of good fatherhood and manhood. "How utterly unqualified to govern others will he be found who has never yet learned to govern himself!," emphasized William Alcott in his advice manual for young husbands as a central rule of life in the young republic. Alcott underscored the magnitude of the accomplishment: "He who governs himself . . . does more than he who commands armies. In fact, there is no victory more glorious . . . than a complete victory over one's self."[27] What self-guidance entailed precisely took on varying forms and changed over the years.

The genre of advice manuals boomed in the early nineteenth century as the population grew rapidly, work and economic conditions changed dramatically, infrastructure expanded, people were on the move, and American society was in a state of flux. Growing geographic and social mobility went hand in hand with the expansion of voting rights to all white men, independent of income and property ownership. This underlined the whiteness of the republican experiment and at the same time fueled skepticism regarding its future success. Increasing poverty, alcohol consumption, and violence in the rapidly growing cities were particularly frightening given the greater political participation of lower-class men. Concern grew that more and more fathers were abdicating their manly duties by abandoning families and thrusting women and children into poverty.[28]

A rising reform movement sought to set counterweights to these worrisome developments. Manuals proliferated that advised men that their life path was not preordained but very much in their own hands, and every boy could become president if only he succeeded in working on self-improvement. Advice manuals repeated constantly how important the functional family was as fruitful ground for the acquisition of diligence and self-control, caution and planning, virtue and faith. The seeds must be sowed in earliest childhood and youth so that the fruit would be reaped in manhood, stressed John Angell James's manual *Young Man's Friend*. Then seemingly difficult duties would be easy to master. Other books agreed that only early education in virtues would prevent a man, and with him his family, from being thrown into the abyss: "Our criminals, our ferocious mobs, our bloody broils, most of the evils that afflict families, cities, and states, may be traced to the neglect of proper early training."[29]

Some even claimed that molding the character of American youth was the most important task in the republic and even in the history of mankind. Fathers were admonished to guide their children through life and teach them appropriate obedience. However, obedience had to be granted voluntarily. It was supposed to be grounded not in coercion, fear, and blind subordination but in the free will of those who were guided and who then learned to guide themselves.[30]

Historian Shawn Johansen has shown how private correspondence stressed the importance of paternal guidance, above all for the self-control and discipline of children. For instance, Ann Brown of Salem, Massachusetts, wrote in 1825 to her seafaring husband that their boys needed the attention and guidance of their father. A few years later, Albina Rich of Maine emphasized likewise in a letter to her husband, who was away from the family to work on railway construction, that her children were good but still "need their Father to help govern them."[31] Sabrina Swain, too, wrote in 1848 to her husband William, who was in California to search for gold, that his daughter, now no longer a baby, needed more and more the guiding hand of her father.[32] William, in turn, instructed his wife from afar in questions of discipline and character formation, which he regarded as the task of a father and as the foundation for the child's responsiveness to any guidance.[33]

Violence

In liberal societies, power is not defined as a means of violent coercion by somebody over somebody (that is at least not its main characteristics), and the main thrust of power is not the sovereign right to kill. Rather, power in liberalism shapes opportunities and creates conditions of possibility that make some choices appear preferable to others. Power unfolds in manifold connections and relations, is diffuse, and has an agency of its own. The ultimate object of power is to make society prosper and grow (which then again is taken as justification for nurturing some people and excluding others).[34] Still, violence has not stopped to exist in liberal societies. Yet violence calls for explanation and justification, and the question of which role violence would play in the guidance of families moved to the forefront of the republican discourse.

In general republican fathers were supposed to guide their families not by force and violence but through love, affection, and persuasion, so that family members would follow their directions happily, willingly, realizing what was best for them.[35] A central tenet was that only those who ruled with a steady hand and self-control would raise children who learned to govern themselves. Tyrannical fathers, who relied on coercion and violence, would reap only violence and hatred. Advice books for parents warned above all against "the relentless use of the rod." Physical violence, when applied in excess, rage, or anger, was rejected more than anything else. The mentioning of the rod in this context was not coincidental, for in nineteenth-century American culture, the rod symbolized relentless, uncontrolled violence. It signaled a loss of self-control and a form of transgression that was also erotically charged.[36]

Unrestrained violence stood for excess and thus for the opposite of self-guidance. Education manuals stressed that those men who applied corporal punishment ran the danger of losing their paternal self-control. Since self-control was seen as a main characteristic of republican manhood, unrestrained punishment was considered not only torturous for the punished but also emasculating to the punisher. Excessive violence was regarded as the practice of barbaric monsters, as leading to widespread brutalization and ultimately to the downfall of the republic. It was seen as a sign of paternal failure to invest in the hard work of steady education that fostered character development. "Govern your child by gentle methods," Artemas Muzzey admonished parents. Then violence would be unnecessary. He emphasized that continuous work on the personality of children was far more effective for teaching them the voluntary obedience of republican citizens, and he explicitly turned away from old practices of forced subjugation: "We can spare the old Puritanic discipline of outward subordination, if we only secure in its stead an inward self-discipline. To promote that vital quality, we need, first, midst, and last, a steady obedience. Let us be gentle and calm, as well as considerate, determined and uniform in exacting that obedience, and all shall issue well."[37]

Historian Shawn Johansen has shown how much these rules have shaped the self-perception of nineteenth-century parents. At the same time, written correspondence between mothers and fathers shows that parents considered their gentle efforts as not always sufficient for fostering their children's self-improvement and for teaching them how to stay on the right path. Gold digger William Swain instructed his wife at home that children needed strict boundaries once in a while, and discipline had to be enforced today in order to avert harsher consequences tomorrow. Corporal punishment was sometimes portrayed as the lesser evil, when compared to waiving self-discipline and virtue.[38]

This could mean that lashings and the withholding of food for days were deemed acceptable, if these measures were meant to teach children to accept the given circumstances so that they could then act "freely" within the given confines. Violence would thus be considered beneficial for a liberal society, if encoded and employed in a specific way. For instance, Francis Wayland, the Baptist preacher and future president of Brown University, wrote in 1831 that he had denied food to his fifteen-month-old son for forty hours to wean him off his mother's breast. This was exceedingly painful to him as a father, he emphasized, but necessary and grounded in paternal love and a sense of duty for "there can be no greater cruelty than to suffer a child to grow up with an unsubdued temper."[39]

Corporal punishment thus remained part of the familial routine despite the pleas to leave the sovereign order behind. William Alcott recommended that republican fathers should act quickly and with precision, like surgeons, when they had to resort to corporal punishment. By using a medical metaphor, Alcott indicated that a painful intervention of this kind ultimately had healing effects and was to be willfully accepted by those who were being punished. Furthermore, parents were advised to punish their offspring hidden from the public. The invocation to punish one's children within the confines of the private sphere and even without other family members being present explicitly mirrored the changing rationale of punishment in republican society. Beginning in the early nineteenth century, penitentiaries were created as sites for the improvement of those who had failed in the art of republican citizenship. Prisons represented a new concept of punishment, executed no longer in exemplary fashion in public space but invisible to the public eye and focused on education and self-improvement. Beginning in the mid-1830s, public executions, once the ultimate tool of sovereign rule, began to disappear (even though this process took a whole century across the country, and when death sentences were executed they often attracted hundreds of spectators, even within prison yards). Both punishment by the state or by the father changed according to the same formula. Resorting to instruments smacking of the premodern arsenal of sovereign power was deemed intolerable, as Artemas Muzzey emphasized: "Great harm is often done by punishing a child in presence of others. The gallows is now, in many cases, concealed from the public; so should the act of whipping be concealed from a family of children. If it must be done, let it take place with the utmost privacy."[40]

According to sociologist Norbert Elias, hiding violence from the view of others is "characteristic for the whole process that we call civilization."[41] For historians, private violence is hard to come to terms with, though statements, such as those by Francis Wayland and Artemas Muzzey, at least indicate how much physical violence ruled behind closed doors. This seems to be confirmed by other sources. In some places, around a fifth of the men behind bars served time for domestic violence. The fact that few of the prisoners came from middle-class backgrounds probably tells us more about the patterns of arrest than about the actual level of violence in theses circles. It can be assumed that middle-class households were reluctant or outright unwilling to talk about violence in their families since it indicated failure in living up to expectations for self-control, self-government, and a loving home.[42]

Already in the first half of the nineteenth century skeptics surmised that the allegedly loving private sphere under parental care even served as a breeding ground for violence. The private sphere was envisioned as a protective zone, yet its removal from public scrutiny also created a space protected from outside witnesses, making the exercise of uncontrolled violence feasible. Thus, it was the privacy of the home where old patterns of sovereign patriarchal rule continued to thrive.[43]

In the era of the revolution and the Early Republic, families became pivotal for the governing of society and fathers served as prototypes of the good republican. This obviously did not spell the end of all forms and practices of sovereign power and rule. Violence continued to exist, most likely also in the middle classes, even if they pointed a finger at the lower classes. It was stressed again and again that poverty, chaos, vice, violence, and alcohol showed how the principle of self-government reached its limit among the lower classes and how fragile the new republic really was. Advice manuals seemed an insufficient means to stem vices across classes. Thus skeptics suggested to strengthen the state and put in place mechanisms and institutions to replace biological parents if they were deemed incapable of giving proper guidance to their families and of producing good republicans.

Failing Guidance and the Paternal State

In the early nineteenth century, a growing number of commentators raised some concern about the ability of men to fulfill their paternal duties and to meet the demands placed on them by liberal society. Critics bemoaned that many men abandoned their families and indulged in alcohol, gambling, and prostitution. Particularly alcohol, consumed in copious quantities in the Early Republic, was seen as the root cause of the loss of control and the spread of violence, the destroyer of a well-ordered, productive, and virtuous home, and thus a threat to the republican experiment. In Philadelphia, for instance, poverty rose dramatically in the early decades of the nineteenth century, and around 90 percent of support for the poor went to single women, often with children, seen first and foremost as a consequence of drinking and unreliable men.[44] The temperance movement, driven mostly by women, can also be considered an effort to foster better self-government among men, interpreted as vital for both families and society. Men were to be rescued from the demonic power of alcohol not only for their own sake but for the sake of the family and the republic.[45] Fathers and also mothers who shirked their responsibilities were seen as hanging like the sword of Damocles over the republic. Furthermore, these fathers, it was generally assumed, were the result of a failing childhood education: "Is a father a drunkard, a libertine, a neglecter of his family and of the duties he owes them? Is a mother given to frivolity, and pleasure, and worldliness, to the neglect of the high mission to which she is called? All may be traced to the neglect of their proper training in youth."[46]

These concerns gave rise to a debate and a reform movement, with the male breadwinner in the lower classes as a main point on the agenda.[47] His unreliability was to be countered by changes in the politics of the poor, which up to then had relied on charity and voluntary aid. Now an emphasis on work, education, and character building gained in strength, much in line with the principles of self-government. Supporting the poor through work was particularly designed to strengthen male self-guidance and by extension the position of the father in the family. Alms were seen as having weakened rather than strengthened that position. Also, middle-class reformers themselves acted like good (political) fathers when they led lower-class men toward better self-guidance in order to escape poverty.[48]

These reformers took on the mantle of experts in self-government, and they felt qualified, even obliged, to guide others. This culture of conduct and counsel has served as a key element of liberal government. "Political" fathers commented, interfered, and gave guidance when moments of familial crisis seemed to threaten individual families and the overall social stability of the republic. In the early nineteenth century, reform of poor relief was part of a larger reform movement that sought to establish a new and adequate institutional structure. Just as the nuclear family was deemed the natural space for developing the ability for self-government, so too did reform institutions such as penitentiaries and poor houses become laboratories meant to provide an environment conducive to the desired effects among those who were said to have failed.[49]

However, reformers stressed that all these institutions faced a tough challenge, and "loose principles and licentious habits," as John Adams had written in his diary in 1778, were best fought against in earliest childhood.[50] After all, different from adults, children were seen as still malleable, toward the good as well as the bad, and indolence and vice in adulthood were seen as the consequence of lacking guidance in childhood. Conversely, diligence and dedication, caution and planning, faith and virtue, and the most difficult of all duties would be easy to fulfill when they were taught from earliest childhood.[51] As a result reformers demanded reformatories for those children, who suffered from a lack of parental guidance, who were described as having gone astray because of their parents' alcoholism and profligacy. Reform societies and institutions were created everywhere to provide juvenile delinquents with the necessary supervision and instruction. A New York reformatory of juvenile delinquents emphasized that "the main design of the Institution . . . [is] to reclaim and reform the children of the State, who, having lost their parents, or what is still worse for them, having intemperate and profligate parents, had, under such circumstances, themselves become delinquent and criminal."[52]

Reformers stressed that they acted in the best interests of the children as well as of all of humanity. Special institutions were to replace dysfunctional families by replicating a functional republican home under the leadership of a good father and a good mother. In 1838, the Pennsylvania Supreme Court confirmed the right of the state to take children away from their parents by asking a rhetorical question and by answering it with a resounding yes: "May not the natural parents, when unequal to the task of education, or unworthy of it, be superseded by the *parens patriae*, or common guardian of the community?" The principle of guidance toward self-guidance thus superseded the family. When the family failed as the crucial link between the individual and society, children would be transferred to the custody of a reform institution, which would then take over the parental role.[53] Reformers saw this kind of interference into family matters as a right and an obligation of the state and of those who knew better. They claimed for themselves the political position of the good father, who was to teach children the proper handling of their own freedom and the pursuit of happiness. For instance, a report from the Society for the Reformation of Juvenile Delinquents in New York stated that "if the agents of our municipal government stand toward the community in the moral light of guardians of virtue; if they may be justly regarded as the political fathers of the unprotected, does not every feeling of justice urge upon them the principle of considering these juvenile culprits as falling under their special guardianship, and claiming from them the right which every child may demand of its parent, of being well instructed in the nature of its duties before it is punished for the breach of their observance?"[54]

Following the concept of the good father, reform institutions were to guide young people onto the right path, through loving affection rather than through violence, yet with violence as last resort. The idea of republican-paternal guidance is expressed in a report of the New York Society for the Reformation of Juvenile Delinquents: "The young offender should, if possible, be subdued by kindness. His heart should first be addressed, and the language of confidence, though undeserved, be used towards him. He should be taught that his keepers were his best friends, and that the object of his confinement was his reform and ultimate good. . . . Obedience thus procured not by stripes, but by a reformation of his mind, will be willing, cheerful and lasting."[55]

Soon, every city, particularly in the Northeast, had its reformatory. Reform efforts by the middle classes and the state were to make up for the lack of familial-paternal guidance, particularly seen as spreading in the lower classes. The institutions were to follow the principles of education in the republican family, seen as the best and "natural" form of liberal governing. Thus, directors of juvenile asylums stressed that "what is needed for the children whom the law entrusts to us is the government of a well-ordered Christian household."[56]

What did reality look like, and what role did violence play in it? "Parental guidance," "paternal goodness," and "manly self-restraint" were among the proclaimed ideals when people talked about reform institutions and their leaders. For instance, Joseph Curtis, the first superintendent of the New York House of Refuge, claimed that his paternal affection transformed his inmates' indolence and vice, almost 90 percent of whom were boys, into "manly self-control" and dedication to work. While boys were being groomed for work, girls were trained mostly in domestic duties.[57]

Corporal punishment was to be the measure of last resort, after gentle guidance, the withdrawal of food, and various forms of confinement. As much as possible, though, the offspring were to be guided without any punishment but instead through kindness and affection. Nonetheless, the rod was always present so that, if necessary, violence was applied in order to create fruitful conditions for the government of children, as pointed out.[58] Corporal punishment was never supposed to get out of hand; that applied to reformers as well as fathers. In the extreme, corporal punishment was interpreted even as an affectionate expression of a good father who wanted to protect his children from standing in their own and in society's way. Reformers were full of self-adulation when talking about punishing children for their own good: "When a child deserves punishment, and will not be won by patient kindness, he is punished; but he soon learns that the spirit with which that punishment is administered is love, and the motive, his amendment."[59]

Further points from debates about corporal punishment in reformatories sound similar to those from debates about family fathers and corporal punishment (which we encountered earlier): the one who punishes is suffering more than the one who is being punished, but must at all times remain in control of himself. Joseph Curtis reassured readers of his report that he never whipped in anger but always with gentleness and in full control of himself, always assuring the child of his benevolence and never losing his temper. The words that he claims to have used in conveying his compassion resonated with the undertones of eroticized violence: "My boy, it is hard, I feel it hard, but the body must suffer to make the mind obey."[60] Several narratives fueled the assumption that corporal punishment was a regrettable but necessary evil and that the one who carried out the punishment was full of love and caring. Curtis once allegedly said to a boy that "you have compelled me to enforce an obedience which should have been willingly yielded. Avoid again subjecting me to the pain you have this day occasioned me."[61]

Reports, testimonies, as well as institutional chronicles reveal that the rod was part of the daily routine in juvenile reformatories.[62] Joseph Curtis kept records during the first years of his tenure at the New York House of Refuge about his regular and uncompromising use of the whip in cases of bed-wetting, disrespect, and unauthorized talking. His successors acted in a similar fashion, even though they all seemed to consort with the principles of guidance toward self-guidance.[63] Even the reform society lauded the superintendents of the institution as good paternal stewards—for instance in the 1843 annual report, which praised David Terry because "he exercises a moral influence over the children, and treats them as one family, over which he is the head."[64]

A liberal order based on the principles self-government was apparently not incompatible with the exercise of violence, neither in theory nor in practice. The ultimate rationale of governing gently was not to ban violence entirely but to keep passions under control and move violent punishment to concealed spaces. Punishing in public was seen as counterproductive, and losing control over one's actions when punishing was considered a signal of the punisher's failure to adhere to the principle of self-guidance.[65] The private sphere, removed from public view and praised as a protective space of love and intimacy, also created room for violence and for the continuation of sovereign-patriarchal modes of rule. At the same time, reformers wrestled with the deplorable conditions and the violence in reformatories and prisons.[66]

Liberal Government and the Family

The revolutionary transformation to a republic was closely tied to changes of the concepts of family and fatherhood. The image of the well-meaning, gently governing, and guiding father perfectly reflected the ideal of the republican. In general, republican government changed the role and meaning of the family from that of a model of the state to that of a switchboard, teaching its members how to handle their freedom properly and successfully. The family connected the individual to society, and this new type of society and its individuals were governed through the family. The family with "breadwinning father," "homemaking mother," and several children soon developed into the normative ideal that was coined by the white middle class. It was seen as especially hazardous for the republic, if fathers and families failed to meet expectations for self-government. Yet many people seemed overwhelmed by the liberal demand to make the best use of their freedom and optimize their existence. However, their difficulties did not necessarily call into question the principle of paternal-familial government. Rather, reformers and state institutions felt called upon to serve as ersatz fathers and to impart the skills of self-guidance.

2

Challenging Love, Marriage, and the Nuclear Family, 1820–1870

John H. Noyes is the father and overseer whom the Holy Ghost has set over the family thus constituted. To John H. Noyes as such we submit ourselves in all things spiritual and temporal, appealing from his decisions only to the spirit of God, and that without disputing.
—Founding declaration of the Oneida Community, November 3, 1846

At the end of their work day, more than two hundred men, women, and children of the Oneida Community gathered in the great hall of their residential building to spend the evening together, eat, and listen to the words of their spiritual and political leader John Humphrey Noyes. The commune had established itself as a utopian experiment over the course of the 1840s and finally settled four miles outside the small town of Oneida on land near Lake Ontario in Madison County, New York. During his nightly "home talks," Noyes taught his followers about life, love, and faith and, above all, held forth on what made a good person, a good family, and a good community. His statements were often printed in the *Oneida Circular*, the community journal, so that they could be read in more depth and were made available to the outside world.

Among his favorite topics were self-improvement and the family. On November 16, 1854, Noyes wrote in the *Circular* that the family formed a perfect bond as long as it was not excessively affected by outside institutions. Noyes viewed modern marriage as exactly such an institution that was detrimental to family cohesion and even destroyed families. Sure, he claimed, marriage created close family bonds, but at the same time it tore them apart over time by separating parents from children, brothers from sisters. The modern marriage confined family bonds to the length of one generation, which is more than obvious to every family man, he explained in another home talk: "Behind him is his own father's family thus falling in pieces, and before him is the certainty that his own family is going to the same fate." In addition, according to Noyes, the desire to isolate oneself as couples and to have an exclusive right to a person destroyed the natural bond within the extended Christian community. Instead, one should look beyond one's own small world to experience boundless true love and fulfillment in the free family of the Lord.[1]

If one followed Noyes's logic, familial living arrangements had gone astray, when, in the early nineteenth century, the nuclear family had attained the status of the ideal, even "natural" form of human coexistence, and as such had become the heart of American society.[2] Noyes denounced nuclear families, the focus on couples, and individual claims to possession—of people or goods—as selfish and the source of evil. His brother George Wallingford Noyes even charged that the dominant form of marriage and family organization raised social and political problems that were in many ways akin to slavery.[3]

Noyes's Oneida Community had chosen a different path. "Every thing that can be shaken will be shaken," Noyes, by then positioned at the head of a postmillennial society and believing in perfecting the world, wrote very self-confidently in December 1852.[4] The Oneida Community allowed neither private property nor marriage between two people or nuclear families, but instead saw communal property and group marriage as the basis for a community of compassion and altruism. The Oneida Community praised that "a community home in which each is married to all, and where love is honored and cultivated, will be much more attractive than an ordinary home." Communitarians saw themselves as social and sexual utopians who acted at the pleasure of God and as good Christians: Noyes preached a so-called perfectionist Bible communism.[5] Their commune, the *Circular* explained elsewhere, united more than two hundred people in perfect Christian love and established a family that was oriented toward eternity rather than just a single generation.[6]

The Oneida Community was founded on a concept of fatherhood that departed substantially from the republican middle-class ideals well established by the 1840s. The Oneidas announced the end of the model of separate male public and female private spheres and greater gender equality, which was praised as beneficial for both men and women, fa-

Figure 2.1. The Oneida Community with Noyes in the foreground. Syracuse University Library, Oneida Community Collection.

thers and mothers. At the same time, the commune was anchored in a notion of God-given sovereign patriarchal power, which had been abandoned by the concept of the social contract and the American republic. Historians have emphasized the importance of contract theory for the conception of marriage and family in the Early Republic and how elements of patriarchy nevertheless continued to exist. The concept of having signed into a contract was taken as indicating a voluntary female recognition of an allegedly natural order. Because of this agreement and on the basis of her virtue, a woman, through the act of marriage, was presented as agreeing to adhere to her husband's greater leadership qualities, while the man committed himself to fulfill these qualities in the best interests of marriage and family. The Oneida Community for its part was a community founded through an actual contract. The signatories, however, acknowledged the unrestricted authority of God and the patriarchal rule of John H. Noyes, who watched almightily over his family. Years later, one of Noyes's sons remembered an autocratic relationship with his father, not at all conforming to the notions of a loving relationship between parents and children that were so predominant at the time: "My father . . . seemed the father of all of us, just as God is the Father of all of us, and my love of him, like my love of God, was rather impersonal."[7]

This chapter shows how the Oneida Community was designed as an alternative to the nuclear family and how it saw itself as the beginning of a new age and a new way of life.[8] A closer look at the Oneida Community will help identify, by virtue of its contrast, the republican, middle-class paradigms of love, marriage, nuclear family, and separate spheres. In addition, the community's alternative way of life laid bare utopian visions as well as the staying power of patriarchal values and offers an important perspective on families, masculinities, and fathers with repercussions far beyond the Oneida Community and the first half of the nineteenth century.[9]

Loving Families and Separate Spheres

In the new American republic, the family emerged as the space where human beings would learn to handle their own freedoms responsibly and in the best interest of society. The republican family was supposed to provide an environment of love, guidance, and instruction among father, mother, and children. Romantic love would meld husband and wife into a monogamous couple, which then formed the germ of the family, the republic and the breeding ground for good republican citizens.[10] Publicly recognized and legally as well as morally legitimized by the marriage vow, this partnership then became the only permissible arena for sexuality, provided it served the objective of procreation. The marriage model followed the template of the contract society, and the marriage contract obliged women to yield to men the government of the family. The system of coverture required that they seize all public activities, at least in theory, in favor of their husbands, including the signing of contracts and the acquisition and ownership of property and other assets. Wives lost all legal standing independent of their husbands, even though they occasionally succeeded in defending their interests against those of their husband. Repeal of the doctrine of coverture was one of the main objectives of early women's rights activists, and in the 1830s various states began to modify their laws to allow greater freedom for women in property regulations and divorce proceedings.[11]

Men and women were assumed to have different "natural" predispositions, abilities, and personalities, which made them particularly well suited for different roles and positions in family and society. Men seemed to be predestined for success in professional occupations and politics. According to Robert Griswold, the role of breadwinner would become the "great organizing principle of men's lives," with work being located outside the domestic sphere step by step.[12] By the same token, women were thought to be predestined to support their husbands in the domestic arena because of their natural inclination toward piety and purity, submission and sacrifice. The home was to be the space where men could recuperate from the hardships of their daily efforts in the public sphere. The middle decades of the nineteenth century established a powerful *discourse of domesticity* that structured the perceptions, lives, and institutional bindings of women and men. The whiteness of this family model under male guidance reiterated the imagination of the American republic as a "fraternity of white men," based on what political scientist Carole Pateman and philosopher Charles W. Mills have described as "sexual contract" and "racial contract."[13]

Historians have stressed that male and female spheres were less separate in real life than nineteenth-century deliberations and advice manuals initially suggested.[14] Women did work for wages, chaired business ventures, and were active in politics, for instance by leading movements against alcohol and slavery. In addition, as mothers they raised young republican future citizens. The concept of republican motherhood reveals the blurred boundaries between the public and private sphere. After all, the political importance of child rearing formed a fulcrum of the political discourse of the young republic.[15]

The public sphere was not exclusively male, much like the private sphere was not exclusively a motherly empire without room for fathers.[16] This was already indicated by the political charge attached to fathers, who were key figures in the government of the family and thus crucial when it came to the overlaps of private and public spheres. The role of provider and protector, which was attached to the father's professional activity outside the home, also shows the overlaps between public and private. In addition, familial engagement was highly important for male identity formation. Despite growing responsibilities outside the home, men tried to meet expectations as husbands and fathers inside the home. They even sent written instructions with regard to child discipline when many miles from home, which ignored any female ability in the art of government.[17]

John Humphrey Noyes and His Family Utopia

Absent fathers, and there were many in the Early Republic, were horrifying for John Humphrey Noyes. First of all they showed paternal imperfection, as he himself had experienced as a son; his father John Noyes, a congressional representative, was often away from home and quite fond of the bottle.[18] Second, absent fathers exposed for all to see the fundamentally fragile nature of nuclear families. Noyes saw love in the nuclear family as insufficiently powerful to bind the individual to their family and community. Instead, he replaced the nuclear family with a large community in the name of Christ, without private property and without exclusive partnerships. This community was supposed to be united and to reach perfection through the power of bodily love among all its members. There must not be property of goods and people in the kingdom of God, and, as Noyes himself stated in a 1849 pamphlet about his *Bible communism*, "the intimate union that in the world is limited to the married pair extends through the whole body of communicants." Noyes vehemently denied any association with the so-called *free lovers*, who in the mid-nineteenth century propagated "free love" as an alternative to the Victorian code of sexuality. Noyes did concede that the human heart could love more than one person at the same time, but he accused the free lovers of fickleness and of lacking manly responsibility.[19]

In contrast to the free lovers, he constructed an image of his own congregation as an orderly and disciplined family and as a moral oasis that demonstrated the possibilities of human, social, and Christian perfection. Noyes was an advocate of *Perfectionism*, which demanded a social and sexual way of life that aspired to a fundamentally pious and thus perfect conduct and attracted followers particularly in Upstate New York over the course of the 1830s. Noyes, of course, claimed for himself close proximity to such perfection, which made him God's best representative on earth who could guide the faithful toward an ideal existence.[20]

From the moment of his conversion to Perfectionism in 1834 until the end of his patriarchy of the Oneida Community in 1877, Noyes was obsessed about propagating his doctrines and preserving them for future generations. He produced an avalanche of pamphlets, reports, guidebooks, and periodicals, and he collected copies of his own writings in scrapbooks.[21] Noyes and his commune were part of the fast-growing communication and transportation network of the early nineteenth century that was spreading from the greater New York and Hudson Valley area to the Great Lakes. Also, the Oneida Community was not the only religious, political, social, and sexual experiment at the time. The Mormon community emerged in the 1820s in the same region as the Oneidas. Another group was the celibate Shakers, whose congregations peaked in the first half of the nineteenth century. In general, the eastern part of the United States, from New England to Ohio and as far south as Tennessee, was in the grip of the Second Great Awakening. Particularly New York had an extraordinary social and religious dynamic, so much so that Charles Grandison Finney, one of the leading religious revivalists, remarked that one could not find another soul in the region in need of spiritual awakening. Contemporaries and historians have highlighted the confluence of spiritual awakenings on one side and political democratization on the other.[22]

In September 1831, it was apparently Charles Finney himself who inspired John Humphrey Noyes at one of his four-day camp meetings in his hometown of Putney, Vermont. Noyes, entranced by the spiritual awakening preached by Finney, abandoned his legal studies and turned to theology at Andover and Yale. As a religious eccentric he drifted for years through New England and New York before returning to Putney in 1837. In New York he spent weeks preaching in the notorious Five Points District, spending his nights on the streets or in one of the boarding houses on disreputable Leonard Street.[23]

In the Five Points District, Noyes experienced a way of life that represented the flip side of what the Early Republic stood for. Growing poverty, prostitution, alcohol, and violence, particularly in the fast-growing metropolitan regions of the country, fueled fear of the excesses of a society based on liberty. Concerns about the failure of the democratic experiment seemed more pressing than ever.[24] Noyes himself had witnessed the fatal consequences of alcohol in his own family home. His father's drinking habits seemed to have become unbearable by the late 1830s.

His alcohol-induced helplessness and mental stupor caused him to fail in his parental duty to be "counsellor and guide of the family," as Noyes and his siblings expected their father to be. But his father was not able to quit drinking and thus save himself and his family from the destructive effects of alcohol. At the time of his death in October 1841, John Humphrey Noyes, who was the eldest son in the family, had already taken over the role of provider, protector, and spiritual guide of the family. He regarded the leadership of the family as a genuinely male task and had fought hard with his mother for this position.[25]

The Noyes family was in no way unusual in its lament over an alcoholic father. The incapacitation of husbands and fathers, the end of successful inner guidance that came with succumbing to alcohol, and its catastrophic consequences for families had become central themes in early nineteenth-century America. Criticism grew that many men led a less than reputable life and were unable to handle responsibly the liberties and responsibilities given to them in the republic. In such families, little was left of the ideal of the caretaker and the art of parental government, and, as was the case in the Noyes family, the role of the father had crumbled. The consequences were disproportionately borne by women and children who in the early nineteenth century made up the vast majority of the urban poor. Alcohol thus represented a major source of a man's loss of control and failed inner guidance and also of the destruction of the orderly and productive home. Many saw in this destruction a direct threat to the survival of the republic. Particularly the women-led temperance movement can be seen as a female attempt to restore male self-control. Women strove to rescue men from the curse of alcohol not just for their own sake but for the sake of the family and the republic.[26]

Reform debates and growing sociopolitical engagement ensued to counteract the destructive effects of alcohol and disreputable conduct on the community. But John Humphrey Noyes was not convinced that advice manuals and reform efforts would solve these problems. In his view, tighter control and stronger mechanisms of guidance were required. As an alternative to unfettered individualism in a—as he saw it—society without proper guidance, he developed a model of a strong community with clearly defined structures.[27] He installed himself as head of this community with a God-given mandate, which he described as the perfect embodiment of Christianity.

John Humphrey Noyes was a charismatic leader.[28] As early as the 1830s, when he was still living in Putney, he began to gather a group of devoted followers, living in the spirit of the religious revival movement. In the commune's founding declaration as well as in letters and other documents, Noyes mapped out his ideas of an alternative to the liberal-republican concept of society. For him, the kingdom of God was an absolute monarchy and he himself was God's right hand, being endowed with authority and demanding absolute obedience.[29] "The Community believed that his inspirations came down . . . from God to Christ," his son Pierrepont wrote in his autobiography, "from Christ to Paul; from Paul to John Humphrey Noyes, and by him made available for the Community."[30] On occasion, Noyes resorted to the use of sovereign-patriarchal force to exact obedience from his followers. He regarded the rod as an appropriate tool to discipline children and adults as well.[31] The erotic connotation of the rod in American nineteenth-century culture has a special meaning in the context of the Oneida Community.

Relationships in the commune were organized strictly hierarchically. Members could rise up in rank through constant self-improvement, eventually gaining the qualification to instruct others in the practice of self-improvement. Yet Oneida's governing practices were not based on the creation of incentives and opportunities. Rather the structure was reminiscent of the colonial puritan order in America, in which authority was passed down in a hierarchical system, from God to chosen ones and fathers, down to sons, and then to servants.[32]

Counter to the sociocultural and political paradigms of his period, Noyes argued that ideal families should be governed like a "miniature monarchy, rather than an example of republican equality."[33] The Oneida Community was configured like an extended family under patriarchal leadership. The commune broke with the nuclear family and the kind of society it stood for, and instead conjured up utopian visions as well as reincarnated elements of the patriarchal past.[34] Maybe its most fundamental break with the existing social order was the dissolution of the two-person marriage and the introduction of a system that Noyes called *complex marriage*.

Complex Marriage

Noyes saw the new American republic, built on the home and the nuclear family and with its powerful discourse on domesticity, less as a sign of human perfection as social beings than as a fatally flawed development. According to Noyes, the division of labor in early industrialization and the development of small two-generation families meant the breakdown of the family as a way of life rather than its elevation to new heights. He saw physically and mentally exhausted men who had no energy left for their families after a long day of work as well as a growing number of unhappy wives as symptoms of this breakdown.[35]

Noyes's critique at least partially overlapped with the first women's movement's at their meeting in Seneca Falls in 1848. The marriage contract reduced women to men's property and denied their existence as persons with independent legal standing. Noyes compared matrimony to slavery—an argument women's rights activists had been advancing for quite some time, strengthened by the fact that women had always played a significant role in the battle against slavery. Noyes supported the abolitionist movement and exchanged ideas with some of its leading activists, such as William Lloyd Garrison, even though abolitionists praised life in the nuclear family as a universal human right and a major argument against slavery.[36]

Noyes celebrated himself as the head of a commune in which men freed women from the bonds of slavery and saved them from the corrosive effects of an existence as wives and mothers.[37] However, Noyes did not regard women's emancipation as the appropriate solution to the deficits of the modern marriage and family life. Wives should not fight their husbands and strive for their own best interests, but both sides should step outside their separate spheres together and provide their children with shared guidance. "Marriage must be replaced by something better, and not merely weakened and destroyed," said the *Circular*, the commune's major magazine, in 1859 about the liberalization of the divorce code in the state of New York.[38] Instead of supporting the individualistic breakup of couples, social bonds should be strengthened by transferring them from couples to the collective. Noyes's solution for the Oneida Community was complex marriage and a community "in which each is married to all." This would strengthen the bonds among all members of the commune and provide better security for women and children since they were no longer dependent on the support of a single male provider and protector. After all, since the beginning of the republic men had proven again and again how poorly prepared they were for such a task.[39]

Sex was to be the element that would closely bind this religious community together. Reciprocal responsibility, the affection of all for all, and the love for the Lord were to be expressed through sex.[40] In the Oneida Community, group marriage and the opportunity for sexual intercourse among all represented the key to breaking up the self-absorption of couples and nuclear families, allowing the entire community to meld together. Oneida claimed that its method succeeded in overcoming immature passions and the idolatrous worshipping of others, as in romantic love and marriage. Furthermore, the concept of communal sex in the complex marriage system contributed to countering capitalist greed, whose focus on property ownership infiltrated two-person relationships. Ego-centric affection, predicated on personal happiness with a single partner, was to be replaced by expressions of true and universalist love among all members of the commune.[41]

When Noyes announced the new marriage system in 1847 as the core of his community, and with it the kingdom of God on earth, he had been developing a new social order for more than a decade.[42] As early as 1837, he had dreamed of a holy community where "exclusiveness, jealousy, quarrelling, have no place. . . . There is no more reason why sexual intercourse should be restrained by law, than why eating and drinking should be."[43] Noyes had first introduced the complex marriage system to an inner circle in the commune, before announcing it to the entire group on June 1, 1847, which would be almost three hundred people at some point. Complex marriage remained in place until 1879.

Communal Property, Work Life, and Home Life

Next to complex marriage, the second pillar of a Christian commune free from competition and greed was communal ownership of goods, coupled with alternative structures of work. Those who entered the commune had to relinquish all exclusive claims to people and goods.[44] Out there, in liberal capitalism, the husband and father was the main link between work life and nuclear family. In the commune, Noyes underscored in its handbook, "the guarantees for women and children are much greater . . . than they can be in any private family."[45] The collective would counter individual weakness and failure to live up to the demands addressed to the male provider. Conversely the burdens on husbands and fathers would be eased by the equal distribution of labor. Noyes condemned the world of separate spheres as emotionally as well as economically unproductive: "When the partition between the sexes is taken away, and man ceases to make woman a propagative drudge, when love takes the place of shame, and fashion follows nature in dress and business, men and women will mingle in all their employments."[46] Men would thus stay with their family and women's abilities—far exceeding those of child bearing and rearing—would be used in the best interest of the community. According to Noyes, the end of separate spheres was a blessing for both sexes and would lead to their complete absorption into the community.[47] Of central importance to him was the return of the man to the center of this new family type since "a family governed by merely motherly feeling is like a wheel with the hub left out."[48] Noyes saw women as too emotional, and a family would be successful only if its unity and harmony revolved around "masculine power and execution at the center." After all, even within a communal arrangement, men's superiority over women and the fundamental male responsibility for the well-being of the entire community had to be recognized. Noyes's utopian vision of family and society thus echoed the patriarchal structure of pre-revolutionary America. This became particularly evident in Noyes's own position in the commune. As the father of all and the representative of God's will, he saw himself as the sovereign of the commune.[49]

Work tasks and schedules in the Oneida Community varied from day to day.[50] Gender division was not practiced rigorously, nevertheless gender stereotypes were reproduced in the division of labor. Women helped with hard labor, but communal dynamics rather than efficiency was the objective. At the same time, Oneidas proudly mentioned that men familiarized themselves with women's work and helped out with laundry, cooking, and meal preparation.[51] In reality, however, kitchen, home, laundry, sewing, and childcare remained the predominant occupation of women in the commune. Women also contributed to the manufacture of small goods, while men or hired hands tended to heavy machinery and transport work, as well as farming and carpentry. Men also occupied leadership positions, and the management of the commune rested in the hands of Noyes and a small circle of chosen elders. Historian Lawrence Foster aptly described gender relations in the Oneida work place as "cooperative subordination."[52]

Noyes expressed the confluence of gender equality with gender differentiation by labeling women "female-man." The Oneida dress code underscored that characterization. Noyes had complained that the Victorian dress style delivered unrealistic messages about women's roles by overemphasizing what was seen as femininity and signaling women's inability to work.[53] Oneida women wore their hair and their dresses shorter than customary. Skirts reached only slightly below the knee, and underneath women wore pants that were bound tight around the ankle, offering greater mobility. These so-called bloomers, existing since the 1850s, were seen as indicators of feminism outside the commune.[54]

Living in a shared house was another necessary condition for life according to the principles of the commune. Life in small separate units signaled to Noyes the disadvantages of the nuclear family. They gave expression to the self-absorption and fragmentation of society. The commune, on the other hand, in 1849 moved into a large house with a communal kitchen, a sleeping area, and a combined dining and community hall, where nightly meetings took place—the so-called family meetings—and where community members listened to lectures of the patriarch. To live under a single roof and share a communal table would bring home the principles of the commune, Noyes stressed.[55]

Once the commune had run profitably for over a decade, its members replaced the wooden house with a stone house.[56] Until then couples, who had joined the commune as couples, had been housed together in half-open sleeping zones; the new arrangement had each member sleep in a single room, an indicator for the complete implementation of complex marriage. The community hall was expanded to fit up to seven hundred people. Another addition was the so-called upper sitting room, which was meant to provide the comforts of a family living room.[57]

The commune also broke with established practices of child rearing. Children stayed with their mothers only to the age of fifteen months, when they moved to the so-called children's department in a separate building. They would continue to spend nights with their mothers until their fourth birthday. Afterward they moved permanently into the

Figure 2.2. The new stone structure, after 1861. Syracuse University Library, Oneida Community Collection.

building where their care was taken up by a specially chosen group of communards with the goal of educating and disciplining the children free from deceptive parental love, more effectively, and in accordance with the values of the community. Noyes regarded parental love, particularly maternal love, as poison for the community, as one of the strongest forces pulling families toward isolation, and as an obstacle to the teachings of God's love. Rather, women should redirect the love for their own child toward the entire commune.[58]

However, Noyes seemed hooked to middle-class conventions, when he declared that child rearing should consist of a balance between maternal affection and paternal discipline. Yet according to Noyes, this balance was rarely ever achieved within the confines of the nuclear family. In the Oneida Community, education was left to specially chosen people.[59] Education and picking the right people for this task were considered of special importance because leniency in childhood would lead to dire consequences in adulthood and could often not be corrected anymore.[60]

When Noyes's son Pierrepont was growing up in the childcare center of the commune, he was under the supervision of a man named William Kelly, who guided, taught, and disciplined the children. The children viewed him as Noyes's representative within a hierarchical system of paternity. Pierrepont described "Papa Kelly" as a strict ascetic man, who during the daily children's meetings would read from the Bible or cite passages from Noyes's *Home Talks*. The themes were supposed to be educational and dealt above all with charity, piety, disobedience, punishment, and self-improvement.[61] If a child had violated the rules of conduct, the entire group received a lesson in obedience and respect for authority. "My soul still bears the scars made by one or two of his [Papa Kelly's] dramatic revelations of eternal fire and brimstone," remembered Pierrepont.[62] With regard to his own biological father, he remembered reverence rather than affection since he was too close to God and in some respect the father of all communards.[63]

The daily work of laundry and child care was performed by women. The gender division of labor within the Oneida children's house thus largely followed traditional patterns.[64] Pierrepont himself saw his own biological mother only once or twice a week, which apparently caused her great pain. But she feared expressing those emotions since any evidence of so-called special love toward one's own biological children was punished by further limiting visiting privileges. *Mommy spirit* and *family spirit* between parents and children were stigmatized, as was the *marriage spirit* between two adults. The exclusive and loving relationship between two individuals, which American society outside Oneida regarded as the glue that held families and societies together, was actively prevented as counterproductive to the utopian experiment. Noyes reported about himself in 1852 that "the feeling of exclusive love, with me, is a thing gone by—-out of mind, and ᵃˡᵐᵒˢᵗ [sic] out of remembrance." Obviously, even Noyes had lingering doubts about the educational practice in the commune, as indicated by the last-minute insertion of the word "almost."[65]

Any deviation from the "community spirit" became subject of the nightly communal meetings in a ceremony called "mutual criticism." Contemporaneous journalist Charles Nordhoff characterized "mutual criticism" as the "main instrument of government" and control in the commune. The practice of "mutual criticism" shared a lot of similarities with Christian confessional rituals, as shown by the fact that Noyes developed the ceremony on the basis of self-improvement practices that he had learned during his religious studies at Andover and that bore some resemblance to earlier Puritan practices.[66]

"Mutual criticism," however, should not be seen as enforced subordination only. For no better opportunity existed for the members of the commune to present themselves to the entire congregation (including themselves) as virtuous than the public inquiry, critique, and spiritual cleansing. It offered the opportunity for self-improvement in front of everyone. After all, the constant striving for self-improvement was regarded as the highest human quality, as "manly spirit [which] not only takes pleasure in the accomplishment of a good change in himself, but in the process by which it is brought about," as Noyes wrote.[67]

The nightly gatherings of self-criticism were prepared by a committee of four, which rotated every four months. With the exception of Noyes, who was deemed infallible and thus above all criticism, at some point everyone had to fulfill the role of critic and criticized.[68] The coupling of criticism and praise was supposed to lead to improvement, and when punishment was called for, it usually came in the form of the curtailment of sexual privileges.[69]

Sex and Male Continence

Sex became the predominant instrument of punishment, control, and regulation in the commune since it represented, according to Noyes, "the vital center of society."[70] Among the Oneidas, sex was meant to be much like the holy communion, a way to bring people together as a community and with God.[71] It was thus absolutely necessary to separate the social from the reproductive function of sex. Furthermore, Noyes was motivated to develop his sexual system by the fact that his wife had suffered through five difficult pregnancies, four of which ended in miscarriages or stillbirths. These experiences were common to many couples during the nineteenth century, and were an incentive to think harder about various techniques of birth control, including sexual continence or coitus reservatus. By perfecting such methods of birth control, Noyes felt, he would not only liberate women from the enslavement of constant pregnancy but also elevate sexual intercourse to a divine art in the service of the Lord: "The separation of the amative from the propagative places amative sexual intercourse on the same footing with other ordinary forms of intercourse, such as conversation, kissing, shaking hands, embracing, &c. . . . differing only in kind by its superior intensity and beauty. . . . The refining effects of sexual love . . . will be increased a thousand-fold, when sexual intercourse becomes a method of ordinary conversation and each is married to all."[72] Noyes's solution for separating "the amative from the propagative" was "male continence," meaning that men abstained from orgasm and ejaculation during intercourse. This practice was meant to prevent pregnancy, and it would also elevate to new heights the sexual desire of women and men and therefore the piety of the congregation. Noyes himself had begun early to practice holding back his orgasm, and he concluded that such self-control was quite possible for him.[73]

He described the ability of a man to have sex without ejaculation as a cultural accomplishment, as a superior taming of natural forces, which separated civilized men from savages. In other words, Noyes saw civilization as the consequence of male sexual self-control, not so very unlikely to Sigmund Freud's later ideas about the concept of culture as the consequence of the sublimation of sexual urges. Noyes enthused about the vision of complete sexual self-control: "It is the glory of man to control himself, and the Kingdom of Heaven summons him to self-control in ALL THINGS."[74] In his mind, male abstention from orgasm and ejaculation during sex marked the highest form of self-control. "Male continence," he declared, "in its essence is self-control, and that is a virtue of universal importance."[75] This is what Noyes saw as the historic mission of the Oneida Community. In Oneida, sex was to be the social bond that tied the community together, made possible through male self-control and male willpower, which in turn was to demonstrate Oneida as an advanced civilization, full of the power of God.[76]

Noyes thus took up central tenets of Victorian sexuality, yet expanded on and moved them in a different direction. He adhered to the nineteenth-century concept of a "spermatic economy," which identified male sperm as the central locus of vitality. The loss of semen was seen as worse than mere waste—it was seen as a threat to the well-being of the male body and mind. Male fitness was threatened to become permanently damaged, which would endanger not only individual men but the growth and success of the community and society as well. It was stated that only a healthy man with healthy sperm would produce good offspring. Therefore, masturbation and uncontrolled sexual intercourse with male ejaculation were seen not so much as a sin but as a threat to individual and collective health and existence.[77]

Male self-control became a foundational force in this "spermatic economy" and in Victorian culture. After all it was in the sexual realm where self-control could best be demonstrated, particularly when considering the assumed great extent of male sexual impulse. It magnified the triumph of restraint in a Victorian culture of moderation.[78]

According to the sexual discourse of the time, occasional sexual intercourse with ejaculation was appropriate only when a man had reached full maturity, which was said to be reached sometime in the third decade of a man's life. It thus corresponded to his occupational advances and his ability to enter into matrimony and provide for a family. Fatherhood thus became an expression of having reached full manhood. It showed that sexual self-rule was intimately connected to professional success in this particular phase of a man's life. Both required self-control and moderation.[79]

The Oneida system of "male continence" fit into the Victorian concept of sexuality and its "spermatic economy." "It is the presence of the seed, and not the discharge of it, that makes the bull superior to the ox," declared Noyes. He vehemently rejected both masturbation and any form of ejaculation outside the female body.[80] Within the system of complex marriage, it was thus not boundless free love, but sexual moderation that became the key to perfection. Ejaculation had to be renounced in order to preserve the strength and health of both sexes, to enhance the pleasure of the sexual act, and to advance male self-control to perfection. Complex marriage thus formed the core of communal life.[81]

Noyes labeled the Oneida Community as a "school of self-control," in which young people learned from older members.[82] Young women entering puberty were introduced to the art of sex by mature men—preferably by Noyes himself—while young men were instructed by postmenopausal women. This would eliminate the threat of pregnancy as a result of involuntary ejaculation by young men not yet able to exhibit the necessary self-control. Inquiries about sexual intercourse were always fielded by men and delivered by women, who occupied top positions in the communal hierarchy and belonged to Noyes's inner circle. He thus always knew who slept with whom. On the one hand this was a system of social control through sex. On the other it made it easier for women to reject male inquiries since they did not have to answer them directly. However, if they declined too often, rejected men's overtures, and lived what was known as the "shaker lifestyle," they were subjected to a critique at one of the nightly community meetings. After all, sex was seen as instrumental to the communal spirit and as a service to God. Men who could not repress their ejaculation were called "leakers" and likewise suffered public criticism and humiliation. They were demoted from men to boys, and were subsequently restricted to having intercourse only with postmenopausal women until they had demonstrated better self-control. The commune was rife with rumors that Noyes himself was unable to refrain from ejaculation.[83]

With regard to birth control, the system of *male continence* seemed to be more effective than expected. Most young women had their first sexual encounter at age fourteen, yet the average age of new mothers was twenty-four. And young women were especially desired as sexual partners. According to surveys conducted in the 1870s, Oneida women had 2.4 children on average, while the average number outside the commune was 3.2.[84]

The system of complex marriage and male continence ended in August 1879, along with the dissolution of the commune itself, leaving only a commercial enterprise in place after 1881. The dissolution occurred as a result of internal conflict around Noyes's succession. Noyes's critics had demanded more transparent rules and had challenged the leader's prerogative to personally introduce female virgins into the art of sexual intercourse.

On one hand, the community was built around core male competencies in liberal societies, such as the ability to self-control and self-government. On the other hand, the collectivization of sex and the idea of complex marriage meant a disempowerment of men, if one applied the standards of the established gender patterns. Noyes stripped men of their essential position as procreators, providers, and protectors of their own families when he stressed a collective responsibility for sustenance and shelter and the end of competition in the working world because jobs in the commune rotated. Also, men did not have to impress women with wealth for getting sexual favors because sex was a spiritual endeavor. Noyes himself, however, occupied an elevated position as the "father to all," expressed through his sexual privileges.[85]

Criticisms and Interventions

Male communards rarely criticized the commune and its leadership, even though concerns and complaints existed from the beginning of the Oneida experiment. One such complaint was recorded by William Gould, who criticized that Noyes's followers were subservient instruments of their leader and that the ties between Noyes and his subordinates were less than fruitful for them.[86] Otherwise, criticism came up in the last years of the commune as the struggle over Noyes's succession heated up. Several men showed to be particularly upset about the leader's privilege to initiate young women into sex. Also, female dropouts from the community denounced the setup of the community around male sexual interests. Young women objected to being obliged to have sex seven times or more per week with men, most of whom they found neither attractive nor desirable.[87]

The rumors that father Noyes relentlessly pursued young girls erupted into open accusations as the commune began to dissolve. During the Sunday meeting on April 23, 1882, Noyes, seventy at the time and living in Niagara, defended himself: "Our institution . . . was avowedly a school for culture in sexual experience and I was the school master. It was my duty as master to attend to all the scholars, at least enough to protect them from evil instruction. And be it observed it was especially my duty to look out for the young, because they are most liable to fall into bad hands & learn bad ways."[88] After all, early puberty was considered to be the time when the devil had the greatest success at planting the seed of evil and when young people were especially in need of firm guidance. Oneida women countered the sexual pressures by creating exclusive spaces where they would nurture close female bonds. The Oneida Community offered ample opportunity for such fellowship since the community was at once openly and tightly structured. These relationships formed an integral part of the female world of affection and ritualized communal practices, much as they were part of the female nineteenth-century world, as described by historian Carroll Smith-Rosenberg.[89]

Neighbors had often been quite critical of the commune's living and love-making arrangements. "Our position as a Community in regard to marriage and the relations of the sexes, has always been more or less an offense to the world," announced Noyes in the *Circular*, as he tried to fortify his congregations against the sharpest outside attacks in March 1852.[90] The attacks had started a couple of years before with the introduction of the system of complex marriage, which led to accusations of adultery against Noyes, after potential new members were appalled upon finding out about the commune's sexual practices.[91] When Noyes faced a criminal conviction and the unrest among his neighbors reached unsettling proportion, he fled with his followers from Vermont to New York. In 1848, the commune settled in the religiously diverse western part of the state on the property of a born-again Christian in the vicinity of the town of Oneida.[92]

But also the new neighbors initially eyed the commune with suspicion and voiced complaints. The *New York Observer* attacked their practices various times. Harshest conflicts occurred between 1850 and 1852, and a court-ordered dissolution of the commune was only narrowly averted. Complex marriage was even abolished for six months and the *Circular* announced that members should return to the "marriage morality of the world." When in the 1860s a new wave of complaints erupted from neighbors, it failed to succeed because the commune was already too tightly integrated into the commercial life of the surrounding community.[93]

Opponents criticized that the commune had a destructive effect on society. They charged that systematic licentiousness in the commune led to the breakdown of family, morality, and the social order: mothers and fathers were not what they were supposed to be. Noyes, they complained, propagated all this through his many obscene publications.[94]

Slavery, Family, and Fatherhood, 1830–1860

I have frequently lectured on slavery, and exhibited the handcuffs, collar, chain, cowhide, and the paddle, showing many friends in this country what constitutes the liberty of the United States of America.

—Thomas H. Jones, letter to a friend, July 15, 1852

Family Man, Slave, and Abolitionist Thomas H. Jones—Part 1

He would be willing to endure any suffering to the end of his days, if only he could free his son from the yoke of slavery, wrote Thomas H. Jones from Liverpool in the Canadian province of Nova Scotia to Daniel Foster, a friend, supporter, and member of the Massachusetts abolitionist movement. "Sometimes I get quite discouraged," the former slave added, but then he would regain his strength to continue the fight for freedom and self-determination for himself, his family, and all enslaved people.[1]

A few years earlier Tom Jones had succeeded in buying the freedom of his wife Mary R. Moore-Jones, but not of their son. In July 1848 he sent his wife and their three younger children, who had been born after her liberation and therefore free, by ship from Wilmington, North Carolina, to New York. Jones had heard rumors that his children's freedom was in danger south of the Mason-Dixon line. Jones himself was still a slave, paying a hundred fifty dollars in yearly rent to his master for his own labor. He made a living as a longshoreman in the harbor of Wilmington, at the time one of the largest coastal cities in the Carolinas. On September 11, 1849, he managed to escape and reunite with his family in New York by stowing away on the merchant brig *Belle*.[2]

With his flight, he crossed several boundaries: from South to North, from slavery into freedom, and from subjugation to humanity and manhood. Journeys, particularly those on ships, held powerful symbolic significance in black history before and after emancipation. As Paul Gilroy has argued in *The Black Atlantic*, movement had been a central theme in the construction of black identity, spanning the Atlantic from Africa and Europe to the Americas. In the mid-nineteenth century, journeys not only served as reminders of the so-called middle passage and thus the abduction into slavery, but also signified the struggle for freedom, rights, and opportunities denied to African Americans in the United States. Maritime passageways could lead south to Haiti, which since gaining independence in 1804 had become synonymous with black self-determination. Or they could lead north, promising a path from slavery to freedom.[3]

Jones is the protagonist of one of the many *slave narratives*, a most important and complex genre in African American literature and history. This chapter argues how his narrative mobilized the power of authentic personal testimony, while adhering to the conventions of the genre itself. Historian Bruce Dorsey emphasizes that the content of *slave narratives* is both "real and yet imagined." The addition on the title page of Jones's publication that his history was written down as told to a friend indicates some of the complications involved in using the text as a historical source for narrating the history of an African American father during slavery. Tom Jones tells his story in the first person in order to vouch for the authenticity of his experience and present himself as an autonomous and empathetic subject. He thus represents the type of human being and man who, in the eyes of his mostly white readers at the time, has all the qualities expected from a good and virtuous Republican citizen and deserves freedom because he seems capable of using it properly. He thus embodies the outlines of an autonomous, well-working liberal subject who elevates himself—and deserves to be elevated—out of "the dependent and suffering condition" of slavery. His role as a father is of special importance in this context, and Jones draws on language that is easily understood by his mostly white middle-class readers in the North of the country.[4] Most family men would easily identify with the feelings and responsibilities expressed in the following passage from Tom Jones's narrative:

> The meeting with my dear wife and children I cannot describe. It was a moment of joy too deep and holy for any attempt to paint it. Husbands

who love as I have loved, and fathers with hearts of fond, devoted affection, may imagine the scene and my feelings, as my dear wife lay sobbing in her joy in my arms, and my three dear little babes were clinging to my knees, crying 'Pa has come; Pa has come.' It was the happy hour of my life. I then felt repaid for all my troubles and toils to secure the freedom of my dear family and my own.[5]

In addition to the tortures suffered on slave plantations, abolitionists condemned above all the practice of tearing apart families as the most brutal and violent aspect of slavery, as aptly described by Harriet Beecher Stowe in her novel *Uncle Tom's Cabin* (1852). The book, which appeared shortly before *The Experience of Thomas H. Jones*, became one of the most widely read novels of the nineteenth century.[6] Families were separated when one partner or a child was sold, and their fate elicited much compassion and sympathy among the reading public. Thus, the reuniting with his family marks the high point of Jones's story, which otherwise is filled with violence, subjugation, separation, but also with the father's journey toward manhood and independence, as he overcomes all obstacles and guides his family and himself into freedom. In his narrative he exhibits all the personal qualities necessary to become a good father and republican, which he was denied by the system of slavery; and he thus qualifies as a republican citizen in the eyes of many of his readers.

Yet the reunification of the Jones family was incomplete in several ways. First, even after the flight to the North, Tom Jones's position remained precarious. He described realizing the constraints on his freedom even north of the Mason-Dixon line as most horrible experience.[7] The notorious Fugitive Slave Law from September 18, 1850, turned the northern states into hunting grounds for fugitive slaves, and all free African Americans constantly feared being deported into slavery under false pretense. Descriptions of fugitives were often arbitrary and deliberately vague. As a result many free African Americans moved farther north into the British territories of Canada, where they would be safe from the law. According to some estimates, between four and five thousand African Americans fled into Canada in the first weeks after the enactment of the law, among them Tom Jones. And even though politicians and abolitionists in cities such as Chicago, Pittsburgh, and Boston assured African Americans that they would protect them from the Fugitive Slave Law, Tom Jones did not feel safe in Boston, not even for a short return visit to see his family. Instead, his wife traveled to Nova Scotia to meet him in the summer of 1852.[8]

Second, the family's reunification remained incomplete as long as their first-born child was still enslaved. In a letter to his friend Daniel Foster, Jones wrote that his wife Mary had received word from North Carolina that the current owner was willing to sell the child to his parents for the sum of $850. But by the summer of 1852, they had been able to raise only $324, with Mary working in Boston and Tom in Nova Scotia. Tom raised money with sermons about his life as a slave, and his letter to Foster, who was a member of the Massachusetts Anti-Slavery Society, was part of the same effort. Jones even considered traveling to England, where he hoped to be able to make more money with his life story. He hoped in particular to use the occasion of the first World's Fair, the Crystal Palace Exhibition in London during the summer of 1851, to advance the cause of abolitionism. However, the best strategy for raising money for his own child, it occurred to him, was to write and sell his own life story about his tribulations as a slave and his struggle for freedom. Thus, *The Experience of Thomas H. Jones* was from its inception already part of a personal and vital commercial operation, and the resulting narrative tried to meet the expectations of a northern, predominantly white readership. By the 1830s slave narratives had become a genre that was to provide testimony to a northern audience about the unbearable conditions of life under slavery, so as to "thrill the land with horror," as abolitionist Theodor Dwight Weld said. For many white northerners, this was the first report claiming authenticity they received about the nature of slavery, its violence, and how it tore apart families of father, mother, and children, who were just being defined as bedrock of a liberal republic.[9]

"I have frequently lectured on slavery, and exhibited the handcuffs, collar, chain, cowhide, and the paddle," Jones wrote to Foster about his experience as a slave and his skill as a speaker. He would thus be able to provide the necessary details for such a slave narrative, in order to further the struggle against slavery and help reunite other slave families. In addition, Jones argued that he had helped disseminate William Lloyd Garrison's radical abolitionist periodical *Liberator* as far as the Caribbean and thus should be able to sell his own story as well. The fact that Tom Jones's name might be associated with the protagonist of Stowe's successful *Uncle Tom's Cabin* was another selling point for his publishers, even though the main characters in each story—the independent man and father Tom Jones who longed for self-determination versus the subservient, sentimental, and effeminate Uncle Tom—had little in common.[10]

Yet it remains unclear whether Tom and Mary Jones ever managed to purchase their oldest child's freedom. The fact that later editions of his book from the late 1850s to the 1880s report on Jones's buying of his own mother's freedom from slavery but say nothing about his son suggests that they might not have succeeded.[11]

The following section shifts the focus from Tom Jones's personal experiences to the narrative structure of his story and its relation to the life under slavery. The goal is to find out more about the relationship between slavery, family life, and the concept of the responsible father as autonomous actor on behalf of his family and seeking to achieve control over his family's destiny. This image of the father in a nuclear family represented the ideal type of the liberal order and served as a yardstick for the recognition of African American manhood.[12]

Black Families under Slavery

Slavery in the American South was the antithesis of a liberal order perceived as consisting of autonomous subjects being guided toward successfully using their freedom. Michel Foucault describes slavery as a "relationship of violence" that "acts upon a body or upon things; it forces, it bends, it breaks on the wheel, it destroys, or it closes the door on all possibilities . . . , and if it comes up against any resistance, it has no other option but to try to minimize it."[13] Eric Foner states likewise that slavery constituted the dependence on the will of others and the explicit denial of the right to self-government. Slavery stood in opposition to political and governmental paradigms propagated during the revolution and the founding of the republic.[14]

This very general claim needs to be qualified in two ways: First, within liberal societies, the ideal of equality and self-determination rarely matched the lived reality. The North had not granted all people equal access to self-government and to the resources of society and the state. Full acceptance of all human beings as citizens and subjects had never been realized.[15]

Second, and conversely, the system of slavery also had some niches of self-government in which slaves would act on their own behalf and exercise some self-control. Slave narratives in particular were determined to argue how slaves were able, within a system based on violence, to carve out such niches not completely dominated by the slave owner and thus exert some degree of "subjecthood." In most slave narratives becoming a subject was a predominantly male experience and often closely associated with the fulfillment of the duties of a father as provider and protector.[16] Victorian middle-class gender norms were taken as the ideal, and they were projected onto living conditions under slavery, even though these were fundamentally different. Separate spheres, for instance, did not exist, and working conditions for male and female slaves differed little, which was seen as effeminating male slaves and masculinizing female slaves.[17]

Nineteenth-century defenders of slavery argued that slaves lacked the ability for self-government and appropriate family structures and that therefore they had to be placed under the sovereign power of a master. Such apologetic voices became increasingly impassioned and fierce since the 1830s, as the abolitionist movement gained strength. For instance, George Fitzhugh sought to present an image of a southern aristocracy of benevolent patriarchs who offered protection and care for immature slaves unable to manage freedom. The strong had the duty to protect the weak, he wrote in *Cannibals All!* This made their domination necessary, even if by coercion and violence: "Physical force, not moral suasion, governs the world," he claimed, expressing the core ideas behind a sovereign power structure that provided recognition as subjects only to a chosen few and was closely interwoven with the idea of *white supremacy*.[18]

Defenders of southern slavery praised benevolent paternalism and racial domination as guarantors of social, economic, and political stability. By contrast, they regarded northern liberalism as a complete failure. Family and fatherhood were also of central importance in the southern white concept of the slave society yet were designed in ways fundamentally different from the liberal nuclear family model. White patriarchs declared the entire plantation as their family, over which they ruled

through direct order, violence, punishment, and patronizing benevolence. The freedom of white male farmers and landowners rested on the
unfreedom of others, and providing incentives for self-government and
the creation of opportunities was not part of their plan. Slave families
were not recognized in their analyses of southern society.[19]

Sociologist Orlando Patterson described life in slavery as "social
death." His understanding of slavery has been criticized as too one-sided
because it does not allow for differences in experiences and suggests
that there existed no room for agency at all among the enslaved.[20] At the
same time it points to the denial of recognizing slaves as human beings
and subjects. For African American enslaved fathers, unfreedom meant
subjugation under a sovereign power, severe constraints on their ability to fulfill the role as provider and protector of their families or to act
autonomously. Enslaved fathers thus lived in a social system that denied
them both the sovereign privileges of a patriarch as well as the governmental privileges of the gentle leader and father.

For many years scholars interpreted slavery as having created a blind
spot in African American family formations precisely where the father
figure was supposed to reside. Analyses of black families lamented lacking fathers, which they assumed led to dysfunctional families and weakened black communities. The roots of this weakness were traced back to
the experience of slavery, which was said to have triggered an increasingly habitualized lack of paternal responsibility.[21]

Three things are important to note in this context. First, these analyses were based on the assumption that the middle-class nuclear family
represented the natural order of things, and thus they asserted its normative and regulatory power. The possibility of different family formations among slaves was simply ignored. Second, declaring slavery as the
root cause of current problems served as a cover-up for continued racism and discrimination. Third, in the 1970s a revisionist historiography
gained momentum and led the historical study of family formations in
slavery in a new direction. This new historiography countered gener-
alizations about dysfunctional families and lacking fathers by closely
examining the diversity of lived experiences in the past. These scholars
presented slaves as historical actors who grappled with the conditions
of their existence and achieved moments of self-determination in their
daily lives. Resistance, struggle, and agency became points of departure

for a new way of thinking and writing about slavery, its history, and the daily life of slaves.[22] Also as of the 1970s historians and anthropologists argued that slaves brought with them traditions and rituals from Africa that influenced the ways in which they organized their family and social life in America, thus leading to a family way of life based on different traditions than the nuclear family (which in fact was not yet that traditional in the first half of the nineteenth century).[23]

Under slavery it was significantly more difficult to live together as father, mother, and children, and slavery placed limits on the ability to find a suitable partner. Choices were few, even on large plantations of the Deep South, also because slaves avoided relationships among extended kin. Often slaves started liaisons across plantations, which meant that even steady partners and married couples would not live together.[24]

In addition, the possibility of being sold or leased to a neighboring plantation or, even worse, to a different region constantly threatened to tear apart couples and families. Slaves were also often given away as part of a dowry or inheritance. After the abolition of the international slave trade in 1808 and the growth of cotton plantations in the Deep South, internal trade from the Upper to the Deep South flourished more than ever. Historian Ira Berlin called this massive internal forced migration a second "middle passage." Even sales within the nearby region would most likely mean the end of a relationship because small distances were hard to cover. For instance, Tom Jones was separated from his first wife Lucilla Smith and her three children because they belonged to different owners, and Lucilla's owner moved from Wilmington to Newbern, only seventy-four miles to the north and still in North Carolina but nonetheless unreachable for Jones. About a year and a half later Lucilla's owner moved to Tuscaloosa, Alabama, making the separation between the father and his wife and children permanent.[25]

Even though subjected to sovereign power, slaves were still struggling to shape their life and safeguard a certain room for maneuver. They established bonds and partnerships against all odds. They set their own rules for courtship and marriage, which might not have transformed their bonds into marriages in the eyes of the white law, yet nonetheless provided them acknowledgment of their own community. Tom Jones, for instance, remarked in his narrative that his marriage with Lucilla Smith was not legal yet nonetheless recognized among slaves: "*We called* it and *we considered* it a *true marriage,* although we knew well that marriage was not permitted to the slaves as a sacred right of the loving heart."[26] Children were often named after parents and other relatives, but particularly after their fathers, in order to establish and document relationships. Larger kinship networks were often more important among slaves than the close bonds of the two-generation family.[27]

The size of the plantation was highly significant for the social organization of slaves and the bonds between them. Wilma Dunaway emphasizes that slave communities of the Upper South tended to be more unstable, given the small size of most plantations and households. Almost half of all sales involved the separation of couples, parents, and children. In the Mountain South only a fifth of all slave families resembled the model of the nuclear family, which historian Herbert Gutman had described as far more widespread, and larger kinship networks were almost nonexistent in this region of scattered settlements and small households. Also, in North Carolina in general most plantations were smaller and had fewer slaves. When Thomas Jones was born in 1805, he was one of 150,000 African Americans in North Carolina, most of whom were enslaved and the majority (53 percent in 1800) of whom lived in households with five or fewer slaves. Less than 3 percent lived on plantations with more than fifty slaves. In 1851 only ninety-one slaveholders in the entire state owned more than a hundred slaves. On both small and large plantations, slaves experienced permanent interferences with their relationships, children, family, and social bonds, including sexual assaults on female slaves and the breeding of offspring. Yet to shed light on the subjugation of slaves does not mean to ignore the many daily acts of resistance, including flight, sabotage, work stoppages, and slowdowns.[28]

The Father, Slave, and Abolitionist Thomas H. Jones—Part 2

Slavery was central to the discourse on freedom in the American republic. Much of this discourse revolved around families, the positions of white and black men within the family, as well as the extent of self-government they were able to exercise in the North and the South. Slave narratives, actually often written or coauthored by white abolitionists, became a central genre in this discourse. They generated images of slaves who were not childlike and subservient at all, but acted as think-ing, decision-making, sensitive, loving, and caring subjects who fought against the external constraints of their existence. Thus, they appeared to be able to live a life in freedom and as citizens of a republic. The narratives often described families, and particularly fathers, who, even though they were slaves, nonetheless had the competency needed to govern themselves and their families, an ability usually attributed only to free white men. Thus, many slave narratives reiterate the competency for governing oneself and the family as a major qualification required for men to act as republicans and subjects, but they did not define this abil-ity as exclusively white. Therefore, slave narratives portrayed freedom as more than the mere antithesis of slavery, but as intricately interwoven with the conditions and skills of using one's freedom properly and pro-ductively to the best of the family and the community.[29]

Tom Jones became so diligent and industrious in the course of time that he would have made Benjamin Franklin proud. Initially consid-ered a burdensome chore of slavery, for him over the years work be-came something akin to a life elixir, precisely from the point in his life when it served his own advancement. Through his industriousness Jones fulfilled the core requirement for a successful and morally upstanding republican.[30] Free labor was considered a central feature of the free and autonomous citizen, and it was considered a white man's privilege. Proponents and opponents of slavery fought over which of the labor systems—the plantation slave labor system in the South or the industrial wage labor system in the North—generated which kinds of coercion, subjugation, and bondage.[31]

Like most slave children, Jones began to work for his master at the age of nine. By that time he had already been sold once and been sepa-rated from his parents. His jobs ranged from feeding horses to taking care of fireplaces. Later he was given the task to mind the store of his new owner. After his master's death, Jones was sold a second time at age twenty-three, for $435 to an attorney named Owen Holmes. He later rented his own labor from Holmes in order to work as a longshoreman in Wilmington harbor, where he would earn up to three dollars a day. He soon was in charge of a crew of three men, among them free people as well. His owner still had to sign off on the labor contracts since a slave was legally not entitled to sign for himself. Records show that his owner protected his slaves against criminal contractual partners. In the 1885 edition of his book, when the sufferings under slavery were less prominent in the narrative, he praised his third owner as a kind of father figure: "He protected and provided for me as though I had been one of his own household."[32]

Jones demonstrated his extraordinary work ethic when one day he received word of his wife having to move away from the city with her owner. Not only did he dutifully report his impending absence to his supervisor, but he also instructed his crew before he left: "Directing my men to keep at their work until I returned, I set out for my humble cabin."[33]

He was, however, powerless to prevent the forced separation from his first wife. Jones learned from this experience, for when he married his second wife, he sought to take their fate into his own hands. Diligent and hardworking and using his room for maneuver, Jones first rented his own wife Mary Moore, and after three years he was able to purchase her freedom. Hard work and the realization of his familial dreams were intricately interwoven in his narrative. Jones managed to assume the role of provider and protector of his loved ones through his work ethic and his foresightedness and thus qualified for republican citizenship.[34]

Jones displayed the same ambition, competency, and daring when it came to education. A second important part of his story revolves around his efforts to learn to read. North Carolina and other slave states prohibited slaves from learning to read and write, and also teaching of these skills to slaves was legally sanctioned. Laws and punishments had always been drastic, and they grew in severity particularly after challenges from the abolitionist movement and the Nat Turner rebellion in Virginia in 1831. "The teaching of slaves to read and write, has a tendency to excite dissatisfaction in their minds, and to produce insurrection and rebellion," the 1831 North Carolina bill stated. Whites who violated the law faced prison and a fine of up to two hundred dollars; free blacks were to be punished with up to thirty-nine lashes in addition to prison and fines.[35]

Those who were literate could read the newspaper, circulate news, and forge passes and identity papers. Literacy was one of the primary weapons against exploitation and subjugation. Furthermore, the ability to read had been an essential tool in the Age of Enlightenment and of

Democratic revolutions. The intellectual and political spirit of the Enlightenment helped people acknowledge and then overcome their own
limitations on their path to emancipated citizenship. Forced illiteracy, in
turn, stood for the enslavement of the mind, the intellectual counterpart
to bodily enslavement and subjugation.[36]

Tom Jones's narrative illustrates the importance of literacy at the very
moment when as a young boy he endured the most brutal beating by
his owner, just so the latter would not find his reading primer. He had
obtained the book under arduous circumstances and even talked some
white boys into helping him make a start, to identify letters and build
syllables. This story closely mirrored that of Frederick Douglass.[37] Over
time the reading primer became Jones's prized treasure, the embodiment of the possibility to transcend the boundaries set for him: "My
days were passing away in very great happiness under the consciousness
that I was learning to read. I felt at night, as I went to my rest, that I was
really beginning to be a *man*, preparing myself for a condition in life
better and higher, and happier than could belong to the ignorant *slave*."
To reveal his secret and his book was not an option for Tom Jones, not
even when under the threat of severe punishment: "Without a moment's
hesitation, I determined to save my precious book and my future opportunities to learn out of it. I knew if my book was discovered that all was
lost, and I felt prepared for any hazard or suffering rather than give up
my book and my hopes of improvement." He was prepared to risk even
physical death for the chance to escape the "social death" of slavery.[38]
His fierce determination to acquire knowledge and his ambition to get
closer to the goal of freedom also demonstrated that he had the potential
to be a good republican.

Literacy increased Tom Jones's independence and opened up new opportunities to further circumvent the rule of his master. Reading about
God inspired him to open up to Christianity. It is noteworthy that his
narrative does not convey any syncretism when it comes to believes and
religious practices, as was customary in slave communities.[39] Rather
Jones wrote about his fascination with the lessons in Christian forgive-
ness given in the New Testament, which must have pleased his readers.
He recalled spending whole nights in conversation with like-minded
people, which again aroused the ire of his owner, who even threatened
to kill Jones if he continued to participate in religious services and

nightly get-togethers. Jones, however, by now seventeen years old, declared again his willingness to die for the chance to move closer to freedom. In a key scene of his narrative he endures the tortures willingly, inspired by his Christian faith, without being affected by them, which again provided him with power over his master:

> Master came down, talked with me a while, and told me he should whip me because I had disobeyed him in staying out all night. He had told me he should whip me if ever I did so, and he should make every promise good. So I began to take off my clothes. He called me a crazy fool, and told me to keep my clothes on till he told me take them off. He whipped me over my jacket; but I enjoyed so much peace of mind that I scarcely felt the cow-hide. This was the last whipping that Mr. Jones inflicted upon me.[40]

Here, too, parallels to Frederick Douglass's story are obvious. Douglass's moment of resistance against his enslavement is among the most famous passages in abolitionist literature. He resists the sovereign force and continuous torture of his cruel overseer through physical resistance. Douglass described the fight against his overseer Covey as a turning point in his life: "I was a changed being after that fight. I was *nothing* before; I WAS A MAN NOW. It recalled to life my crushed self-respect and my self-confidence, and inspired me with a renewed determination to be a FREEMAN."[41] Different from Douglass, Jones disempowered the violence of his master through Christ-like endurance. From that moment on, the whip could no longer harm him. Like Douglass, though, Jones described how his triumph over his master's violence strengthened his desire for freedom and self-determination, which was described as equal to the chance for self-improvement. "I still felt a longing desire to improve, to be free."[42]

By embracing work, education, and Christian religion, Jones became the embodiment of a responsible, reflecting, and diligent man, who even under the most difficult of all circumstances acted deliberately and with determination and thus generated an image of himself as a subject capable of mastering his own freedom. As told by his narrative, this process of subject formation was meant to appeal to his readers, and it climaxed in a fourth arena, the family. We need to recall how apologists for slavery often evoked the failure to fulfill parental duties and the alleged nonexistence of black family life. Thus the striving for familial togetherness was of major significance within slave narratives.[43] The multiple family separations endured by Tome Jones exposed readers to the cruelty of slavery. His struggles on behalf of his family and his strategic operation for keeping them together presented him as a good, caring father who knew the art of government and made a potentially valuable member of a republic.

Tom Jones's narrative begins with a brief sketch of his home and his parents. Until he turned nine his parents were able to provide him with a happy childhood, a common theme in the live stories of slaves:

> I remember well that dear old cabin, with its clay floor and mud chimney, in which, for nine years, I enjoyed the presence and love of my wretched parents. Father and mother tried to make it a happy place for their dear children. *They* worked late into the night many and many a time to get a little simple furniture for their home and the home of their children; and . . . [to protect them] from the storm and the cold. . . . I have heard them [my dear parents] speak of their willingness to bear their own sorrows without complaint, if only we, their dear children, could be safe from the wretchedness before us.[44]

In the same passage Jones draws a link between his parents' feelings and his own as a father and thus establishes fundamental continuities about parenthood and humanity, which apparently are presented by the narrative as of timeless validity and as existing across all boundaries. Loving and caring parental and particularly paternal emotions were seen as part of a *conditio humana*, which was passed from parents to children and which slaves shared with particular intensity:

> I can testify, from my own painful experience, to the deep and fond affection which the slave cherishes in his heart for its home and its dear ones. We have no other tie to link us to the human family, but our fervent love for those who are *with* us and of us. . . . I remember, and now fully understand, as I did not then, the sad and tearful look [my parents] would fix upon us when we were gathered round them. . . . I am a father, and I have had the same feelings of unspeakable anguish, as I have looked upon

my precious babes and have thought of the ignorance, degradation and woe which they must endure as slaves. . . . I love those children with all a father's fondness. God gave them to me; but my brother took them from me, in utter scorn of a father's earnest pleadings.[45]

Tom Jones condemned the tearing apart of families as inhumane. In the remaining forty pages of his narrative he tells the story of repeated separations of children from their parents and the struggle to reunite and keep them together, a story that culminates in Jones's reunion with his family.

His literacy, Christian faith, and diligence are presented as instruments that empowered the slave Tom Jones to educate himself and take up the struggle for his family's existence. Of equal importance for the success of his story are the determination, character, skill, and virtue, which aided him in overcoming all obstacles. Even though Jones describes the desire for family togetherness as natural and deeply engrained in all human beings, his narrative demonstrates that for a slave it required particular qualities to fulfill that desire for himself and his family.

When Tom Jones at twenty-three reached what his readers most likely regarded as close to the ideal marriage age, he stated, "My heart yearned to have a home, if it was only the wretched home of the unprotected slave, to have a wife to love me and to love." Though acutely aware of the pain and desperation that befell an enslaved husband and father, he nonetheless desired love, partnership, and the private sphere of a home, which, just like the middle-class ideal, would serve as a sanctuary from the horror of life "out there." The slave's striving for this ideal might have been even more urgent than the white middle-class man's, Jones surmised: "It seems to me that no one can have such fondness of love and such intensity of desire for *home* and home affections, as the poor slave." He wanted to make plans for the future with a partner, even though he knew that he had little control over it: "And yet I sought to become a husband and a father, because I felt that I could live no longer unloved and unloving."[46] Living in a loving partnership was portrayed as a fundamental timeless desire of human beings, not as an ideal and type of living arrangement that came to dominate in the early nineteenth century.

Jones's first marriage to Lucilla Smith lasted around five years, when the family was separated by the sale of Lucilla and her three children. Tom and Lucilla had always felt that the threat of separation was hanging like the sword of Damocles over their heads, and yet they never gave up hope for a better future, possibly even freedom, particularly for their children. Jones wrote that he even contemplated suicide in his sorrow and loneliness after the separation, as he spent day and night thinking about his family.[47]

After four years of despair, Tom Jones could no longer live in solitude. Before he married Mary Moore, however, he formalized his separation from Lucilla Smith, a detail that demonstrated his sense of honor and virtue. We know the rest of the story, showing how love, marriage, and the yearning for a family are intertwined with the qualities of liberal citizenship and how they challenge the sovereign-power structure of slavery.[48] This time Jones took precautions, somewhat immodestly putting both his own contribution and the divine blessing on the same level: "*She* [his second wife Mary Moore] has been rescued from slavery by the blessing of God and my efforts to save her." What followed then was the story of a man who—driven by love and enabled by his education, diligence, and Christian faith—took up the battle with fate, putting himself in the role of the head of his family, as provider and protector, and ultimately overcoming the yoke of slavery. After purchasing his wife's and his children's freedom, he undertook his own escape north into freedom, everything well planned and coordinated. "But alas! it was not long before I found that I was not yet free. I had not yet slipped from the chain," he complained at the end of his life story. "I found that my wanderings were not yet ended." His flight to Canada, the continued separation from his family, and the enslavement of his oldest child brought home to the readership that Tom Jones would continue to suffer as long as slavery existed.[49]

Self-Government and Sovereign Power

Tom Jones's struggle for self-determination and family reunification was fought in permanent conflict with the sovereign power of his master. During his youth his master's power was articulated through the repeated use of corporal punishment. The narrative lists torture after torture from his first whipping at age nine to his last one at seventeen. Readers expected to encounter such brutality since its depiction represented the harshest critique against slavery while at the same time inducing a shuddering and delightful horror in them. Physical violence and the threat of death were classic instruments of sovereign power. In slavery, its most significant tool was the whip, but there were others such as "handcuffs, collar, chain, . . . and the paddle." Jones sarcastically described them as a sign of American freedom.[50]

In the American Revolution, revolutionaries depicted their withdrawal from the orbit of sovereign power and force as their own transition from slavery to freedom and to manhood. It is thus no coincidence that Tom Jones recounts in his narrative how he was able to overcome the physical violence of his master when, at almost eighteen years of age, he was also in the bodily process of becoming a man. Even if he was still the property of a slave owner, he nonetheless had since his childhood built up counterforces. Literacy and Christian faith had helped him shape a new sense of self. His hard work, diligence, intelligence, and virtue allowed him to withdraw from his master, countering his power with a form of self-rule that led him and his loved ones through careful planning and precaution into freedom. His struggle for family, its unity and reunification, coalesces with the republican vision of good fatherhood. Even the slave narrative itself contributed to this coalescence both because the act of writing was central to his taking his life into his hands and becoming an emancipated subject and because the narrative became a means through which he hoped to unite his family and purchase his fourth child's freedom.

Thomas Jones is thus portrayed in his own narrative as a man who earned full distinction through the qualities of self-government in the best interest of himself and his family. He thus appeared as having the potential of being an ideal citizen of the republic, the opposite of the image of the immature slave unable to handle his own freedom, alluded to in the apologetic writings of the South. Thus the narrative needs to be understood as an intervention into the struggle between slavery and freedom and into a conflict between different societies built on different concepts and practices of power.

Teasing out this role of the narrative does not mean to say that enslaved men did not desire to be fathers who cared for their families. It also does not deny that they carved out niches of self-determination and acted strategically in support of their own advancement. At the same time, it is obvious that Tom Jones portrayed himself (or was portrayed by others) as a loving, caring, providing, strategically acting, and self-disciplined father at precisely the historic moment when the struggle for the end of slavery climaxed. Slave narratives were at the same time imagined and yet quite possibly real narratives of life stories, which, through the narrative form and within the specific republican and abolitionist discourse, would become testimonies for the illegitimacy of slavery as well as for the slaves' ability to use freedom properly and to the best of themselves, their families, and the republic. Furthermore, the narratives turned the family into a space where freedom and personal responsibility were lived and learned, exactly in line with the republican imagination.

Exposing how much Thomas Jones's slave narrative revolves around the middle-class model of the family helps make sense of this facet of the abolitionist movement and of the way its critique of slavery worked. It revolved around a model of a liberal society with a particular type of family and the father in its center. Abolitionists criticized slavery also because it denied this family model, leveled gender differences, dissolved separate spheres, and was said to make men and women barely distinguishable in their chores, their functions in the community, and their identity. Male slaves did not live as men were expected to live, female slaves not as women were expected to live, critics charged. Tom Jones's narrative confirmed and at the same time countered this constellation by conjuring a middle-class republican family model including the requisite gender divisions. The narrative presents a father who secures his family's freedom, who invokes divine inspiration because he rescued his family from slavery. Likewise, the narrative portrays his wife as passive, one who lets herself be rescued and who is proud of her husband because he is able to read and write and holds promise for a better future for all.[51]

Slave narratives have been analyzed as reiterating a hegemonic family model that was gaining momentum among the white middle classes of the early nineteenth century. Moreover, philosopher bell hooks has criticized slave narratives for their validation of patriarchy because many of them focused on male agency and experience, particularly the fulfillment of the paternal role as provider and protector. She describes slave narratives as the root cause for the notion that African American liberation had to be achieved and showcased through the empowerment of black men, a demand and political program that would gain momentum in the 1960s.[52]

4

Daughters, Fathers, and the Westward Movement, 1850–1880

I insisted that I could do the driving and hauling just as well as any hired help. My father permitted me to try. He mixed and loaded the mortar, and I hauled it, put it into buckets, and hoisted it up to the scaffolding to him. True enough, the work was soon done.
—Mollie Sheehan, age seventeen, spring 1870, San Juan Capistrano, California

Of Myths, Fathers, and Daughters

Since early childhood Mollie Sheehan had been on the westward trail with her father. In the early 1850s the Sheehan family moved from Kentucky through Indiana to Illinois, where her mother died soon after the birth of her younger brother. "I can dimly remember my father crying and crying," she recalled many decades later to her own daughter who recorded her memories on paper.[1] After her mother's death she lived with many different people: relatives, friends, her father, and later her stepmother Anne and several siblings. They moved through Iowa, Missouri, Colorado, Montana, and Utah, until they finally reached San Juan Capistrano in California. Mollie summarized her father's life with the following observation: "At the age of forty-six he had reached his last frontier in California, on the very shores of the westward flowing sea where lay the shadowy line between civilization and the sun."[2]

Mollie's synthesis of her family's journey from Kentucky to California, as recorded by her daughter Margaret, invokes an image of the frontier that resembled Frederick Jackson Turner's famous vision from 1893.[3] Turner described the settlement of the American continent as a dynamic movement from east to west in which white men pushed the frontier between civilization and wilderness steadily westward until it reached the Pacific Ocean. The frontier experience, he argued, had produced a specifically American type of civilization. Twenty-one years after the Sheehans had begun to build their homestead on the Pacific Coast in California, the 1890 US census declared the settlement of the continent as complete and the frontier as closed, what prompted Turner to declare the end of the first great era in American history. Nevertheless, the idea of white male conquest and settlement of an allegedly wild, untamed, and empty wilderness continued to be of great importance for the American nation-building myth.[4]

This myth was intimately connected to a vision of a republic consisting of free and independent farmers who as God's chosen people would occupy the land west of the thirteen original states to advance America's continental expansion and settlement. "Those who labour in the earth are the chosen people of God," Thomas Jefferson famously wrote in the early 1780s in his *Notes on the State of Virginia*. Historians speak of an agrarian myth of American expansion, driven by the idea of robust and independent small farmers who find a home in the allegedly empty territory and would turn the virgin continent into a civilized garden. A half century after Jefferson, the journalist John O'Sullivan further developed this vision by calling the expansion over the continent all the way to the Pacific America's "manifest destiny."[5] He elaborated this concept of manifest destiny at a time that also saw the beginning of a three-decade-long period of extended migration across the continent to the Pacific Coast. From 1840 to 1870, between a quarter and a half million people, about the population of New York City at the time, moved on the Overland Trail, roughly the same route the Sheehans had taken, through Indiana, Illinois, Iowa, and Missouri to Oregon or California.[6]

For the past decades, historians have pointed to the contradictions inherent in the romantic narratives and myths of frontier and western migration. They have stressed that the land was not uninhabited at all and exposed the westward movement as a project of settler-imperialist conquest that included the subjugation and extinction of the Native American population and needs to be seen as an integral part of global imperialism. In addition, they have emphasized the diversity of people living in the West, which included Latin Americans and East Asians in addition to Euro-Americans coming from the eastern United States.

Furthermore, historians have pointed to the gendered connotations of this vision of the West that told of male conquest of a virgin land and thus contributed to the construction of a male nation.[7]

Since the 1970s, women historians have emphasized that women's agency was often ignored in these narratives, even though many thousands of them participated in the westward trek and left numerous diaries and letters.[8] More recently gender histories have underlined, how male-oriented frontier societies were or at least had been conceptualized and portrayed as such. The West was defined as a space for male regeneration, which was of utmost cultural, social, and political importance far beyond the nineteenth century. In fact, even after the so-called end of the frontier, the West continued to be mobilized as a locus of white male rejuvenation and a remedy for the modern crisis of masculinity. Going West was offered up as a strategy for healing and regeneration in and through nature for men, who had become worn down by the responsibilities of the modern urban society. Modern stories of the West were filled with heroic trappers, hunters, ranchers, cowboys, Indian fighters, and conquerors, even though the majority of westward migrants were small farmers, many of them husbands and fathers. However, it was mostly lonesome riders and adventurers who were elevated to the status of mythic and emblematic figures of the West, not the fathers who with wife and children eked out a living in the harsh environment—for instance, like Mollie's father James, by building the railroad across the continent, by supplying the gold diggers on the mining frontier with goods, or by growing fruit and vegetables.[9]

When it comes to the westward movement, we encounter at least three myths—stories that shape one's assumptions about past and present and thus mold one's own thinking and talking.[10] First, we encounter the vision of the frontier man as a lone hero who left home and hearth behind in search of an adventurous life in the West. But many men on their westward journey fought hard for their own and their family's bare survival, most of them as farmers. Second, when thinking of farmers going West, we need to acknowledge that this was no innocent agrarian movement, but rather was linked to ideas about Anglo-Saxon exceptionalism and part of a broader settler imperialism. Third, the history of the westward movement cannot be reduced to a history of male experience.

This chapter first embeds the westward movement into the history of fatherhood and argues that going west and being a husband and father were by no means mutually exclusive.[11] At the same time the kinds of life families and fathers led on the frontier barely matched the model of the nuclear family. Moving westward often meant living in a variety of family configurations. Second, the chapter is told from the perspective of Mollie Sheehan, a girl who spent her childhood and youth on the trail. Placing a child at the center of the narrative of westward migration allows us to move beyond a history of triumphant male individualism.[12] The girl's perspective reveals that the West and the frontier were far from exclusively male. Yet at the same time it is striking to what extent even Mollie's own accounts of her experiences are interwoven with a male-dominated frontier narrative and are very much focused on her father. Reading Mollie Sheehan's memoirs shows the diversity of experiences of people on the frontier as much as the power of the frontier myths and their focus on male actors. On one hand, Mollie becomes more self-confident in her portrayal of her own contributions and strengths as she grows older, on the other hand she still describes the westward movement and the building of the homestead as a male project. In her rendering, it is her father who brings civilization to the wilderness and order into chaos, by building a home and thus creating the structures for their life as a family. It is her father who moved the alleged frontier between civilization and wilderness and who reached his last frontier in California.[13]

Whether the ambivalences in her story are a product of her own experiences or a result of the fact that she recorded her memoirs in 1929, a time of heightened romanticization of the frontier, cannot be determined. The fact that autobiographical accounts of childhoods spent on the frontier are almost always recorded many years later is a problem common in western historiography since it began over two decades ago to include children's perspectives in their accounts. Most of them have to be seen as retrospective accounts *about* childhood and not reflections *from* the perspective of childhood.[14]

Families on the Westward Trek

In 1840, James Sheehan arrived in the United States from Cork County, Ireland. The Irish were already the largest immigrant group at the time,

Figure 4.1. Mollie and James Sheehan. 97-0003, Archives and
Special Collections, Mansfield Library, University of Montana.

even though the potato famine was still years away. A few years later, in
Louisville, Kentucky, Sheehan married Ellen Fitzgibbon, who had just
come to America from Limerick in Ireland. They had a daughter in 1852:
Mary Catherine Fitzgibbon Sheehan, called Mollie. Shortly thereafter
her brother Gerald was born. The family then moved to Indiana.

The social environment in which Mollie grew up changed often and
dramatically over the next few years. In her childhood and youth she
did not experience the kind of nuclear family stability that was already
well established as a middle-class ideal by then. First the Sheehans were
joined by a widowed uncle and his three children. Soon after Mollie's
brother died in an accident, then the uncle, after that a newborn sister,
and two weeks later her mother. Weakened by the birth and with their
house burned down, the mother fell ill with pneumonia. In these early

years of the Sheehan family, the father had been away to Illinois for a while, probably without his family, for work in railroad construction.[15]

Father, daughter, and the three orphaned children of her uncle then moved on to Ottumwa, Iowa, where they lived for over a year with a family called Lauder. Whether or not the Lauders were close acquaintances of the Sheehan family is not clear from Mollie's memoirs. During this time Mollie developed close ties to some of the members of the Lauder family. Yet when her father lost his job, he and Mollie moved to an Irish farmstead and left Mollie's two girl cousins temporarily behind with the Lauders. By then their older brother was already a grown man and married. Father and daughter lived as boarders on the Irish farm. During this time Mollie was especially close to her father. The two slept in a single bed, and she accompanied him on occasion to dances in the neighborhood.

The next stage of their journey brought life changes yet again. Together with her two cousins they moved to St. Joseph, Missouri. On the eve of the Civil War they lived on the plantation of her father's cousin. Mollie and her cousins were cared for by a slave woman, who Mollie called "Mammy Caroline." She became Mollie's closest kin, especially after her father had remarried and moved with his new wife Anne Cleary to Colorado to start a mining business, leaving Mollie behind in Missouri. Colorado's first gold rush had just begun. For over a year Mollie lived without her father on the plantation, which the slaves left soon after the outbreak of the Civil War in April 1861. She recalled missing her father terribly during that time, having taken him for granted until then, as she stresses in her memoirs.[16]

The path of the Sheehans was in many ways typical of the westward movement during that period. While going west, starting from the East Coast or somewhere close to it, settling first in areas in the Midwest and then moving along the Overland Trail, most families lived in various kinship constellations, stopping in different places along the way for shorter or longer periods, before picking up and moving on. About three-quarters of those who wrote down their life stories had begun their trek to Oregon, California, or the mining towns of the Rocky Mountains somewhere in Indiana, Illinois, Iowa, or Missouri—exactly where the Sheehans had lived. By the early 1860s, there no longer existed a single route as it had been the case in the early 1840s, when the first treks made their way west. The variations grew with every new passage. Over time, more and more migrants also traveled as single families or in small groups. And it became quite common to leave children temporarily or permanently with relatives or friends, much like the father of the Sheehans had done.[17]

In the fall of 1861, Mollie's father returned to Missouri in order to take his daughter to Colorado. They spent six weeks together on the Overland Trail. In Colorado, he again left her for a few weeks with friends, before taking her to Nevada City, about forty miles west of Denver. There Mollie lived with her father, her stepmother, and her younger half sister Katherine. Mollie's father remained her main confidante, even if he was often away on business trips as a shipping agent for gold prospectors in the frontier regions. Retrospectively she characterized him as "loving but stern" and as a man "who believes that a man is the master of his home and makes his belief the practice of his household."[18]

Soon after, Mollie and her family moved northwest to Montana, first to Bannack, then Alder Gulch, and eventually Helena, which at the time was a new gold prospecting camp that had been established as a town only six months earlier. Mollie experienced Helena's first boom phase between the summer of 1865 and April 1869, when the population reached over four thousand, before declining to thirty-one hundred when many people, including the Sheehans, moved on.[19] These years were for Mollie a time of social stability, even though her father was still often absent, sometimes for months at a time as his shipping business delivered goods to frontier towns along the Montana trail from Fort Benton in the north to Salt Lake City in the south. Also, for a year and a half he worked in railroad construction again, this time in Utah, almost five hundred miles away, where he participated in the completion of the transcontinental railroad. In March 1869, about two months before the Union Pacific and Central Pacific railroads met in Promontory Summit in Utah, James Sheehan briefly returned to Helena.[20]

His return meant packing up the family's belongings once more to move for another six months to a railroad construction site in Corinne, Utah, the logistics hub of the Union Pacific Railroad. Until the completion of the transcontinental railroad the Sheehans supplied the railroad workers with food and thus earned the funds for a new beginning, this time in San Juan Capistrano near Los Angeles. Mollie remained with her parents for two more years before, at the age of nineteen in late summer of 1871, she began a teacher training program at the Convent of St. Vincent de Paul in Los Angeles.[21]

During the first eighteen years of her life, Mollie Sheehan moved a total of around forty-five hundred miles between Kentucky and California; she lived in fourteen different places, with the longest stay in a single place lasting roughly four years. This was not unusual for people on the frontier.[22] As a railroad worker and shipping agent, her father spent months and even years away from his family, yet still Mollie saw him as the one constant in her life, which was otherwise characterized by continuous change. She lived with relatives and friends, as a boarder, in cities and on the frontier, on a farm, on a plantation, in tents, and with an always changing cast of caretakers. During her childhood she lost her mother and two siblings, replaced eventually by a stepmother and two half siblings.

Westward migration, whose core phase lasted from 1840 to 1870, is one of the defining collective experiences in American history. At the very same moment in history, the nuclear family had become the hegemonic norm, being considered the anchor of the republican society and the best locus for virtuous upbringing. Mollie Sheehan's life story shows that families who moved West rarely lived in circumstances that approximated this norm. Let us now zoom in on each member of the family to see to what extent they lived a life according to the predominant family and gender norms of the times.

Fathers, Mothers, Daughters

When focusing on the father, we can clearly see how his efforts to secure the livelihood of his family shaped their path. Many other memoirs written by women confirm this experience of the Sheehans.[23] The Sheehans followed the promise, directed at men, that the building of the railroad, the harvesting of riches at the mining frontier, and the cultivation of the fertile soil in California would secure their families' livelihood. However, father Sheehan could never alone fulfill the role of the provider. Wife and daughter contributed to the family income. In addition, the family's restlessness over their sixteen-year journey on the westward trail was a direct result of the father's recurring lacking success to provide.[24]

Even the young family's first leg of the journey in 1853–54, from Kentucky to Indiana, was prompted by the fact that the father had received a contract as a worker on the railroad, which had attracted thousands more, mostly Irish and German immigrants. During the 1850s the rail network grew massively in the old Northwest. The Ohio & Mississippi Railway established a connection between Cincinnati, Ohio, through Indiana to East St. Louis in Illinois. James Sheehan followed a call by the O&M beyond Indiana and moved with the railroad construction crews to Illinois. It is unclear from Mollie's recollection whether the family joined him or not. At the time, it was quite common for fathers to leave their loved ones behind temporarily to work on construction projects, such as canals, roads, or, as in this case, railroads.[25]

Mollie's life path continued to be determined by her father's work. While Mollie's recollections are vague during this period, it seems that railway construction again prompted the Sheehans to move to Iowa. The railroad reached the small town of Ottumwa in September 1859. Interruptions in construction and unemployment during the extremely cold winter of 1859–60 seemed to have forced father and daughter to board themselves and their horses and mules on a nearby farm until father Sheehan followed another job opportunity in road construction and then as a shipping agent in St. Joseph, Missouri.[26]

After only a short stay in Missouri, he embarked on the Overland Trail—leaving Mollie behind—to Colorado, where he set up a business supplying goods to gold prospectors. Thereafter he followed the miners westward, conducting his supply business, stopping in Bannack and Alder Gulch, Montana, where gold was discovered in the summer of 1862. Based in Alder Gulch and Helena, he delivered goods into the frontier regions of the Montana trail, extending about 280 miles north to Ford Benton and about 480 miles south to Salt Lake City. His journeys lasted from days to months, at times under dangerous, even life-threatening conditions. Corruption and bankruptcy forced him to return to railroad construction and to again leave his family behind to work in Utah, where the Union Pacific and Central Pacific connected.[27]

Despite his frequent and lengthy absences, Mollie's father nonetheless sought to remain in charge of crucial family decisions: "I never questioned my father's authority. I never argued. I always obeyed," Mollie stated, remembering that her father, immediately upon his return after an eighteen-month absence, dissolved her engagement to a man ten years her senior. Mollie was sixteen years old at the time, and her engagement was not unusual. In some frontier regions the average age of marriage for women was 17.4. Also, Mollie had secured her stepmother's permission before.[28]

Already before the dissolution of the engagement, her father had asserted his control over the lives of his family members, even though he was absent most of the time. For instance, he arranged for his family's move within Alder Gulch away from the main street, where they had run a boarding house, in order to prevent contact of his wife and daughter with single men of questionable character. He also forbade Mollie to sell flowers in hotels and other public places in town or to socialize with gold diggers.[29]

Her father's trade and logistics business was risky and constantly prone to crisis. While he was circumspect about possible roadside attacks and armed himself for protection, the frequent corruption and fraud by partners and subordinates forced him repeatedly into bankruptcy. One of his coachmen made off with an entire shipment, including carriage, forcing him to take up a new job in Utah. While he was gone, his shopkeepers in Helena and Blackfoot City, three hundred miles away, embezzled all of his goods and money, so that the family had to leave Helena shortly after his return in search of a new existence. At the end of the 1860s Helena's first boom period was coming to an end anyway. The Sheehans moved to Corinne, Utah, where they established a new boarding house close to the major railroad construction site. Within six months they had saved enough money to move on to California and buy farmland. It was quite common for frontier families to grab opportunities for quick money in order to finance the next step in their effort to secure their existence.[30]

James Sheehan steered his family in the direction of San Diego, which at the time was rumored to be a booming town. Yet their journey ended instead near Los Angeles in San Juan Capistrano, after news reached him that the rumors about San Diego were false. The California boom of the 1850s and 1860s was already in decline at the time, and increasing socioeconomic insecurities in the area contributed to the growing resentment against Chinese immigrants. The Homestead Act of 1862 enabled Sheehan to purchase 160 acres of land from the federal government. However, disputes persisted into the 1870s between local, mostly Mexican, and immigrant, mostly European, settlers over murky property rights that had festered since the US incorporation of California between 1846 and 1848. Legal disputes stretched over almost two decades, leaving many Mexican rancheros bankrupt. When Sheehan bought land in 1869–70 he incurred the wrath of his Mexican neighbors, and he secured a legal deed confirming his ownership of the land in US courts.[31]

When Mollie's father had reached his last frontier in California at the age of forty-six, for the first time in his life Sheehan worked as a farmer, tilling the land and planting corn, potatoes, and fruit, including wine grapes. For the umpteenth time he tried to build a homestead for his family, which had, as so often before, taken temporary shelter in a makeshift tent. With his last money he paid a carpenter to build the house, completing the project together with his now grown daughter.[32]

Historians have shown that social and gender relations in the frontier regions of the Overland Trail both resembled and differed from those on the East Coast. Even though James Sheehan had the ultimate power of decision in his family, it is debatable whether he was the central figure in his family's government. He also did not fill the role of provider and protector, as was expected from men in a gendered society of separate spheres. Even if the respective tasks for men and women on the trail still followed gender divisions, women who undertook the westward journey took on tasks that did not conform to the notions of Victorian womanhood. And even if on the trail women were mostly responsible for cooking and laundry, they also chopped wood, carried water, steered carriages, and took on whatever tasks necessary. Scholars agree that the division of labor was more equitable on the trail than in those parts of the world that proselytized separate spheres.[33]

Women were a minority on the trails as in most frontier regions. For instance, in 1870 in the mining frontier town of Nevada City, where the Sheehans lived for a while, there were 28 women to 643 men.[34] By that point in time, the proportion of women on the trail had been rising for quite a while since the 1850s because more families and larger groups undertook the journey. Nonetheless for every woman on the trail there were between five and seven men. For women, the westward move meant making do without female networks of a kind that shaped their lives on the East Coast, which revolved around church, schools, and social tasks. Mollie too complained on occasion that there were few girls around. In a highly mobile and male-dominated society, there was not so much opportunity to create social networks among women. As historian Paula Petrik explained, this also applied to communities on the mining frontier such as Helena, where the Sheehans spent several years. Overlapping gender spheres could lead to both greater gender equality and greater patriarchal power.[35]

Looking more closely at Mollie's stepmother Anne and her position in the family confirms these gender patterns. According to Mollie's recollections it was primarily her stepmother who fulfilled the domestic tasks on the trail. She cooked and washed the laundry; she made the makeshift tents and log cabins more homey by putting up curtains between parents' and children's areas to create at least some privacy.[36] She did not steer the oxen carriage, but Mollie's father hired a coachman for the second carriage; and when James Sheehan was absent, she did not take charge of his business dealings, or at least not that we know of. His hired employees led the business into bankruptcy. Mollie never mentioned any involvement of her mother's with the supply and logistics business.[37]

Yet this does not mean that she did not contribute to the family income; she did so in her own way, though. She served meals to gold prospectors in her home, sold cakes, and offered warm meals in various other locations; she rented out rooms or ran a kitchen for railroad workers, often with Mollie's help. In frontier societies, the income of wives and older children was indispensable to the survival of the family. Mollie's recollection says little about her father's second marriage, yet we learn that it happened quickly. It was obvious that a new wife would contribute to the family income and ease the burden of a widower with a child and other children in his care. The text suggests that the relationship between Mollie's father and his second wife Anne was less intimate than one would expect from a loving partnership.[38]

Women in frontier regions were above all employed in the service sector, working independently and making independent decisions, just as the Sheehan women. Otherwise survival would not have been possible given the father's frequent absences, for such long periods, and so far.[39] The spectrum of female service work was broad, ranging from room and board to sex work. The boundaries between these areas were often fluid, and it may have been considered disreputable to run a boarding house and to feed paying guests in one's own home. Still, in Helena in 1870, about a fifth of all households engaged in that practice. Nonetheless, those who opened their doors to strangers endangered their own respectability, as prostitutes, too, regularly invited their clients to their own homes. Brothels became more common only toward the end of the nineteenth century. When Mollie left Helena in 1869, around sixty prostitutes lived in the city. Many of them had their businesses on Clore Street, where Mollie lived with her family. In her own recollections, however, she studiously avoids to mention their presence in the neighborhood.[40]

Father James Sheehan sought to put limits to Mollie's and her stepmother's self-government. He often reversed decisions made by the stepmother in his absence, whether they were permissions to attend dances "without his escort and protection" or concerned Mollie selling flowers in hotels or other public venues, her cleaning sluice boxes for miners, their running the boarding house in Alder Gulch, or her first engagement to her fiancé Peter Ronan in Helena. Again and again her father interjected and asserted himself, as Mollie put it, as "master of his home [who] makes his belief the practice of his household," especially when he feared for the respectability of his wife and daughter.[41]

Most of the time the Sheehans did not live up to the nuclear family ideal, and still Mollie's descriptions convey a sense of a familial striving for a loving and caring togetherness, much as it was envisioned in the predominant middle-class conception of the family. Retrospective projection seems to have played a vital role in this respect.[42] She repeatedly portrayed her father as her provider and protector, even though she laments his frequent absences and often writes about her loneliness.[43] She describes her father as the one who sought to keep away from her the danger of the frontier, the cold, the accidents, and the potentially deadly encounters with Native Americans, by arranging for armed guards for the trek or cutting Mollie's long hair. He also tried to shield her from other dangers common in frontier societies, particularly from other men. His objections to Mollie's entrepreneurial activities in the city have already been mentioned. Her father appeared to have been much stricter than her stepmother. He restricted both women's freedom of movement, action, and self-government.[44]

Nevertheless, Mollie's life appeared to have been shaped quite early by a mixture of self-guidance and paternal authoritarian supervision. Her descriptions also demonstrate how much she projected middle-class norms onto the representation of her own life. School and education was one such area. Already at the beginning of the journey she remembered that her father sent her to school whenever possible. Mollie also grew up with books, despite the mobile nature of her home. She read not only the Bible but allegedly also Shakespeare and Byron. She went to the theater whenever she could. Her father apparently envisioned sending her to the East Coast to a secondary school. Her recollections reveal the great importance school and education held for her. At the age of fifteen, while living in Helena, she opened up her own small school, where she taught about fifteen children for some time.[45]

Mollie's teaching initiative showed her creativity, engagement, and contribution to the family's material existence. She received $1.25 per student per week. Work, even when playful, was her steady companion. Already at age nine, when she traveled with her father on the Overland Trail to Colorado, she helped out wherever she could. She set atop the carriage, fetched water, and collected wood or buffalo dung for the fire, which is a topic of almost all childhood accounts of the frontier experience. She also describes with a tone of playfulness the sale of flowers in the city or the cleaning of gold diggers' sluice boxes. Over the years her involvement became more serious. Sometimes she was helping her father, yet many of the jobs she remembers doing she took on only during her father's absences. In addition, she worked closely with her stepmother rather than her father, looking after tenants in their boarding house, and feeding the railroad workers in Utah. Servicing railroad workers was abhorrent to the seventeen-year-old, since the men made sexual advances regularly, as she recalled. "My pride was deeply wounded. I hated waiting on the table."[46]

As Mollie grew older, she became increasingly her father's main assistant and confidante, more so than her stepmother, if her recollections are to be believed. She worked tirelessly side by side with her father, helped loading and unloading the carriages, steered the mule team on the way to California, and helped her father cultivate the land and build the homestead.[47]

Particularly their time in California is filled with hints to a mutual affection between father and daughter, their closeness as they worked together in the fields, their mutual trust, love, and "comradeship," which is a term usually reserved for male relationships. The father, in turn, showed a level of emotional attachment to the daughter that at the time might have been considered unmanly. The daughter, furthermore, kept the books for the family and thus had the best oversight over the household's finances.[48]

Commensurate with her growing competency, Mollie increasingly made her decisions more independently, though always in consultation with her father. This included the decision in the late summer of 1871 to move to Los Angeles fifty miles away to pursue an education, as well as the decision to renew her relationship with her former fiancé Peter Ronan from Helena. Even though she sought her father's approval, even showed him Ronan's love letters, she knew as well as her father that she needed to forge her own path and that her father was no longer the person who decided which path she would take. "I think, Pa," she apparently said to him shortly before her departure, "that I am old enough now and have sense enough to choose what I shall do."[49]

On January 14, 1873, Mollie left the family farm and returned to Helena together with her husband Peter Ronan. Mollie was twenty years of age, still young, when she married, but not as young as many other frontier wives. With letters and poems, through friends and hearsay, she had managed to maintain the relationship with Ronan over four years, which by all accounts was described as romantic, but also accompanied by many insecurities. In the second half of her memories we learn how Mollie remained strong and self-confident as a wife. She managed the family's affairs and contributed to the government of the family. Nonetheless, her marriage marked a moment of transition from one network into another, with the new one focused no longer on the father but on the husband as protector and provider. She accompanied him on his path until his death in October 1893. In a letter, composed about six months prior to their marriage, Ronan laid out his manly promise, which reflected his understanding of his role as husband and future father: "You will never regret your choice, for from this day forth all my care and industry will be employed for your welfare; all my strength and power will be exerted for your happiness and protection."[50]

Frontier Myths and Other Imbalances

The heroic narrative of the frontier claims that in the course of the westward movement male initiative and creative energy transformed nature into culture, building America out of wilderness. Over the years, this frontier narrative became a myth that shaped America's understanding of its past as well as its presence, guided many of its political actions, and nourished its social and cultural identity.[51]

In the following chapters, we will see time and again how Americans in the nineteenth and twentieth centuries conjured up the frontier as a place of rejuvenation and empowerment for American men in particular. Increasingly distant memories invoked an image of America built on a specific notion of male strength shaped at the frontier. This was not necessarily the strength of the family man and father but rather the strength of the combat-ready rugged individualist. These two core concepts of masculinity, the father figure and the frontiersman, placed at times contradictory demands on men.

Mollie Sheehan's recollections both complicate the history of the frontier and westward expansion by showing cracks in the myth as well as reproducing some of its core aspects. Stories like hers show first of all the diversity of people moving across the continent. Second, they show that many men who moved west are hardly to be seen as embodiments of the heroic frontier myth. James Sheehan was no trapper, bear hunter, Indian fighter, or cowboy. He was, from Mollie's perspective, first and foremost a father, who eked out a living in railroad construction and trading before finally settling down as a farmer. In addition, he was continuously driven westward toward California primarily by bankruptcies and crises, rather than by a heroic desire to expand America's reach on the continent. He suffered several setbacks, which was quite common, as shown by Mollie's husband Peter Ronan, who also suffered financial ruin several times in his lifetime.

Obviously, how families moved across the continent, which path they took, and their timing were largely determined by the father's work opportunities. We know from Mollie's recollections that even though she and her stepmother contributed to the family income, it did not alter where or when they moved. Nevertheless, the Sheehans did not adhere to the model of the nuclear family, generally seen as the keystone of the

American republic. The only constant in their life together was the permanent instability of their circumstances.

Mollie Sheehan thus provides insight into the life of a family on the frontier, which reinforced and at the same time contradicted the dominant ideals of fatherhood and republic. She portrays James Sheehan as a caring father who nonetheless leaves behind his child (and by extension the family) for long stretches of time, placing her with friends and wider family, before entering into a second marriage. He failed repeatedly in his role as provider and constantly relied on family members to secure their existence; nonetheless he often acted in a patriarchal and authoritarian manner and made major decisions in the family. Nevertheless their life still opened up numerous spaces for stepmother and daughter to act independently without having to adhere to paternal orders. Still, until his death in October 1888, James Sheehan always acted on the assumption that it was his responsibility to govern and rule the family.

Mollie Sheehan, too, tells the story of westward expansion and of life on the frontier as predominated by a natural quest for nuclear family life and its related values. She barely mentions unregulated sexuality, violence, corruption, and fraud in the frontier regions. Prostitution on the frontier, and particularly in Helena, is only hinted at marginally in her narrative, even though it was a thriving business. Her story instead is built around themes such as hard work, diligence, church, family, as well as romantic love, which together are presented as having transformed western wilderness into civilization.[52]

Being a Father and a Soldier in the Civil War, 1861–1865

We were standing in an open field, under the shot and shell
of these batteries, for half an hour, before we moved for-
ward, and a good many soldiers were killed all around me.
One poor fellow had his head knocked off in a few feet of
me, and I felt all the times as if I would never see you and
little sister again.
—Letter from Private John Camden West to his son Stark
West on his fourth birthday, July 8, 1863, after the Battle of
Gettysburg

John Camden West was one of over three million men who between 1861
and 1865 fought in the American Civil War. Around 900,000 took up
arms for the Confederates to fight for secession and slavery, and around
2.2 million for the Union, including 189,000 African Americans. Born
and raised in Camden, South Carolina, West had followed his brother to
Texas in 1855 at the age of twenty-one. At the beginning of the Civil War
the vast majority of his extended family still lived in Camden, one of the
oldest cities in South Carolina and an important trading post and center of Kershaw County in the midlands. The family of his wife Mary E.
Stark, whom he had married on April 14, 1858, came from South Carolina's capital Columbia, not far from Camden. South Carolina's plantation
system had continuously expanded since the late eighteenth century.
The dominant crops were rice, particularly in the midlands, and cotton
in the upcountry. At the beginning of the Civil War, about 67 percent of
Kershaw County's population were slaves, surpassed in proportion only
in the coastal regions of the state.[1]

When John West moved into the vicinity of Waco, Texas, he belonged to the Anglos who brought slavery to the region. Even though
he worked as an attorney and school principal in Texas, he nonetheless owned slaves, and as the master of the house he felt responsible for

their instruction. West did not manage a plantation, yet his letters and recollections reveal a deep connection to the specific way of life he had known among the southern gentry of the Deep South. West felt a close bond with South Carolina, which was the first state to secede from the Union, on December 20, 1860, after the election of Abraham Lincoln.[2]

When the first shots of the Civil War were fired in April 1861, there was no question that John West was going to defend the culture of the South against what he interpreted as the incursions of the Union. His idea of freedom meant that the rebellious southern states had control over their own social, economic, and political order and above all that white men had the freedom to own slaves. His understanding of white freedom was thus built on black unfreedom.[3] West was aroused by battle euphoria, as were many other men, and he was among the first to enlist in the Fourth Texas Regiment. However, just before he was to move out with his regiment, the president of the Confederate States appointed him district attorney for West Texas. Jefferson Davis felt that West's contribution to the rebellion was bigger in politics and the law than on the battlefield. Several times afterward West volunteered for military service again, and each time he was ordered back into politics. In his own recollections, he wrote that those close to him also questioned whether as a husband and father he should volunteer to serve at the front. After all, casualties were extremely high—more than a quarter of the Confederate soldiers died on the battlefield or from injuries and disease in field hospitals. In the end, West ignored their advice and joined the troops, as so many other married men and fathers did.[4]

Of all Confederate soldiers, 6 percent came from Texas, and even if his home state of South Carolina was fifteen hundred miles away, West regarded it as his duty to join the bloody battles in the East. It is said that particularly the Texas elite with close ties to the Deep South were prone to seeing the Civil War as a battle for their way of life. In the spring of 1863, West could no longer be held back. He wanted to prove himself as a man by banishing the enemy from "our soil," as he put it in his diary on April 14, 1863, when he was on his way to Virginia to join Hood's Texas Regiment. Texans had acquired the reputation of being General Robert E. Lee's sharpest weapon. West's further notes that day allude to the tensions he felt between the demands of being a father and of being a citizen-soldier: "To-day is the fifth anniversary of my wedding day, and

I have thought often of my dear wife and little ones and wished I could be with them, but I am resolved not to remain quietly at home another moment while a foe is on our soil."[5]

West must have known of the bloody nature and heavy casualties suffered in the Civil War battles when he made his way to South Carolina and Virginia in the spring of 1863. The number of casualties at the time had risen to 290,000, and Robert E. Lee, the commanding general of the Army of Northern Virginia, lamented that the many accounts of casualties among the Confederates lowered the morale of his own troops and strengthened that of the Union.[6] Several brigades were decimated by more than half in battles. John Bell Hood's Texas brigade lost 280 out of 500 men in the Second Battle of Manassas, August 28 to 30, 1862. In Antietam on September 17, 1862, 60 percent of the entire division was decimated. The day became known as the bloodiest in American history, with 6,000 deaths and 23,000 casualties overall. At Gettysburg at the beginning of July 1863, when John West himself took part in the battle, the Texas brigade suffered 600 casualties. "The slaughter on both sides was terrible," a witness wrote on July 9, 1863.[7]

According to more recent estimates, the Civil War resulted in 750,000 to 850,000 casualties.[8] In this most deadly war in American history, men died not only on the battlefield but also from many other causes such as disease, exhaustion, malnutrition, and poor medical care. Casualties were highest in the South, where most of the battles took place, which also strongly affected the civilian population. Of all southern men between the ages of thirteen and forty-three, 60 percent served in the Confederate Army. If one also takes into consideration the great numbers of disabled servicemen, abandoned families, widows, and orphans, pretty much every American family suffered pain and loss during the Civil War. In the South, the war itself, the loss of a great proportion of the white male population, and the end of slavery meant a fundamental upheaval of social, gender, and family structures.[9]

The focus of this chapter is the interdependencies between battlefront and home front. The diary and letters of John Camden West will help to make visible the tensions but also the interdependencies between being a father and a citizen-soldier from the perspective of a southern family man. It is important to note that military service was inextricably intertwined with citizenship, male identity formation, and whiteness—also in the Union. Even though African American men had fought in every American war, in general, proving oneself as a worthy citizen by fighting for one's country was a white privilege, and only those who demonstrated the right and willingness to serve in the armed forces were granted recognition as good citizens.[10] For African American men, joining the Union Army in the Civil War meant a most important step in their struggle for the recognition of their manhood and their claim for citizenship.[11] The fact that white men from southern slave societies went into battle with the conviction that they were fighting for their liberty and against oppression underlines that professing liberty did not necessarily, at least not in the eyes of white southerners, contradict a society based on racism, exploitation, and slavery.[12]

Frontline Experiences

On April 11, 1863, a day before his twenty-ninth birthday, John West and four companions set out from Waco, Texas, to Richmond, Virginia, where they planned to join the Texas Regiment. Early diary entries reveal his deep emotion and eager anticipation of his upcoming war experience. He had the sense, as he wrote, of becoming a man for the second time in his life. Even if the bloody battles and enormous losses of the previous two years had left the troops increasingly beset by battle fatigue, he emphasized that he was willing to make any sacrifice in the fight for the freedom of his country. West wrote these lines on his fifth wedding anniversary, making sure to include his family in his pledge, for the cause of the South was, in his mind-set, "the holiest cause that ever fired the breast of man."[13]

However, within the first two weeks of his journey, his visions of military heroism gave way to a more mixed emotional state. At the end of April, while on route in Natchitoches, Louisiana, West heard rumors about how the war had developed and about the presence of Union troops in various parts of the country. The closer proximity to the battlefront seemed to have filled him with worry about the uncertainty of what lay ahead in the coming days and weeks. His entries oscillated between the desire to join the battle rather sooner than later and the desire to spend another peaceful day with his wife and children. On April 28 he wrote that "this position [of uncertainty as to when exactly the fighting will begin] gives me too much time to think of home." Over the remainder of his journey he continued to associate his home and wife with peace, calm, and sweetness.[14]

After five difficult weeks, West reached Columbia, South Carolina, where his extended family lived. He had a reproduction of a photograph of his wife made, which he then carried with him wherever he went. He hoped to gain comfort from the daguerreotype, whenever he was overcome by thoughts of possible death in battle.[15] Thoughts of death remained with West constantly, particularly once he reached the Texas Brigade near Richmond on May 24, 1863. Passionate descriptions of the martial heroism of the troops, who did not shrink from the threat of death, and assertions of his own willingness and readiness to give his life in battle were accompanied by daily readings of the Bible and pleas for divine protection. The picture of his wife Mary also seemed to have been elevated to the status of a religious talisman, which was quite common among soldiers. It helped West overcome his nagging fears. His letters also tell of the excruciating monotony of camp life as well as the daily tortures of military service: he complains about long marches, fatigue, injured feet, hunger, lice, and insects, but hardly mentions military training, drill, or other preparation for battle. His entries ended temporarily on June 9, 1863, when West was ready for battle for the past ten days and heard its sounds in the distance. "Perhaps I may see my first battle to-day or to-morrow—will it be the last?"[16]

It took another three weeks before West had his first engagement. Between July 1 and 3, 1863, West and 150,000 other soldiers participated in the Battle of Gettysburg. A turning point in the Civil War, Gettysburg became a key moment in the historical memory of the nation, in part because it was the site of President Lincoln's memorable address four months later, when he invoked the unity of the nation in the service of freedom. Both sides together suffered around 50,000 casualties at Gettysburg, among them 8,000 fatalities. John West's brigade lost 150 of its 350 men.[17]

In the days immediately following Gettysburg, West was likely not aware of the irony that his first real battle engagement, eagerly anticipated but also feared, was at the same time the point at which the war turned against the South. The day after Gettysburg, July 4, Confederate rebels lost the Battle of Vicksburg, Mississippi, around a thousand miles southeast of Gettysburg. These two battles appeared to have sealed the fate of the Confederate cause, as Union general and future US president Ulysses S. Grant concluded in his memoirs.[18] West heard about these defeats and their grave significance only much later. He was emotionally greatly affected by the battle, as he wrote to his son Stark on July 8, from the battle camp near Hagerstown, Maryland, on the eve of his son's fourth birthday. In the letter, which his son was supposed to read years later when he was about to become a man himself, West relayed the blood, suffering, and dying he had witnessed. He regarded it as his paternal duty to impart these thoughts to his son as he was coming of age. Not shrinking from violence seems to have been considered as important a manly quality as the ability to lead a wife, family, and household. The father described in greatest detail the horror of the battle around him, the whizzing bullets and fallen bodies. But he also explained to the boy, whom he called "my little man" and "Master," how he was supposed to instruct his mother in the household, giving him a sense of being the trustee of his estate.

The father's sense of duty to educate his son through demonstrating his own strength also emerges in the letter he wrote the next day to his wife. There is hardly any mention of the violence of the battle in this letter, and the little there is refrains from heroic pronouncements but rather emphasizes the suffering in the days after, the hunger, and the rain, which left everyone drenched to the bone. In an almost whiny tone, West stressed how impossible it was to provide even a minimum of comfort to a soldier.[19] He was apparently unaware that supply shortages plagued not only the Confederate Army but the southern home front as well.[20]

In the following weeks West continued to lament the poor conditions of life in the Confederate Army. At the end of July he wrote to his wife that his clothes were wet through and through, without a dry set to change into, and that he had countless blisters and an infestation of lice—a misery he shared with most of his fellow soldiers. By then he had also heard of the defeat at Vicksburg, which prompted him to be more pessimistic about the South's chances for victory. Nonetheless he displayed a fundamental sense of optimism toward his wife, which was however a thin façade. For on the same day he wrote to his brother that following Vicksburg he would rather stay west of the Mississippi, "closer to Texas and closer to my family." He also indicated to the attorney general of the Confederate States that he was ready to return to Texas, if there was need for his services. Even though West did not speak of desertion, after Gettysburg and Vicksburg more common among Confederate troops, the majority of his letters and commentaries increasingly interspersed platitudes professing perseverance and strength with hints of skepticism, disappointment, and obvious longing for his family and his Texas home. There was little sign of optimism and confidence in victory.[21]

In mid-August, his letters revealed one more fleeting moment of confidence, when he emphasized how much his stamina had improved. "I am stronger and in better health than I ever was in my life," he wrote to his wife. Hopes for personal rejuvenation as a man through battle as well as for the rejuvenation of a heroic masculine nation briefly reasserted themselves.[22]

These brief moments of confidence were accompanied by descriptions of growing despair, morphing into a fatalism that guided him through the next battles. The next test came at Chickamauga on the border between Tennessee and Georgia, on September 19 and 20. In war memoirs, the Bible in the breast pocket became a favorite myth as life saver, preventing a bullet from penetrating the carrier's body. For John West, it was the handle of his bayonet at Chickamauga:

> The bullet hit the handle of my bayonet, which had not been in my belt two seconds, and knocked the handle entirely off. It was driven against me with great force, blinding and sickening me so that I fell and was supposed to be fatally wounded. It seems to me that a thousand bullets and grapeshot tore up the ground around me. As soon as I was able I crawled to a tree and afterwards to the rear, to the field hospital in a barnyard, where I remained all night. I was pretty sore but able to march, so I went back to the line of battle early next morning. I thought of Waco and its peaceful days and the sweet-faced, innocent children on their way to church.[23]

The Battle of Chickamauga led right into the Battle of Chattanooga. The entire campaign in southeastern Tennessee and northwestern Georgia would continue for another six months, culminating in a November 1863 nightmare defeat for the Confederates, bringing their rebellion closer to an end. "Gloom and despondency" hung like a shroud over the entire South, as Mary Chestnut wrote in her war diary at the end of the year.[24] John West used almost identical language, describing the few letters he received from his wife Mary as "gloomy and despondent." Even if he thought of his own letters as still sounding positive, they no longer delivered optimism, much less euphoria. At best they expressed faith and gratitude for having survived this long. Soon after West returned to describing his own circumstances as wretched. The brigade, he noted, lacked supplies, and many had to fend for themselves without footwear.[25] He felt homesick and battle weary, a feeling he shared with many men in the Confederate Army. He mused that maybe there was something good that would come out of experiencing the horrors of the war since it made the blessings of the home seem all the brighter. These reflections anticipated the overarching significance that home and particularly white women would acquire in the post–Civil War South.[26]

His fantasies about home, his sweet wife, and his obedient children proliferated at year's end. On February 19, 1864, he was finally honorably discharged from the army and made his way back from Tennessee to Waco, Texas, where he arrived on April 20, 1864—just about a year after he had left.[27]

Home-Front Perspectives

Historian LeeAnn Whites described the Civil War as a crisis of the gender and social order of the American South. By the war effort, the position of white men as masters of their plantations was called into question in several ways, even before the end of slavery.[28] First, there were the battlefront experiences of soldiers. White men's position in southern society depended in large part on the ways in which they processed their war experience. Second, as the war dragged on, women assumed to an ever-greater degree the affairs at the home front, which again challenged male hegemony in general. A South Carolina woman spoke in February 1865 of living through "queer times" because there were no men around to protect women from the wickedness in the world. It goes without saying that she referred to white men only in this passage.[29]

White southern women supported the war effort from the outset. They often endorsed their husbands' decisions to enlist, sometimes overcoming their own anxieties and worst fears.[30] In addition, women contributed in several ways to the production of essential war material. They knitted and sewed and took over the management of the homestead, plantation, and administration. Many white southern women for the first time in their lives engaged in productive labor.[31] On occasion white women also made adjustments to the existing economic and social structures and adapted modes of production to the needs of a subsistence and supply economy in wartime. This required not only technical know-how but also a considerable amount of organizational skills and agency. In addition, white women became politically active, for instance, through various fund-raising activities.[32]

As the war wore on, living arrangements in the South shifted more dramatically, and white women were engaged in the war in an even broader range of activities. First, several women followed their husbands to the frontlines and battle sites in order to be near them during the fighting. The Wests too had contemplated such a move. While John initially instructed his wife in how to organize the journey, suggesting that she leave all the slaves behind and that she not incur too much debt, he decided after Gettysburg that his wife was better off staying in Texas. A move with part of the entire household from Texas toward South Carolina in the summer of 1863 also would have meant going against the current, since Texas had become a preferred destination for many refugees from the regions east of the Mississippi, particularly those who wanted to bring their property, including their slaves, to safety.[33] There were more causes why women were on the move and why living arrangements changed. Toward the end of the war an increasing number of women were fleeing the fighting and destruction of the battlefront areas. Some moved in with relatives and friends away from the frontlines, others hosted refugees in their own homes, and still others formed new communal living arrangements in order to better cope with the disruptions caused by the war, the absence of their husbands, and other losses.[34]

Second, women provided and cared for soldiers. Caring for the growing number of injured and maimed men absorbed ever greater time and effort. Thousands of women volunteered at field hospitals and makeshift care facilities or nursed wounded soldiers in their own homes. It was a grave misconception to assume that the suffering of war did not reach the home front, as some of West's remarks seemed to suggest. At the same time, from the outset of the war many southern women cared for troops who were passing through on their way to the battlefront by offering them drinks and supplying them with food rations. These activities demonstrated the involvement of women in the war effort, but they also showed the acceptance of war making as a male endeavor for the protection of wives and children, while women, in return, offered nurture and care.[35]

Many forms of white female engagement contributed to undermining white men's position as the arbiters of the organization and functioning of southern society. John West himself praised women's contribution to the war effort only much later with great pathos. During the war he imagined his wife and women in general as not particularly productive members of southern society, despite the fact that when he fell seriously ill shortly after his departure for the front he was nursed back to health by a female acquaintance. Without her aid, he would probably never have reached his regiment. Even though he had depended on female engagement, he never applied that experience to his own wife. In his eyes Mary remained the beauty and muse whose purpose was to support her husband's well-being and social advancement though soft words and a friendly disposition, rather than through hard work.[36]

John West saw his home as a place of sweet dreams, peace, and sensual pleasures, the contemplativeness and idle bustle of white femininity.[37] This image stood in stark contrast to the violence at the front. The more explosive and terrifying life in battle became, the more urgent were his praises of his wife's aesthetic arts. He thus stressed over and over how much he loved her Latin language skills and her musical abilities, encouraging her to keep practicing. Furthermore, he admonished her to feed the chickens and turkeys and to encourage the children to study hard—everything else should be left in the hands of the Lord. We do not know how Mary actually managed her own affairs and the affairs of the house in the absence of her husband. We can see, however, that in his letters John never addressed her as someone who was able and ready to take her life into her own hands and who presumably was well informed about the state of the war effort. In letters to his mother and sister, he instead portrayed her as fragile and in need of protection, one who should be spared the horrific details of the war and for whom he still had to care for, even though he was more than a thousand miles away and hardly able to cope with his own problems.[38]

There were few moments in which West addressed his wife as the leader of his household in his absence. Even then he did so with a clear understanding that he represented the organizational center of the home with the authority to dispense advice from afar about how to govern the home, the family, and their households. Such moments related primarily to the supervision of slaves, which appeared as a more difficult challenge as the war wore on. First, with him being away, the power structure of the household seemed weakened, and, second, particularly after President Lincoln issued the Emancipation Proclamation on September 22, 1862, slavery was falling apart.[39] Furthermore, since the summer of 1863, the South's defeat appeared more and more likely. John West instructed Mary to demand obedience and diligence from children as well as slaves by invoking the authority and spirit of their father and master, revealing his assumptions that African American fears were akin to those of children and that he did not see them as rational actors. Only once did he give his wife advice about how she herself could exercise authority. In his November 15 letter he wrote, "Make them obey your rules, but do not make your rules severe or numerous. Do not have too many rules on any subject, but have one universal rule; you must be obeyed. Then be cautious how and what you order."[40]

In general West did not place much faith in the abilities of his wife and instead placed responsibility for the present and future in God's hands. Like many of his fellow soldiers, he appealed to God to protect him and his loved ones and implored his wife to have faith in an afterlife together. "I have left you to take care of yourself," he wrote in a July 27, 1863, letter to Mary, "and you must not be disturbed about me. God will take charge of both of us." His own existence as well as the existence of the South thus became part of a larger timeless order, and references to various Bible passages reveal the fluctuations in the assessment of his current circumstances. At the end of May 1863, just after he had reached the Texas Regiment, he was sure that he would soon die. Referring to Jeremiah 49:11, he pleaded for God's protection of orphans and widows. Half a year later, after he had survived both Gettysburg and Chickamauga, his faith grew that he would in the future be reunited with his family. He relied on Jeremiah 29:11 to express his newly found faith in God's promise of future happiness.[41]

Aftermath

When John Camden West published his diary and letters in 1901, both the Civil War and Reconstruction had been over for years and the South had returned to what was praised as home rule by reactionary voices. Step by step southern states implemented a system of segregation, ensuring that African Americans, even after their constitutionally guaranteed rights had been established, would not be able to fully participate in the public and political life of American society or have access to the same resources as white citizens had.[42]

The decades after the Civil War saw the reconstruction of white southern manhood. Cultural, social, economic, and political relations were reestablished around white men in the center of society. White women were again put on a pedestal and worshipped as the incarnation of the old and the new South. In this spirit, West dedicated his book to the women of the South who, as he wrote, through their smile, inspired the soldiers at the front, through their scorn and derision forced cowards to enlist, and through their tears, their devotion, and their prayers provided strength and comfort to "the weak, the weary and the wounded." "Their sacrifices, their toils, their fidelity, their sufferings entitle them to the love, admiration and gratitude of posterity, which ought to be demonstrated by the erection of a shining shaft of marble—white, pure and chaste—whose apex shall kiss the clouds."[43]

Texas alone counted sixty-eight such monuments, the first one in 1893 in Waco. And even if many of the funds for these monuments were collected by women's organizations, they nonetheless were meant to demonstrate men's respect for white femininity. Through the erection of these phallic monuments, they reestablished white manhood as the center of southern society.[44] John West could not have formulated it more pointedly. The hard, white, and pure monument asserted the reclaimed power of white masculinity and patriarchal dominance, not the least through its deference to southern white femininity. The sacrifices, sorrows, and faithfulness of women during the war were said to demand expressions of love, admiration, and gratitude now and forever. An order based on whiteness and racially defined purity was supposed to rest on male strength and female chastity. It revolved around the central figure of the white patriarch, who guaranteed the protection of wife, sister, mother, and daughter and who secured a racist hierarchy that would persist for a long time. A key component of this order was the ongoing exploitation of black women and to deny black men an equal opportunity to provide for their families, to guide them, and to protect them.

6

Bachelors in Urban America, 1870–1930

He had a knowledge of young men's hearts and a sympathy
with them as had no other man I had ever met. As I recall
my feelings toward Mr. McBurney at that time I can easily
understand how so many men say that Mr. McBurney was a
father to them. Not having any children of his own, he made
all young men children to himself.
—Henry Orne about Robert R. McBurney, 1899

In the summer of 1854, Robert McBurney arrived in the United States
from Ireland. Barely eighteen years of age, he disembarked in New York
Harbor, alone and without family, like so many other young men who
had made the overseas journey or were flocking to America's growing cities from the surrounding countryside. McBurney would never
marry or have children. As a bachelor who escaped familial guidance,
he was considered deserving of special attention in a society, which was
governed through the family. At the turn of the twentieth century, the
bachelor came to embody many of the social and cultural transformations in an increasingly urban and modern world. This world opened
up space for new ways of living, just as it developed new strategies to
hedge them.

McBurney was a bachelor to the core, but still he was not quite a
"ladies' man," as his colleagues emphasized. He never stole the heart of
a woman; rather, as director of the New York Young Men's Christian Association, he was more familiar with the hearts of young men than any
other, as Henry Orne, his successor, would write.[1]

The YMCA was McBurney's "family," which he led with paternal care,
as Orne pointed out. Another former protégé described his relationship with McBurney like that of a son to a father.[2] The YMCA was one
of several homosocial fraternities and clubs that flourished in the late
nineteenth and early twentieth centuries. It stood for social work in that

time period and was meant to serve as a Protestant antidote to the urban temptations to which unmarried men between the ages of fifteen and forty were especially susceptible. At the same time the YMCA represented a type of society whose close-knit ties consisted not of the family but of homosocial, and at times homoerotic, forces.[3] By the turn of the century, according to historian George Chauncey, the YMCA was a prime meeting spot for New York's "gay male world."[4]

The same period saw how the sexual sciences gained shape, which made the many bachelors an object of academic scrutiny. A system of sexual categorizations was developed and over the course of the twentieth century would acquire great importance for the government of society with all the inclusions and exclusions provided by it. The sexual sciences, how they related to the social and sexual transformations of the era, and how they shaped the perception of the bachelor are outlined at the end of the chapter.[5] At first, we begin with Robert McBurney and how his life was shaped by various experiences, which illustrate the myriad living arrangements of unmarried urban men in the second half of the nineteenth century. There were his experiences as a migrant, his various housing arrangements as a New York bachelor, and his diverse homosocial connections. At work and in private, he gathered around him a group of like-minded men from the YMCA administration, but also many young men from the city, with whom he wanted to share some of his life experiences when they came to the YMCA. Soon complaints surfaced that the male world of the YMCA was not an adequate social instrument to counter the temptations of the city. Instead, it was seen as a breeding ground for homoerotic entanglements and considered as belonging to the modern urban world of vice.

The unmarried man was seen as the counterpoint to the husband and father, as a completely different character with a completely different way of life. He was not beholden to the all-important principle of family government and thus embodied a social and sexual threat to society. The urban centers in particular were often seen as erotic and exotic, with myriad possibilities for alternative life and love arrangements, which eventually would be classified as "unnatural" by the sexual sciences. As constitutive other, the bachelor demonstrates how the sexual, familial, social, and political were intimately intertwined. A close look at the bachelor reveals even more sharply the central role of fatherhood in

American society and how embattled it really was. As a countermodel, the bachelor was as much part of the normative armory as the father figure himself.[6]

Bachelors in the Early Republic

In the Early Republic, unwed men were seen as eccentrics, good-natured yet somehow unrefined and lacking in social skills. Bachelors were thought of as being on the unhappy side themselves as well as contributing little to the happiness of others. They were unfamiliar with the private sphere of the family, which was so important for the self-perception of the middle classes. Egocentric, often acting irresponsibly, whiling away his time in coffeehouses, prone to the subculture of the parlor, lonesome and misanthropic in old age, those were the typical assumptions about lifelong bachelors. They were considered hardly able to fulfill either the familial and sexual or the social and political duties of citizenship, thus turning them into a social problem. The celibate single man who gave up the physical pleasures in the service of the common good seemed an exception to this. His renunciation of marriage and family was seen as a particular kind of independence, which might have made him into an even better and more virtuous national citizen than a good father could be. The narrow line between recognition and skeptical uncertainty when it comes to the character and peculiarities of the bachelor becomes clear when going into the personal history of Robert McBurney.[7]

The single man was quite a common phenomenon in American history. First, this was a result of immigration, which accelerated markedly in the 1830s and consisted to a considerable degree of single young men. Second, the American ideal of individual male freedom prompted men to move westward, preferably on their own and unattached.[8] They were largely driven by the opportunities of the frontier, seemingly free land, railway construction, and the gold rush. In the middle of the nineteenth century, the proportion of unmarried men in frontier towns and districts ranged between 30 and 70 percent, even higher in mining towns. Also, in large coastal cities, such as San Francisco, Boston, and New York, around one-third of all men were single, and among those between the ages of twenty-five and thirty-five, the proportion was about

50 percent. Most bachelors lived in working-class neighborhoods of the city, such as the Lower East Sides of Detroit and New York. To be sure, the bachelor of the Early Republic was not so much a bohemian or misanthrope as a poor migrant worker or adventurer who could not afford a family or who did not want one because it seemed to stand in the way of his goals.[9]

The Age of the Bachelor

However, the so-called age of the bachelor began only after the Civil War, with the years between 1880 and 1930 as the golden age of bachelor subculture.[10] This diagnosis by historian Howard Chudacoff does not so much refer to the sheer number of bachelors as to the fact that even commentators in the last third of the nineteenth century saw the bachelor as a social, cultural, political, and sexual phenomenon of great historical significance. In 1868, the *Nation* asked why male bachelorhood had become so widespread that philosophers, statisticians, and social commentators as well as mothers and daughters racked their brains about it. In his search for a cause, the author J. Bixby referred to the "growing self-assertion, masculinity, independence" of increasing numbers of women who made marriage increasingly unattractive for men.[11] In addition, flourishing trade, increasing communication, and a generally greater wealth made bachelorhood attractive, above all in modern cities, where physical, mental, and aesthetic stimuli, which were better enjoyed without the burden of marriage, abounded: "The city is the habitat of the single. The country town or even the small city is an uncongenial clime for the species. The single must have public amusements and public resorts, and these only flourish in great cities."[12] It was said that the bachelor needed the city and the city made bachelorhood attractive. Those who were tied to family and home missed out on a good part of the urban quality of life. Of course, Bixby warned, urban centers could also drag single men down into a morass of wicked pleasures, where cheap and unseemly substitutes for the joy of marriage were found easily. The nightly visits to disreputable districts offered the middle and upper classes guilty pleasures that in subsequent decades became ever more popular and were generally referred to as "slumming."[13]

Already in 1868 Bixby described the urban bachelor as a representative of modern society *avant la lettre*; as a friend of the flapper, the exuberant and highly stylized young woman in high heels with a cigarette hanging out of the corner of her mouth; as a lighter version of the Great Gatsby in real life as he gained popularity from the late nineteenth century into the Roaring Twenties.[14] The so-called Bohemian, who flaunted rules and habits with great ease, was born in the mid-nineteenth century in New York's Greenwich Village. By the 1920s he had become an established fixture within American culture and society, "an object of desire or ridicule, but a fact of American life," as Tom Lutz writes.[15] Popular culture abounded with recipes for single men, fashion advice for the admirer of distinguished clothing and fine shoes, and there was even—if only short-lived—a magazine for bachelors, complete with drawings of relaxed men smoking cigarettes in the company of attractive women. The "single blessedness" was desired and admired but at the same time mocked as a "grotesque misconception." Either way, the bachelor was on everyone's lips.[16]

In the late nineteenth century and early twentieth, observers repeatedly described the bachelor as a specifically modern phenomenon, among them Ernest W. Burgess, a leading scholar of the Chicago School of Sociology as late as in 1934.[17] Half a century earlier, J. Bixby had already characterized bachelorhood as the effect of modernization and civilized refined tastes for sensual and aesthetic pleasures. Other commentators were more skeptical and fearful of a loss of control and order. They regarded the bachelor as a representation of the darker side of modernity. Their concern grew when the 1890 census revealed that 41.7 percent of all men above fifteen and 20 percent of men around forty were unmarried. Chicago, a rapidly growing city with a reputation for being a hotbed of vice, alone counted more than 170,000 single men in 1890, a figure topped by New York already in the 1860s, and the upward trend continued in the coming years.[18]

Fear of bachelors merged with a fear of a society that responded to their sexual needs and desires, which could potentially replace the sphere of family and domesticity. Cheap restaurants catered to bachelors' need for food, barbers and bath houses for their hygiene, and saloons, clubs, pool halls, dance halls, and amusement parks to their leisure as well as sexual desires. Female companions in these places were often, though not always, prostitutes. Industrialization provided more job opportunities for women, who now enjoyed greater independence outside of familial control yet earned too little to be able to fully enjoy the amusements of the modern urban social world. As so-called charity girls, they were willing to let wealthier male patrons treat them to an evening out in exchange for sexual favors.[19] As early as February 1866, a memorandum from the New York YMCA produced a detailed list of the danger zones in the city: 653 pool tables, thirteen theaters, countless gambling parlors and lotteries, 7,786 bars, and 223 music halls with 1,193 female bartenders, many of whom offered sex for money and serviced around 29,900 customers daily. In addition there were allegedly 730 "real" brothels in the city, where 3,400 prostitutes worked. Brothels and seedy boarding houses were often the only places that welcomed bachelors with open arms, YMCA director William E. Dodge stressed.[20]

The Bachelor Robert McBurney and the YMCA

The first sexual revolution was under way in the final decades of the nineteenth century, and it encountered some strong opposition.[21] The YMCA was a leading crusader in this fight, and the notorious Anthony Comstock expanded on YMCA activities in his fight against the circulation of obscene literature in the early 1870s.[22] The ambiguity of these struggles becomes visible by taking a closer look at the YMCA and Robert McBurney. The New York YMCA and particularly "Brother McBurney" largely financed and propagated Comstock's moral crusade. In order to further strengthen Comstock's activities, the New York YMCA founded the Committee for the Suppression of Vice, with Robert McBurney and his YMCA colleagues Cephas Brainerd, Morris K. Jesup, and Charles E. Whitehead as members.[23] Through his activities in the committee as well as in the YMCA, McBurney fought at the front lines in the battle against urban vice. At the same time it was bachelors like McBurney and their way of life that were seen as a danger to the existing social, cultural, and sexual order.

In the summer of 1854, McBurney arrived in New York, seventeen years of age, coming from a small town in northern Ireland. It was the end of the great wave of Irish migration to the United States, in which at times half of all immigrants were coming from poverty-stricken Ireland.

In 1854 there were 101,606 Irish among the total of 427,833 immigrants. More than half of them had no education, and around 20 percent was classified as "laborers," another fifth as farmers. The male surplus was around 35 percent, the largest proportion of which was between sixteen and forty years of age.[24]

As a young Irishman without an education who opted to stay in one of the major cities on the East Coast rather than moving West, McBurney typified the kind of immigrant that elicited growing concerns. Lawrence L. Doggett, a contemporary of McBurney's, fellow YMCA member, and historian, described McBurney's youth in his 1902 biography as penny-less, jobless, and lonely. At that time the "lonely stranger in the city" was the subject of a powerful discourse on the dangers of urban life.[25] At the time of his arrival McBurney seemed headed for a life as a low-wage, single, rootless man who would make a living as a day laborer and who would find shelter in one of the cheap, overcrowded tenement houses in the seedy area around the Lower East Side. His early New York years, Doggett wrote, were an apprenticeship of sorts, where he would have the experiences that would prepare him for his later life as an advocate: "He knew young men—their temptations, their struggles, their needs, their possibilities, their peril. He had been alone in a great city, he had been without money, and almost without friends. He knew what it was to need work, he knew what it was to overcome temptation."[26]

But on the day of his arrival McBurney was taken under the wing of a former teacher from his hometown who had come to New York shortly before him and who introduced him to the new YMCA, founded only two years earlier. The founders of the Young Men's Christian Association had intended to offer a religiously inspired counterweight to the moral and cultural erosion they saw occurring as a result of migration, ur-banization, and industrialization. These developments seemed to change the working and living arrangements of young men for the worse. The YMCA sought to position itself not in opposition to the urban environ-ment but as a safe place within it. It reacted to the dangerous tempta-tions of urban life and offered young men an inner-city meeting point, and missing family guidance was to be balanced by Protestant guidance within a tight network of all-male relations. In short, a Christian male clubhouse was to replace the saloon and at the same time provide an alternative family. In the YMCA physical exercise became a key to moral

Figure 6.1. Robert McBurney. Kautz Family YMCA Archives,
YMCA of Greater New York.

Protestant enhancement, and historian Clifford Putney sees in the mid-
nineteenth century the beginnings of a muscular Christianity, nurtured
by a rising number of male fraternities in American society.[27]

In his first eight years in New York, Robert McBurney worked as shop
manager for a hatter.[28] In addition he immediately joined the Methodist
Episcopal Church on Mulberry Street, began teaching Sunday school,
and helped out at the YMCA, located two blocks away on the second
floor of the Stuyvesant Institute on South Broadway. During this time
he moved along the edges of the Bowery, where, according to his biographer, "the gates of sin stood wide"—theaters, saloons, and other places
of temptation and violence that were rumored to present an explosive
threat for young lonely men new to the city.[29]

After eight years in New York, Robert McBurney's life took an important turn, when, in 1862, he took a position as a librarian at the YMCA. According to his biographer it was through this position that he learned from experienced men the art of leadership and thus prepared for a life dedicated to the education of other young men. Up to that point McBurney had had a rather introverted personality, as one of his mentors at the YMCA stated, and his extraordinary qualities had barely been recognizable. Yet male relationships across generations, even outside the family structure, were seen as extremely important for bringing his qualities to the fore, as is told by the following passage from McBurney's biography: "Somewhat similarly it may be said that the men who accomplish their work through influence upon other characters and the direction of other men must first themselves be influenced and developed by contact with others. Such education McBurney received by coming in contact in his young manhood with a group of strong and leading characters."[30]

The very special bond among men was seen as a key to success. McBurney himself counted his attractiveness to young men as his greatest asset, which he could cash in on and prompted him to make his job at the YMCA his life's task. It seems that it was not only the way he affected young men but also the affection he himself felt for young men that made life in the YMCA so attractive to McBurney. Several reports mention a "young English sailor boy" on Christmas Eve 1863 who apparently represented a special experience in McBurney's life but who also stood in for thousands of other often sad and homesick young men who remembered McBurney's warm disposition. McBurney would approach men in parks or on trains and did not stop until he had won them over to the YMCA.[31]

A few years later McBurney was named one of the secretaries of the New York YMCA. He spent the years until age thirty-three living in the household of his mentor and YMCA director Cephas Brainerd and his wife at 190 Nineteenth Street East. This created some distance to the seedy Lower East Side. The communal life and work of Brainerd and "Mack," as the former called him, appeared to have been quite close and mutually influential.[32] According to historian Howard Chudacoff, it was quite common to rent a room from or live in the household of close acquaintances or relatives, especially among bachelors of higher social status. Also, McBurney's upward social mobility somehow matched with where he lived in the city.[33]

Figure 6.2. The YMCA building on the corner of Twenty-Third Street and Fourth Avenue. Kautz Family YMCA Archives, YMCA of Greater New York.

McBurney's next step on the social ladder was to move into a bachelor apartment, which showed unmistakably the class difference to the workers and lodgers of the Lower East Side and stood for the life of the bohemian. Such an apartment was seen as the crowning achievement of bachelorhood and meant that even without a family the single man could create comfort, warmth, and intimacy unknown to a tenant or lodger.

Comments said that single men in bachelor apartments were "better housed than any other class of persons in town." Most apartments consisted of a small bedroom and a salon big enough for some artwork and an eclectic mix of furniture, which were considered typical for bachelors of a higher social status. Kitchens were usually not included in these abodes since a bachelor tended to take his meals in one of the many pubs, which could be found on pretty much any city block in New York with various levels of quality. At most he would use a shared kitchen included in many of the apartment buildings for single men. In this respect New York was a trailblazer. The first building of its kind was the

Stuyvesant Apartments, which opened on Eighteenth Street in Midtown, then a middle-class section of Manhattan and only a block south of Mc-Burney and Brainerd's home.[34]

In 1870 Robert McBurney's dream came true of living in his own, very special bachelor apartment, as Richard C. Morse, soon one of his closest confidantes at the YMCA, wrote.[35] Five year earlier, the directorate of the YMCA had erected a new building on the corner of Twenty-Third Street and Fourth Avenue, designed according to the specific needs of the organization and consisting of five stories topped by a tower. The building would be remembered in New York history as the McBurney-YMCA. It included classrooms, a library, and sports and swimming facilities, which were seen as fortifying the social, intellectual, Christian, moral, and physical stamina of young men.[36] Because of the perfect lighting conditions, the tower room was first used by an artist. But McBurney was apparently so obsessed with the idea of moving into the YMCA and so fascinated by the view of the city from the tower room that nothing could deter him from making his home in that tower, not even the directorate of the YMCA, which was concerned that his health could suffer if there were no boundaries between his personal and work lives. In 1870 "father McBurney," as he was called by then, moved into the tower, while several, mostly younger employees of the growing YMCA staff moved into a room on the floor below him. One of McBurney's friends later remembered that "this room contained two double beds and was not infrequently occupied by four young men who were either McBurney's associates on his staff or among his group of intimate friends."[37] His longtime companion Richard Morse would live there for five years, and he commented on the life together this way: "I took the room below, and then we came together in the closest relations we had ever had. I helped him and he helped me in every possible way. Eugene Peck came into the work as his assistant, and after him Henry Webster. We were all together, aware of course, of one another's failings as well as of one another's excellences. . . . We never thought of separating; it was essential that we should be together."[38] The vertical structure of the living arrangements in the house, with McBurney at the very top, the staff a floor below, and the young men of the city in the stories below them, mirrored the fraternal conception of the YMCA, in which more experienced YMCA members were seen as *primus inter pares* who im-

Figure 6.3. Robert McBurney's tower room. Kautz Family YMCA Archives, YMCA of Greater New York.

parted their skills and experiences to those "below" them.[39] At the same time the tower apartment symbolized McBurney's upward mobility in several ways. His social climb corresponded to the step-by-step moves from Downtown to Midtown and then into the uppermost rooms of the new YMCA building.

With a smaller bedroom and a more spacious salon, the McBurney tower matched the expectations for a typical bachelor apartment. Furthermore, McBurney was always impeccably dressed, another known quality of bachelors. At the time of his death he owned 110 ties, seventy-seven handkerchiefs, mostly silk, and fourteen pairs of shoes. His housekeeper remarked that she had never seen a man more obsessed with his clothing.[40] He also surrounded himself with books (mostly religious texts and advice manuals of all types) and decorated his room with all sorts of curiosities, including hunting trophies, souvenirs, old prints, heavy rugs, and antique furniture. McBurney's predilections and the interior furnishings of his apartment corresponded to the contemporary expectations of urban bachelor designs. Single men of elevated social status had the reputation of amassing a lot of knickknacks to create an ostentatious and often supposedly Oriental living atmosphere that combined images of the bachelor bohemian with those of the urban homosexual and the cosmopolitan connoisseur. The male consumer was thus marked as a cultural, social, sexual, and territorial border crosser. These perceptions of bachelors also alluded to ideas about the Oriental and its specific sexualized connotations. They became mutually reinforcing because they were both located outside the realm of what was considered normal in Western society. It might have just been a coincidence that, apart from business trips and camping, fishing, and hiking excursions, McBurney's only longer trip led him to Palestine, which was not only the holy land of Christianity but also the site of ostentatious bachelor fantasies about the Orient.[41]

McBurney's tower parlor would soon gain fame beyond the city limits as a place for national gatherings. As described by his biographer, McBurney not only looked after the young men of New York but also gave advice to YMCA secretaries from across the country, much like a shepherd toward his flock, a relationship that Michel Foucault identified as a "pastoral" form of power and a basic building block of the liberal government.[42] McBurney was often associated with the figure of the encouraging as well as strict father, making his image complete: "He was as watchful as a father over his fellow-secretaries. He encouraged them, and whenever he thought they needed it, he reproved them." In his apartment he also hosted friends overnight, as Morse recounted. Jacob T. Bowne from the international committee of the YMCA confirmed that McBurney always invited him to stay overnight when he was in New York. Other YMCA managers echoed those observations, stressing that they would discuss the most creative and important matters early in the morning, while McBurney shaved or got dressed. One recollection showed the great intimacy that existed among the men: "The time to see him was in the morning. Come to his room and wake him up—not too early—and while he was dressing his mind was free, and he could advise."[43]

This arrangement of male companionship and close working relationship disrupted the prevailing familial, heteronormative concept of how a good living arrangement was meant to look like. Yet the male community also functioned as a surrogate family in which the members learned from each other and cared for each other in sickness. In the manner of a typical fraternity, the men undertook group excursions into nature, for instance to go fishing or camping. Members also mourned the loss of any member who left the community. McBurney's friends remembered that he had gone through days of solitude in the tower and indicated that he had battled through "many trials of faith–earnest wrestlings in prayer, many battles with self."[44] For instance, when one of his staff members, H. P. Anderson, left New York in 1889 for North Carolina after only three years because he was suffering from lung disease, McBurney was said to have cried, and Anderson recalled, "He showed to me that day a heart of love that no one has shown me except my own mother." Nothing hurt McBurney more emotionally, however, than seeing his longtime companion Richard Morse enter into marriage at the age of forty in June 1883. One of his colleagues remembered that "he seemed to feel as if he were left alone." McBurney himself described his apartment in moments like these as a "miserable old bachelor's lot."[45]

Homosocial and Homoerotic Moments in Bachelorhood

The biographical and autobiographical writings of McBurney and other YMCA men offer rich material for queer readings. In general, they are full of references to "looking after young fellows," to his fondness for "unruly boys," to his own "attractiveness to good-looking young men," to "temptations" and "tenderness" in his interactions with them, and to the fact that he touched them and gave them guidance. "It was wonderful how he touched and influenced young men," one observer noted.[46] Young men were repeatedly presented as the only thing giving meaning and purpose to McBurney's life. Accounts of the shared lives of the YMCA secretaries with each other, who at times referred to themselves as "the boys," were also full of references to intense feelings and intimate situations among them, such as the early morning routines of getting up and shaving, the sharing of sorrow and joy, friendly touches, mutual care, and the nightly gatherings in McBurney's tower parlor. What was possible among men was absolutely impossible between men and women as long as unmarried. A woman's visit to a bachelor apartment, not to mention an overnight stay, was considered disreputable.[47]

Letters between the men also show their intimate ties. The greetings in the letter exchanges between McBurney and his colleague H. Thane

Miller in Cincinnati or James McConaughy in Harrisburg between the 1870s and 1890s make this obvious. In 1873 Miller addressed McBurney in a friendly but still rather formal way with "My dear Mr. McBurney." The following year he addressed him as "dear old boy," then as "My dearest Mc.," "My dear good old Mac," and finally, when McBurney was traveling in Europe, as "My ocean-tossed brother, . . . Oh' how much I wish, I were with you," and "My dear old beloved, you have an ocean full of love from my never failing fountain of affection," and finally "my beloved foreign tramp." By 1892 it had turned into "my darling Mac."[48] McBurney for his part signed the letters to McConaughy "with best love," or "I often think of you and miss you very much." In the mid-1870s, McBurney tried everything to bring McConaughy to New York. The letters expressed intimacy and an emotional affection of the highest order between the men, and yet they also included occasional greetings to or from McConaughy's wife.[49]

The wider historical context reinforces a queer reading of Robert McBurney's life in New York City. He had spent years on the Lower East Side, which had the reputation as a hotbed of vice, where men amused themselves with charity girls or hooked up with prostitutes. Beginning in the 1870s, the Lower East Side and the Bowery also became known for encounters among men. It is hard to imagine that Robert McBurney did not know the gay bars, establishments, and hotels. We cannot say this with certainty, but it would have been hard for him to miss the signs on Mulberry Street, Bleeker Street, and the Bowery. In addition, the boarding houses where he lived in his early New York years were often sites of diverse male living arrangements. Even though McBurney put increasing social and geographical distance between himself and the Lower East Side, it did not necessarily mean that he never returned to this or similar areas in town. First, his new abode on the corner of Twenty-Third Street and Fourth Avenue was not too far removed, and the notorious Tenderloin District was just north of Twenty-Third. Second, McBurney was always looking for young men, as his colleagues noted, which presumably would have frequently led him back into the Bowery. Third, many middle-class single men from Upper or Midtown Manhattan, who lived in bachelor apartments or led a married life, regularly found their way to the Bowery, where they would go slumming or lead a double life by entering the urban gay male world at least for a while.[50]

YMCAs themselves became prime spots for men looking for men. Originally conceived as a Protestant shield against urban temptations, they soon became favorite hangouts for men who desired other men. Historian George Chauncey dates the beginning of this development in the 1890s, when the New York YMCA set up sleeping halls for men. Likewise, historian John D. Gustav-Wrathall points out that in the last decade of the nineteenth century YMCAs became "sexual laboratories" for young men.[51] The New York YMCA's athletic and bathing facilities, established twenty-five years earlier, had already offered ample opportunity for homoerotic and sexual encounters among men. As early as 1870 concerns were raised at the New York YMCA about how to deal with this. The directorate was obviously pleased to see the popularity of the athletic facilities among young men. Physical exercise was fundamental to the mission of the YMCA, which wanted to develop better citizens, good Christians, and real men. Yet particularly the athletic facilities appeared to encourage forms of interactions considered problematic by the leadership of the house. This led to the introduction of four male supervisors who were to ensure strict adherence to the rules of conduct. Exactly what kinds of rules had been violated is not mentioned in the records.[52]

In the 1880s leadership of the New York YMCA itself became the target of critics, who regarded the bachelor life of the New York directors as homoerotically charged and thus problematic. Their criticism was prompted by the upcoming festivities on the occasion of the fiftieth birthday of Robert Weidensall, chairman of the international committee of the YMCA and living in New York at the time. The intimate male relationships within the New York leaderships seemed to worry the general secretary of the Indianapolis branch, John C. Brandt. He voiced concerns about Weidensall's career in a letter to his Chicago colleague W. W. Vanarsdale, who was in charge of coordinating the birthday celebrations for Weidensall.

Historian John D. Gustav-Wrathall has reconstructed the complex history of this particular concern in its multiple variants. The criticism included many innuendos of homoerotic entanglements, which were so blunt that Weidensall himself and others within the YMCA leadership considered them unseemly and inappropriate. Actually, two versions of Brandt's denunciatory letter exist: one in handwriting, with a passage that directly attacked Weidensall and his bachelor life, talked about immaturity, denounced the bad influence of other imperturbable bachelors, and derided McBurney in the sharpest manner; and another typeset version, which omitted that very passage. The erasure of the passage below is marked by a handwritten "omit" in the margins of the original letter:

> Weidensall is fifty is he? Just think of it. It seems but yesterday when we all thought we were boys. Isn't there some mistake? Why he is not even married yet. . . . Here he comes and says he is fifty and this important business of life is not yet attended to. It ought to have been done at least twenty five years ago. I am sure you will agree that we would not have thought this of one so conscientious and devoted to every known duty as this dear Brother of ours has always shown himself to be. But here is another sad example of the influence of Associates. If in the early days of our association work we could have kept Weidensall away from Morse & McBurney and altogether under good wholesome western influence all this might have been different. It is some encouragement that Morse has seen his error repented and is now trying to undo the mischief of nearly a life time. But McBurney seems to be as obdurate as ever. Here he is right along side of Weidensall. Fifty years and no wife yet. I think some of you Chicago Brethren ought to lay aside all other matters for a year if necessary and teach these boys a thing or two. These young gentlemen should be shown up in their true light. They will be the ruin of the country if they are not stopped. You see already how . . . many of our brightest and best are going in the same wretched way.[53]

Several claims made in this passage would resurface later in discourses of the sexual and social sciences: same-sex affection as a sign of immaturity; a negative influence of male cohabitation and desire on others, as if it was a communicable disease; the importance of individual "good moral conduct" for the advancement of country and culture; the alleged moral purity of the American West in contrast to the disreputable eastern cities.

The omission of the above paragraph may have had several reasons: First, during the festivities several eulogies to Weidensall were presented, among them excerpts from Brandt's letter. Organizers obviously wanted to avoid any reference to the sexual connotation of all-male living arrangements, and a sanitized typed version ensured that this would be the case. Second, Weidensall was known to have cared a great deal about his legacy. When he began to sort his papers at the beginning of the twentieth century, the power of the sexual scientific discourse increased, and the number of unmarried YMCA-leaders decreased markedly. He might have worried about the negative effect such allusions to the homoerotic context of his living arrangements possibly would have had on his posthumous image. Over time it seemed to become ever more important to avoid the ambiguities that usually accompanied the "Life with Young Men," and instead hide them in the dark regions of the "closet."[54]

Weidensall obviously preferred to be remembered as a celibate social worker who in the spirit of the Christian mission had renounced sexual pleasures and had therefore remained unmarried rather than as crossing sexual boundaries and as connected to the gay male world. It is surprising that the handwritten letter even survived among Weidensall's papers. Either way, the multiple versions of the letter reveal that contemporaries were aware of the growing homoerotic connotations of the life within the YMCA. They either condemned them or tried to cover them up, depending on the nature of their involvement.[55]

The controversy might have been a result of the change in perspective in the early twentieth century, related to an increasing power of the discourse on sexology. In the nineteenth century, a significant proportion of YMCA secretaries had remained unmarried, particularly in New York. This began to change at the turn of the twentieth century, when the YMCA attempted to create different living and working conditions for its secretaries. There seems to have existed a general concern about the leadership potential of unmarried men, who were said to suffer from irresponsibility and immaturity in their own personal development by then. The effort to achieve change appeared to bear fruit, for by the 1930s, almost the entire YMCA leadership was married.[56] Nevertheless, the reputation of the YMCA as a "gay cruising spot" still grew in the early twentieth century. The same was true for the vibrant and sexually diverse nightlife in the city, whether downtown in the Village or uptown in Harlem. Jazz, cabarets, gay shows with their popular "pansy acts," and drag balls offered amusement for New Yorkers, regardless whether queer or straight. From the 1930s on and during the Great Depression, homosexuality and gay culture were increasingly interpreted as signs of failed excesses of consumption and mindless pleasure seeking and branded as immoral and transgressive.[57] Of major influence on the interpretation of sex and its transgressive power were the social and sexual sciences. At the fin de siècle, they were shaping a new kind of knowledge on sex in the United States, being extremely powerful in the urban centers of the country.

Sexual and Social Sciences

In 1886, the same year that YMCA leadership circles began to express concern about the closeness of the men at their New York branch, Richard von Krafft-Ebing published his study *Psychopathia Sexualis.* Seven years later an American translation came out, and another seven years later Random House published Havelock Ellis's *Studies in the Psychology of Sex.* In 1909 Sigmund Freud presented his sexual theories in five lectures at Clark University in Worcester, Massachusetts. By then, Freud's theories were well known in America, and leading psychologists, among them William James, had been following Freud's work since the 1890s. Representatives from psychology, medicine, the media, and the public were curious about what Freud had to say, and his lectures were well received. Freud's journey to America in 1909 has been seen as critically important for the international debate about his theories within the academic and general public. Beginning in the 1910s psychoanalysis and sexology were nowhere more popular than in the urban centers of the United States. Freud himself often lamented the superficial reception of his theories in the United States, which he regarded as broad yet shallow.[58]

Krafft-Ebing's, Ellis's, and Freud's ideas and theories differed substantially from one another, and they were only three positions in a much broader discourse. Since the 1880s a number of researchers on both sides of the Atlantic had contributed to the shaping of a wide field of knowledge on "sexuality." Despite the diversity of ideas, these efforts had several things in common. First, they reflected a specifically modern understanding of scientists' ability to develop objective knowledge about things, humans, and conditions, and thus bring order into the diffuse forms of life and libido. Second, these voices constituted a new, broad, pressing, and diverse field of sexuality, which interacted with the diversity of sexual life, thriving above all in urban areas between the 1850s and the Roaring Twenties.[59] Third, scientific observations about sexuality led to the shaping of norms, which divided sexual activity into variants deemed "healthy" or "pathological." Scientific conceptualizations of sexuality quickly proliferated in popular culture and thus became available to a broader public. Furthermore these new theories and their popularized versions urged men and women to scrutinize others' and their own sexual behavior and analyze their most secret desires in light of this newly popularized sexual knowledge. It was easy to turn oneself into the object of one's own research. In the 1920s American publishers planned a sourcebook with extracts from psychoanalytic and sexual scientific writings with an introduction by Freud, though he himself found the idea dubious.[60]

The sexual scientific discourse moved in two directions at once. First, it brought forth an intense description and documentation of different modes of sexuality, which then became categorized as such. Second, it used these modes to define what seemed "natural" and "normal" and thus was of highly normative power. This meant the recentering of the heterosexual family within a by then scientifically grounded order that in general showed manifold sexual options.

In the 1890s a concept of sexual drive was developed that uncoupled the close connection that had existed between sexual desire and procreation. The concepts of homosexuality and heterosexuality emerged gradually and referred initially to any sexual desire and sexual activities outside the realm of the romantic marriage ideal, transcended monogamy, and were not geared toward reproduction and thus transgressed the boundaries of what was considered to be "natural." In the case of homosexuality, the desires and activities were geared toward same-sex partners; in the case of heterosexuality it was partners of the opposite sex. The 1901 *Dorland's Medical Dictionary* defined heterosexuality as "abnormal or perverted appetite toward the opposite sex." Until well into the twentieth century both heterosexuality and homosexuality connoted the manifestation of sexual desire that was seen as pathological.[61] The urban bachelor embodied this modern order predicated on pleasure and the consumption of bodies. These aspects were deemed problematic since regardless of whether the desires of bachelors were directed to the same or the opposite sex, they were considered outside the realm of "normal" and monogamous marital relations and their unpredictable effects were seen a potential threat to the social order.

These overlaps between the sexual and the social, advanced and consolidated above all by Freud's theories, are of particular importance for a history that seeks to understand how society is governed through the family. Even if these theories acknowledged the power of the libido, they were also highly normative insofar as they told contemporaries in no uncertain terms which kind of sexual behavior was acceptable, appropriate, and correct. If the desire was focused on the opposite sex and furthermore directed toward the sexual organs as the locus of sexual gratification, it was assumed that one had undergone a successful and "healthy" sexual development form childhood to adult maturity. Everything else, such as oral and anal sexual pleasure, was acknowledged as existing yet considered as a developmental stage that was immature, underdeveloped, less than civilized, and, after all, pathological when it came to adults.[62]

The family was seen as the social and cultural space in which children and youth would mature from polymorph to exclusive, from oral to anal and ultimately genital, from a childlike to an adult desire, from nature to culture, from the biological to the social, and from the primitive to the civilized. According to Freud and other sexologists, only the nuclear family offered the opportunity to develop a "healthy" and "appropriate" sexual desire directed at the opposite sex, through a complex process of desire and rivalry, of wrestling with incestuous lust and patricide. Only these structures of desire were defined as being grounded in "normality," and as leading to cultural and civilizational advances and social stability. Rarely did Freud use the explicit term "heterosexuality," yet he significantly contributed to its categorization as a "healthy" mode of opposite-sex desire. The sexual and the social thus became intertwined in new ways placing the family at its core. Even though the bachelor represented the embodiment of modern culture, shaped by urbanization, industrialization, consumption, sexual diversity, and scientific thinking, he remained at the margins of this culture. For in the decades around the turn of the century, which was known as the age of the bachelor, a sexual-scientifically grounded certainty developed that only the nuclear family would provide social and cultural stability. This certainty would unfold even greater power in the following decades.

The overlaps of sexologist and sociological discourses can be exemplified by a volume on the bachelor, published in 1934 by Vanguard Press in New York. In his chapter of the book, Ernest W. Burgess, one of the leading scholars of the Chicago School of Sociology, described the bachelor as "peculiarly a phenomenon of modern times." The book's title, *The Sex Life of the Unmarried Adult*, announced as clearly as possible what this book dealt with. A panel of experts from various academic fields commented extensively on sex among unmarried people. The theme and approach were seen as specifically "modern," which Erich Fromm, one of the volume's reviewers, deemed "highly remarkable." Among the disciplines represented in the volume were sociology, economics, anthropology, literature, medicine, psychology, and others. According to psychologist Ernest R. Groves, the volume underscored that in past years, and partly because of Sigmund Freud, we had learned "that sex has a larger meaning for the human career than appears on the surface." Particularly the Chicago School had paid increasing attention to sexuality, and its scholars had examined through interdisciplinary work in the urban laboratory the relationship between "sexual and social pathologies" (the title of one of the courses taught by Burgess at the University of Chicago). Through a myriad of individual studies, sociologists at the Chicago School aimed at identifying "urban personality types" that they defined through their relationship to the sexual.[63]

The bachelor was seen as one of the leading urban personality types of modernity. One of the possible facets of his sexual life was the same-sex relationship, which by now was called "homosexual" and which Burgess had described as a socially, psychologically, and/or biologically conditioned phenomenon. According to Burgess various new and peculiar forms of sexuality were an effect of the modern urban environment, and they often consisted of short and peripheral contacts among people—homo- or heterosexual—drifting in and out of the city. Burgess described the bachelor as the representation of a modern urban society, a corresponding popular culture, greater gender equality, and greater social mobility. At the same time he recorded a higher proportion of unmarried men among criminals, the mentally ill, the disabled, and those suffering from sexual disease. Bachelorhood thus, according to Burgess, was, regardless of its sociocultural acceptance, still associated with a higher level of dysfunction within society and thus a lower level of success in life. Burgess concluded his essay in the volume by stating that married life was still the preferred form of sexual relations, even if one acknowledged the existence of sexuality outside the parameters of marriage.[64]

In 1935, a year after the publication of the volume, the Committee for the Study of Sex Variants was founded in New York. Funded in part by the Rockefeller Foundation, it included social scientists, urban studies scholars, and eleven physicians from different medical subspecialties, including endocrinology and psychiatry. The committee sought to explore the various sexual behaviors in the city, primarily by examining the biographies of forty research subjects between the ages of twenty and sixty-four. These subjects were to provide their own life stories and be thoroughly described, photographed, and classified.[65]

The New York study appeared in 1941 in two volumes spanning more than a thousand pages, which demonstrated how scientific endeavors resulted in the classification of "the homosexual" as a species: men desiring men were observed, analyzed, standardized, categorized, and recorded as deviant and psychopathic.[66] According to the chair of the study, the psychiatrist George Henry of the New York Payne-Whitney Psychiatric Clinic, the gay male world was populated by this deviant sexual type. This type, the study determined, had never reached the level of maturity described by Freud and was a byproduct of the modern world, whose complex demands for the building of a well-ordered family he could not master. As the study continued, families that still managed to exist in this environment were often dysfunctional and their developmental deficits and pathologies often carried over from one generation to the next. The only remedy appeared to be the support for and establishment of stable nuclear families, in which children provided the opportunity to learn the respective natural gender roles modeled by their parents. This study linked concepts of sexual pathologies, dysfunctional families, and social chaos, creating a powerful imagined threat to the social order of the twentieth century.

Bachelors were paradigmatic for an increasingly modern and urban society. Robert McBurney's biography is representative of the complex and ambiguous living arrangements of single men. Since the end of the nineteenth century, men like McBurney and their living arrangements faced increasing suspicion. The emerging sexual and social sciences exerted a new type of power, which at once contributed to the first sexual revolution and the classification and scientific specification of a supposedly deviant sexuality. They tied the sexual to the social and the political, with the family as the crucial link of this assemblage.

Immigrant Families in Urban America, 1880–1920

Your first duty to God is to serve your father. But what's an old father to an *Amerikanerin*, a daughter of Babylon?
—Bernard Yezierska to his daughter Anzia in New York, 1920

Jewish Migration to the Lower East Side: Diversity, Unity, and Upheavals

In 1894, twelve-year-old Minnie Goldstein traveled with her mother Brayndl from Warsaw to New York. Minnie was one of about 135,000 Central and Eastern Europeans going to America that year.[1] Unlike her father Hershl, who had arrived a few years earlier, Minnie had to enter through the immigration inspection station on Ellis Island, which had been built years earlier in the shadow of the Statue of Liberty. More than twenty-five million people arrived between 1880 and 1921, the year of the Emergency Quota Act, most of them from Southern and Eastern Europe, Catholic or Jewish, and escaping poverty, discrimination, and pogroms in their home countries. The Jewish population in the United States grew from a quarter million to around four million in this period, and by then most of them hailed from Eastern Europe.

Minnie and her parents stayed in New York City, which became home to the largest Jewish community in the world during this time. On the eve of World War I, about a quarter of New York City's five million inhabitants were Jews. About three-quarters of them lived on the Southeast Side of Manhattan, in the area between East River and Delancey Street. Just three blocks south of Delancey, on Hester between Essex and Ludlow, Minnie's father Hershl ran a small store. By the time Minnie and her mother reached New York, he had found a small apartment in one of the tenement houses. The Jewish residents shaped the Lower East

Side, adjacent to other ethnic neighborhoods, such as Chinatown and Little Italy.[2]

Jewish migrants' personal histories were diverse, as demonstrated by the 223 autobiographical sketches that were sent in 1942 and 1943 to the New York Institute for Jewish Research (YIVO) in response to a writing contest that asked for stories about immigrants' success or failure in America. Authors tell about their motivations for leaving their home country and point to their accomplishments in America. Minnie Goldstein wrote one of them.[3] The diversity of Jewish experiences is also reflected in the almost fifteen hundred interviews that the Ellis Island Oral History Project conducted in the 1970s with Jewish migrants, as well as in memoirs, short stories, and novels that tell of life on the Lower East Side, in New York, and in America.[4]

Even if the autobiographies, interviews, memoirs, and personal histories were diverse, they nonetheless came together in a common narrative that depicts Jewish life on the Lower East Side as a rite of passage that lasted for about forty years. In Jewish memory, Hasia Diner writes, the period on the Lower East Side was seen "as narrow bridge between slavery and freedom, between the Egypt of Russia and Poland and the promised land of America." When the Williamsburg Bridge, sometimes called the "Jews' Bridge," opened in 1903, it served as a threshold, both symbolic and real, from the Lower East Side out to Brooklyn, on the other side of the East River. When Minnie entered the writing contest of the YIVO-Institute, she reported that she had a family and raised children who had acquired university degrees; that she had taught herself reading and writing, owned several apartment buildings, and had moved on to Providence, Rhode Island.[5]

Yet the mythical success narrative also shows tension and upheaval, often with the family and long periods of separation at its center. For many years Minnie and her mother had to fend for themselves in Warsaw without her father. He struggled for four years to build a life in New York before he could afford to send for his wife and child. Many families left behind grandparents and siblings in the home country, while in the new country conflicts often arose around family relations and between the generations.[6]

When Minnie arrived in New York in 1894 the living conditions of the immigrants in the tenement houses had become an important object of intense observation and documentation. Concern over "moral malaria," discussed by the New York City Council as early as 1857, was nearing its peak in 1880.[7] Given the increasing power of social Darwinist racism, the mass immigration from different cultural and ethnic background cried out for close scrutiny, analysis, and reform. Racist stereotyping and social reform efforts overlapped, and few embodied this better through their writings and work than the journalist and social reformer Jacob Riis.

The fears of observers like Riis also revolved around family upheaval, but of a very different kind than those in the Jewish community. Riis spoke of the "murder of the home" in the tenements and of the slum as a cancer. "The tenements touch the family life with deadly moral contagion," he wrote, stirring up a scary scenario, when theories about disease and contagion enjoyed great scientific and political authority.[8]

Riis's lament about the death of the family home in the tenements had three major reference points, which frame the structure of this chapter. First, the reform discourse diagnosed a lack of privacy in the tenements and thus the loss of what was considered the core of a home. Virtuous, republican characters and citizens would not be able to thrive in such cramped living conditions, where the private was public and the public sphere encroached on the private. A second problem seen by Riis was poverty and labor. Poor working conditions and low wages meant that fathers could not alone serve as providers for their family but that all members of the family had to contribute to the family income. The work itself, whether sewing or cigar-making, was often done at home, which further blurred the boundaries between private and public. Third, reformers grew concerned about raising children in such an environment. If children grew up without the moral guidance of a nuclear family, and if their lives were shaped not by schooling and education but by work and neglect, reformers worried, America was heading toward a gloomy future. Immigrants such as Minnie Goldstein had a very different self-perception, and they sought to find ways of navigating between two very different worlds.

This late nineteenth- and early twentieth-century world that they encountered seemed coined by a thriving scientific racism and a racist understanding of the body politic, its productivity and "health." A growing army of experts with knowledge in social sciences, health sciences, and economics analyzed the American body politic and created a broad knowledge base for progressive innovation and reform.[9] Public health, working conditions, schooling and education, housing, leisure spaces, tenement buildings and public parks, hygiene, water quality, air and nutrition, and above all the dis/ability of the poor and underprivileged to have control over their own lives were on these experts' agenda. Theodore Roosevelt, New York City police commissioner then governor of the state and later American president, arranged for Riis to serve as adviser to New York mayor William F. Strong, praised him as "New York's most useful citizen," and invited him to the White House on several occasions.[10]

Biological considerations, anthropometric research, and racial charts began to differentiate with ever more detail among human groups and their alleged dis/ability for self-government, drafted a hierarchical spectrum of assumed races, and construed collective characteristics—such as moral, intellectual, and civic qualities—from physical features, such as skin color and body shape. Since the late nineteenth century, such charts constructed a broad spectrum of shades, and they were also used to categorize new immigrants. Just as the 1890 census introduced various grades of blackness for African Americans, so did immigration officials, beginning in 1899, introduce various races for European immigrants at American entrance points: Italians were divided into southern Mediterranean and northern Alpine peoples, and Jews were recorded as "Hebrews."[11]

However, positioning Jews on this spectrum proved to be difficult. Historian Eric Goldstein shows how since 1880 they became increasingly defined as "pathological others," and how they vacillated in a space between whiteness and blackness with the influx of new Eastern European immigrants. Jacob Riis described Jews as "the lowest of the whites" with only marginal civic abilities. That most of the new immigrants from Eastern Europe spoke Yiddish, a language not well known in the United States, reinforced those assumptions. At the same time, many progressive reformers welcomed the challenge to "whiten" these Jewish immigrant "in-between peoples," as historian David Roediger has called them. Even if Riis gradually changed his mind over the years and later spoke of a Jewish potential for development as well as calling Jews "material for citizenship," their "whitening" process was to take off only in the 1920s, after their immigration had been drastically restricted. Minnie Goldstein had already purchased a ticket for her half brother's passage to New York when the Immigration Quota Act came into effect, claiming a generic whiteness of the American population. He never made it to America.[12]

Jacob Riis and the Reform Discourse

In 1870, young Jacob Riis came from provincial Denmark to the United States and eked out an existence doing odd jobs, before embarking on a career as a journalist. Between 1877 and 1890 he worked as a police reporter at the *New York Tribune*. His office was located on Mulberry Street at the intersection of Chinatown, Little Italy, and "Jewtown," where, according to Riis, standing at the corner of Bayard Street and doing a 360-degree turn would present a view from Palestine to southern Italy. Colleagues soon praised him as the "best-known and most widely read expert [on] life in the crowded districts of New York."[13] Riis thought of himself as a preacher and missionary who, instead of going to foreign countries, stayed on the Lower East Side, where more people were in need of enlightenment than in any other place in the world. He criticized urban mischiefs and called on people to improve their living conditions, their community, and themselves. His work blended progressive-reformist critiques of the exploitative structures of the modern urban order, advice on the improvement of conduct in life, and racist observations, infused with the social Darwinist discourses of his time.[14]

Riis was also a pioneer in social photography. Numerous photographs were meant to make his observations seem more authentic and his books more attractive. Riis published his findings in articles in books and magazines, but also through slide shows, which he usually presented in churches and YMCAs throughout New York and the northeastern United States. His first illustrated lecture about life in the slums, given in January 1888 at the Amateur Photographers Association in New York, received a lot of attention in the media and among his listeners. According to a commentator from Asbury Park, New Jersey, the images were strange and different, allowing Riis's audience and readers to undertake a visual excursion into the slums, a journey into the underworld, to observe the filth and chaos of the tenements up close, without having to physically travel there. In addition to this voyeuristic armchair slumming, several philanthropists and tourists actually toured the slums, sometimes perceiving life there as picturesque.[15]

On the following pages, Riis serves as a vehicle for a closer examination of the nexus among migration, Jewish life and the Lower East Side, and reformist scenarios of familial and sociocultural decay. We will scrutinize first how he portrayed the private sphere in the tenement houses, second how he commented on the conditions of poverty and work there, and third what the lives of children in the slums meant to him.

"Anglo-Saxon civilization is founded upon the family," the *New York Tribune* declared with an air of apodictic certainty in a review of *How the Other Half Lives*. Those who did not have a family home were seen as tainted in their citizenship and manhood. "No home, no family, no morality, no manhood, no patriotism!," Riis wrote in the *Atlantic Monthly* describing the consequences of losing a private abode.[16] He made sure to stress how closely the private was interwoven with the public. "To the home it comes down in the end,—good government, bad government, and all the rest. As the homes of a community are, so is the community. New York has still the worst housing system in the world."[17] In the spring of 1903 in a lecture in Philadelphia, he elaborated on his ideas about the relationship between individual, family, and state: "You cannot herd human beings in battalions and expect them to develop the qualities of individuality, of character, that make citizenship upon which to build the Republic that shall be the hope of to-morrow as well as the shelter of to-day. . . . No, brethren, upon the home rests our moral character; our civic and political liberties are grounded there; virtue, manhood, citizenship grow there. We forget it to our peril. For American citizenship in the long run, will be, must be, what the American home is."[18]

In the nineteenth century ideas about the essential goodness of the private sphere were tied to a particular spatial order: a separate paternal bedroom was regarded as especially important, as was a separate room for personal hygiene and toilets. However, these would be standard at best only in middle-class homes, even though they were generally propagated as necessary. "Decency," a travel guide for New York announced in 1872, did not exist in the slums of the city, and little changed about this perception until the turn of the century. Only white middle-class residents could afford such a living arrangement, which shows, also with regard to the tenement houses on the Lower East Side, how class and racial distinctions intersected. Only those who could afford a measure of privacy in their homes could be considered white, morally upright, and worthy of citizenship in a kind of society, in which individualism and freedom also meant having privacy in certain situations. Tenements, on the other hand, where sometimes nine or more people were crammed into two rooms, represented, according to Riis, the exact opposite, and they were "with its crowds, its lack of privacy, . . . the greatest destroyer of individuality."[19] Journalist Parke Godwin underscored this in the *New York Post* in 1879: "They are the homes where intemperance is nursed, crimes are nourished, the modesty of girlhood is crushed, and the innocent instincts of childhood are stifled in their birth."[20]

When Jacob Riis published his most famous book, *How the Other Half Lives*, in 1890, the overcrowded tenement homes and their detrimental effects had been on the agenda of city officials for several decades. As early as 1857 an official report stated that the increasingly crowded tenements housed ever more people in ever smaller units at overpriced rents, forcing them to live hand to mouth, unfettered in their morality, inconsiderate in their habits, degenerate, filthy, impoverished, not unlike the panhandlers in the city. Soon dozens of physicians and inspectors descended on the neighborhood every summer on behalf of the Board of Health in order to patrol, control, take stock, and educate.[21]

At the outset of his book, Riis reminded readers about the report from 1857 as a way of pointing out that the conditions had not improved since then. To the contrary, they had gotten worse. There now existed more than 37,000 tenement houses, often with front and back houses, even more cramped than before, with close to 1.25 million residents. No area of the world had a denser population than the Lower East Side with 290,000 people per square mile. That same year the Census Bureau had announced the closing of the frontier and declared the North American continent as fully settled because it counted at least two residents per square mile in the West. While Riis denounced greedy speculators who exploited unknowing immigrants, he nonetheless connected cramped ways of living, moral decay, and racially infused otherness into a single problem. The tenements, he emphasized, were inhabited by "a queer conglomerate mass of heterogeneous elements," which was everything but American. Especially the blocks north and south of Delancey Street and between the East River and the Bowery, which had for the past few years been home to Polish and Russian Jews, were so packed with people, Riis lamented, that there was no resemblance to homes with a private sphere at all.[22]

Consequently, people exhibited their private lives on the streets. Foreign food smells of garlic, cabbage, and others wafted through the quarter and were interpreted as signs of poor hygiene, much as the laundry that was hung up in courtyards and between houses, which led to fears of disseminating infectious diseases. Men who congregated on corners for small talk were seen as a sign of male indolence, and children who played in the dark hallways as indicators of neglect and broken families. Closeness and alienation were always connected to moral decay, the threat of epidemics and fire, as well as high child mortality, which in some tenements was as high as 50 percent in the first year of life, a figure that observers mentioned over and over again. Even if concern about tenements had existed for decades, it seemed that in 1890 the Lower East Side had sunk into a most dangerous cesspool or had grown into an out-of-control cancerous tumor in the American collective body.[23]

Critics lamented endlessly about life in the tenements. There was a shortage of lavatories and washrooms so that tenants had to use shared bathrooms in the courtyard, associated by reformers with poor hygiene. In the hot summer months, when, as Riis warned, children's diseases turned into deadly epidemics and people died like flies, tenants moved out of their overheated, often windowless, apartments onto rooftops in order to catch a little bit of a nighttime breeze. Women and men lay side by side: restless, sweaty bodies, who panted for a bit of air and some sleep, Riis wrote turgidly, using ambiguous language.[24]

Furthermore, almost every family took in additional boarders in order to pay the exorbitant rent. This was a double burden, considering the already tight living quarters and the often doorless rooms, sometimes subdivided only by curtains. Many boarders frequented the cheap lodging houses and ate in the two-cent restaurants, which were considered even more disreputable with regard to health and morality. Lodging houses and cheap restaurants stood for the opposite of family life. Besides prostitutes, lodgers were regarded as the most dangerous carriers of infectious diseases, which would then spread among the families in the tenement houses and destroy the last vestiges of a family structure. Critics often omitted the fact that most of the lodgers who stayed with families were either relatives or *landslayt*, the Yiddish term for people from the same hometown or region.[25]

A second criticism of the lives of migrants and their family structures revolved around working conditions on the Lower East Side. The constant influx of new people without means swelled the ranks of workers on a daily basis, making also unions hostile toward new arrivals. Riis and other muckrakers tied their laments about the poor conditions in the tenements to stereotypes of "swarthy Italians" and "Hebrews." But they also denounced the greed of profiteers who exploited the ignorance and lack of organization among immigrants and who raised rents to exorbitant levels while depressing wages. If rent for two rooms was $7.50, and thus more than a week's wage for the father of a family, then it should come as no surprise that many parents were driven to despair, insanity, and even suicide. This, in turn, would lead to even more mass impoverishment and would threaten individuals, families, and all of society at once: "Here as everywhere, the welfare of the State is consistent with humanity towards its citizens," an article in *Scribner's Magazine* about poverty in cities pronounced. In contemporary discourse, poverty, alcohol, impurity, vice, crime, and fraud merged into the single concept of "pauperism," which threatened society as a whole. Pauperism became a central topic of all social questions and had distinct racial connotations.[26]

Reformers also criticized high rents and starvation wages because they impeded the whitening of the Eastern European Jewish immigrants. In principle these reformers acknowledged that Jewish migrants had the potential to become productive members of the American body politic precisely because of their close familial ties and their alleged ingrained diligence.[27] Furthermore, well-established Jews who lived uptown strove to install structures and philanthropic organizations, to advance the assimilation of the more recent Eastern European Jewish immigrants. It is important to keep in mind that most of the immigrants not only were unfamiliar with the United States but also came from politically autocratic systems and from small towns in agrarian regions of Eastern Europe called *shtetls*.[28] They found it especially difficult to make their way in New York City. Jewish organizations, such as the Hebrew Immigrant Aid Society (HIAS), were supposed to help with the transition. Volunteers went out to Ellis Island in order to offer support to new arrivals, who often spent their first night in HIAS emergency shelters. Assimilated Jews were also motivated to help because they feared that the general classification "Hebrew" would lead to the demotion of their own status in the United States and thus force them onto a lower rung of the "civilizational ladder." They thus pursued a dual objective: to aid Eastern European Jews in their assimilation process and to maintain their own position in American society.[29]

The scenario of poverty and poor working conditions was very much seen as tied to the loss of the family and the father's position. Low wages made it impossible for fathers to fulfill their assigned role of being the provider of the family. Riis and his colleagues stressed this over and over. With regard to life in the tenements, they arrived at several conclusions. First, mothers and children were also gainfully employed, which Riis considered the end of the home as concept and reality. Wages for women were often as absurdly low as thirty cents per day, yet absolutely necessary for the survival of the family.[30] If one or both parents became unable to work, it was said, then the family likely plunged into absolute poverty, despair, alcoholism, complete neglect of children, and reliance on welfare. This, in turn, would lead to pauperism. Riis constructed the image of an urban socially fraudulent "welfare queen," and Ronald Reagan could not have invented her better eighty-five years later. While Reagan zeroed in on single black mothers as the prototype of the social parasite, Riis identified the migrant widow, "whose husband turned up alive and well after she had buried him seventeen times with tears and lamentation, and made the public pay for the weekly funerals."[31]

Most Jewish immigrants worked in textile and cigar production, which was done primarily as piecework in homes and not in factories. This allowed manufacturers to lower the cost of production and circumvent legal regulations. Whole families were pressed into sub and subsub enterprises, which ignored the legally grounded ten-hour workday. Furthermore, nobody asked whether child laborers were below the legal working age. The home as workplace as well as the incorporation of the family into the wage labor system exposed the failure of the provider model for many immigrant fathers.[32]

The mechanization of the textile industry and its proliferation in 1880s New York went hand in hand with the large Jewish immigration. Spurred on by a sweater, a kind of supervisor, who stood between home worker and employer, hundreds of sewing machines hummed along in countless apartments and sweatshops from morning to night in so-called Jewtown. As Riis wrote, they were operated collectively by all members of the family, "shut in the qualmy rooms, where meals are cooked and clothing washed and dried besides, the livelong day."[33] The competition and the work, the sweat and filth, desecrated the home as the locus of morality and purity, of intimacy and regeneration: "Domiciliary temperature is parboiling," warned Richard Wheatley, who regularly wrote about conditions on the Lower East Side in New York magazines such as the *Century*. "Dirt breeds disease. Foul air poisons life at its sources," if the home becomes the place of work. "It is idle to speak of privacy in these 'homes,'" Riis remarked. "The term carries no more meaning with it than would a lecture on social ethics to an audience of Hottentots."[34]

Directly related to the loss of the private sphere, the failure of the father as provider, poor work conditions, and poverty in general was a third area of concern: children's life experiences in the urban tenements. Over the years Riis paid special attention to the theme of childhood on the Lower East Side (or rather the loss of what had been construed as childhood in the nineteenth century). In 1892 he published a book titled *The Children of the Poor*. Progressive reformers feared that without a private home life it was impossible to raise morally upright and healthy children who would mature into good citizens. After all, the home was considered the key to "good citizenship."[35] The all-important ability to self-guidance, they stated, was taught mainly in families. In response, philanthropic organizations such as the Children's Aid Society and the National Child Labor Committee were founded to protect childhood. Riis, too, reiterated this concern quite often: "For, be it remembered, these children with the training they receive—or do not receive—with the instincts they inherit and absorb in their growing up, are to be our future rulers, if our theory of government is worth anything."[36]

Riis and his fellow reformers observed abominable conditions on the Lower East Side and painted a grim future. Children who managed to survive the first year of their lives grew up in filthy basements and overcrowded rooms without windows, which they had to share not only with several siblings but also with strangers who sublet. Parents often worked from morning till night, and the children roamed the dark hallways of the tenement buildings or the filthy alleys. Reformers complained that they panhandled, bartered, pilfered, joined street gangs, and drank left-over beer they found in the two-cent restaurants. If they lived entirely on the street they were often from fatherless families, Riis observed, or had an alcoholic as father. Around fifteen thousand children lived permanently in one of New York's orphanages or public shelters. According to historian Sydney Mintz, during this time the number of children who became wards of the state rose from sixty thousand to over two hundred thousand. Reformers sought both to protect children from the dangers of urban society and to protect society from children, who, through lack of supervision, became a threat.[37]

Riis and his colleagues conceded that a father could hardly be blamed for sending his son to work in one of the small factories on the Lower East Side, even if the boy was too young to work. "It was either the street or the shop for the boy," one father replied to the accusations, declaring that breaking the law against child labor was easier for him than losing his boy to the streets. "What indeed was there to say?" Riis concluded rhetorically.[38]

Child labor was a central concern of progressive reformers years before the New York teacher and journalist Lewis Hine exposed the practice in America through his photographic reportage. Hine became most famous for documenting child labor everywhere: in factories, mines, and steelworks, on farms, and in the street barter system, from Maine to Texas. Starting in 1904 Hine taught photography on Ellis Island, where he and his students took thousands of pictures. Two million children, according to some estimates, were employed in the early twentieth century in the whole country. Child labor was most definitely not a problem only on the Lower East Side, nor is it exclusive to the turn of the century. This shows a closer look at the early phase of the capitalist market economy, the beginnings of industrialization, the agrarian sector, and forced labor such as slavery.[39] Nevertheless, reformers charged that particularly migrant children in turn-of-the-century New York worked and rarely went to school.[40] Lower East Side children who did not work in the local shops and factories usually did piece work at home. In the textile and tobacco industries, all family members contributed, regardless of age and gender, as Riis underlined: "Men, women and children work together seven days in the week in these cheerless tenements to make a living for the family, from the break of day till far into the night."[41] In the end child labor would become such a vital element of the family income only because families became production units and homes became sites of production. To be sure, factories too constantly disregarded child labor and work hour rules, but especially the work in homes made abundantly clear how much these legal constraints existed on paper only.[42]

Minnie Goldstein and Others

From the perspective of Jacob Riis and the reform discourse, people on the Lower East Side were without their own agenda and without agency. Their kind of self-government, their decisions to move in one direction or another and to adhere to norms and principles that maybe differed from those that dominated in the United States did not appear in his reports, even though he always tried to get as close to his objects of investigation as possible. Participant observation was getting highly popular among anthropologists at the time. But even if his contemporaries regarded him as the greatest expert on life in the slums, the tenements and their inhabitants always remained alien and exotic to him. In order to overcome that obstacle and make his observation appear more participatory and his reports more authentic, Riis hired assistants such as Robert Leslie, who talked with residents of the Lower East Side and observed them closely. A person like Leslie was particularly well suited for such a task since he himself was born and raised on the Lower East Side as a son of Russian immigrants, with an alcoholic father and seven siblings (an additional four did not survive), at 5 Hester Street, on the same street block where twelve-year-old Minnie Goldstein moved in 1894. Like his neighbors, Leslie had lived in a tenement without toilets and running water. As a child he had made money by selling newspapers on the streets and preserved apples in the notorious sweatshops. When he grew older he received support from a Jewish aid organization. He worked for Jacob Riis on Ellis Island and went on to study chemistry, supported by a fellowship, eventually earning a PhD at the Johns Hopkins University in Baltimore, Maryland.[43]

Robert Leslie embodied two narratives of so-called new immigrants to America: the slum story of being seen as a hazard to the American body politic and the success story of a second-generation Jewish migrant becoming "white." Because of his apparently "authentic" experiences, he was of great value to Riis as a field worker as well as historical witness in oral history projects of the 1980s. Of course over the years experiences turned into memories, in which some elements resonated stronger than others, thus shifting the overall image of the past.[44] On occasion immigrant memories of life on the Lower East Side, as recorded in oral history projects or autobiographical testimonies, reveal the same patterns as the reformist discourse at the turn of the century. Yet they also reveal that the immigrants' way of organizing and experiencing their lives differed from the way presented by Jacob Riis.

Therefore I revisit the three areas previously addressed through Jacob Riis's lens, but this time approach them from the perspective of people such as Minnie Goldstein and Robert Leslie and how they deal with issues of privacy and intimacy, working conditions, childhood, and family experiences. These examinations include memories of life experiences before and after migrating to the United States, memories that changed from generation to generation.

In their home countries in Galicia, Lithuania, Poland, or Russia, most Eastern European immigrants to America had never lived in conditions that met American reformers' expectations of privacy and intimacy. The concept of family was more broadly defined and shaped by the experience of diaspora, which affected Jewish life also before emigration to the United States. Minnie Goldstein, for instance, had lived in Warsaw with her mother in a single room after her father had left for America. At the same time she was very close to her grandmother and half siblings, even if their relationship was often strained. Families of several generations and branches frequently shared small houses, which often met only the most rudimentary needs. Interviews tell of huts with only a dirt floor and no running water. America thus meant simply the continuation of life in cramped conditions. Most migrants were used to not have separate spheres that would have allowed intimacy in bed- or bathrooms. This remained a prospect for years later, when one was able to move to Brooklyn or uptown into the Bronx.

Since new immigrants mostly came from small towns, they might have been used to cramped quarters, but not to overcrowded neighborhoods in urban multifamily dwellings. Esther Sheinman, who arrived in 1905 from Białystok, an industrial center in Russian Poland, found the different houses and floors of the tenements so identical that she had occasional difficulties finding her way back to her own apartment. Many others recalled the bustle in the tenements: constant shopping, taking out the garbage, and fetching firewood or water were just some of the chores to be completed.[45]

Residents supported each other in order to master the day-to-day chores. They coordinated the shopping, baked bread together in shared ovens, exchanged information, and supported newcomers. A social structure that tied together landslayt in a communal network that encompassed neighborhoods as well as spanned across the Atlantic was central to survival in the diaspora. Riis's later writings show that he recognized the tight community of extended family and neighborhoods as a kind of practice run on the path toward citizenship. Such a wide network of family, kin, and neighbors was especially important for migrants because they were often separated from partners and close family for a prolonged period, possibly forever, when they moved from Europe to the United States. Alienation was a common experience. Julia Greenberg, for instance, recounted that she no longer knew her father when she reunited with him after years. "I was afraid of him. I wouldn't speak to my father for a long time before I got used to the fact that he was my father."[46]

Communal living beyond close family relations also played a role when taking in additional boarders. Necessary in order to be able to pay the rent, boarders often were distant relatives or acquaintances of acquaintances who were new to the city, needed a place to stay, and wanted to bypass the lodging houses. After having spent the first night in a shelter run by the Hebrew Immigrant Aid Society (HIAS), Minnie's father stayed several years as a boarder with a Jewish family on Hester Street. He used the kitchen with three others as his sleeping quarters, while the children moved into the parents' bedroom. Almost all interviewees had similar stories of residing as newcomers with sister, uncle, acquaintances for the first days, weeks, months, or even years, and how later they took in newcomers themselves. Accepting help from the HIAS or similar agencies, especially upon first arrival, was also quite common.[47]

By taking in new arrivals, immigrants did not counteract family obligations but fulfilled them. They followed principles of hospitality and
religiosity and thus ensured survival in times of separation, transformation, and waning structures. Many autobiographies and memories
show how making room for the *mischpoche* meant showing respect for
relations of kinship and friendship rather than the desecration of the
private home. Family thus meant not nuclear family but a much wider
kinship network.[48]

Historian Eric Goldstein describes bonds in the Jewish community as
especially strong. Jewish immigrants from Eastern Europe initially felt
only little urge to rise in the ranks of whiteness precisely because they
did not see themselves in competition with other migrant groups. Their
self-identification as Jewish was so strong, observers noted, that they did
not react to Anglo-American demands to define their level of whiteness.
Furthermore, most Jews operated in a world of work with little competition from other groups. This changed for second- and third-generation
immigrants, who, as a result of their success in education and work, followed different paths and faced more severe competition with others.[49]

A closer look at the working conditions and at poverty in general
reveals that most historical witnesses recalled experiencing poverty in
their life. Minnie Goldstein even stressed that "I cannot remember a
single day of my childhood when . . . I had enough to eat—even here in
America."[50] In Europe poverty was largely the result of settlement, educational, and labor discrimination, to which Jews were subjected, as well
as growing anti-Semitic pogroms. Russian men also fled to America to
escape brutal conscription practices, particularly relating to the 1904–5
Russo-Japanese War.[51]

Widespread poverty had various consequences for the family order
and for their migration practice. First, few families could raise enough
money for all members to emigrate to America at the same time. Even
though Minnie's father sold all their belongings, he had only two dollars
in his pocket when he arrived in the United States. The first thing he did
upon arrival was to sell his fur coat, a wedding gift from his father and
thus of both economic and sentimental value. For two years her father
eked out a living on the Lower East Side, trying out and failing at several
jobs before he opened a small shoe store on Hester Street. He began to
send money to his wife and daughter back home and after two years had

saved enough to buy passages to America for both. Their son had to stay behind with his grandmother.[52]

In almost all families fathers went first in order to gain a foothold in the United States. Not always did the families back home trust the fathers. For instance, Goldstein wrote that back home her father had been a Yeshiva student who enjoyed studying the Torah and Talmud and was not very successful in his mother-in-law's business. Upon his departure, his wife told him that he was a weakling, that he did not know a single trade and thus was unlikely to make it in the United States. This judgment contained undertones of the concept of the "muscle-Jew," a new type of Jewish man who embodied strength in life in contrast to the "Talmud-Jew."[53] In Poland Minnie Goldstein's grandmother presided over the family. Her personal history represented a kind of American dream in Poland since she worked her way up from an orphaned childhood to becoming a successful business woman. Minnie followed a similar path when she would later, in the United States, manage a business while married with a family. Other contemporaries also recalled the traditions of male-Jewish learnedness and their consequences for family structures. "My father was a scholar. My mother was making a living for all the children," Clara Larsen remembered in an interview about her life in Russia. Another immigrant uttered a similar statement about her father: "He was a scholar. He didn't do anything [in Russia]."[54]

In Eastern European Jewish families, certain traditions shaped different work, provider, and gender relationships than what was expected within the American model. What American observers regarded as a deficit in Jewish families were instead often practices rooted in historical and cultural traditions that differed from the American norms of gender, family, and society. In Jewish families in Eastern Europe, the role of provider was less exclusively focused on the family father. It was thus not seen as paternal failure and a sign of familial and social destabilization when all family members contributed to the family income. Nonetheless, these families regarded the role of the father as central, and migration to the United States unsettled these structure in various ways. Some worshipped the process of Americanization; others lamented it as a Babylonian break with tradition. In one interview Morris Abrams recalled how his grandmother warned the then nine-year-old he would lose at least part of his Jewishness when he would leave his village in today's Belarus for America.[55]

In the United States the focus on fathers as head of their family was often further strengthened by the fact that they usually had a head start in familiarizing themselves with the customs, rules, conditions, and language of the new country. Yet children often adjusted faster than their parents to life in America and would soon take over the family affairs. "Too often relations between father and son are reversed," Jacob Riis noted, "and the father must depend on the boy . . . [because] he is and remains a stranger, never even learning the language."[56] Still, by the time families followed, fathers often had secured an apartment and a job and would offer advice for the journey in their letters. Fathers also usually traveled to Ellis Island to welcome their family and certified to authorities that the new incomers' livelihood was secured at least for the first month of their stay. Goldstein also wrote of her father's desire to finally acquire the status of provider in the United States, which he associated with ideas about manliness and equality of opportunity. He supposedly said upon deciding on emigration that he wanted "to go to a country where I can work hard and make a living for my wife and children and be equal to everyone." It is quite possible that both these passages in Minnie's narrative were more a projection of her own attitudes many years later. After all, she articulated her father's wish after she had already lived in the United States for about half a century and had herself been married for several decades to a man who had a hard time finding his way in the labor market.[57]

The situation in New York was quite difficult, and immigrant experiences were manifold. Accordingly, the narratives about working lives in the New World vary. They range from fathers as sole earners in the family, working fourteen hours a day in order to make ends meet, to mothers who managed the affairs for the family and together with their children became the main wage earners of the household. Some talked of working conditions that felt like paradise compared to what they had experienced in their homeland or even in London. Others perceived them as unbearable, so much so that they soon left the city again.[58]

Some accounts of work life were also accounts of childhoods spent on the Lower East Side, which is the third area of concern in this section. Minnie Goldstein was twelve when she began helping her father in the shoe store on Hester Street. Fortunately her father worked independently and the store was located opposite their apartment. Minnie also helped her mother, who exclusively tended to housekeeping.[59]

Some recalled such parental division of labor that seemed to adhere to the model of separate spheres.[60] Most, however, noted that it took the labor of all family members in order to safeguard survival since wages were so low and rents so high. Some children worked for a few cents an hour in sweatshops and factories and had to hide whenever inspectors came looking for evidence of illegal child labor. Others, much like Minnie, helped in stores or slaughterhouses, where, besides a meager wage, they might secure a few scraps of discarded meat. Minnie wrote that she worked in the sweatshops of the textile industry without her parents' knowledge in order to be more independent of her father and mother and escape her own misery. Still others sold newspapers or helped their parents, who worked as peddlers or sold candy, drinks, cigarettes, and other items in one of the many kiosks. Girls often worked as servants in German-Jewish households. Still others recalled how individual family members or entire family networks sewed garments at home.[61]

Particularly striking in these accounts is the fact that these individuals did not perceive their experiences as a decay of the familial order or as part of a social catastrophe—in stark contrast to most American reformers. They mostly saw their communal work as a bond that kept families together and enabled them to survive under difficult circumstances in the New World. Retail trade, the textile industry, and cigar production attracted many Jewish migrants because they would perform their work independently at home in small groups, with at least some degree of flexibility. Many interviews and personal testimonies addressed the fact that this work was not possible without colliding with traditional Jewish or modern American family patterns. In one interview Sadie Chaplan pointed out that her learned father finally had to contribute to the family income in the United States by rolling cigars. When asked how her father fared with this new occupation, she responded, not without a touch of schadenfreude, "Well, he couldn't help it. He wasn't going to sit in the synagogue all day like he did in Europe." In another interview Frank Shelibovsky stressed that the circumstances of the family's life changed little after the death of their father in 1926: "Oh, it wasn't much harder because he wasn't the main producer. He never made anything, the highest was three or four dollars a week. Can you make a living on three or four dollars a week? That's why we all had to go to work."[62]

Most of these interviews were conducted in the last decades of the twentieth century with people who had arrived as children around 1900. Many of the autobiographical texts sent to the YIVO-Institute in the early 1940s also drew on childhood memories. Almost all of them indicated a shift in perspective from one generation to the next. If asking fathers about their experiences had still been possible, results might have been different. The memories of Sanford Sternlicht, a professor of literature who himself grew up on the Lower East Side, provide a glimpse of this. He identified the synagogue as a kind of retreat for Jewish fathers where they could at least temporarily escape the demands of society and family. Sternlicht wrote that his father found it humiliating to never have been able to offer his family financial security: "After twenty-five years of backbreaking work, he was still at the immigrant's starting point."[63]

The mythical narrative of entering the promised land rests on the assumption that second- and third-generation Jewish migrants will have found their way in America, much like Minnie Goldstein, her children, or many of those who told their stories in interviews or through other venues about their life paths. However, such "whitening" of Eastern European Jewish immigrants would happen only once their numbers were restricted by the immigration laws of 1921 and 1924. Thus, historian David Roediger speaks of the "dialectics of whiteness."[64] It is of critical importance to this narrative that many children and grandchildren were able to take advantage of educational and career opportunities, in spite of all the obstacles and constraints they were facing. Anzia Yezierska, for instance, came to the United States without speaking English; she worked in sweatshops but also went to various schools and finally to college.[65] Likewise, Minnie Goldstein, who could not read or write when she came to New York as a twelve-year-old, attended night school for a short period, acted at times against the will of her parents, and ultimately succeeded, not until she reached adulthood, in teaching herself reading and writing. She started with Yiddish and learned to write in English only later. Many Jewish children seemed to have had similar experiences.[66] Nonetheless, many of the interviewees recounted how they, much like Minnie Goldstein, eventually left the Lower East Side, either across the Williamsburg Bridge into Brooklyn or uptown into the highly desirable Bronx.[67]

Minnie Goldstein's parents tried to prevent her schooling. Many interviewees recalled such generational conflicts and the fear of parents that their children would break with traditions and ways of life or would just begin to talk more English. Historian Steven Mintz sees a reversal of generational roles, with children taking over the management of family affairs and, at least to the outside world, appearing to hold the reins in the family. While one generation strove toward Americanization, the other vilified it, sometimes calling it "Babylonian godlessness."[68] Others lauded the educational zeal of their parents, who appreciated the opportunities for their children, particularly sons, in the United States, opportunities they themselves never had as Jews in Russia or Poland. In most cases the intermittent school attendance of children was often less a result of heritage or religion than of family income and social status. On the eve of the First World War, Eastern European Jewish children made up the largest single ethnic group, with 37 percent in the city's elementary schools and 53 percent in the public high schools, even though the curriculum ignored Jewish culture.[69]

Historian Eric Goldstein argues that the often less than enthusiastic attitudes of first-generation Jewish immigrants toward American schools on the one hand and the high proportion of Jewish children in schools by 1920 on the other are not necessarily contradictory. Rather, they indicate differences between generations. While first-generation immigrants saw schooling as well as mastery of the English language as a threat to Jewish identity, the second generation focused more on the process of becoming white. Growing participation in American society and access to its resources were of great significance for this transformation.

Yet integration into American society often ended where family planning began. A New York study for the years 1908 to 1912 concluded that 98.83 percent of married Jews had chosen a partner from within their own community. This might have been the result either of rigid exclusion or of one's own striving for some kind of tradition. Even Minnie Goldstein, who regarded her Americanization as a complete success, tried to prevent the relationship of her son with his non-Jewish fiancée. "I told him that she seemed like a very nice girl, and also very pretty," she reportedly said to her son, "but, after all, she was not Jewish." For years her son kept his mother in the dark about the nature of his relationship, before he married his fiancée against his mother's will. "This hit me very hard," Minnie Goldstein remembered in her account. As much as ten years later she still expressed her concerns about her sons' loss of Jewishness through marriage to Christian women.[70]

"An Excessive Waste of Human Life"

This chapter has shown how an entire arsenal of experts and authors claimed that the family served as the medium through which the individual connected to the body politic. The family grew in importance even as mass migration of people who were characterized as ethnically different altered the composition of the American population. Their otherness seemed to manifest in different family organization and different ways of living. Reformers and political administrations watched the crowded and seemingly un-American way of life in neighborhoods such as New York's Lower East Side closely, and they concluded "that the excessive waste of human life in this city is dependent upon preventable causes."[71]

The assumption about different abilities to determine one's own future was part of a racially conceived social order. One consequence was the gradual regulation and exclusion of unwanted immigrants, climaxing in the immigration laws of 1921 and 1924. Another was the assumption that many of these immigrants would, over the years, become "whiter" and thus learn the skills needed to be recognized as good citizens. This seemed to be hampered by their lives in the tenements with their exploitative ownership and rental structures, but also by the power of traditions and of living patterns that were explained through racist stereotypes. The efforts to deal with the lack of a private sphere on the Lower East Side, a missing focus on the father as provider in the family, and a less than ideal environment for child rearing oscillated between exclusion and assimilation.

The best single solution to these manifold problems attached to life on the Lower East Side seemed the strengthening of the nuclear family structure through reform efforts. The nuclear family was not just the living arrangement deemed most appropriate for reproduction and thus of utmost importance for the effort to maintain what was considered a racially pure population. It was also the site where productive citizens of a liberal republic were supposed to be molded. Criticisms and reform efforts thus revolved around the absence of this particular structure in Jewish family life in the tenements, around its effects on the American body politic, and around the potential for a cure.

Reformers lamented the lack of good government in the Lower East Side. As remedies, experts and reformers, clubs and organizations, institutions and agencies provided knowledge and engagement; they arranged offers of help and regulations in order to eliminate shortcomings and ensure the establishment of what they saw as an appropriate sociocultural order in the tenements. A precondition for immigrants to become, if not entirely white, then at least whiter, was to adhere to the normative model of the American family. Furthermore, Jacob Riis emphasized that the responsibility to provide for and protect children had in essence always rested with the state, and thus he claimed the power of the *parens patriae* doctrine. But according to Riis, the state had often taken this responsibility too lightly and left parental prerogatives untouched.[72]

8

Indigenous and Modern Fathers, 1890–1950

Joe Friday was always my inspiration. He could turn my
imagination on about Indians.
—YMCA secretary Harold Keltner, July 1946

The Y Indian Guides: A Program for Fathers and Sons

Joe Friday, or Chief Caribou by the Ojibwe Indians, made his living by
guiding white men through the woods of his home region along the
shore of Lake Temagami, north of the Great Lakes in Ontario. Among
his clients in 1923 was Harold Keltner, the director of the South Side
Young Men's Christian Association in St. Louis. Keltner had embarked
on the long trip from Missouri to Ontario in search of wilderness and
the great fishing and hunting grounds in the region. One story, which
became part of the founding myth of the YMCA Indian Guides, has
Friday and Keltner gathered around a campfire contemplating the different positions of fathers in their respective cultures. Friday, according
to the story, expressed concern about the modern American father,
particularly his relationship with his son: "To the Indian, his family is
everything. Our fathers personally taught us the dangers of the trail.
Little braves tagged big braves for years before they ventured forth on
their own. The American father gets into an automobile; blazes away
in one direction, while his son, with an eighty horse power engine at
his command, tears off in another . . . often without being prepared for
the dangers ahead; without having been taught good sportsmanship and
thoughtfulness for others."[1]

Regardless of what actually transpired between Friday and his guest
that evening, it stirred Keltner's imagination. The vision of a Native
American father who showed his sons the secret of life in the woods of
North America matched Euro-American romantic ideas about indig-

enous life and even grew in strength with the closing of the frontier. The emergence of a fast-paced modern society generated much uncertainty and a sense of crisis, fueling the idealization and romanticization of nature and everything that was associated with it.

Keltner and Friday found themselves at the crossroads of this historical transformation, coined by three major elements. First is the idealized admiration of the indigenous population, which reached its apex at precisely the moment of their near extinction, confinement onto reservations, and efforts to assimilate their children into American society.[2] Second is the growing critique of modern life, condemning the loss of engagement with nature and wilderness, which were regarded as fundamental to America's identity.[3] This corresponded with a new educational philosophy for American children that, based on the assumption that boys in particular had a natural wildness about them, would grant them space within nature to grow. The hope was to escape the dangers of overcivilization.[4] Third is complaints that the division of labor in modern society removed fathers from their children's daily life: "White men build cities, Red men build sons," Friday is supposed to have summarized the modern dilemma, according to a YMCA retrospective.[5] A growing movement in the 1920s and 1930s sought to counter this dilemma and promoted "modern fatherhood." Fathers were encouraged to become more involved in the day-to-day chores of their families and the children's upbringing and thus be different from the earlier model of middle-class detached fatherhood. The popularization of Freudian theories in the 1920s further enhanced a notion of how problematic and regrettable was fathers' absence from their children's and particularly their sons' lives.[6]

Harold Keltner described Joe Friday as hunter, trapper, guide, philosopher, and Christian. In 1925 he invited him to St. Louis so he could speak to fathers and sons. "The Indian is a creature of imagination, so natural to a boy, and at least dormant in the man," Keltner declared. He hoped that listening to Friday would generate among fathers and sons an unfettered fascination with and heroic admiration for the Indian way of life as well as a stronger attachment to each other. Local newspapers reported, tongue in cheek, that enthusiastic fathers crowded around Friday so closely that their sons did not even get to see him. Keltner developed visions of fathers and sons who, modeled on Indian ways, would regularly venture out together in groups, "doing, exploring, learning together," according to a contemporary commentary. Its author saw in these precepts a decisive improvement on the modern American family life, as she revealed in a rhetorical question: "Would such an organized group [of fathers and sons] furnish that missing link in the modern American home?"[7]

Friday would come to St. Louis and stay for some years. He participated in the creation of the YMCA's Father and Son Indian Guide Project, inaugurated in October 1926 in Richmond Heights, a suburb of St. Louis. Eight fathers with their sons, aged between six and eight years, made up the first "tribe," which took its name from the Osage. They got together every other week in order to celebrate pseudo-Indian rituals, tell each other hunting stories, and bond through play, building projects, and outdoor activities at the "crabgrass frontier" of their suburban gardens.[8] The Father and Son Indian Guides with group meetings, camping trips, annual conventions, instructions, craft brochures, and motivational pamphlets were among the most successful programs of the YMCA. They still exist today.[9]

This chapter discusses the origin and design of the Indian Guides. It connects them to the three trajectories of historical transformation outlined above: the romanticized admiration for Native Americans, the back-to-nature movement, and the invention of modern involved fatherhood.

The American Indian and the "Teddy Bear Patriarchy"

It is surprising that Harold Keltner and the YMCA leaned on American Indians as models for white American fatherhood. After all, Euro-Americans had never before seen indigenous men as having the ability for leadership required of father figures in the republican mold. Europeans on their westward march instead had seen them as part of the wild, uncivilized natural world that had to be subjugated, eradicated, or at least tamed, as part of the fulfillment of divine providence, manifest destiny, and the conquest of the North American continent.[10]

Besides bloodthirsty and wild, Native Americans were portrayed as children in need of guidance, help, nurture, and protection coming from a white father figure in order to guide them to the path of survival. Individual indigenous people were infantilized as much as whole communities and cultures. Native Americans were generally seen as sticking to a childlike stage on the scale of human development. Observers described the modes of thinking, living, and working among indigenous peoples as signs of civilizational backwardness, supposedly legitimizing supervision as well as subjugation. The relationship between the indigenous population and the US settler empire had a strong paternalistic note, with Christian missionaries and US politicians claiming for themselves the role of father figures. This position was akin to a well-meaning yet sovereign patriarch who showed his children the right path but at the same time reserved for himself the right and duty to mete out harsh punishment if the indigenous population did not obey. Often this was taken as legitimizing a policy of removal, relocation, and killing. Thus, in the nineteenth century indigenous men were portrayed both childlike and as a threat to civilization, yet never as exemplary, caring, and strong fathers who led their children and their community into a secure future.[11]

The politics of paternalism gained further momentum after Native American communities had been defeated militarily in 1890. Educational and assimilationist policies were intended to alienate from their own culture and way of life those Native Americans who had survived war, removal, and confinement in past decades and instead condition them for a life according to Euro-American patterns. Following this paternalistic logic, Native American survival was possible only if they reorganized their lives in the image of the American middle-class family model.[12] In light of this policy of extermination through assimilation during the late nineteenth century and early twentieth, it appears all the more puzzling to hear the eulogies for Native American fathers and the apparently positive effects of their harmonious and nature-loving child-rearing methods, as the Indian Guide program was preaching since the mid-1920s.

Central to the strategies of assimilation and reeducation was the so-called Dawes Act of 1887, which deprived Native Americans of about two-thirds of the land granted them within the reservation system. The law granted plots of land to men and thus approached and installed them as heads of families in order to create a newly structured family order with gender specific divisions of labor in line with the Euro-American ideal. The vision of private property in the form of landownership in conjunction with agrarian labor expanded in the Anglo-American imagination into a mythical civilizational force, even if farming as lived experience declined in significance during the late nineteenth century. However, this concept of landownership and men as farmers and providers for their families was incompatible with most indigenous cultures and their understanding of land and masculinity.[13]

A second central element of the assimilation policy was boarding schools. Established in 1879, the Carlisle Indian Industrial School in Pennsylvania expanded by the end of the century into a comprehensive system of boarding schools where Native American children were separated from their families and kin and from their language, traditions, and cultures and taught Euro-American values and practices. A 1920 survey showed that almost half of all Ojibwe who lived inside the United States had attended one of the boarding schools, where they were meant to internalize American values and leave their traditional way of life behind. Besides the state-run boarding schools, several hundred day and missionary schools added to a system of "education for extinction," as historian David Adams had called it. Not until the 1930s did parents gain a greater say in their children's education. Even if some Native Americans were able to use the boarding schools for their own purposes, such as to mitigate poverty or gain a better understanding of the rules in a white-dominated society, this does not at all change the general nature of the institution.[14]

While the boarding schools pursued the politics of reeducation and the extinction of all Indianness, the Indian Guides touted romantic, allegedly natural Indian ways of education as a way to establish closer bonds between fathers and sons and counter the increasing sense of crisis and degeneration in modern society. We need to keep in mind that when Harold Keltner and Joe Friday began to imagine the great accomplishments of Indian fathers, it was customary to take Indian children from their families in order to mold them in the Euro-American image. Just as small boys in American suburbs began to memorize and recite short stories in indigenous languages, their counterparts in the boarding schools had to speak exclusively English. This also happened in Friday's home country Canada, where the boarding school system functioned much the same way yet was carried more heavily by the efforts of missionaries.[15]

The mythical ideal of a harmonious Native American father-son relationship furthermore ignored, as did the Indian Guide program in
general, the diversity of indigenous ways of life. It relied on stereotypes
of the other that were removed from historical context and appeared
to be regionally and culturally uniform and historically static. It relied
on an ethnic typology that veered into racism, similar to the Orientalism showcased by Edward Said. Ideas about Native Americans' appar-
ent closeness to nature as well as the image of the noble savage became
central features of this typology that were largely the product of Western
projection rather than an accurate reflection of indigenous reality.[16]

With regard to family life, many Indian tribes traditionally lived in
family configurations that hardly served as models for the nuclear family structures within US society. Nuclear family concepts and structures
were of little significance for Indian societies.[17] This was true in various
ways for Cherokee in the Southwest, Kiowa on the Great Plains, Crow
in Montana, and Yakima in the Northwest, to name just a few tribes.
The Cherokee, for instance, had traditionally lived in matrilineal family
structures, and a maternal brother or uncle occupied the most important male position in the life of a child. This system had changed only
since the early eighteenth century, influenced by settlers, missionaries,
and the increasing power of European political structures.[18] As late as
1877 Crow Indian agent George W. Frost lamented that the Crow were
practicing polygamy. They would completely ignore marriage vows, and
the men would take as many wives as they could support. By 1900 many
tribes were still living in extended kinship structures.[19]

The Ojibwe were among the few tribes organizing their life more
strongly in nuclear family structures, a practice that made them quite
unusual among the indigenous tribes of North America, according to
historian Nancy Shoemaker. Yet Ojibwe also practiced polygamy if men
were able to afford several women.[20] Still, the Ojibwe Joe Friday was
taken as vision of an authentic Indian for the YMCA program and its
goal of nuclear family stabilization. He became a blank canvass on which
Americans could project their fantasies of an ideal type of Indian, and
most likely it was a coincidence that an Ojibwe became the point of departure for the Indian Guides anyway.[21]

In the early twentieth century some Ojibwe indeed still made a living from hunting, fishing, and gathering fruits in the woods, despite

reservations, removal, and school programs. This was true for Ojibwe south and north of the US-Canadian border, and highly unusual among Native Americans at that point in time. Traditionally, Ojibwe boys were indeed trained by fathers, but also by uncles, older brothers, and cousins, to find their way around the woods and in the spiritual realm, which stirred the respective YMCA fantasies. Physician, writer, and Dakota activist Charles Alexander Eastman, or Ohiyesa, wrote about this during his travels through the land of the Ojibwe in 1910. Since the mid-1890s Eastman had worked for the YMCA, the Boy Scouts, and the Camp Fire Girls, and he had contributed to developing the first outdoor programs with an Indian theme for city kids. Eastman had also pledged to preserve Native American knowledge for Euro-Americans. During his journey through Ojibwe territory he collected artifacts and tools, which were displayed in American museums. These artifacts then served as models for the skins, vests, drums, pipes, and other items that YMCA boys crafted together with their fathers at home.[22]

Harold Keltner from the YMCA considered the experience of roaming through the woods with an Ojibwe on a hunting and fishing trip an authentic Indian one. He was obviously not aware of or ignored those voices who argued against the glorification of Ojibwe life in the early twentieth century as authentically and timelessly Native American. Some critics stressed how much Indian daily life was shaped by Euro-American influences and modern forms of poverty. The entire nineteenth century had brought to the Ojibwe tribe a conflict-laden history of forced step-by-step changes in their living arrangements, brought about by growing pressure from Euro-American settlers, missionaries, and politicians. Ojibwe signed more than sixteen contracts with US agencies over the course of the nineteenth century and lived in seven reservations, and every time they had to accept further restrictions on their sovereignty as well as their opportunities for hunting, fishing, and general mobility.[23] North of the border, Canadian policies toward the indigenous population were also shaped by land confiscations, missionary work, and assimilation, both during British rule and after the founding of the Canadian dominion in 1867. Canadian officials pressured indigenous populations into adopting an agrarian way of life, sent them to boarding schools, forced them onto reservations, and in general worked to undercut traditional living arrangements and customs.[24] Thus the daily life of the Ojibwas was shaped by the interaction with and struggle against an increasingly dominant Euro-American culture. The uncontaminated purity that Harold Keltner and the YMCA Indian Guide Programs imagined did not exist.[25]

Yet it was precisely this purity and a kind of rejuvenation that increasing numbers of American men during these years associated with life in the wilderness and on the frontier and that they believed to find among American Indians. They also sought such experiences through the acquisition of set pieces assumed to represent Native American culture in watered down form. These forms of appropriation can be traced back through the nineteenth century and beyond.[26] Yet in the late nineteenth century, when the number of Native American had shrunk to below a quarter million, admiration for indigenous culture among Euro-Americans reached a high point. At this time, a new wave of enthusiasm about the West was gaining momentum. After all, Frederick Jackson Turner's frontier thesis from 1893 claimed a productive encounter between civilization and wilderness on the frontier from which a distinctly American culture, society, and character had emerged, which surpassed all previous in quality and potential. Contrary to the discourses on European colonialism, *going native* in the United States did not necessarily mean a precipitous descent into the *Heart of Darkness*. The exchange with indigenous people rather signified a core element of a borderlands and wilderness experience, which became glorified as the wellspring of American energy and exceptionalism.[27]

Yet after the so-called closing of the frontier, the active foray into "nature" on the American continent continued, undertaken by more and more men at the turn of the century. In a climate of fear about overcivilization and neurasthenia going native for a while was considered the best way toward regeneration and a fortification against the diseases of modernity. Keltner was in good company when he, as a city person, made his trip into the wilderness. Since Theodore Roosevelt had first traveled from the East Coast to the Dakotas in 1883, numerous men had moved west in order to recharge their batteries and re-create themselves as men. As Keltner's trip into the Canadian woods shows, it was not necessary to venture into the American West in order to experience the frontier. One could also go north into Canada or simply venture out into the surrounding woods close to home. What mattered most was to shape oneself by encountering nature. Roosevelt helped galvanize the conservation movement by creating national parks such as Yellowstone and making nature more accessible, often at the expense of Native Americans, who in most cases had to leave the national parks.[28] During the same period Americans began to engage Native Americans as nature guides, in an effort to have a nature experience they considered even more authentic. Tourism became a source of income for American Indians.[29] Another result of the go-west phenomenon in new guise was a plethora of scientific and popular studies.[30]

Another way of encountering wilderness even after the closing of the frontier was the consumption of writings, pictures, shows, or artifacts. The West went East in the form of numerous anthropological and natural science studies, popular science publications in magazines such as *National Geographic*, dime novels, and adventure stories for boys. These written sources created indigenous fantasies, which then became glorified as an integral part of an imagined past and present.[31] Extensive collections of photographs, film material, and other artifacts were displayed in exhibitions and museums in the modern metropoles, further consolidating the idea of Indian American culture as both alien and indigenous.[32] The exhibitions included displays of symbols and of objects of daily life. They served as templates for fathers and sons, who in their YMCA groups crafted copies of amulets and other items, and as models for the forms of communication, rituals, and behaviors fathers and sons practiced and staged in special performances.

Real-life Native Americans were presented in popular Wild West shows. Sioux chief Sitting Bull was a major attraction of Buffalo Bill Cody's show in 1885.[33] World and other expositions showcased indigenous life. The display of indigenous populations in various forms, performing dances, demonstrating their craft, and reenacting traditional camp life, was often part of anthropological exhibitions, and it was meant to reproduce ideas about civilization and progress by contrast. In Chicago in 1893 one could purchase the speech by Potawatomi Chief Simon Pokagon, printed on birch bark; in Omaha in 1898 one could observe Native American tribal camp life; and in St. Louis in 1904 one could have one's picture taken with the Apache chief Geronimo.[34] In San Francisco in 1915 James Earle Fraser's larger-than-life statue, titled *The End of the Trail*, garnered great attention. The hunched-over figure of an American Indian on his horse became a visual marker of the end of an epoch, which Euro-Americans were now invited to mourn as well. Soon copies of the sculpture were turned into bookends and ashtrays; it was printed on porcelain and postcards; and it showed up as a comic strip in one of the Indian Guide brochures.[35]

These elements were signposts of a broader movement that manifested itself in multiple forms and locations. Images of the "wild," of "nature," and of "the indigenous" did not just function as the "other," used to define what was understood as American through difference. They were at the same time presented as an integral part of America, of "the American" and its own history. They were hailed as a source of strength for a society seeing itself as threatened by overcivilization at precisely the moment when the end of the Indian was mourned. Philosopher Donna Haraway called this movement the "Teddy Bear Patriarchy," in reference to its foremost proponent Teddy Roosevelt. It advocated mastering the forces of nature as a way to strive for male rejuvenation in the name of racial and national perfection. The American Indian became a crucial element in this new domesticated version of "nature," which was constructed as nature in the moment of its appropriation.[36]

Teaching Boys to Be Wild

Efforts to appropriate "wilderness" were no exclusive privilege of grown white men. Prevention was of utmost necessity, experts assumed, in order to escape the traps of modernity. Renowned psychologist and pedagogue G. Stanley Hall, cofounder and first president of Clark University and host to Sigmund Freud during his 1909 visit to the United States, developed an educational concept that he compared to an inoculation against the softening, weakening effects of overcivilization and neurasthenia. Influenced by the physician Charles Beard, Hall saw neurasthenia as a psychosomatic effect of the excessive demands of modernity and of a Victorian pressure for self-restraint. He speculated that if boys were to spend more time in nature, it would lead to strengthening nerves, body, and spirit. It would help protect them from civilizational malaises and thus ultimately foster men's all-important self-control. Boys needed free spaces in order to act out their natural wildness. A closely supervised "going native" in the domestic wilderness protected against the serious effects of being contaminated by modern life.[37]

Hall relied on the widely accepted theory that every individual went through the various stages of human development, or to be more precise, of one's own "race."[38] All individuals would, in the course of their lives, pass through the stages from savagery to civilization and would advance as far as the specific developmental stage of their specific "race." This concept meshed with contemporary assumptions that identified indigenous people as children and European Americans as men. Hall believed that white boys should be allowed to act as "primitives," as the "primitive" in the boy represented to him a glimmer of hope in a crisis-prone overcivilized modernity.[39]

Hall's challenge to teachers and pedagogues to cultivate wildness in boys up to the age of nine incurred mixed reactions, from enthusiastic support to serious skepticism. However, Hall's theories were part of this powerful, romanticizing "back to nature" movement. For instance, a camping trip was considered a journey into the past with the goal to help boys, through an education in nature, gain manly strength and thus restabilize American society. Camping for boys became immensely popular in the 1880s.[40]

Sending kids to summer camp for the strengthening of body and spirit and as prevention against the corrupting effects of an increasingly urban life became common practice. The YMCA was among the leading forces in this movement. After 1910, it gained further momentum through the Boy Scouts of America and since 1912 also through the Camp Fire Girls, which offered a similar program geared toward girls. By the time the boys of the Indian Guides regularly undertook nature trips in the 1920s, the camp culture had become firmly established.[41]

The camping eulogies of the Indian Guides mostly ignored that girls, too, went into the woods in droves. Much like the boys, they were to contemplate within nature the wellspring of life, which girls were to find at the "campfire," being an outdoor version of the hearth and home. Girls' and boys' camps thus drew on and performed middle-class gender norms, making them seem natural and thus timeless in the woods.[42]

Camps were even considered "ideal life in the woods for boys," as Edward S. Wilson, a pioneer of the movement, had stated as early as the 1890s. They represented a locus for men's boyish wilderness fantasies, documented by the fathers' enthusiasm for Joe Friday. The camps became playgrounds where individual boys could find out how successful they were in groups and acquire leadership skills and dependability, all through mastering life in "nature" and "wilderness."[43]

American Indian themes carried great importance in these camps. Already in the 1890s, the YMCA secured the support of Native Americans such as Charles Eastman. Ernest T. Seton, author of adventure stories, self-made youth counselor, and cofounder of the Boy Scouts of America, had in 1902 started a youth organization called the Woodcraft Indians, which organized camp life according to Native American precepts and rituals, or rather what was considered to be Indian life in folkloristic imagination. Much like the later Indian Guides, boys would master challenges, earn points, and win prizes. The whole game system was given an authentic sheen through Indian terms and names. In the 1910s, the indigenization of summer camps expanded before becoming predominant in the 1920s and 1930s.[44]

More was at stake in these Indian Guide programs than the mere fact that a few boys played Indian with their fathers. Wilderness, nature, and the indigenous other became incorporated into concepts of Euro-American subjectivity. The Indian Guides epitomized a movement that sought to unearth a seemingly natural essence of America's identity under the many civilizational layers piled on by modern society. This nature movement became entangled with a new fathers' movement that gained momentum in the 1920s and stressed the extraordinary significance of fathers in the successful upbringing of their children and particularly of their boys. The active father who plays a critical role in shaping his son's development is an important precondition that needs to be considered in order to better understand the Indian Guides and their success.

Sons and Fathers Forever United

A favorite opening for an Indian Guide meeting was to sing "pals forever." To the tune of the favorite children's song "Clementine," fathers and sons swore eternal friendship and the leitmotif of their organization, seeking to make "boys stronger," "dads younger," and "mothers happier." The lyrics declared that with the mythical power of American Indianness, fathers and sons would go through life together. "Through the days and through the years / we will wander side by side / pals forever, pals forever / the Great Spirit is our guide."[45]

In the fall of 1926, William Hefelfinger, the first chief of the first tribe in Richmond Heights in suburban St. Louis, invented the slogan "Pals Forever." When the Indian Guides gained momentum, the YMCA had already been operating with various Indian-themed projects for several years.[46] Among them were the aforementioned summer camps, with some support from Native Americans in preparing and designing Indian themes. Other types of father-son programs had also existed since the early twentieth century, in order to counteract the effects of modern urban life, alienating fathers from their sons.

The Indian Guides for the first time brought these two themes together, fusing paternal engagement with Native American romanticizing. Until then most father-son activities of the YMCA had had an outdated musty quality to them. They had included communal dinners, lectures, religious services, and visits to a special, if small, father-son library. In February 1918, the YMCA had organized its first father-son week, in order to motivate fathers into showing continuous engagement. The weekly program also included outdoor activities; a "frontier day" was added to the already existing "Church Day." Presidents Warren G. Harding and Calvin Coolidge lauded the great importance of these programs.

The YMCA also used short questionnaires to motivate fathers to become more involved, demonstrating to them how little they knew about their sons and their abilities. One informational pamphlet from the early 1920s noted in a psychologizing tone that the most important aspects of their boy's character lay hidden deep beneath the tousled hair, dirty hands, and holes in their pockets. The most important task for fathers was to reveal those hidden characteristics that lurked below the surface and out of plain sight and find "normal" ways to express them.[47]

The YMCA's efforts to involve fathers more directly in the education of their children and especially of their sons was part of a larger shift, which Ralph LaRossa described as the *Modernization of Fatherhood*. Admonitions to fathers not to neglect their families over their jobs are as old as the concept of separate spheres and the idea of the male provider. On the other hand, nineteenth-century middle-class fathers had not left families as far behind as has long been suggested. They often regarded their place within the family as most important in their lives.[48]

Nonetheless fatherhood was now becoming more infused with emotions and demanded a greater involvement of fathers in various familial tasks, from work around the house to childcare and children's education. Various groups now demanded making the gendered spheres more porous, or rather acknowledging their already existing porosity. The women's movement demanded better recognition of women's contributions to the workforce, which should manifest itself as well in greater civic equality and the right to vote. By the same token, men should play a greater role in daily family activities, above all as supporters of their wives. "Get involved" was a common message to men in advice manuals, studies, and the newly created *Parents Magazine*, which was first published in the 1920s. Between June 1932 and December 1937, *Parents Magazine* included a column speaking to men directly. The engaged, loving, and playful "dad" was propagated as a complement to "father," who was more strict and first and foremost the provider for the family. In reality, however, the playful dad role was often limited to activities with his children on one or two Sundays per month or a few minutes before or after dinner.[49]

The father movement of the 1920s reflected cultural and social shifts. It revealed the growing popularity of Freud's theories, which suggested that children needed a father to achieve a "normal" development of their personality. At the same time fathers were admonished to learn to act as fathers, otherwise children remained fatherless, even if fathers were physically present. The period also saw the first men's groups whose goal was to acquire and exchange vital knowledge about dealing with children. They paid special attention to fathers' relationship with sons rather than girls. "Boyhood is calling to its father, and boyhood cannot wait," the popular writer Edgar Albert Guest stated. "If I lose this opportunity to be his comrade I may lose him forever."[50]

The practices of father-son bonding as they had existed until then were severely criticized. Lectures, dinner banquets, or shared church attendance had not borne the desired fruit. Afterward fathers patted one another on their backs, congratulated one another about how much they had engaged with their sons, while they had probably engaged more with other fathers and each other's businesses. And as Harold Keltner observed while working on the Indian Guides, most of the work was probably done by mothers anyway, since they prepared the food for the banquets in their own kitchens.[51] At the same time, fathers who were seen as overly engaged with their children and families were ridiculed as "maternal fathers." However, the new ideal of the engaged father and pal did not ask for sharing the tasks of child care equally with mothers. Rather, the "dad" was to function more as playmate who did craft projects with his son or conquered nature. This is precisely where the Indian Guides came in since they captured the trend and situated themselves at the nexus between indigenous veneration, the new outdoor movement, and engaged fatherhood. All this came together in the slogan "Pals Forever."[52]

For the launch of the first tribe in the Indian Guide program, the organizers wanted to win the most respected men in the suburban community of St. Louis. Fathers with higher educational status and families in stable communities were more easily won over to the project, for which Friday was to lend authenticity.[53] In the following years organizers of the Indian Guides made efforts to convince fathers and sons to participate in existing tribes or to establish new ones. They did so by reaching out to churches, schools, and neighborhood associations. Mothers, too, were seen as extremely important for the development of the Indian Guides, since they would motivate their husbands and get the neighborhood networks involved.[54]

By the end of the 1920s, ten functioning tribes had been established.[55] From the suburbs of St. Louis, the Indian Guides expanded into Missouri, Kansas, Illinois, and Indiana, before they officially became a national YMCA program in October 1936. Friday advertised the program all over the country. In 1940, 97 tribes existed in twelve states ranging across the country. By 1947 they had expanded to 149 tribes in seventeen states, and by 1959 to 5,784 tribes in forty-three states. By the mid-1970s, the Y Indian Guides had become the YMCA's most successful program with 26,000 groups and about half a million active members.[56]

When the Indian Guides finally became a national YMCA Program, it received a state-of-the-art administrative structure. Four regional zones were established; a program brochure was created with participants' experiences and other stories of interest; and local delegates were invited to an annual meeting at the so-called longhouse, named after the traditional Iroquois community building. It created the impression that the extended YMCA family came together at the annual meeting. The

Figure 8.1. Joe Friday (middle row, fourth from right) and Harold Keltner (middle row fifth from right) on a promotional tour in 1944. Kautz Family YMCA Archives.

gatherings included executive committee sessions and meetings with discussions recorded in minutes. Somewhat ironically, then, a back-to-nature program, conceived by romantic visions of primitivism and the American Indian, now availed itself of the modern strategies of organizing and administrating.[57] The increase in members and tribes after World War II indicates that the ground became even more fertile during the Cold War for the expansion of such a project of civic education. Soon a study was commissioned at the University of Chicago's renowned Sociology Department to gauge the effectiveness of the Indian Guides program. Surveys among youth members were to determine which programs they liked best and why, meant to allow leaders to fine-tune and adjust the program accordingly.[58]

The Indian Guides targeted boys between the ages of six and eight. Boys between nine and eleven could join the Friendly Indian Program, which used Indian traditions—or what was imagined as such—in order to build character and promote civic skills. One difference was that the older boys attended without their fathers. They were supposed to learn to act independently, honor country and flag, attend Sunday school and church, engage in prayer on their own, get good grades in school, complete all work joyfully and reliably, watch their health, and help others: "Play square, work square, and be square" was the slogan of the Friendly Indians. The

Friendly Indian, they were told, practiced self-control in order to become a good citizen. He thus was expected to mature in two ways: first from child to man, and second from (childlike) Indian to man.[59]

The Indian Guides were also meant to teach boys how to become good citizens. During the opening ceremony the tribe pledged "to be clean / to complain never / to put the other fellow first / to be silent while elders speak / to love the sacred circle of my family / to love honor and truth / to be reverent / to see the beauty of the Great Spirit's Work."[60]

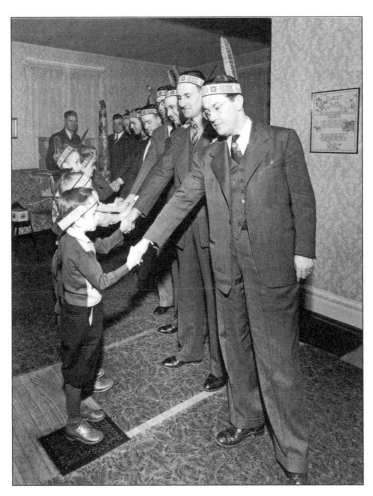

Figure 8.2. Fathers and sons during an evening event for the Indian Guides, ca. 1950. Kautz Family YMCA Archives.

Figure 8.3. Indian Guides at a pledge of allegiance ceremony from a 1950 brochure. Kautz Family YMCA Archives.

The Indian Guides sought to school both sons and fathers through shared activities so that they practiced how to act in groups, to adhere to a specific value system, to learn manliness and social leadership qualities. Boys were to experience a stable father figure with whom they would identify and who would show them how to explore and conquer the world for themselves. Boys learned "that they really are masculine men," according to a historical retrospective from December 1950. By this time, psychological theory had gotten even more influential, and the era of the Cold War and McCarthyism saw an even greater urge to produce loyal citizens.[61] But also in earlier decades the program was apparently so impressive that a visit to a tribe or longhouse was enough to convince critics. For instance, an initially skeptical YMCA director from Illinois wrote in the late 1930s that the whole program represented much more than a "game of playing 'Indian,'" and for fathers the program was a "school in leadership."[62]

Fathers and sons met every two weeks with their tribes. In order to make fathers really attend, a strictly enforced rule said that sons could not attend without their fathers.[63] Meetings were held in one of the father-son team's houses so that the entire family's and particularly the mother's support was ensured. Mothers prepared cookies and snacks, and they often pulled the strings from behind the scene through ideas, motivation, and organization. Elaborate invitations in natural designs, sometimes written on animal skins or withered parchment, were more often the result of mothers' involvement than fathers'. They often guided the tribe or at least their own father-son team with such skill that fathers did not notice and claimed for themselves the glory and success of their tribes and the Indian Guides in general. The leadership circle of the YMCA, however, recognized the central function of mothers for the program and repeatedly recommended internally to involve mothers in jobs that were only seemingly marginal, in order to help get the Indian Guides off the ground and provide some structure.[64]

Meetings themselves were rather formal, with staged opening ceremonies and many additional rituals designed to strengthen father-son unity. Only when both were successful as a team did they win certificates, pins, patches for their jackets, and other insignias. The YMCA also offered suggestions in colorful brochures about how to vary the meetings, for instance with adventure stories, games, or Indian-style drumming.[65] Almost all activities were described in manuals and handicraft brochures, offering support to urban white-collar fathers who might not know how to mount an animal hide over a drum case or light a fire without matches.[66] If the weather was right the tribe would meet in backyards around a campfire or in nearby woods. Every two or three months the tribe congregated at a particularly beautiful or historically significant location for a large "powwow," with mothers and sisters also participating, "in fact with the entire family and friends, thus imitating a real Indian situation," William Hefelfinger wrote. During winter, these powwows consisted of lectures on American national parks, or the tribe went to the local movie theater to see an adventure movie. A favorite was the 1950 movie *Broken Arrow*, which is a founding film of Hollywood's "Indian Cult."[67]

Once a year tribe members embarked on a multiday camping trip. These ventures into nature were particularly useful in conjuring up the idea of an ahistorical unity between father and son and regaining some semblance of authenticity, which modern citizens were purportedly in danger of losing. Hefelfinger described euphorically the nightly campfires when looking back on the first years of the Indian Guides: "In all my years of camping in the open there are no occasions which thrill me more than on those nights when fathers and sons together sit around the same fire and discuss the same problems and joys together as primitive man has done from time immemorable. The purity of the boys' dreams inspires the fathers and the wisdom of the older braves tempers the judgement and actions of the younger."[68] Through their worship of nature and their search for timeless authenticity in a modern age of constant movement, the Indian Guides subscribed to and emulated the cult of American Indian identity. The father-son relationship would thus be marked as timeless and original to all being, providing a solid foundation for confronting the threats of modernity. The program tapped into the fascination with all things Indian, a fascination that had been spreading among boys and girls for some time and had become associated with activities such as hunting and fishing as well as nature in general. Harold Keltner explained, "The Indian symbolized all of these interests to both father and son."[69]

The Native American myth as well as the myth of Joe Friday as the indigenous creator of the Indian Guides were continually developed over the years. They were reinforced by the purported Native American practices in the Indian Guides, as well as by stories of Native American boys who had blind faith in their fathers and thus managed to navigate safely through the rough waters of youth to mature into young men who themselves would shoulder responsibility. Keltner repeated the story of the Indian boy passing dangerous rapids with the help of his father's advice over and over, and he attributed it sometimes to Friday and at other times to a nameless "young Indian in the far North," somewhere on the last Canadian frontier. The story connected the power of instruction, modeling, and trust to a primeval relationship between father and son and used the Indian myth as a symbol to reinforce its significance.[70]

When the Indian Guides became a national program after 1936, interest in Friday by YMCA leaders waned markedly. The YMCA continued to send Friday regularly on speaking and publicity tours, but the leadership was also interested in keeping costs down and in limiting Friday's initiative and independence.[71] The managers of the national program at times mocked his enthusiasm for the Native American cause and suggested cutting down his engagement to provide only the folklore for the father-son connection. He was officially introduced as "one of the last real Americans" on the frontier when he went on speaking tours, visiting a different city every day. Internal evaluations stated that Friday was at times irritating and poorly organized, "but he can stir up the desire in fathers to get going with some kind of a Father and Son program. You must capitalize on this desire."[72]

When these discussions took place in the late 1930s and early 1940s, Friday was on the cusp of becoming a living myth among YMCA members. Articles in the *Long House News*, the journal of the Indian Guides, expressed great admiration for Friday, and a meeting with him or a visit to his home seemed to have been the most cherished experience of every tribe. Friday became the mythical Ojibwe who lived in the legendary Hiawatha Lodge on Lake Temagami in Ontario, received the occasional visitor, or appeared at meetings in order to tell stories, but otherwise caught giant fish when paddling in his birch canoe on the Canadian lakes. In February 1951, Friday was awarded the medal of honor at the national longhouse in Chicago for his lifetime service. When he died four years later at age sixty-two, he was described in the YMCA bulletin as an empathetic Ojibwe "who taught the civilized white man how to raise his sons." Friday would live on in the memories of the many tribes of the Indian Guide program, "until our country again learns that a father's job is to teach his sons how to become men." A Joe Friday memorial fund was established later to financially support the project. He was interred on Bear Island on Lake Temagami, and the epitaph on his grave stone commended him for building bridges between two civilizations.[73]

It is somewhat ironic that Friday's home and final resting place had also been the site of the last armed rebellion of indigenous people against European intruders in North America. In 1898, the Ojibwe of Bear Island had resisted their subjugation.[74] This is most certainly one of the coincidences in the story of Joe Friday, but it reminds of the fact that he was not just a myth but also a human being and historical actor who had the power to resist. Also, his personal history confirms that drawing a sharp distinction between colonizers and colonized is too simplifying.[75] The records of the YMCA show how he brought to the

"COME ON DAD, LET'S GO."

Figure 8.4. From a 1956 graphic booklet on the Indian
Guides. Kautz Family YMCA Archives.

Indian Guides a persistent and unwavering support for imparting elements and behaviors, which he considered part of his own culture, increasingly conceptualized as pan-Indian. Tova Cooper states that this
might be seen as a strategy to preserve moments of Native American
existence within modern America. Shamoon Zamir makes a similar argument with regard to the Crow Indian Alexander B. Upshaw, who as
an anthropologist and translator supported the photographer Edward
Curtis. Upshaw posed for a romanticized staged photograph as an Indian warrior with feather headdress and beaded necklace. This act might
be interpreted as a way for Upshaw to use Curtis's project toward his
own ends and within the opportunities available to him.[76] Upshaw and
Friday might have seen their collaboration with Curtis or the YMCA as
a chance to speak out and also to be heard.[77]

Historian Brenda Child noted that even the boarding schools are fully understandable only when also examined against the backdrop of indigenous agency. For instance, sending their children to a boarding school may have helped indigenous parents to cope with their poverty.[78] Friday, too, had economic motives. The Indian Guide program provided him with an opportunity to make a living. Records show how he negotiated about expenses and financing when he went on speaking tours. He demanded room and board and a per diem of ten dollars. Friday also attempted to stretch out the financing phase for as long as he could in order to get as much as possible out of these trips. His YMCA partners, however, had little sympathy for this maneuvering. They described him as greedy, just as they complained about Friday's sense of entitlement to promote the program just the way he thought right. The program managers did not want the "authentic voice" to reach quite that far. All they wanted was an inspiration that stimulated the imagination of their clientele.[79]

"Come on Dad, Let's Go" . . .

. . . the boy yells to his father, who stands at the edge of a cliff looking into the abyss. The landscape below looks like a prototypical western landscape, such as Monument Valley in Arizona. As in so many other cartoons used to promote the Indian Guides, in this one from 1956 father and son are dressed in Native American garb. The image of the father on his horse is a likeness of James Earle Fraser's famous 1915 sculpture *End of the Trail*. And much like Fraser's sculpture, which signified the decline of Native American culture, the caption below the cartoon warned that father and son and with them American society were at the "end of the trail" if dad was too busy to develop this most important relationship with his son. Together, they would have to overcome the abyss between them.[80]

The cartoon unites the three elements that together made up the Indian Guide program. First, it builds on a uniform understanding of indigenous culture in an Orientalist manner, in order to steer father and son toward each other and away from the abyss. Early twentieth-century critics blamed modernity itself for bringing father and son to this crisis point as well as for having pushed much of the Native American population and their culture into the abyss. The allusion to the *End of the Trail* connects the two elements—the destruction of Native American culture and the sense of crisis in father-son relations. The myth of an idealized Native American culture and the specter of its collapse are invoked to rescue American society from its own demise.

Second, it is the young son who proposes a wholesome going native and an outdoor adventure together. Monument Valley became the quintessential locus of western imagination only after John Ford's 1939 movie *Stagecoach*.[81] Also, viewers of the cartoon were aware that the Indian dress was no more than dress-up, leaving no doubt about the transient nature of the moment and thus the healing power of going native. After all, going native was desirable only in a narrowly contained form. This was underscored in a highly ironic manner when in December 1950 the YMCA meant to honor the first Indian Guide camp ever in St. Louis at its twenty-fifth anniversary by declaring it a National Y Indian Guide Reservation.[82]

Third, the cartoon presents father and son as able to move away from the abyss only by acting together. Discussions of the father-son relationship drew increasingly on popularized psychoanalytical theories, symbolism, and vocabulary. It became increasingly common to talk of high cliffs, unknown territory, and dangerous currents in life, which men could master only if they had grown up in a "normal" and wholesome way and been able to follow the example of their father. Since World War II, the Indian Guides had engaged with a powerful discourse that focused increasingly on fatherless boys, who were presented as socially and sexually without direction and thus in danger of turning to a life of crime or homosexuality.

In the 1970s the program was more timely than ever. First, images in the Indian Guide brochures increasingly showed African American boys; second, the program reacted to the new gender politics by integrating the Indian Father and Son Guides into a broader Y Parent Child Program. In December 1979, the national leadership of the YMCA stressed that families needed to be seen as the molecules that built the substance of sociocultural stability.[83]

9

Unemployed Fathers in the 1930s

When a man cannot provide for his family and makes you
worry so, you lose your love for him. A husband has to have
four qualifications—first, second, and third he should be able
to support a family, and fourth he should have personality.
—Mrs. Garland, Newark, New Jersey, 1936

Mirra Komarovsky and the Sociology of Crisis

Mrs. Garland was mother and wife in one of fifty-nine families
observed and surveyed in the winter of 1935–36 by Columbia University sociologist Mirra Komarovsky. For her dissertation Komarovsky
conducted extensive interviews with families of mothers, fathers, and
at least one adolescent child, each between twenty-five and seventy
typed pages.[1] Her aim was to determine how a man's position in the
family changed when he was long-term unemployed and unable to
provide for his family. The Great Depression, which hit the United
States after the October 1929 stock market crash, triggered this question, and its urgency was underlined by countless examples of faltering
family providers plagued by self-doubt and social marginalization.
Komarovsky emphasized that the subjects of her survey considered
the role of provider as crucial in the life of men, husbands, and fathers:
"It is the man's duty to provide for the family. This pattern is apparently taken for granted by the cultural group to which our families
belong." She continued that the ability to fulfil that role was "the very
touchstone of his manhood."[2] The development of wage labor over the
course of the nineteenth century had contributed to this particular
family formation that reinforced the economic dependence of the family on a male wage earner. The figure of the breadwinner had become
central for modern society, revolving around male leadership and con-

nected to the notion of society as based on a contract among free, independent, and responsible men.[3]

Komarovsky became a successful sociologist in twentieth-century America. She already considered herself a feminist while studying as an undergraduate at Barnard College, and her later work was instrumental in our understanding of gender-related discontents and the attendant instability in the gender and social order.[4] The relationship between gender—and masculinity in particular—and the perception of a gender and social crisis was a central concern to her, and it is at the center of this chapter as well. Particularly Komarovsky's 1950 article "Functional Analysis of Sex Roles" was ahead of its time in its demand to think of gender, its attributes and functions, as flexible, dynamic, and central to the social order. She rejected the idea of a natural gender division as a stabilizing force in society. She argued against the by then dominant paradigms of role theory in sociology, which will be shown as of crucial importance for gaining a better understanding of the crisis notion and its effects.[5]

In the 1930s Komarovsky was a doctoral student at Columbia University and the International Institute for Social Research, where she worked on her dissertation under the supervision of Paul F. Lazarsfeld on the subject of unemployed fathers in the Great Depression. Lazarsfeld had coauthored the 1933 Marienthal Study, an examination of the sociopsychological effects of unemployment on the village of Marienthal in Lower Austria. Marienthal was considered a pioneering study because of its encompassing view of a community forced to confront the fundamental social and cultural problem of the unemployment of almost the entire village. Hans Zeisel, one of the coauthors of the study, pointed out that the analysis of the individual is of utmost sociological interest when the existing order loses its structural clarity in a single dramatic moment.[6] Calling this moment of social disintegration a crisis of individual and collective proportions is more than a descriptive act, but a call for political action. According to philosopher Jürgen Habermas, "To conceive of a process as a crisis, is tacitly to give it a normative meaning—the resolution of the crisis effects a liberation of the subject caught up in it."[7] Thus, by describing a situation as a crisis, the state prior to the so-called crisis is declared desirable, and the implicit and often also explicit goal becomes to return to that state in order to experience a kind of healing and to gain new strength. Those who identify a crisis as a collective phenomenon usually dismiss differences among historical actors and their experiences, and they ignore that a crisis for some might mean liberation for others.

At the beginning of the 1930s, American politicians, intellectuals, and researchers spoke endlessly of a crisis, and they thus framed social disturbances in pathological terms.[8] Developing a successful therapy required first of all a precise diagnosis based on solid research. In 1933 the Rockefeller Foundation, impressed with the Marienthal Study, brought Paul Lazarsfeld to the United States on a two-year fellowship. Lazarsfeld, who would stay in the United States for good, worked for the Federal Emergency Relief Administration (FERA), one of the first New Deal aid organizations, and later also for the National Youth Administration (NYA) in New Jersey. In 1936 and 1937, he also served as director of the Research Center at the University of Newark (now Rutgers), before arriving at Columbia University in 1939 by way of Princeton University.[9]

It is therefore no coincidence that Komarovsky chose Newark for her study, as she was able to recruit the families for her study through her collaboration with Lazarsfeld and FERA. Of the eighty-nine families she contacted, fifty-nine were willing to work with her. Komarovsky had always considered herself a qualitative sociologist. In-depth interviews allowed a closer look, she stated at one point in the 1960s, and thus made possible very special insights: "The reader catches the tone, the intensity of feeling, the overtones of pride, embarrassment, humor, irritation, the association of ideas, . . . the immediacy of experience."[10] She applied specific criteria for her choice of families: all her subjects were born in the United States, Protestant, and white, and all families had a father, a mother, and at least one child over ten years old. The fathers had to be skilled workers or low-level white-collar workers who had, before the depression, been the sole breadwinners in their families. They had to have been out of work for at least a year and had to be on relief.[11]

Komarovsky's study thus focused on so-called ordinary families of the so-called common man, defined by her colleague Ruth S. Cavan in her own study on unemployment as white Anglo-Saxon Protestant (WASP) men of the "upper-lower and lower-middle class." The common man and his family also stood at the center of most other sociological studies of the time, exploring the economic crisis and unemployment.

The general assumption was that the traumatic effects of the crisis were most devastating in this social class, particularly among family fathers. Obviously, class, gender, and race structured the perception and analysis of the Great Depression and its effects. In fact the crisis scenario of the 1930s focused on this particular social group, which was at the center of attention, as will be discussed in more detail below.[12]

America in Crisis

After the beginning of the Great Depression in the United States in October 1929, unemployment rose dramatically, reaching fifteen million in 1933, or about 25 percent of the labor force. In addition, millions of families had lost their savings in the stock market crash and subsequent bank failures. Until then unemployment had been considered an individual problem. As a social and economic problem it had been of minor importance, and no systematic unemployment statistics existed.[13] While the Republican government under Herbert Hoover still trusted in the market's ability for self-regulation, since March 1933 Franklin D. Roosevelt provided government aid through the multiple programs of the New Deal. The goal was to offer economic, social, and moral support to American citizens. Roosevelt had already stressed in his campaign that he considered work and security to be more than mere facts and words but "spiritual values," and the Great Depression meant more than an economic crisis.[14] The New Deal's broad spectrum of social and work programs were designed to not only grant material support but also strengthen the self-esteem of those affected. The programs targeted particularly white men of the lower middle and upper working classes, and New Dealers were above all concerned about curing the low self-esteem of white male fathers. Harry Hopkins, chief coordinator of the New Deal work programs, asserted that "most of our family habits and customs are constructed around the central fact that the father is the breadwinner. He must be respected."[15] By centering her study around men as fathers and heads of families, Komarovsky validated this concept of society.

On the eve of the depression, Newark had seen decades of industrial growth and expansion. Around 1930, it had more than 440,000 inhabitants, the first skyscrapers were signs of prosperity, and an imposing skyline was seen as a realistic project for the future. The city was unprepared for the depression, when wealth and employment sank precipitously. Not until 1931 did the city begin, hesitatingly, to set up state and municipal work and support programs. Indigent families received seeds so they could plant vegetables on surrounding grazing land. In the summer of 1932, 38,000 Newark citizens signed up for the New Jersey state work program, yet only 10 percent were hired on a temporary basis. Across the state the average per capita income sunk by almost half between 1929 and 1933, and in 1937 official unemployment numbers stood at 287,000. In Newark alone more than 90,000 were on poor relief in 1935.[16]

Men in Crisis

Komarovsky explored the effects of unemployment on American families in a northeastern industrial city with a long history of growth. Her selection of survey subjects was guided by the nuclear family ideal and relied on the help of FERA. Komarovsky's investigation focused on the common man who embodied the aspiration for autonomy and social mobility through hard work. The study design thus reaffirmed the lower middle-class, white, Anglo-Saxon, Protestant man as the center of society threatened by the Great Depression. Social scientist E. Wight Bakke puzzled in 1940 over how persistent the belief in male autonomy and responsibility as core strengths and values was: "It is a strange paradox— this survival of the basic conviction that a man is responsible for his own economic success or failure in the midst of a multitude of experiences to the contrary, and in spite of the realization that one's destiny is controlled from another world occupied by legislators, employers, bankers, police, probation officers, and politicians."[17]

Such limits on male self-determination were shown clearly by the visible dependence on money from others (family members or state aid). According to Jürgen Habermas, "The idea of an objective force that deprives a subject of some part of his normal sovereignty" was considered a driving force of a crisis.[18] It appears as if the loss of sovereignty caused by the widespread unemployment of the 1930s was particularly severe for men of the lower middle class. Men of higher social status, other studies found, could shoulder financial losses better without seeing their position as provider and head of their family fundamentally endangered.[19]

Komarovsky analyzed the reciprocal relationship among economy, society, and gender, among depression, changes in family relations, and the crisis of masculinity and fatherhood. She was above all interested in how the loss of a father's privileged position in the family might lead to a sense of crisis and a decline in his self-esteem, and vice versa how the father's sense of crisis and a decline in his self-esteem might have been the cause of internal family transformations.[20] In her book she concentrates on thirteen of the fifty-nine families in her study, precisely those in which the father's position had experienced a dramatic shock, and she summarized, "It must be stated that the downfall of the husband was due most frequently to the loss of his earning power."[21]

Among her survey subjects, the Adams family showed the complex relationship among wage labor, family positioning, and crisis mode particularly clearly. Mr. Adams was sixty years old at the time of the interview, eleven years older than his wife. A daughter, nineteen, and son, seventeen, still lived at home. Even before the depression hit, Mr. Adams had not been a reliable breadwinner. Particularly his excessive alcohol consumption had led to repeated periods of unemployment in the 1920s. With the onset of the economic crisis he became permanently unemployed, and beginning in 1933 the family depended on government relief. Mrs. Adams was now the family's main wage earner. She worked as the custodian of her apartment building, sold doughnuts and vegetables, and sublet a room. Her nineteen-year-old daughter also contributed to the family income; the son is rarely mentioned in the interview. Social scientist Ruth Cavan stated that particularly these kinds of changes in the family wage earning structure increased tensions, even though the income from wife and children clearly reduced economic hardship and should have been welcomed.[22]

A look at other families in Komarovsky's study shows that in such cases it was most often older sons who took on an increasingly central position in the family. The demotion of the father often manifested in small things in everyday life, such as a change in the seating order at the dinner table. Seventeen-year-old son Henry of the Brady family confessed to Komarovsky that after three years of unemployment he could no longer bring himself to respect his once authoritarian father. "He is not the same father, that's all. You can't help not looking up to him like we used to. None of us is afraid of him like we used to be. That's natural, isn't it?"[23]

Another interviewee, forty-seven-year-old Mr. Patterson, lamented, "The tables are turned." Before the depression he had earned between thirty-five and forty dollars a week as a warehouse manager, but for the last four years he had been unemployed. For the last eighteen months he had been on government relief. The changes in the Patterson family as a result of the father's unemployment reveal particularly well how fathers experienced themselves, their families, and society as being in a crisis. Mr. Patterson could not bear asking his eighteen-year-old daughter for bus fare or money for tobacco. While the father was without income, his daughter earned $12.50 per week at Woolworth. Mrs. Patterson worked as a cleaner at a doctor's office. If we assume that she earned about the same as her daughter, the family would have had an annual income of about $1,300, which in 1935–36 was about average for American families.[24] To be sure the family income of both the Patterson and the Adams families was lower than it had been before the depression. But at least the Adams family enjoyed greater economic security despite the father's long-term unemployment, what should have improved the overall situation in the family, maybe except for the father. While before the depression Mr. Adams had spent a good portion of his income at the local pub, now his wife controlled the money, placing the household on a much more secure financial footing than before. She received ample advice about how to run a household from journals and popular magazines, and the increasingly popular science of home economics sought to educate women in particular in becoming efficient consumers who were able, with limited funds, to secure an adequate living standard (an increasingly popular term since the 1910s) for their families.[25]

Quite obviously, unemployment of fathers led to a loss of clarity in familial, social, and political structures.[26] They took on many different forms, when the traditionally male domain of breadwinning no longer rested in the hands of men. Being a man and being manly no longer worked in tandem, which cultural studies scholar Sabine Sielke has described as a core element of the crisis of masculinity.[27] The fathers in the Adams and Patterson families were devastated by the changing constellation of the family structure. The upheaval of the family balance went hand in hand with the upheaval in their own personal balance, which led to a sense of crisis, particularly among fathers. "Unemployment and depression have hit Mr. Patterson much more than the rest of the family," Komarovsky stated. Mr. Adams himself pronounced most pointedly that the control center of the family lay no longer with him but still with the person who brought in the money and controlled the finances: "There certainly was a change in our family, and I can define it in just one word—I relinquished power in the family. I think the man should be the boss in the family. . . . I tried to be the boss in the beginning. . . . But now I don't even try to be the boss. She controls all the money, and I never have a penny in my pocket but that I have to ask her for it. . . . I toned down a good deal as a result of it. How did it all come about? Very simple. I stopped earning money."[28]

Several other family members shared that understanding. While before every purchase, every meal, every financial decision gave a sign of masculine-paternal power, the father's unemployment now reversed the power configuration. Countless acts in everyday life exposed and deepened the erosion of male power. Paying for deliveries at the door, buying groceries, paying for bus fares, and desiring tobacco or affection or sex were now interpreted by the male interviewees as acts of subjugation. When one of the husbands revealed to Komarovsky that "a man is not a man without work," he also revealed the sexual aspects of his perceived emasculation.[29] Many men saw their dependence on their wife's income or on government relief as the biggest humiliation of their unemployment. A wage-earning wife and mother was now seen less as a sign of female success than as an indicator of male failure.[30] Other sociographies found that fathers avoided going to government relief agencies for as long as possible. They would consider accepting government relief only when they had reached the third of five stages of social and psychological destitution, described by sociologist E. Wight Bakke. Bakke called this stage "disorganization," when economic efforts, social relationships, and other family activities had been reduced to a minimum and the authority of the father in the family had withered to almost nothing.[31] Furthermore, most of the government relief agents were women, which magnified the shift in the gender order. These female relief agents wielded a kind of authority, which men found difficult to submit to. Aggressive behavior of relief seekers toward the agents was apparently quite common.[32] Male loss of power, the sense of personal failure, and the shifting gender order were often perceived as more humiliating than the economic hardships. This is also illustrated by the testimony of another unemployed father in Komarovsky's study. Mr. Scott remarked that "before the depression . . . I wore the pants in this family, and rightly so. During the depression I lost something. Maybe you call it self-respect, but in losing it I also lost the respect of my children, and I am afraid I am losing my wife."[33]

At this point it is most important to change the perspective and look more closely at how wives positioned themselves in these situations. Mrs. Garland revealed bluntly that even before the economic crisis she did not appreciate her husband's personality but that his financing of house, clothes, car, and vacations consolidated his position and his prestige. Forty-three-year-old Mrs. Patterson, too, stated that she had always felt that she deserved a higher living standard than her husband could provide. But only the Great Depression offered her a chance to articulate her disaffection with her husband. Mrs. Adams was most direct in articulating the opportunity to finally break up the social and gender order, and she regretted that she had not spoken up earlier: "If I had only not been so soft in the beginning. If I had only set my will against his. But there was no use trying before [the depression and his unemployment]."[34]

Women's statements show how they were striving for opportunities to exert influence, to make choices, and to determine future paths independently. A look at families such as the Garlands, Pattersons, and Adams demonstrates that what was perceived as an upset in the established balance and loss of clarity for one family member was perceived as an opportunity for another. Jürgen Habermas claimed that "only when members of a society *experience* structural alterations as critical for continued existence and feel their social identity threatened, can we speak of crises." There is no doubt that the structural transformations of the 1930s were "critical," yet not all members of society perceived these transformations as a threat. To the contrary, some perceived the challenges to and the "disintegration of social institutions" as a promise and an opportunity.[35] Sociology and politics preferred to look at white men of the lower middle class, and thus their analysis and programs underscore the constellation as threatening. Their perspective prompted the restrengthening of men as providers, despite the fact that women and also children quite obviously experienced the changes of the 1930s differently than their husbands and fathers. Yet given the predominant analytical and political perspective, only the restabilization of the male provider promised to restrengthen American society as a whole. Economic crisis, social crisis, crisis of masculinity—they all were considered intertwined, and their resolution was considered a common goal.

New Deal Policies

Examining the New Deal policies reveals that restoring the father as wage earner of the family seemed vital to the consolidation of the social order. In political and public debates, women were commended for putting their feminist aspirations on hold and instead, in light of the crisis, were asked to refocus their energies on hearth and home. The argument that unemployment would disappear as soon as women would leave the labor market quickly gained traction. Views like these were frequently presented in the media as well as in countless letters to President Roosevelt and the federal government.[36] Critics often asserted that families required only one income in order to secure survival. Even if only few demanded the explicit exclusion of women from the workforce, there was no doubt that most considered the procurement of a family wage as privilege and responsibility of men. By contrast, money earned by women was seen as spare change, which only invited excessive consumption and was, after the end of the Roaring Twenties and in the midst of the scarce thirties, denounced as decadent. Indicative of the dominant thinking at the time was the advice of the president of Barnard College (Mirra Komarovsky's alma mater) to its female graduates in 1930, saying that they should closely monitor their own material needs before they chose to enter the job market.[37]

Political measures to combat unemployment and poverty were also geared toward the male provider. Municipal and state authorities pressured women as early as 1930 to give up their jobs in the public sector. In 1932 the Hoover administration passed the Federal Economy Act, which required that married women in government positions would be laid off first if their husbands were also employed by the federal government. Within a year sixteen hundred wives lost their government jobs and schools laid off female teachers and refused to hire wives. Even if President Roosevelt appointed Frances Perkins as secretary of labor and had in his wife Eleanor a committed women's rights advocate at his side, the policy of excluding women from the labor market continued after FDR's election. For instance, social security was tailored specifically to male forms of employment, and agreements with numerous industrial branches within the framework of the National Industrial Recovery Act allowed for lower wages for women.[38] The focus on male employment continued in the various work projects of the New Deal. The Works Progress Administration paid men five dollars per day, while women had to make do with three. Employment of women would not exceed a sixth of all jobs in the program, and since only one member of the family was allowed to hold a WPA job, it was usually the man in the household. Studies about the WPA were also explicit in this demand. According to social scientist Donald S. Howard, who until 1936 had worked for the federal government and the WPA, it was necessary "to put some brake upon women's eagerness to be the family breadwinner, wage recipient, and controller of the family pocketbook."[39]

Other works programs had similarly gender restrictions. In the fall of 1934, 1.6 million Americans received work relief from the federal government through FERA. Among them were only 142,000 women, 8.875 percent. The Civil Works Administration never employed more than 7 percent women, and the Civilian Conservation Corps, which was hailed as the New Deal's most successful program, was exclusively male. The CCC hoped to mold productive citizens through work in and on nature in a six-month training program. A central element of the project was to teach young men responsibility for their families by forcing them to send almost their entire income home.[40]

The basic decision to combat poverty through work relief rather than direct financial or material relief also relates to the gender-specific aspects of New Deal crisis management. Already during his campaign, Roosevelt had praised work as a value whose importance exceeded securing a family's material existence. New Deal programs therefore were designed to accomplish not only the mitigation of social destitution but also the stabilization of the morale of male providers. The president explicitly described the unemployed as innocent victims of external forces over which they had no control. Roosevelt, as well as Harry Hopkins, committed New Dealer and head of the works programs, stressed repeatedly how important it was to help families regain their ability to help themselves and particularly to give male heads of households the feeling of self-determination.[41] Socio- and labor-political measures followed a model of society that circulated around the working husband and father at its core. While relief and welfare were seen as forms of effeminate dependence, work programs were assumed to strengthen an order of free (white) men in accordance with American self-perception since its founding. A WPA job repositioned men as providers at the center of society, as Komarovsky was also told by the Smith family. Being a man became synonymous with being manly again.[42]

It seems at first surprising that this political program faced a dynamic in which for years more women, even married women, had been pushing into the workforce. Visible since the late nineteenth century, this trend continued in the 1930s. In 1890 around 3.7 million women above the age of fifteen worked for wages. In 1930, at the beginning of the depression, that figure had risen to 10.6 million, and by 1940 there were 13 million female wage laborers of a total of 53 million. In 1930, around a third of wage earning women were married (3.1 million). Of all married women, 11.7 percent were employed. During the Great Depression both the absolute and proportional share of women in the workforce grew. By 1940 the number of employed married women had increased by almost 50 percent to 4.6 million, around 15.3 percent of all women. The vast majority of these women lived with husbands whose yearly income was below a thousand dollars.[43]

Thus, the number of working women, including married women, grew during the depression, despite a general focus on the male provider, and these figures did not even include women like Mrs. Adams, who worked as a custodian, sold homegrown produce, and rented out bedrooms. It is also most likely that the figures did not include Mrs. Patterson, who cleaned a doctor's office. The proportion of women in the shadow economy was large.[44] Some regarded married women's employment as detrimental for the family as the "traditional unit of our civilization."[45] They painted an alarming scenario of an emasculated society and prophesized the widespread demise of unsupervised youth into juvenile delinquency, a topic that would gain traction in the postwar period.[46] Others simply regarded it as an economic necessity and saw no direct competition between male and female wage earners since they predominantly worked in different branches. There was a caveat in these arguments though. Mary Anderson, for instance, longtime chairwoman of the Women's Bureau within the labor department, argued that married women had to work as long as economic necessity within the family demanded it. Even Eleanor Roosevelt stated that most married women worked "only because a husband is ill or has deserted them, or . . . there may even be fathers, mothers, sisters or brothers to be supported." Even though these women challenged men's status as sole breadwinners in the family, they characterized women as emergency or supplemental wage earners, a position that reaffirmed male employment as privileged.[47] Voices like that of social scientist Lorine Livingston Pruette, who argued that competencies of women in the labor market meant an enrichment for the development of family and society that should not do without them, were rare.[48]

The Impact of Race

Around 15 percent of all married women were employed during the Great Depression. The proportion was much higher among African American married women, with around 39 percent, even though their opportunities for work diminished significantly during the economic crisis as a result of greater competition even for the lowest jobs. Statistically harder to account for were the roughly 60 percent of African American women who worked in service in places like Newark.[49] This section discusses the meaning of race for the unemployment policies of the New Deal. Racist discrimination in the social security system established in the 1930s has been well documented by other scholars.[50] Therefore, this section focuses on how the meaning of poverty changed in the 1930s, what this meant for black families, and how this affected the search for political alleviation of the hardships of the Great Depression.

Concepts of poverty and blackness have been closely intertwined in American history. However, in the 1930s public depictions of poverty were overwhelmingly white. In contrast to stereotypes of welfare cheaters, drug users, and criminals, who all were overwhelmingly portrayed as black, images of poverty in the 1930s depicted the so-called undeserving poor, in other words those whose lives were upended by outside forces and who could not be blamed for the condition they found themselves in. These poor, it was suggested, deserved attention and help, not the least because their fate was tightly bound up with the fate of the nation.[51]

At a time when poverty was seen as a national crisis requiring a national cure, African Americans were largely ignored by those observing and diagnosing this crisis, even though many of them were among the poorest of the poor. The common man, placed at the center of almost all sociographies, including Komarovsky's, was presented as white. The assumption of the whiteness of skilled blue-collar and low-level white-collar workers, who were in need of support in this time of crisis in order to save America, was rarely called into question. The various studies on unemployment in Great Depression thus not only recentered men as fathers in family and society but conceptualized them as white as well.

Why were African American fathers and families in Newark ignored by Mirra Komarovsky? As an expanding industrial city, Newark was fourth in the nation after Detroit, Chicago, and Cleveland in the number of African American migrants it attracted from the South. By the end of the 1930s, around 10 percent of Newark's population was black, mostly living in the Central Ward, an inner-city district. Many of them worked in private households, as service personnel or drivers, but the expanding industrial sector had also recruited African American workers from Alabama, the Carolinas, and Tennessee. In the 1920s, more than half of African American men worked in Newark's steel industry, such as Benjamin Atha Steel or Carnegie Steel. However, they often held the lowest paying jobs in these industries. Even though prior to the Great Depression employment among African Americans was near capacity, it did not banish poverty from the Central Ward. The economic downturn in the 1930s hit the African American community doubly hard: they were the first to be laid off, and they were seen as newcomers in the community and incurred growing hostility in this period of increasing destitution.[52]

Strategies such as taking in boarders or pooling households, described by sociologists as a specific response to the hardships of the depression among white families, had been common in black families for a long time. In addition, it had been common practice within African American families to secure the family through a second or third income from wives and older children. For instance, caring for boarders had traditionally been the women's contribution to the family income. Life became still harder for African American families in the 1930s since white women, such as Mrs. Adams and Mrs. Patterson, now applied for the very jobs black women had done before. The average yearly income of a black family during the depression was $655, significantly below that of white families as well as below the income of $903 considered by the WPA as subsistence level.[53]

Even though the depression hit many African Americans hard, their poverty did not mean a "systemic alteration," no decentralization through a sudden and unexpected blow from outside, no "disturbance of system integration," no loss of "sociocultural identity," and no "experience of structural alterations as critical," all of which are crisis indicators according to Jürgen Habermas.[54] To the contrary, poverty among black families appeared to have been inherent in the system. For decades African Americans had developed survival strategies and a more flexible social and family structure geared toward times of hardship, leading contemporary observers to the conclusion that even though black poverty was economically challenging, it was an integral part of the black life experience. Furthermore, if the position of African American fathers was challenged by the Great Depression, it was considered far less threatening to society at large; in fact it only consolidated existing stereotypes. Those who spoke of a crisis among black men assumed that it did not appear to be one brought on by the depression. Thus, they saw hardly a reason to study the effects of the Great Depression on African American fathers.

However, the 1930s produced a number of sociological studies about the life of African Americans in the United States, among them classics such as E. Franklin Frazier's 1939 *The Negro Family in the United States* and Gunnar Myrdal's *An American Dilemma*, published in 1944. However, both studies did not deal—at least not exclusively—with the effects of the Great Depression on fathers, family structure, and social order. Rather, they traced the origins of African Americans' difficult living conditions to slavery and thus outlined a constellation that might have been difficult for a particular social group, but did not represent a specific problem of the 1930s. Instead it appeared to have existed forever. Frazier described African American life as one of familial dysfunction. Myrdal perceived it as an "American dilemma" that belonged to America as much as the common man, who represented the center of society. Hegemonic white and subordinate black positions were thus reiterated. There was no mention of a crisis-type shock in African American lives caused by the Great Depression, even if Myrdal at the end of his study predicted a reevaluation of the African American status and a transformation of society as a result of World War II. The sociological analysis of African American fathers in the Great Depression was no crisis diagnosis; their situation wasn't seen as crisis at all. There certainly existed suffering, yet no one demanded a remedy, nor a revolution (not yet), which would have been the alternative response to a crisis.[55]

Mirra Komarovsky and the Sociology of Crisis

Social systems, Jürgen Habermas states, are characterized by a high level of stability and modifications have to stay within certain ranges. Once those ranges are transgressed, the system is assumed as being in a crisis, which in the end threatens its viability. Crises can be of truly historic significance since "the boundaries of this range of variation are manifested as boundaries of historical continuity."[56] Thus, diagnosing a crisis does not necessarily initiate restabilizing, life-sustaining measures but may instead indicate a critical transition period, after which much, if not everything is fundamentally different.[57]

Yet particularly in medical, economic, and political contexts, historical subjects are urged, because of the normativity of the crisis concept, to take countermeasures, stabilize the system, and maintain historical continuity; anything else would mean revolution. This call for countermeasures comes across as particularly urgent, when a crisis occurs in what is assumed to be a "natural" order or system. A crisis of the "natural" order of things, a transgression of its tolerated boundaries, appears as an existential threat. A combination of a general crisis in society with a crisis in the gender order appears all the more threatening, if the gender order is conceived as "natural," as it used to be for a long time, seemingly based on fixed biological preconditions. Cultural theorists Stuart Hall and Kobena Mercer diagnosed a "crisis of identity" that subjects experienced when the naturalness of the gender order was called into question, because "something assumed to be fixed, coherent and stable is displaced by the experience of doubt and uncertainty."[58]

Most sociologists who had diagnosed a crisis in the 1930s urged measures toward recentering and restabilizing the existing social order, which was considered to have become derailed and robbed of its stability and its assumed naturalness. It is important to note that experts could as well have acknowledged that what was perceived as a crisis by some was seen as an opportunity by others, as some women's statements in the Komarovsky study indicate. Yet this would have required a willingness to think about the changes in the family and gender order in new and different ways, to overcome its assumed naturalness, and to strive for historical transformation, or at least accept it.

However, quite obviously, in the 1930s hardly anyone was yet prepared for this different line of thinking. The fundamental challenge to the white male provider model during the Great Depression instead triggered the renewed proclamation of its centrality and necessity to society. Why, one has to ask, were there so many sociographies about white men written and barely any about the effect of the depression on women, just as there were almost none about African Americans?[59]

In this context, it is hardly surprising that the 1930s saw the rise of theories about gender roles as well as of masculinity studies, putting men center stage and assuming a "natural" gender order.[60] Among these sociographies, Komarovsky's makes a complex contribution with regard to the crisis concept. On one hand it presents white middle-class families and how they are affected by the Great Depression. At the same time it also shows how creative individuals were in dealing with the crisis, hinting at least at the possibility of a more substantial transformation of the social order.[61]

In the 1930s Komarovsky's work pointed in this direction kind of vaguely. In the 1950s her gender sociology urged transformation rather than inertia, change rather than continuity. Her book *Women in the Modern World* (1953), above all, prompted insiders to name her "the real Betty Friedan."[62] The contemporary reception, however, was largely skeptical. After all, the decades after World War II saw a renewed striving for strong fathers, the topic of the next chapter.

10

Fatherhood in World War II and the Cold War, 1940–1960

You think you're something special because a hell of a long while ago you were a good paratrooper. And now all you want is security, and life insurance, and money in the bank to send the kids to college twelve or fifteen years from now, and you're scared because for six months you'll be on trial on a new job, and you always look at the dark side of everything, and you've got *no guts*!
—Betsy Rath to her husband Tom, around 1955

Every morning Thomas Rath takes the 8:26 train from Westport, Connecticut, to his job in Midtown Manhattan. Every afternoon at five o'clock he returns to Westport, where his wife Betsy greets him at the train station. He is one of the many men in gray flannel suits, spilling out of the train, briefcases in hand, alone in an amorphous mass, as the sociologist David Riesman wrote in *The Lonely Crowd*.[1] While Tom earns the money in the family ($7,000 a year), Betsy takes care of home and children. They live with their three children and a dog in one of the leafy suburbs, where the streets are called Greentree Avenue and the like, where everyone drives family-friendly station wagons and drinks martinis during happy hour and where husbands help their wives do the dishes before bedtime.

Tom epitomizes the father in the postwar world, when living conditions of many Americans came closer to the ideal of the nuclear family than ever before or since. "The 1950s was a profamily period if there ever was one," historian Stephanie Coontz comments on the normativity of the nuclear family, which became a concept in family sociology only around this time. Until then this ideal had never been a reality for the majority of the American population. Yet even if the 1950s were an exception, they have been summoned repeatedly in battles over family values as a time when families were just as they should be, as a time when families became the major stabilizing force in American society, thus fulfilling their "natural" destiny.[2]

Yet these seemingly ideal lives of Tom and Betsy Rath also exposed the rifts and fissures that accompanied the long 1950s from the end of World War II to the presidency of John F. Kennedy. Even in 1950s America the nuclear family was accompanied by discontent and insecurity. When Betsy accused Tom of having an insurance mentality, of having no guts, she echoed a powerful discourse proliferating in popular news media, among public intellectuals, and in the social sciences. A number of voices lamented the softening, conformity, and inflexibility of men stuck between white-collar jobs in corporate offices and the consumerist family life in the suburbs. "Security" as well as "insurance" became euphemisms for a lack of self-guidance and emasculation, as will be shown in this chapter. It's best to not even hope for great things to happen, Tom explained his life philosophy to Betsy, "then you won't be disappointed if nothing does happen."[3] In these suburban communities of the 1950s, not much was left of the wilderness spirit of the frontier that was supposed to have shaped America in such significant ways.[4]

Tom Rath was emblematic of all those men who every morning left their standardized single-family homes in their standardized suburbs, clad in standardized gray suits and hats, to work as "corporate clones" in standardized large office buildings, only to return to their standardized families every afternoon.[5] Even though men appeared to have fulfilled their destiny as breadwinners, they also appeared to plunge into a new crisis, this time a crisis of masculinity that was symbolized by the image of the man in the gray flannel suit: standardized, unmotivated, concerned about material security, risk averse—in short without "guts," as Betsy complained.

Tom Rath is *The Man in the Gray Flannel Suit*, the protagonist in the novel by Sloan Wilson, Harvard graduate, World War II veteran, journalist, and writer. The story was first published serially in *Collier's Magazine* in 1955 and then as a book. A year later Gregory Peck and Jennifer Jones starred in the Hollywood version.[6] According to reviews, book and film brought across the sense of a new and fundamental malaise of American manhood and fatherhood after World War II. The magazine *Look* wrote that Tom as a young family man "must meet the challenges that confront *nearly every man*."[7] The "the man in gray" was conjured up in press reports as well as academic studies as a shorthand for the new crisis of masculinity and society.

The dynamic as well as the fragility of this constellation can be understood only against the backdrop of family, fatherhood, and being a soldier in the Second World War. Betsy herself opens her attack on Tom with the contention that Tom's great days as a paratrooper were over. Later in the story we learn how difficult it was for Tom to make the transition from citizen soldier to family man. Repeatedly he is plagued by flashbacks to his wartime service, when he dozes off on the train to work. The other men in their gray "uniforms" and with their expressionless faces remind him of his comrades just before they jumped out of the plane. These experiences are still very much with him even ten years after the end of the war. When Betsy assumes that Tom has had a great time as a paratrooper, she articulates a common misconception of American men's wartime experiences.[8]

This chapter begins with briefly looking at the conflicts of being a father and being a citizen-soldier in the Second World War and at the efforts to achieve a smooth transition of veterans into family men. Yet its major focus is on the Cold War and the nuclear family in the nuclear age and on the complaints about another male crisis and its remedies.

Fathers, Families, and the Second World War

Historians have shown how in the Second World War the nuclear family gave concrete expression to the abstract values of freedom and democracy. It allowed the filling of war aims with tangible personal meaning. The explicit linkage between political aims and the private world of the family mobilized support and sacrifice for the war in the American population.[9]

Publicity campaigns and propaganda strategies helped fuse ideas about a liberal society with the American way of life and the ideal of family, and associate all with the war effort. The Office of War Information (OWI) ran more than a hundred campaigns in cooperation with private corporations. Around half of all commercial ads included patriotic themes, and it seemed that the family was the most patriotic of all themes. War bonds, for instance, were advertised as a good financial investment (for the extra cash now in everyone's pocket as a result of war production), and their purchase was often directly linked to images of family happiness in one's own home. The campaigns further stressed how important war financing was for a speedy return home of fighting fathers and sons.[10]

Safety, security, and family were presented as privileges of a liberal society, whose continued existence had to be defended militarily. Norman Rockwell's illustrations of President Franklin D. Roosevelt's four freedoms, published by the *Saturday Evening Post* and in an OWI-campaign in the spring of 1943, were a case in point. "Freedom from fear" and "freedom from want" depicted intimate scenes of family bliss: parents watching over their sleeping children, while German Luftwaffe planes were attacking London, and grandparents serving Thanksgiving dinner to their children and grandchildren.[11]

The linkage between military engagement, family bliss, and liberalism faced a big dilemma, however. Even though Americans were told to go to war to protect strong and healthy families, they experienced the weakening of the family as the war took away fathers from their families, possibly never to return. Sociologists, psychologists, and psychoanalytically inspired public intellectuals noted that without a father children, boys in particular, lacked good models for a "healthy" and socially productive upbringing. They worried about war as a threat to strong and stable homes, and they conjured up the specter of momism: children without direction, coddled and softened by single mothers, yet also neglected since women took on the male role of breadwinner during the war and were too often absent from home. A menace of the war were dysfunctional families without fathers, with promiscuous mothers and with children without direction. Particularly boys, some critics feared, would descend into criminality or homosexuality without the guidance of fathers.[12]

The increase of women in the workforce—it rose by 60 percent as a result of the wartime industrial boom—and the deployment of fifteen million men appeared to transform the social and gender order. Three-quarters of working women were married, and many of them had children. Even if absent fathers and working mothers were seen as socially destabilizing, as men went to war, women were called on to fill jobs in offices and factories.[13]

Both male functions, as fathers and as citizen-soldiers, could not be fulfilled at the same time. In the fall of 1943, the Seventy-Eighth Congress debated this dilemma, prompted by concern about rising juvenile delinquency, assumed to be related to the war and the absence of fathers. The Senate Committee on Military Affairs deliberated whether it should prohibit the planned drafting of fathers into the military.[14] Sexologists and psychologists fueled concerns on Capitol Hill by connecting family relations to the sexual, social, and political development of children. Before 1943 fathers had been exempted from the draft, and draft boards had given priority to the protection of families. The military was now arguing that the growing war effort demanded the readiness of every man, including fathers. Pentagon officials could not and would not do without the six million fathers between the ages of eighteen and forty-four.[15]

Democratic senator Burton K. Wheeler (Montana) proposed a bill against drafting fathers. He argued that fathers' contributions to the war effort were most efficient as leaders of families and on the home front rather than with a rifle in their hands on the battlefront. They were indispensable at home for the stability of families and society. Boys in particular would become delinquent and veer from the moral straight path in female-headed households because of a lack of conduct. Because today's boys were tomorrow's fathers, America would enter a vicious cycle by turning fathers into GIs. The drafting of fathers would cause the demise of families and with it the demise of the middle class, the foundation of democratic society and of the American way of life. Thus, this step would leave the country vulnerable to totalitarianism. "After all, the home is the backbone of a democratic republic, is it not? . . . If you destroy the home and the family, you destroy your country, you destroy America."[16]

Congress ultimately gave priority to the military's needs and rejected the proposed law. However, even after the fall of 1943 boards tried to avoid drafting fathers, and when demobilization began fathers were given priority as well.[17] After the war the predominant concept of an adequate social and gender order suggested a policy that would, after twelve years of economic crisis and four years of war, support nuclear families and build a society around the father as provider. Already in the summer of 1944 Congress had passed the so-called GI Bill, designed to strengthen veterans in the areas of work, education, and homeownership and thus build a society around the nuclear family with the father in its center.

Coming Home

The Roosevelt administration had begun to propagate a postwar male-centered education and social policy even before the American entry into war. On June 22, 1944, only two weeks after D-Day, the president signed the GI Bill into law. The package was designed to ease veterans' (98 percent male and 96 percent white) return into civilian life. Families representing the nuclear family were seen as the backbone of democratic society, as the nexus between male success on campus and at the workplace and American liberalism.

The GI Bill imagined veterans as fathers with families, even if most of them were single at the time of their discharge.[18] Starting a family, it was assumed, was good for veterans' readjustment to civilian life and was what they would naturally want. Everything else was considered a failure and discussed in psychologizing terms, as threatening veterans with amputation and castration.[19] In order to turn soldiers into family men, veterans received weekly unemployment support, college tuition, preferential treatment on the labor market, and favorable credits backed by the federal government for the purchase of a home or a farm. The GI bill encouraged and helped veterans to get a degree, get a job, own a house, and thus start a nuclear family. By strengthening male veterans it sought to build a society centered around a broad middle class consisting of straight families, whose fathers had privileged access to education, work, and property.[20]

The GI Bill further strengthened a trend toward marriage and family that had already begun at the outset of the war. In Sloan Wilson's book about the man in the gray flannel suit, Tom and Betsy were among the couples who married in 1941, when he was only twenty years old. During the war some got married because they had not been able to afford marriage before during the economic crisis of the 1930s, others because they wanted to declare their commitment toward one another before he headed off to war, and still others to avoid being drafted. After the war marriages boomed. More Americans got married at a younger age than ever before (average age was 20.5 for women and 22.5 for men). Married partners received tax breaks, and the birth rate rose to an average of 3.2 children per married couple, higher than before. The Raths with their three children represented pretty much the average American family.[21]

After the war, women vacated 2.5 million jobs or were demoted in the workplace hierarchy. Returning men filled the roughly seven million new jobs in the now expanding civilian production of goods, allowing them to reclaim their positions as providers.[22] Women were expected to make way for strong men and strong families and thus to contribute to the stabilization of society after a period of social disorder through depression and war. Magazines and other publications dismissed working wives as abnormal, as a "disease," and as a menace to a stable social order. Femininity and the independence that came with wage labor were now seen as a "contradiction in terms." Women would, it was assumed, find their "natural" fulfillment only through home and hearth and motherhood.[23] Even though this was far from being the reality for numerous non-middle-class and mostly nonwhite women, politicians and commentators demanded a focus on nuclear families with fathers being in charge.[24] Fictional families like the Raths and the Cleavers from the popular TV show *Leave It to Beaver* presented powerful examples. Betsy Rath, for instance, was described by Sloan Wilson as "a conscientious household manager" who carefully weighed solutions to all problems, consulted advice manuals when one of her children was stricken with the chicken pox, and consulted with her husband in the evenings. In addition to advice books, mothers could rely on magazines, such as *Good Housekeeping* and *Parents Magazine*, for advice on how to build a comfortable and secure home that could offer refuge to war-weary veterans and serve as a fortress for a moral society.[25]

Responsible fatherhood was now hailed as the key to successful manhood more assertively than ever before, and the life of the nuclear family was more than ever regarded as the natural order of things. Men who started a family were demonstrating maturity, next to "togetherness" a key term of the time. In 1947 *Parents Magazine* wrote that "being a father is not 'sissy' business," a euphemism for effeminacy and homosexuality, but "the most important occupation in the world." Likewise, philosopher and social psychologist Harry Allen Overstreet argued in his 1950 study about *The Mature Mind* that "a man is immature if he regards the support of a family as a kind of trap in which he, an unsuspecting male, has somehow been caught." According to a survey from the mid-1950s, less than 10 percent of Americans felt that unmarried people could be happy, and a popular advice manual declared that "the family is the center of your living. If it isn't, you've gone far astray."[26] Any path other than heterosexual marriage with children was seen as flight from civic responsibility, as a pathological and socially destabilizing departure from the straight path toward upright and normal living. It was thus fitting that Tom Rath's first assignment in his new job was to craft a speech about a new initiative to tackle mental illness in America. It offered a way to address the widespread postwar discourse on war-related mental scars among veterans, but also signaled the pathologization of all forms of living outside the nuclear family.[27] Morris Zelditch, sociologist at Columbia University in the 1950s, summarized the "reproductive consensus" and the gender division in Cold War America in the following way: "Father helps mother with the dishes. He sets the table. He makes formula for the baby. Mother can supplement the income of the family by working outside. *Nevertheless*, the American male, by definition, *must* 'provide' for his family. He is *responsible* for the support of his wife and children. His primary area of performance is the occupational role, in which his status fundamentally inheres; and his *primary* function in the family is to supply an 'income,' to be the 'breadwinner.' There is simply something wrong with the American adult male who doesn't have a 'job.'"[28]

Tom and Betsy Rath can be seen doing the dishes together while discussing the issues of the day. In contrast, men without families were accused of fleeing the natural responsibility of fatherhood, of leaning toward homosexuality, and of lacking manly resolve in the new Cold War battle against totalitarianism. After 1945 heterosexual manliness was connected more closely with liberalism and capitalism than ever before, supposedly demonstrating the ability to take on responsibility to conduct oneself and others in a free society. Homosexuality was associated with communism, with the loss of individuality and of freedom, and with totalitarianism instead. McCarthyism and the House Un-American Activities Committee mostly targeted citizens whose way of life did not fit the normative mold. In this context Tom Rath represented an ambivalent figure: on the one hand he epitomized the heteronormative family-oriented men, yet on the other his lack of motivation and self-guidance, his lack of drive, and his reluctance to take risks made him look weak. Shortcomings of this sort did not match the image of the upright man, suggesting the arrival of a new "crisis" of masculinity.[29]

The question of motivation, needs, desires, and aversions gets played out in Sloan Wilson's novel with respect to homeownership. Tom and Betsy had purchased their current home in 1946, when Tom had taken his first job after the war. The house was located on nondescript Greentree Avenue in suburban Westport, filled with consumption-oriented, martini-sipping middle-class families. There were ink stains on the wallpaper and a crack in the wall had the shape of a question mark.[30] The novel does not state whether Tom had purchased the home with the support of the GI Bill, yet it would have been likely for a man in his circumstances. The bill fueled the suburbanization of America, settling new neighborhoods with straight nuclear families, more than ever regarded as building blocks of American society.[31]

Thirteen million homes were built between the mid-1940s and the mid-1950s, almost all of them in the suburbs of major metropolitan areas with a population that reached forty million by the early 1950s. Housing sales reached their peak in 1951 and 1955, with almost 1.7 million sold homes each year. State and federal authorities invested in the expansion of the electrical grid and built a total of eighty thousand miles of roads, linking suburbs to cities, making the idealized suburban family life possible. A continuously growing and white middle class lived in suburbia, which was by the end of the 1950s about a third of all families in the United States.[32]

Suburban life was clearly structured, with a given place for every member of the community, determined by skin color (white), class (middle), gender, sexuality (hetero), and age (middle age). A favorite suburban abode was a ranch-style family home with garage, TV set, and barbeque in the backyard, where dad would grill red meat and mixed drinks such as martinis or highballs were consumed, perhaps with one's like-minded neighbors. Communities adopted generic names such as Greenbelt (Maryland), Park Forest (Illinois), or Clear Lake City (Texas). Satirists quickly invented alternative names such as "fertility valley" or "rabbit hutch." Levittowns, maybe the most famous suburbs in postwar America, built in Pennsylvania, New Jersey, and New York, were named after their developer, Arthur Levitt. Levittowns consisted of 17,400 units, priced at $7,900 each, with garage, television, and the so-called panorama window, through which mother would watch her youngsters playing in the backyard while preparing meals in the kitchen. Fathers could spend weekends finishing the attic for extra space, giving each house an individual touch. With a minimal down payment and long-term loan, the monthly mortgage of one of these smaller houses was between fifty and sixty dollars a month. Levitt sold exclusively to white Americans. They paid less than most black residents paid in rent for their inner-city apartments. African American veterans experienced general and widespread discrimination on the housing market and when trying to access GI Bill benefits or to get credits.[33]

Gray Flannel Suits

Tom Rath seems to have everything a man could wish for: a caring wife, three children (and a fourth in Europe, which would eventually expose all the dissonances in the happy family façade), a job, a house, and a car, including, over the course of the story, an upward move to a better job and a more spacious house. His experience appeared to match perfectly the predominant expectations of a natural male life trajectory in Cold War America. Nonetheless, he is beginning to feel a nagging emptiness, a lack of motivation, and a feeling of living a life without deeper meaning and being worn down by the demands of family in suburbia and his corporate job in one of the tall office towers in the city. His wife Betsy feels similarly. She too seems to have everything she wanted to fulfill her "natural" destiny of strengthening America's social fabric: a caring husband, children for whom she could care, and, over the course of the story, a more spacious home. But Betsy is also plagued by a feeling of discontent, which leads her to contemplate consulting a psychotherapist. Years later journalist Betty Friedan would articulate this female discontent in her book *The Feminine Mystique*. Friedan's book helped launch the second wave of feminism in the United States. For women of Betsy's time, however, one assumed that the emptiness could be filled by upward mobility and faith in one's husband and marriage.[34]

Tom himself articulates his existence between emptiness and outsized expectations in a key passage of the book. As part of a job interview he is asked to write down what he considers to be the most important qualities about himself and his life. "Is there anything in particular you want me to tell you about?," he asks his interviewer, the personnel manager of the United Broadcasting firm, who responds with a short "yourself." Alone in a room Tom struggles to put something about himself on paper. This task alone is of elemental significance in a culture that gave more and more credence to psychoanalysis. Tom cannot think of anything other than his experience of violence in the war or the little drab house in which he lived—all things that would not make his application any more attractive. In addition, these were things he wanted to leave behind, that paralyzed and motivated him at the same time. Tom sidesteps this autobiographical trap by trying to take the perspective of others. He decides not to write down what he himself regards as important but what he thinks his potential employer regarded as important.[35]

This was typical for Tom and the other men in gray flannel suits. He had become an expert in developing strategies to keep his own opinion to himself until he had found out what his bosses wanted to hear. In a moment of self-reflection he wonders about "how smoothly one becomes, not a cheat, exactly, not really a liar, just a man who'll say anything for pay."[36] Those who have to take care of their family in the modern working world, he explains to Betsy, have to learn to maneuver carefully. Sloan Wilson makes Tom reproduce critical comments by social scientists and public intellectuals from the first half of the 1950s. David Riesman, for instance, had identified the other-directed conformist who was all alone in a mass of people. "Other-directedness" had replaced the ideal of "autonomy," and it became associated with the feminization of American society.[37] C. Wright Mills came to similar conclusions, arguing that the white middle-class man no longer acted on his own, to take a position was no longer part of a man's identity: "The white-collar man is the hero as victim, the small creature who is acted upon but who does not act, who works along unnoticed in somebody's office or store, never talking loud, never talking back, never taking a stand."[38]

In 1950s America, no one yet worried about "other-directed" women, yet "other-directed" men were considered a serious problem.[39] Among men, other-directedness was considered a sure sign of softening and feminization, putting men outside the heteronormative as well as liberal-democratic realm. Women, homosexuals, and communists were expected to submit to the will of others, but "real" men were not. Emasculated fathers were therefore seen as a threat to the stability of the liberal capitalist order. The main dilemma was that precisely those living arrangements touted as desirable and even natural after the Second World War were also seen as the source of emasculation: the standardized home in standardized suburbs, leaving for work on the same commuter train every single morning, staying in standardized cubicles in nondescript office buildings from nine to five, following the directions of others. After their return home, these men would play a little with their children, eat dinner, and watch sitcoms or game shows on TV. Were such men still manly? What had happened to the ideal of manly American incentive, the pioneering spirit that had allegedly been building over centuries among men who were constantly pushing into new regions, searching for unknowns, and taming the wilderness? Tom Rath epitomized what had happened to these men. Nobody expressed his dilemma better than his wife Betsy. Betsy pressured Tom into overcoming his sleepy discontent and strive for more wealth and a larger house, which was finally made possible by her husband's new job. At the same time, she was not at all happy with Tom's strategy to accommodate everyone else in order to advance in his job, to negotiate his way through difficult situations. "I wanted you to go out and fight for something again—like the man I married [before the war]. Not to turn into a cheap, slippery yes-man," she charged. "You're talking like a typical American woman," Tom retorts. "You want it both ways. 'Don't play it safe,' you say, and 'can we get a new car tomorrow?'"[40]

Lamentations about another "crisis" of the American man grew louder, when the crisis of the 1930s was barely over. Standardized suburbs and conformist work environments threatened to suffocate men in their gray flannel suits, contemporary critics warned. Virile and individualized manhood was crushed under pressure to conform, given the burden of having to provide for one's family. Fewer and fewer men seemed to be willing to forge their own path and accept setbacks along the way; instead there was significantly more conformity.

Tom Rath became the archetype of male conformity, submissiveness, and other-directedness. Book and film reviews described him as emblematic of his generation. *Look* magazine noted that several "young white-collar heroes" shared his fate and confronted the same challenges. *Life* stated that Tom Rath was, like so many of his male fellow Americans, caught in the "gray flannel trap."[41] Almost all reviews lamented that the American man stopped being a real man. Instead, he had become a "professional yes-man" and "unprincipled robot."[42]

The man in the gray flannel suit soaked into sociology and the discourse on the gendered society. William Whyte referenced Tom Rath in his 1956 study on the *Organization Man*, whom he regarded as "paradigmatic of corporate life in America." That same year the *Woman's Home Companion* worried that "if [the masculine drives] are always and completely inhibited—the man in the gray flannel suit will stop being a man."[43] Such widespread emasculation was seen as dangerous, particularly because the Cold War made the nexus between autonomous, assertive masculinity and the liberal order seem more important than ever before. Maintaining America's strength required powerful men, said the predominant assumption of the 1950s. *Look* reflected the general tenor when it brought out a special feature in 1958 on the theme of conformity. Under the title "The American Male: Why Is He Afraid to Be Different," it read, "One dark morning this winter, Gary Gray awakened and realized, he had forgotten to say the word 'I.' . . . He had lost his individuality. In the free and democratic United States of America, he had been subtly rooked of a heritage that Communist countries deny by force."[44]

Playboy magazine, first published in December 1953, was a powerful voice in this discourse. Within less than three years the print run went from seventy thousand to over a million, and by the mid-1960s it was among the most widely read magazines in the country with over four million copies printed, just behind the *Saturday Evening Post* and *Reader's Digest*. "We aren't a 'family magazine,'" declared its publisher Hugh Hefner. Its articles argued consistently that "conformity, togetherness, anonymity" meant the slow death of real men. They warned against the "gray flannel mind," the embodiment of the crisis of masculinity and the feminization of America.[45] The cure was, according to the magazine, to exchange the ethics of the fatherly breadwinner for that of the hedonistic playboy. For in contrast to the man in gray, the playboy went through life self-assured and beholden only to his manly and assertive lust for consumption. The gray flannel was exchanged for silk or linen, the functional station wagon for the fast sports car, the suburban ranch-style house for the bachelor apartment in a high rise in the city (as shown in the magazine in the fall of 1956 as well as in several Hollywood comedies), and one's own wife for a pliable and devoted Playboy bunny.[46]

The bachelor was back. On one hand *Playboy* countered the dominant paradigm of a society centered around family and father and instead worshipped a Bohemian lifestyle. *Playboy* showed how a man could be heterosexual and very manly without getting married and becoming a father. On the other hand it seemed ideal reading material for living room rebels who continued to practice the routine of their own suburban existence yet enjoyed an occasional escape into another world, one that fathers and providers were apparently lacking in their lives and that made them feel like real men again. They could fantasize about wearing silk instead of gray flannel, and maybe even about catching a playmate since (as the magazine repeated endlessly) they were just like the girls next door.[47]

Tom Rath's life story was widely known for its conformity. Yet his daily struggle with his war memories received relatively little public attention. The war had become part of America's collective memory as the "good war" in which young Americans fought against totalitarianism and turned into universal heroes. The struggle against totalitarianism continued almost immediately after the war against the communist regimes behind the Iron Curtain, and veterans had little opportunity to process their wartime memories and to heal their wounds. Public silence was accompanied by veterans' silence, which contributed to the consolidation of the heroic version of the war in collective memory.[48]

Tom wants to forget the war, yet every day he finds himself returning to its key moments in his memory. "I was what we have to have in our country, what they call a citizen soldier," he tries to explain to his wife. "One day a man's catching the 8:26 and then suddenly he's killing people, and then a few weeks later he's catching the 8:26 again. It'll be a miracle if it didn't change him in some way." Initially Betsy shows little understanding for the troubling memories of fear and of the seventeen men Tom killed in the war. Eventually the rift between citizen-soldier and provider threatens to tear him apart when, at his new company, he meets an old war buddy who reminds him of his wartime liaison with an Italian woman, Maria, and reveals to him that she bore his child. Tom eventually gathers the courage to face the past and the present and confesses his wartime infidelity to Betsy. After a dramatic falling out, they reconcile and resolve to jointly take on the responsibility for the child and by extension for their life together as a family. With Betsy's help,

Tom makes a conscious decision in favor of family, and not as part of a conformist routine. Tom continues to live the suburban life, but he has succeeded in regaining self-guidance and control over his life.[49]

Challenges to the Life in Gray

While Tom's war experience was rarely debated, the story of his submission to the conformist pressures of the postwar period received great attention and had long-term repercussions. One of the strongest views on this subject of conformity came from the writer Norman Mailer, who relished the opportunity to challenge apathy and a lack of admiration for what he considered real masculinity. He targeted the emasculation of America in the 1950s most sharply in his *White Negro*, first published in 1957 in *Dissent*. The purpose of this new magazine was, in the words of its editors, to be radical and "to dissent from the bleak atmosphere of conformism that pervades the political and intellectual life of the United States."[50]

The content and tone of Mailer's article were indeed radical, an ode to the urban outlaw as the last remaining embodiment of man, who had escaped the death by conformity in 1950s America. "Slow death by conformity" was at least as dangerous as "instant death by atomic war," Mailer quipped in this latest crisis diagnosis. The American man must rediscover the rebel in himself, he demanded; he must rediscover living in the present, beyond assimilation, job security, and mother's hearth. According to Mailer in 1950s America only urban outlaws were battling the constraints of conformity, by living on the streets, escaping corrosive luxury, pushing daily to the limits of their existence, fighting for bare survival, and looking death in the eye. Honorable street battles would preserve manliness in these effeminate times. The principle of movement was, in Mailer's eyes, more important than its direction: the important thing was to stay in motion because motion kept the body warm. Mailer presented a glowing plea for a reconsideration of the somatic in order to recover that which he described as the core of a real man's existence. Only those who walk the fine line on the edge with an eye always toward the possible end would experience such corporeality. Past and present, according to Mailer, had outfitted the African American man with the body and the guts necessary to cope with violence and lead the way out of the crisis. "The cameos of security for the average white: mother and the home, job and the family, are not even a mockery to millions of Negroes," he continued.[51]

Mailer's ode to the black man living on the edge was full of racist stereotypes that will be looked at in greater detail in the next chapter. It also needs to be seen in the wider context of America's ambivalent love for rebellion and a corporeal masculinity. In 1950s America the psycho- and sociopathic *Rebel without a Cause*, much admired by Mailer, is a source of both much middle-class anxiety and enthusiasm within youth culture. The Beatniks, who represented the cultural avant-garde, challenged the conventions of heterosexual monogamy, despised consumption, and had nothing but contempt for the constraints of work and suburban life. While the Beatniks occupied the margins of American society in the 1950s, actors like Marlon Brando in *The Wild One* (1953) and James Dean in *Rebel Without a Cause* (1955) were widely admired as virile young men without the nagging responsibilities of fatherhood. They dismissed authority and were full of sexual urges and potentially violent. Dressed not in gray flannel suits but in black leather jackets and white T-shirts, occasionally soiled by blood, they went searching for models of masculinity, which their conformist fathers could not offer. "What can you do when you have to be a man?" asks James Dean alias Jim Stark in *Rebel Without a Cause* of his father who is dressed in an apron and crawls on the floor, trying to pick up broken dishes. "Now you give me a direct answer. . . . I need one!," he implores his father, even though he knows he won't get one.[52]

Also, the 1950s were more diverse and not as uniformly heterosexual as it appears on the surface. For instance, the Kinsey reports, published in 1948 and 1953, issued findings about masturbation, sex within and outside of marriage, and hetero- and homosexuality. Instant best sellers, they seemed to suggest that the sexual practices of Americans were so diverse that what had been regarded as perverted behavior was in fact quite widespread and thus "normal." Kinsey even showed to his readers that the boundaries between hetero- and homosexuality were quite fluid. Also, gay and lesbian organizations formed in this period, triggered by the sexual dynamics of the Second World War, when many young people of the same sex spent long periods of time in close quarters with one another. Of note was also the example of Christine Jorgensen, whose sex change garnered a lot of attention in the 1950s. Jorgensen pointed to what was possible. Last but not least, in spite of all the talk of men in crisis, many men in the 1950s continued to live their lives between office and suburban homes, and they liked to drink martinis, eat steaks from the grill, and look at *Playboy* without necessarily experiencing a sense of crisis.[53]

In 1960 the Democratic candidate for the presidency John F. Kennedy raised hopes for a renewal of American manhood. Kennedy represented youth and dynamics and thus a welcome change to the tranquilized 1950s. When Kennedy accepted the nomination at the Democratic convention in Los Angeles, Norman Mailer wrote full of enthusiasm in *Esquire* that Superman had come to the supermarket: "[With] discipline and savvy and go-go-go, sound, drilled, never dull, quick as a knife, full of the salt of hipper-dipper—a beautiful machine."[54]

Kennedy cultivated this image, presented himself as a war hero and an athlete, hid his various ailments, was seen as a womanizer, and played with associations of his own sexual potency. At the same time and despite all the emphasis on his virility, he succeeded in presenting himself as a model father and family man. He and his wife Jackie often posed in family pictures, and images of his children playing under his desk in the Oval Office are legendary. Kennedy's success and enduring myth might be at least partially grounded in his successful fusion of fatherhood with a dynamic, masculine leadership style, or, to put it differently, to wear gray suits and yet still demonstrate determination.

Kennedy's opponent in the fight for the presidency was Richard Nixon, who, though not much older, had a harder time ridding himself of the negative attributes associated with the gray flannel suit. Symptomatic of Nixon's image was his famous kitchen debate with Soviet premier Nikita Khrushchev in Moscow in 1959. Nixon used the modern kitchen, generally considered the best place for conversations between husband and wife in America, to tout the completely furnished American home as a telling sign of the superiority of the United States over the Soviet Union and of capitalism over communism, and he asked Khrushchev, "Would it not be better to compete in the relative merits of washing machines and color TVs than in the strength of rockets?" Kennedy immediately seized the opportunity to associate Nixon's benign suburban rhetoric with stagnation and crisis, and claimed for himself the power to overcome the crisis in a highly sexualized rhetoric, alluding to a more powerful masculinity. Kennedy advocated for pushing the limits and searching for new frontiers, for instance in space and weapons technology, and he added rhetorically, "Mr. Nixon may be very experienced in kitchen debates. So are a great many other married men I know. . . . I would rather take my television black and white and have the largest rockets in the world."[55]

11

Families, Fathers, and the Black Community, 1950–2010

This bitter earth
Well, what fruit it bears
What good is love
mmmm that no one shares
And if my life is like the dust
oooh that hides the glow of a rose
What good am I
Heaven only knows
—Clyde Otis, "This Bitter Earth," 1960

Killer of Sheep by Charles Burnett—Part I: 1977

In a scene from the 1977 movie *Killer of Sheep*, Stan dances slowly with his wife to the tune of Dinah Washington's "This Bitter Earth," their figures a silhouette in front of the kitchen window. While the wife, who remains nameless in the movie, touches her husband's naked upper body, at first cautiously and then with increasing affection and desire, Stan remains stoic, with almost apathetic distance, united in the same room with her, moving gently together yet distant nonetheless, while Dinah Washington sings "what good is love—that no one shares?"

The scene invokes and contradicts images of the black body, connected since slavery to ideas of physical strength and sexual desire. Stan is naked and strong yet also weak at the same time—apathetic and seemingly immune to all affection. For almost the entire movie, Stan is unable to respond to his wife's gestures and approaches when she seeks to be close to him, tries to attract his attention, or gently flaunts her beauty. He is exhausted from hard labor at the slaughterhouse; exhausted from the daily struggle for survival of his family in the Watts neighborhood of Los Angeles. The area looks as poor in 1977 as it did in 1965, when riots had broken out, laying bare the frustration and anger about continued poverty, exploitation, and police brutality. After eight days of riots, thirty-four dead, a thousand injured, eleven thousand arrests, and property damage of more than thirty-five million dollars, government officials raised serious concerns about the potential for violent revolution.[1]

Over a decade later, conditions in predominantly black neighborhoods such as Watts had improved little, making a mockery of President Lyndon B. Johnson's war on poverty that should have improved opportunities and living conditions for poor, disadvantaged, and marginalized members of society.[2] Stan describes his frame of mind when he repairs the kitchen floor at home after a long day at work: "I have worked myself into my own hell; unable to close my eyes. I can't sleep at night, no peace of mind." His friend Oscar quips in response, "why don't you kill yourself, then you'll be a lot happier," receiving a faint smile from Stan. To give up, to evade his responsibility, is not an option for him.[3]

Stan's situation reminds of the Memphis sanitation workers and their famous protest in April 1968. Charging that they earned too much to die and too little to live, they fought for better working conditions and

Figure 11.1. Still from *Killer of Sheep* (dir. Charles Burnett, USA, 1977/2007).

higher wages, but also for respect as human beings and men. During their demonstrations they repeated the simple yet poignant slogan "I am a man," pointing to that being a man meant being able to support one's family through the fruits of one's labor. The dynamic of collective anger that had resonated so deeply in 1968 had all but dissipated in 1977. The rage had turned inward. Stan fought in isolation.[4]

Stan (played by Henry Gale Sanders) is a father in his thirties living with his wife (played by Kayce Moore), his teenage son Stan Jr., and five-year-old daughter Angela in a small house in Watts. His days are spent trying to be a good provider and fight against poverty and other adversities and against his own despair and depression. After the physically and mentally exhausting work at the slaughterhouse he tinkers around the house or searches for a working engine for his car. Like Sisyphus, Stan struggles against overwhelming odds without giving up. "You keep going because it's the only thing you can do," Charles Burnett describes his movie's protagonist. "That defines you as a man, gives you dignity."[5]

The car in particular becomes a symbol of Stan's struggle to overcome the confines of his existence. In his struggle for spatial mobility, he is overpowered by repeated failures, standing for the hurdles he encounters in his struggle for social mobility and for becoming part of the middle class.[6] The weekend excursion with family and friends ends with a flat tire, with no spare tire available. The purchase of a new engine for the car culminates, according to philosopher bell hooks, in the "most tragic moment" of the film, representing an "existential metaphor for the black exilic experience." The hard-earned engine, multilayered symbol of mobility, falls off the bed of his pickup and breaks apart. As hooks notes, "It's like when you go step out in everyday life to do something, a basic chore, but it matters so much to you, you put your heart and money on it, and it fails. This is so symbolic that this particular moment stands out. It evoked such a deep sense of failure—of not being able to beat the odds."[7]

Burnett presents several moments in black everyday live in post-civil-rights America, which together create an almost insurmountable obstacle course. According to filmmaker Arthur Jaffa, the movie shows "that existential quality of black life in the vernacular" as well as the impossibility to overcome those spatial and social boundaries. Stan's friend Gene remarks in a resigned manner, "Ain't nothing we can do to fix it" when the broken motor lies on the road. What at first seems a laconic comment about the broken motor is also a comment on black life in America. Stan fights tirelessly against the social and discursive confines of his existence, but despite his best efforts he loses control over his life again and again. An essential component of being a man in a liberal society thus remains unattainable to him.[8]

Killer of Sheep is not a documentary, but the characters are inspired by friends and family with whom filmmaker Charles Burnett had lived in Watts. In the movie they interact with an environment of violence, destruction, and disappointment, but also of mutual support and perseverance. Even though the events in the film are fiction, they are close enough to lived experience that they could have happened. The mode of shooting on-site, much of it with a hand camera, give the film a documentary feel. In addition, the sequencing of scenes without a linear plot creates the impression of detached observations rather than the narration of a structured story. The direct tone of the dialogue and the use of lay actors further consolidate that impression. It seems as if Burnett had taken the principles of postcolonial history and the history of everyday life to heart, which mean to give voice to those without a voice so that they can tell their own stories and, as pointed out by Erich Leon Harris, speak out truths about life in America.[9]

Burnett was influenced by Italian neorealism, particularly Vittorio de Sica's *Ladri di biciclette* (1948), and British documentary film.[10] Burnett's borrowing from European traditions is noteworthy because it demonstrates his search for alternatives to Hollywood filmmaking traditions. *Killer of Sheep* portrays an African American working-class family, which does not match black stereotypes propagated by American history, film, and media for over one hundred years. Examples of the latter include D. W. Griffith's racist epic *The Birth of a Nation* (1915) and the TV series *Amos 'n' Andy* (1951–53, 1954–66), but also the 1970s blaxploitation movies.[11]

During his time at UCLA Burnett was among the founders of a group called LA Rebellion, which sought to invent a new type of film, in which African Americans were not marginalized as problems or presented as threatening but portrayed as individuals with agency.[12] LA Rebellion was part of a wider movement that developed new cultural and aesthetic forms of dealing with repression in the context of antiracist and global anticolonial struggles. Other initiatives besides LA Rebellion included the Watts Writers Workshop, the Watts Prophets, and the Jazz collective Pan Afrikan Peoples Arkestra.[13]

Killer of Sheep was Charles Burnett's senior thesis at UCLA. It was shot in twenty-five days and had a budget of ten thousand dollars. It was not commercially distributed until 2007, when the film was highly successfully re-released, after Burnett could finally afford to purchase the rights for the soundtrack. Yet still in the 1970s and early 1980s, successes at US and European film festivals, among them the 1981 critics award at the Berlin Film Festival, indicated that Burnett had created a most important and powerful film. In 1990 *Killer of Sheep* was among the first fifty films placed in the Library of Congress's National Film Registry, receiving the accolade of being a "significant element of our cultural patrimony and history."[14]

Against the Stereotypes: Sex and Violence

Killer of Sheep did away with long-standing stereotypes of African Americans. When in the summer of 1965 various groups of artists and writers explored black living conditions in Watts, mainstream media portrayed them as radical and unable to restrain their anger and aggression but never as thoughtful or critical. This stereotype of angry and threatening black masculinity has a long history, which became magnified in the 1960s with the black power movement and its militancy.[15]

This focus on black men's bodies and physique can be traced back to slavery. A predominant image of black men in times of slavery was one bred for hard work, with a potential for violent rebellion, yet often overlaid with an image of a loyal, simpleminded, "ever cheerful, infantile Sambo." It was assumed that such men were capable of survival only under white tutelage. Their status was one of "*anticitizen*," as historian David Roediger states.[16] Historian Martha Hodes shows how African American stereotypes shifted with emancipation and the possibility of African Americans' greater political and economic participation. After the end of slavery the image of the aggressive, violent, and hypersexual black man gained momentum and moved to the forefront. Fears ran rampant of politically active black men who would endanger the existing social order and who, liberated from bondage and without external control, might now exact revenge by lusting after white women. Fear about sexual aggression of black men against white women became intricately intertwined with white fear of black freedom and former slaves' aspiration to participate in the political, economic, and cultural life of the polity. Liaisons between white women and black men became symbolic markers of the erosion of the racial and patriarchal order and were thus considered by large parts of the white population as a nightmare. The long history of white sexual aggression against black women was studiously ignored. Political, economic, and sexual power were intertwined; citizenship and civil rights corresponded to specific, sexualized ideas about race, manhood, and a man's self-perception as protector, provider, and property owner.[17]

So-called anti-miscegenation laws were passed in thirty-eight states, and the historical record counts over five thousand lynching victims in the United States, most of them African American men who were hunted down, tortured, mutilated, and killed by white mobs mostly in the South between 1880 and 1920. These mobs claimed for themselves if not the legal then at least a vigilante right to protect white women from alleged transgressions by black men and to exact revenge in case of an alleged assault. These assumptions about their own righteousness given the stereotype of sexually aggressive black men proved persistent, even if the immediate trigger for a lynching often lay elsewhere.[18]

Historian Grace Hale shows how lynchings were part of an emerging modern media society in the American South, which facilitated a particularly rapid circulation of representations of African Americans. Newspapers, photographs, postcards, and artifacts helped publicize lynchings and disseminate images of allegedly violent, sexually impulsive African Americans. Plays in theaters and movies, such as D. W. Griffith's *The Birth of a Nation*, lauded the good old South of the slave era and lamented its demise. African Americans were presented as infantile simpletons, cunning sexual predators, or loyal servants to white masters and good souls—yet rarely ever as critically reflective, earnest, and caring human beings.[19]

These racist stereotypes have never been simply accepted but rather have always been criticized and contested. In the early 1890s Ida B. Wells countered this self-perception of white male mobs as protectors of their wives and daughters against black barbarians. Rather, she argued, they themselves were the barbarians and the act of lynching was a barbaric practice destroying black social and family bonds. The National Association for the Advancement of Colored People (NAACP) advanced similar arguments in their fight against lynching. They provided an alternative interpretation of the many lynching photographs. In white southern households, picture postcards were found on kitchen walls or in family albums and seen as evidence of responsible and protective white men, while the NAACP magazine *The Crisis* frames the very same images as showing bloodthirsty white mobs who hunted and tortured innocent African Americans to death.[20]

In the 1920s the Harlem Renaissance offered artistic, musical, and literary expressions of this critique. The Great Migration of African Americans from the South into northern, midwestern, and western cities led to new black neighborhoods in Harlem, New York, on the South Side of Chicago, and in Watts. Charles Burnett's family had moved to Los Angeles from Mississippi, and in *Killer of Sheep* Stan, his wife, and his children show repeatedly their close ties to the rural South of their past. On the one hand they want to leave this past behind because it meant poverty and subjugation, but on the other it is part of who they were.[21]

The Great Migration led to greater and more vociferous criticism of the racial violence against African Americans. Yet it also transported the image of the angry dangerous black man from the rural South to the urban North. The 1933 movie *King Kong* presented an allegory for the dangerous displacement of a physically oversized "black ape" who lusted after white women and who came across as both out of place and pitiful in the urban jungle of the metropolis. In his 1940 novel *Native Son* writer Richard Wright turned the story into a critique of African American living conditions in the ghettos of the metropolitan areas outside the South. Drawing on the plot of *King Kong*, Wright created with Bigger Thomas a young man who is overwhelmed by the tensions between poor and rich and by the different life paths and expectations. The stereotypical accusation against black men of lusting after white women is burned into his consciousness. The fear of being discovered in the bedroom of the daughter of his new employer leads him to commit his first murder, even though there is no sexual connection involved. Frantz Fanon, postcolonial critic *avant la lettre* and among the first scholars of black masculinity, commented that "in the end, Bigger Thomas . . .

responds to the world's anticipation."[22] In the novel Bigger grows up without a father. Wright himself was influenced by sociologist E. Franklin Frazier from Howard University, who described absent fathers as the cause of a lacking sense of direction particularly among young men.[23]

Seventeen years after Wright portrayed the urban African American violent offender as a product of a racist society, the writer Norman Mailer celebrated the black outlaw as the last manly hero in a degenerative consumer and family-oriented society. Mailer urged his mostly white 1950s readers to overcome their confines and live a life beyond conformity, security, and family togetherness. Only the daily struggle for survival on the street would keep real men alert. In his essay on the *White Negro* Mailer reiterated racist stereotypes of uncontrollable black physicality. Mailer worshiped the black urban outlaw as embodiment of true masculinity, outside the constraints of security, beyond "mother and the home, job and the family." He was not interested in the struggling black working-class father or the civil rights activist. But according to Richard Wright and also Charles Burnett, African American urban manhood between 1940 and 1980 was defined less by militancy than by despair; it was less orgasmic than sexually debilitating. Norman Mailer seems to have missed that.[24]

Mailer's writings impressed Eldridge Cleaver, whose collection of essays *Soul on Ice* became a political manifesto for the era. Cleaver found Mailer's essay prophetic since it cut to the core of white weakness and black strength. Clever advocated for recapturing black manhood as a political strategy and as a goal, for which one had to be willing to destroy the world, to target white man's innermost fears, and to see the rape of white women as an act of resistance, for which one had to practice on black women. Cleaver used the stereotype of the oversexualized black man as a political strategy: "Rape was an insurrectionary act. . . . [By raping white women] I felt I was getting revenge. From the site of the act of rape, consternation spreads outwardly in concentric circles. I wanted to send waves of consternation throughout the white race."[25]

He felt that only once he had succeeded in escaping the shame of his centuries-long denied manhood, in overcoming the pain and humiliation of the defeated warrior and the wounds of castration, would he be able to stand tall, face the black woman, and fulfill his male role as protector and provider. For Cleaver, the flight from southern plantations to northern and western cities hardly brought relief to African American men. For black women it was now time, conjectured Cleaver, "to put on your crown, my Queen, and we will build a New City on these ruins."[26]

Cleaver's manifesto culminated in a motif that had been raised thirty years earlier by E. Franklin Frazier and that Charles Burnett would address ten years later in his *Killer of Sheep*, even though very differently, namely the (dis)ability of African American men, partners, and fathers to shape their and their families' lives in the urban ghettos. In 1968 Cleaver preached aggression and violence in a visionary scenario of the future full of pathos and optimism. Burnett, on the other hand, has Stan turn his frustrations inward. If at all, Burnett at most allowed a faint glimmer of hope that happy couples and new communes would emerge out of the urban ruins of Watts.

At about the same time when Burnett shot *Killer of Sheep*, female black social and cultural critics condemned the pompous-patriarchal machismo in the style of Eldridge Cleaver as antifeminist and counterproductive. Writer Michele Wallace argued in 1979 that Cleaver was interested not in the equality of all human beings but rather in the black-masculine appropriation of white male power. The result was the continuation of female oppression and a new era of violence, hysteria, and confusion. In her book *Black Macho and the Myth of the Superwoman* she also deconstructed passages from Norman Mailer's *White Negro* and denounced both black and white machismo.[27]

Few white men and women shared Mailer's enthusiasm for the black outlaw who was transgressing the confines of his existence. To the contrary, this male type became a widely disseminated horror scenario, particularly with the radicalization of the civil rights movement, with Malcolm X, and with black power.[28] While black power advocates attracted quite a few supporters among white intellectuals and students, they were mostly portrayed as militant and ready for violence in the media. They were rarely described as activists who struggled for better living conditions in their community or who advocated for social policies, housing rights, or the strengthening of African American families.[29] This is particularly true for the Black Panther Party, which became the most visible emblem of black radicalism, militarization, violence, and the will to revolution. One of the first branches of the Black Panthers outside of the original group in Oakland was formed in Watts.

While the Panthers took on the function of male protectors and pa-
trolled black neighborhoods in order to protect residents from excessive
police violence, white journalists continued to write stereotypical stories about black men, portraying them as endangering the social order
through violence.[30]

Until the 1970s journalists hardly picked up on the community work
and grassroots campaigns of the Panthers, activities geared toward tasks
traditionally reserved for families. Yet most party members were at work
on educational and social projects, medical care, and breakfast programs
for school children. Eldridge Cleaver himself emphasized at the end of
1969 how much his own perspective had changed over the years with
respect to initiatives such as the breakfast programs. He praised them
as a second step toward a revolution, for they meant "liberation in practice," pointed the way out of poverty, and shifted the parameter of the
system. Historian Peniel E. Joseph noted that above all the increasing involvement of women had made the close connection between economic
inequality, racism, and misogyny more visible. Male Panthers for their
part recognized the social programs and neighborhood engagements
as opportunities to claim for themselves the role of collective provider
in addition to that of the armed protector. Men saw themselves as caring for the well-being of the community. "On Meeting the Needs of the
People" was the title of one of Cleaver's essays in which he praised the
breakfast programs as a revolutionary measure. Even Elaine Brown, one
of the first recruits and since 1974 chairwoman of the Panthers, who
could be quite critical of the gender segregation in the Panther's day-to-
day chores, was quite fascinated when she joined the party by black men
taking on responsibility for the community.[31]

Against the Stereotypes: Fatherhood

When *Killer of Sheep* came out, sociologists had long been writing about
an alleged lack of responsibility and a failure of black men as fathers.
Daniel Patrick Moynihan's 1965 study, *The Negro Family: The Case for
National Action*, moved the image of incompetent and absent fathers to
the center of the political debates about African American family, masculinity, and civil rights. Lyndon Johnson drew heavily on Moynihan's
analysis in his famous speech at Howard University on June 4, 1965.[32]

When the Moynihan Report was made public, critics immediately noticed its explosive implications for the civil rights struggle. African Americans' discontent with living conditions in black ghettos had just culminated in the riots in South-Central Los Angeles. In the white public eye, Moynihan's findings were soon considered the foundation for the Johnson administration's approach to urban violence.[33]

Moynihan identified a pathological condition within the African American family as the main problem of black communities. He drew on traditional notions of the importance of the nuclear family for the development of character and social competency: "The family is the basic social unit of American life; it is the basic socializing unit." Therefore, he continued, the disintegration of the African American family was "the fundamental source of the weakness of the Negro community at the present time." This weakness, he surmised, was above all the result of the systematic undermining of the male position since slavery. The black woman, E. Franklin Frazier had already written in 1939, was the "mistress of the cabin."[34] The connection between male self-conduct, family conduct, and collective well-being was emphasized. Different from the 1930s, black poverty received greater attention because it was considered to be the source of a broader crisis in American society as well as of the radicalization of the civil rights movement. Among the leading indicators of black poverty was an unemployment rate on average twice as high as among whites; in some communities it reached 30 percent. A second indicator was that 24 percent of all black children were born out of wedlock; the proportion of female-headed households grew steadily, interpreted as confirming the thesis about black matriarchy. Fathers were criticized as absent or unable to fulfill the role of provider, and black families as more dependent on social welfare such as Aid to Families with Dependent Children, which was de facto available only to single mothers,[35]

Moynihan diagnosed a crisis of masculinity, family, and society among African Americans, with its origins in the history of slavery, segregation, and racism, which, he argued, hit black men harder than black women. Black women were often characterized as dominant and thus considered at least partly responsible for black men's malaise, rather than seen as victims of violence, oppression, and discrimination during slavery and segregation. Moynihan criticized that the buildup of a strong father figure had been impossible under slavery and that this altered family constellation was carried into the post-slavery period and to his present. Borrowing popular Freudian language, Moynihan pointed to the lack of male role models for adolescent boys, particularly in the inner cities, making a positive development for these boys less likely and the drifting into criminal behavior more likely. Mailer's heroic black outlaw thus returned in the guise of the sociopathic product of dysfunctional families built on matriarchal structures—much as the juvenile delinquent of the war and immediate postwar period was portrayed as the product of absent fathers. The result was the image of a pathological black community that was turning into a problem for America as a whole, as demonstrated by the riots in Watts and elsewhere.[36]

The White House paid close attention to the Moynihan Report during the Watts riots. It subsequently described dysfunctional African American families as the source of the unrest and young men from broken families as its motor. Moynihan deflected attention from the ongoing socioeconomic and racist discrimination suffered by African Americans as well as the structural demise of the inner cities, also caused by the government subsidizing the white flight.[37] Instead he tried to explain the unrest in Watts as a habitual self-perception among African American men to have failed as providers and protectors for their families—a deficit that was said to have turned into aggression, which in turn was interpreted as a typical reaction among men without self-conduct and self-control. This interpretation drew on the various stereotypes of African American men while ignoring the socioeconomic and political problems and discrimination of the postwar period. Some critics immediately pointed out that Moynihan appeared to blame the victims, and his report inspired a counter-historiography of the African American family during slavery and reconstruction. Various studies challenged Moynihan's historical interpretation by documenting alternative family structures in great detail, including kinship networks and socio-familial cohabitation.[38]

It is important to note that Moynihan drew on a list of studies of African American and Euro-American scholars from various disciplines. Among them were Stanley Elkin's work on the history of slavery, Gunnar Myrdal's findings in *American Dilemma*, and the work of psychologist and family researcher Kenneth Clark, whose term "tangle

of pathologies" Moynihan borrowed in his own study.[39] Most important for Moynihan, however, was the work of E. Franklin Frazier, who is
often regarded as the intellectual father of the Moynihan Report. Frazier
himself was influenced by the Chicago School of Sociology and was regarded as the intellectual heir of W. E. B. Du Bois. The latter's 1908 study
of the black family inspired Frazier to write him a letter in which he
praised the work as a foundational document for black family sociology.
Similar to Frazier and later Moynihan, Du Bois had found long-term
destructive effects of slavery on the structure of the African American
family, and particularly on the self-conduct of black men.[40]

The list of studies interpreting the dysfunctionality of the black family and the emasculation of black men as rooted in the experience of
slavery is long and varied. While the works of Du Bois, Frazier, and
Moynihan countered widespread interpretations about innate inabilities
of black men, they created a scenario of habitualized behavior of dominant black women and deficient black men. By doing so they exculpated
racism, discrimination, and political decisions made in their immediate
past and present. In *Killer of Sheep* Charles Burnett presented a different
narrative.

Killer of Sheep by Charles Burnett, 1977–2007

Twelve years after the Moynihan Report and the first riots, Stan's life in
Killer of Sheep in Watts suggested neither the triumph of black masculinity nor the end of black poverty. As Burnett was shooting his movie
in 1977, *Time* published a feature on poverty in America. The article
prophesied a return of urban violence, yet this time with no safe place
on either side of the barricades. It said that far from the American
dream and value system, a different world of poverty had emerged in the
mostly black inner-city ghettos, isolated from the rest of America. Just as
American mainstream media began a campaign for "moral leadership"
and called for reestablishing white heterosexual Christian male dominance in American society, it portrayed black everyday life as shaped by
male inertia, unemployment, welfare dependency, dilapidated housing,
broken furniture, poor nutrition, illness, alcohol, drugs, violence, and
crime. American society seemed in greater danger than ever before.[41]

After almost a quarter century of the civil rights movement and a decade of the war on poverty with an increase of spending on social welfare, work, and educational programs from $1.4 billion a year in 1960 to $15 billion in 1976, and despite the growth of a black middle class, a large underclass of marginalized and underprivileged African Americans existed, as *Time* reported.[42] About half of all black families lived in inner-city ghettos, a third of them below the poverty line of $5,500 a year for a family of four. Unemployment among African Americans stood at 13.2 percent, twice as high as among whites. In neighborhoods like Watts, unemployment topped 50 percent in 1982. The feared "underclass" lived in neighborhoods like these, and in the white American public it became synonymous with fraud, indolence, violence, and promiscuity. In public discourse racial stereotypes about black men and women melded with class characterizations, social discrimination, and political marginalization.[43]

With *Killer of Sheep* Burnett produced a critical intervention into this discourse and politics. First of all the film describes the life of an African American nuclear family, particularly its father Stan, in Watts. It shows Stan's struggle to make ends meet, to preserve his dignity, for self-determination and for respect as a person with an independent voice. The movie does not reveal how much Stan earns, yet it makes clear how important it is for Stan not to be seen as poor, to be able to provide for his family, and to improve his lot. At various points in the film Burnett addresses the discourses on the black family, the underclass, and African American masculinity, on providers, poverty, and an environment of violence; and he offers more nuanced visions on African American urban life in 1970s America. Stan's friend Bracey asks him mockingly whether now that he wants to fix up a second car, he considers himself middle class. Stan gets agitated and sets himself apart from those who are really poor: "I ain't poor. I give things away to the Salvation Army and you can't give things away and be poor. We may not have a damn thing some of the time but if you want to see someone who is poor, go around to Walter's and they live like chickens. . . . That ain't me and damn sure won't be."[44] In such moments, when striving for self-determination and prosperity, Stan embodies the pursuit of happiness, ingrained in American society as a personal and political goal. Yet he has to recognize over

F.11.2. Still from *Killer of Sheep* (dir. Charles Burnett, USA, 1977/2007).

and over again how his efforts to improve his status and to overcome the constraints in his existence are frustrated by the burden of a persistent spatial and social immobility. For even if Stan fights hard to escape poverty, his efforts never suffice to leave the ghetto behind, to overcome the racist patterns and the zoning of American cities. The crack in the motor and the flat tire epitomize the impossibility of poor black inner-city residents to reach the suburbs and become middle class.[45] Stan, however, musters the strength to keep going and not give up. This strength comes in part from his job at the slaughterhouse, giving him a sense of status and self-esteem. It steels his determination to not give up the fight, even though it drains him emotionally and sexually. Stan is no absent father. His determination to improve his and his family's living standard is in many ways a quintessentially American virtue.[46]

It is not easy for Stan, despite having a steady job, to serve as male role model, as his interactions with his adolescent son Stan Jr. show. The boy hangs out on the streets with a youth gang, plays with a BB gun, and roams around the crime-infested neighborhood. As an adolescent who drifts purposeless through life, he embodies the potential failure of fatherly leadership in family and society, even though he grows up in a nuclear family and not with one of the roughly 2.4 million single mothers, who were disparaged as "welfare moms." Over the course of the 1970s, these "welfare moms" moved to the center of the debates about black poverty. Ronald Reagan used the term "welfare queen" in his 1976 presidential campaign as a specter of all that was wrong with the welfare state, and she stood beside the "deadbeat dad" as a symbol of the demise of black family structures.[47] Since the 1960s, sociologists, the public, and political leaders had been blaming the social welfare system, designed especially to support single mothers. Aid to Families with Dependent Children, critics complained, created a culture of poverty and encouraged parents to use children as a source of income and motivated fathers to leave their families behind.

The nameless wife and mother in *Killer of Sheep* is anything but a prototypical "welfare mom." She worries about her son, who is exposed to many dangerous situations in Watts, dangers that emanate above all from the men who live in her neighborhood. She teaches her children to stay away from the conversations among these men, so as not to be drawn in to their shady business dealings. She wants to prevent these men from serving as role models for her children. At the same time she is no matriarchal figure in her household, acting like the "mistress of the cabin." Instead, she acts when necessary, for instance, when her husband

Figure 11.3. Still from *Killer of Sheep* (dir. Charles Burnett, USA, 1977/2007).

runs the danger of being pulled into a criminal scheme. When two men named Scooter and Smoke show up at her doorstep, looking and behaving like prototypical hustlers, driving a huge and shiny black car, wearing black leather jackets, sunglasses, and hats, trying to convince Stan to participate in a murderous plot, she steps in and out of the house. A conflict ensues in which both sides, wife as well as the gangsters, invoke conflicting images of manhood. The wife stands by the house, the gangsters on the curb, and Stan sits in between on the veranda looking up at them.

"You be a man if you can, Stan," Scooter urges, emphasizing that he himself grew up with a martial concept of manhood. "I mean, an animal got its teeth and a man got his fist. A man got scars on his face for being a man. And ain't nobody going to run over this nigger." Smoke adds, "Look, all we trying to do is help this nigger. You can't live if you are afraid of dying. Am I right?" Stan's wife vehemently rejects this martial-animalist self-conception with an undertone of mockery. After all, she stresses, they were living in a civilized world and not in the jungle. "Why do you always want to hurt somebody? . . . You use your brain, that's what you use. You're not an animal. . . . And who are you," she asks Stan, appealing to his sense of self, "to sit there and let them do this?"[48]

The film's depiction of an African American working-class family in mid-1970s Watts is full of nuances. Again and again it confronts stereotypical conceptions of masculinity and femininity when it shows incidents from Stan's and his wife's life: him being half naked yet weak at the same time; the men handling the motor clumsily during transport, leading to the fateful accident, which is at the same time an effect of overpowering circumstances; or the decisive action of the wife, who otherwise is anything but dominant in the house, at just the right moment. Burnett plays with and breaks up the existing stereotypes.

This is already evident in the central premise of the movie, which revolves around an African American nuclear family and its provider father. This nuclear family with female homemaker and male breadwinner is enveloped by love, but it does not contain within itself the solution to all problems. Daily life remains difficult, the path out of the ghetto is unclear, and moments of happiness together are hard to come by. The father works himself into exhaustion and despair for the family, but the fruits of his labor are not enough to break through the

Figure 11.4. Still from *Killer of Sheep* (dir. Charles Burnett, USA, 1977/2007).

barriers of his barren life. Work gives him self-esteem, but at the same time it makes him physically and mentally ill. Though Stan is physically strong, he is far from hypersexual. He has nothing to confess, he tells his friend Oscar. "I've done a lot of things, but nothing yet to make the devil blush."[49] The film rejects the glorification of violence and ghetto machismo. Stan's disillusion finds expression in despair and emotional isolation, not in coolness, anger, or violent aggression.

Charles Burnett thus relates to the subtler and more complex voices in the discourse on black men and fathers: voices like those of the Memphis sanitation workers who in 1968 fought for higher wages and better working conditions, who also melded manhood, the provider role, and the striving for social opportunity.[50] Or voices like those of black feminists, among them Michele Wallace and bell hooks, who in the 1970s began to fight black machismo in the civil rights movement while simultaneously condemning social and cultural discrimination of African American men.[51]

When in March 2007 *Killer of Sheep* was shown for the first time in a remastered version at the IFC Center in New York, critics were euphoric. The film was an "American masterpiece," the *New York Times*

218 | FAMILIES, FATHERS, AND THE BLACK COMMUNITY, 1950-2010

wrote, and the *Washington Post* commented on Stan, "He just survives, managing a quick nap and a smile to indicate that he's going to be okay." Film critic Stuart Klawans wrote in the *Nation* that the film was substantial in the real sense of the word. It was so substantial and weighty that one might consider putting it on a scale.[52] The burden carried by the black worker-father was so heavy "that he no longer smiles, or rests, or makes love to his wife."[53]

Critics did not just praise the artistic quality of Burnett's movie. They also commented on the continued explosiveness of the debates about African American families and black fathers since the first showing of the movie decades earlier. Obviously, a critical public felt a strong urge to counter the negative stereotypes of familial demise, welfare queens, and deadbeat dads with more nuanced portrayals of African American family life, femininity, and masculinity.

Debates about the black family had grown even more controversial in the 1980s, when Ronald Reagan propagated individual responsibility and introduced a policy that capitalized on shrinking the state apparatus. Self-government and responsibilization became a mantra, accompanied by a broad social, cultural, political, conservative Christian movement whose central focus became the family. Critics vociferously demanded the dismantling of New Deal and Great Society social programs. Conservative analysts and politicians declared that these programs only encouraged indolence, dysfunctional families, parents unwilling to work, and truant children who learned nothing but crime and promiscuity. The programs themselves were portrayed as the source of urban poverty. They pointed out how the social malaise was worsened by rapidly rising divorce rates, an increase in the number of single mothers, unsupervised children, and an extraordinarily high rate of teenage pregnancies in comparison to other industrialized countries.[54] This was generally seen as a quickening demise of "family values," which conservative critics blamed on the permissive spirit of the 1960s. The nuclear family was romanticized as the ideal antidote and projected into the American past as the "natural" historical foundation for American society.[55]

What held true for families in general held true especially for African American families. Talk of dysfunctional and broken families proliferated everywhere, including the assumption that the weakness of the black family was above all the result of black men's lack of responsibility and leadership and that its consequence was social misery and impover-ishment. A frantic wave of actions and publications ensued in the 1980s, in which a coterie of experts and politicians demanded "a cure" for black families, called on "the real black family" to show itself, and borrowed genocidal terminology to express their fears of the "extinction of the black family and the black race." Census data at the beginning of the new millennium created new fodder to keep the discourse alive. The 2000 US census found that 69 percent of all African American children were born to unmarried women; 55 percent lived with only one parent, com-pared to 23 percent among whites; and only about 40 percent of African American adults were married.[56]

The many voices in this discourse are hard to systematize since they included white conservative think tanks; black intellectuals, some more conservative others more liberal; white politicians and political consul-tants; black community organizers; and many others. Together, they created a cacophony of voices that revolved around the demise of the black family, generating grave concern about the effects on the black community, the "black race," and even human civilization. For instance, one of these voices was Kristin Taylor, between 1987 and 1990 media consultant in the Reagan and Bush administration and author of a book on black fatherhood. She called for "the healing" of the black family, thus asserting its pathological condition. She blamed male failure and de-manded they develop healthy concepts of manhood. Taylor urged men to relearn hard work and to become protector, provider, and friend. She held up ten commandments to give expression to the spiritual charac-ter of this mission, each being introduced with a promise exacted from black men.[57] Another voice was that of Mark Anthony Neal, African American intellectual who referred to himself as a "feminist dad." He celebrated fatherhood as the "fullest expression of our masculinity," his-torically denied to African American men. But, Neal proposed, the time had come for the "new black men."[58] A similar but more conservative argument was advanced at a conference at Morehouse College in 1998. Participants issued a "call for action" and declared in a religious tone a "shared mission" to overcome the weakness of the black man and the black family. Here too ten commandments were formulated to help ac-complish the goal. Another call to action came through the Million Man March, which brought several hundred thousand men to the Washington Mall on October 16, 1995, to repent, to show strength, to promise improvement in getting their lives back on the right path, and to better support their families and their community. The march excluded women and nonblack men and all men whose philosophies of life did not include being a provider and protector for their families.[59]

Countless other projects, studies, interviews, and books of all kinds contributed to this discourse, including many that demanded the recognition of alternative concepts of African American families rooted in African history. Almost all these writings found points of connection that linked individuals to couples, to family, to community, and ultimately to civilization. Psychologist and education specialist Daryl M. Rowe wrote of "one of the most significant challenges . . . in this era."[60] A liberal society founded on self-control and self-guidance, governed through the family; a gender order that defines self-control and self-conduct primarily as male competencies—such a society regards dysfunctional families and faltering or absent fathers as the epitome of personal and political failure.

This conflict continued, as for instance heated reactions to the award-winning 2009 film *Precious* show. The film portrays the life of an African American teenager in New York in the 1980s who is raped and impregnated by her father and abused by her lazy alcoholic mother, whose mission is to educate her daughter in becoming a good welfare recipient. Precious ultimately is able to escape the abuse with the help of a group of light-skinned social workers, who point the way toward self-reliance and a better life. Film critic Armond White characterized the movie as a sociological horror show filled with clichés. No film since D. W. Griffith's notorious *Birth of a Nation* from 1915 had humiliated black people and families as much as *Precious*. Mark Anthony Neal worried that the long history of negative stereotypes had contributed to the persistence of assumptions about African American inferiority and had cemented the position of African Americans at the margins of society. Sapphire, the author of the book on which the movie was based, countered that by then Michelle, Sasha, Malia, and Barack Obama were living in the White House. The images in *Precious* were, according to Sapphire, not the only ones circulating in public: "Black people are able to say 'Precious' represents some of our children, but some of our children go to Yale." The author also pointed out that the post–*Cosby Show* era had begun. Bill

Cosby was seen as "America's dad" who from 1984 to 1992 presented to an American audience week after week a black version of the white nuclear family model. Cosby also published a best-selling book on fatherhood and issued a plea to black men, families, and communities to get on the path from victims to victors. In 2018 Cosby was convicted of sexual assault, like so many other powerful men, no matter the color of their skin.[61]

Enthusiasm for the first black family in the White House was widespread but not universal in the black community when it came to its role as family model. First, some critics commented that the Obamas presented an American family life that hardly matched reality any longer. The Obamas reiterated a powerful norm that should have been abolished long ago and that served to politically, socially, and culturally demote many African American men and families. Second, Obama himself repeatedly intervened in the debates about black families and fathers. In 2004, when he gave a speech as an aspiring young senatorial candidate at the National Democratic Convention, he celebrated family values, hard work, and inner-city women and men who knew how important parenting was—much as Michelle and he knew in Chicago. "[These people] don't expect government to solve all their problems," he asserted. "They . . . will tell you that government alone can't teach our kids to learn."[62]

Obama's 2006 book *The Audacity of Hope*, about the future of America, offers more comments on black families. In one chapter he describes the conflicts with his wife and the birthday parties of his daughters, tying them to the debates about black families. Family values matter, is the tenor of this chapter, and it requires multifaceted everyday effort to maintain the family. Obama considers family of utmost importance, both politically and for the reanimation of the American dream. This particular chapter stands side by side with others about the party system, values, the Constitution, politics, faith, race, and the global order. Its position in the overall context of the book underlines the political significance of the family.[63]

As presidential candidate Obama offered further commentary on black families when he used Father's Day 2008 to remind specifically black men of their duties as fathers. At that moment in his campaign he had come under fire for his relationship with Reverend Jeremiah Wright and his radical rhetoric and politics. It was at this point that he resorted to the theme of African American fatherhood. "Any fool can have a child," he admonished his audience on June 15, 2008. "That doesn't make you a father. It's the courage to raise a child that makes you a father." To take on permanent responsibility meant the difference between boy and man, Obama continued, and too many African American fathers acted like boys and not like men. To call a black man "boy" was extremely controversial and reminiscent of the humiliation African American men had experienced in the era of slavery and segregation. Moreover, the process of maturing from boy to man had since the American Revolution served as an allegory for the ability and willingness to take on personal and political responsibility. Obama thus played with the complex reciprocity between fatherhood and good government that had linked family and manliness for more than two centuries to the political arena and had determined who was included in and excluded from the body politic. As *Time* pointed out, even if he spoke foremost to black families, his audience included the white voting public. The repeated self-presentation of the Obama family as a locus of happiness but also of conflict that was carried out and overcome contributed to the political renown of the president.[64]

The reaction to Obama's admonition to black fathers in 2008 was as varied as the discourse on the black family in general. Battle-tested civil rights activist Jesse Jackson expressed outrage at the comments, and African American intellectual Dedrick Muhammad lamented Obama's "post-racial racism."[65] On the other side was Kay Hymowitz of the *Washington Post*, who predicted that Obama, by virtue of his own family example, would significantly advance the fight for political equality in the country.[66] Bill Cosby too praised Obama for his remarks. Cosby himself had incurred criticism for creating a "black comfort zone" for white viewers with *The Cosby Show*. Media scholar Linda K. Fuller argued pointedly that *The Cosby Show* presented *Leave It to Beaver* in blackface. *The Cosby Show* sold a white ideal to a white audience, but pretended that it was black.[67]

Obama's book *Audacity of Hope* itself addresses *Leave It to Beaver* and thus the epitome of the white nuclear family ideal of the 1950s and beyond. Having grown up without a father himself, Obama describes the family of his then future wife Michelle Robinson as just such an ideal family, reminiscent of the glorified 1950s. A visit to the Robinson family felt to Obama as if he had dived into the middle of *Leave It to Beaver*. However, Obama also points out that the image of homey bliss with its gender-specific conventions was until today a burden to many men and women and how hard the Robinsons had fought against racist barriers, which were never shown on TV.[68]

Charles Burnett's *Killer of Sheep* shows precisely these barriers and how an African American family tries to cope with and overcome them. Burnett himself stated that the film showed impressions in the life of a family in Watts as they had never been seen on television. He thus gave voice and visibility to people who in the 1970s were still barely heard and seen. The film's protagonists represent multidimensional characters, not stereotypes. Even though Stan experiences failure on and on, he keeps trying to determine his own life, fulfill the expectations and demands placed on a father, and beat the odds. This message is foreshadowed in the opening scene of the film, which shows a father lecturing his fearfully shivering son: "You'll soon be a god damn man, so start learning what life is about now, son."[69]

12

Queer Parents and Fatherhood Movements, 1970–2010

It's time to talk again about family, hard work, integrity and
personal responsibility. We cannot be embarrassed out of
our belief that two parents, married to each other, are better
in most cases for children than one.
—Vice President Dan Quayle about family values and the
TV character Murphy Brown, May 1992

Queer Families and Reflections on Values

Bernal Heights is among the most desirable neighborhoods in San
Francisco. Located in its southeastern part, it mostly escapes the fog
that typically envelops the rest of the city, and those who climb to the
top of the steep hill are rewarded with a beautiful view over the bay and
town. The neighborhood has the reputation for being lively and family-
friendly at the same time. The people who live in Bernal Heights have
arrived. They get up early in the morning, have steady jobs, own their
home, and appreciate the local park as well as the nearby hip Mission
District, even if they rarely go there anymore.

At the time of the interview in 2010 Heidi and Ren had lived in a
house in Bernal Heights near the park for about ten years, with their
daughters Isabella (ten) and Teddy (five), two dogs, cats, chickens in
the backyard, and a tenant. Both have jobs, one as a math teacher at
a middle school in a blighted neighborhood, the other as a librarian
for two different schools. Ren describes their life in the neighborhood:
"We know everybody on the block. We have lived here for ten years.
We have a block party. We go to the meetings of the block party, and
talk about the cars getting broken into. . . . I don't think a single person
on this block thinks even twice about the lesbians on the corner with
the kids and the dogs." Heidi adds, "We are not the only lesbian couple;

we don't stick out." Ren reflects further: "The lesbians with kids, they live here in this neighborhood. We're like, you know . . . : we're like a stereotype."[1]

Heidi and Ren belong to a large group of gays and lesbians, who view marriage, family, and parenthood no longer as the embodiment and motor of heteronormative repression but as a major step in their lives and to full civic recognition.[2] Heidi and Ren are not married, but live together in a civil union.[3] Next to gay marriage, early twenty-first-century debates about civic equality particularly revolved around the right to serve openly in the military.[4] "I'm very anti-military and anti-war," Ren claims, "marriage and war, . . . I didn't choose those two issues. . . . But how could you disagree with that? Of course we should have the same rights." Queer critics compared the long heteronormative battles against gay marriage to the anti-miscegenation laws during slavery and segregation.[5]

By founding families, queer parents are positioning themselves no longer at the margins, but at the center of society and the social order. They encounter strong opposition from conservatives who lament the demise of the traditional family, and in particular from the heterosexual father movement that emerged in the 1990s and saw the women's movement and lesbianism as its main enemies Through its activism and dynamic the fatherhood movement has garnered great media attention and publicity and filled sports stadiums and the Washington Mall, whose monuments embody the political values and ideals of the republic. What is the relationship between queer families and the so-called most recent crisis of masculinity, fatherhood, and family values? Do male cries of crisis, combined with self-accusations and pledges toward conscientious fatherhood, contribute to the return of heterosexual men to the center of family and society?[6]

These questions are addressed in this chapter. Heidi and Ren, their daughters Isabella and Teddy, and their fathers Mike and Shum help shed light on new and different family formations in the twenty-first century. The wider context of their portrait will be provided by the contradictory political movements, from the LGBT movement to the heterosexual fathers' rights movement. First, however, I provide a broad overview of the history of same-sex relations since the mid-twentieth century.

Counterculture, LGBT Movement, and the Bay Area after World War II

When Ren and Heidi moved to the Bay Area in the late 1980s and early 1990s, San Francisco had a long established reputation as the capital of same-sex life in the United States if not worldwide. Ren arrived from New York, where she had been a political activist connected to the AIDS Coalition to Unleash Power, also known as ACT-UP. ACT-UP had formed in New York in 1987 with the goal of garnering greater public attention for AIDS and ending its stigmatization with spectacular actions such as the occupation of the New York stock market. Ren was also among the hundreds of thousands of protesters who in October 1987 participated in the Great March on Washington. The politically and culturally conservative climate during the Reagan era and the continued stigmatization and exclusion of homosexuals in general, and HIV-positive individuals in particular, had galvanized people and reinvigorated the struggle for gay and lesbian civil rights.

The 1986 Supreme Court decision in *Bowers v. Hardwick* also generated fierce protests for upholding the criminalization of oral and anal sex between consenting adults. The queer community went to Washington with a long list of demands, among them the legal recognition of same-sex partnerships and reproductive freedom. "Love Is What Makes a Family," one of the buttons at the march read. Reproductive technologies, such as artificial insemination, were since the 1970s geared toward heterosexual couples encountering male infertility. For lesbian women they were officially unavailable. Ren realized in the late 1980s that she wanted to be in the queer center of the country, which is why she moved to San Francisco in 1989.[7]

Heidi arrived around four years later. She had grown up in rural Michigan and Arizona, then went to college in Maine and at the University of Mississippi. Ole Miss was considered one of the most conservative institutions of higher learning in the United States. Historian John Howard points out that in the second half of the twentieth century even Mississippi provided spaces for same-sex encounters, above all at its universities. Still, Heidi emphasizes that "the South was hard for a young gay person to live." The story of her youth is at once a story of queer provincial life and at the same time a story of urban attraction, with the latter being a dominant narrative in queer historiography. Heidi ultimately decided that "the Bay Area . . . just felt like the place I needed to move to."[8]

Historians trace the origins of San Francisco as a hub of sexual diversity as far back as to the gold rush in the mid-nineteenth century. Around the turn of the twentieth century a gay male world had grown, with bars, clubs, hotels, and entire streets and neighborhoods serving as spaces for same-sex encounters and the construction of individual and community identities.[9] Some women lived in a marriage-like relationship, independent of any male support, in so-called Boston marriages.

World War II is considered a watershed moment in the queer history of San Francisco. Its harbor became a gathering point for young men waiting to be shipped off to war in the Pacific. Before embarking sailors wanted to enjoy one last night on the town, which led to the expansion of the bar scene in the city. The military environment and the theaters of war themselves created homosocial spaces far removed from the small-town worlds known to most young GIs.[10] In World War II women worked in predominantly female offices and factories. When they began to serve in the military in 1943 by joining the Women's Army Corps, immediately rumors came up about sexual transgressions. Parents feared that daughters who served in WAC would either be abused as prostitutes to satisfy male soldiers' sexual lust (much like the Japanese comfort women) or turn into masculinized lesbians.[11] WAC and the US military redoubled their efforts to present a straight image of the armed services, revealing how serious their concerns were, but also how homoerotically charged the atmosphere was in the military. Thousands of GIs received so-called blue discharges, which, while not signaling a dishonorable discharge or criminal misconduct, nonetheless represented sexual transgression and meant stigmatization and the loss of privileges such as the benefits of the GI Bill. As historian Margot Canaday argues, the wartime struggle for a straight army transitioned seamlessly into the Cold War struggle for the straight state.[12]

In Cold War America a straight liberal-capitalist society seemed to require a straight gender order. It was considered a given that (above all male) homosexuality signaled the submission of the self to conduct from others, in contrast to the active self-conduct of heterosexual men, which was said to climax in successful fatherhood. Non-fathers were feared more than ever. In the nuclear age, nuclear families with men and women who demonstrated their unambiguous preference for heterosexuality were considered more important than ever. The Cold War struggle against communism on the home front meant persecuting suspected homosexuals. This witch hunt put enormous pressure on men and women to conform to sexual and family conventions. Even small deviations from the straight path could pose a threat to one's social, occupational, and political position.[13]

However, the sexual conformity of the postwar decades was not as clear-cut as generally assumed. For instance, the best-selling Kinsey studies from 1948 and 1953 documented same-sex experiences among broad sections of the American population. In December 1952 Americans were fascinated by the story of Christine Jorgensen, who underwent sex change surgery. In addition, successful literary works, plays, and films, such as Tennessee Williams's 1955 *Cat on a Hot Tin Roof*, inspired queer readings.[14]

At the same time an avant-garde subculture spearheaded by the Beatniks broke with literary, social, and sexual conventions and experimented with drugs and alternative life and love styles. Many of their adherents settled in the North Beach area of San Francisco, between Chinatown and the harbor, which had been a gay neighborhood for quite some time. After the war had ended many GIs returned to San Francisco, and the city became a magnet for young people who found it hard to fit into the postwar heteronormative matrix. Other cities too developed and consolidated queer spaces, among them New York, Chicago, and Washington.[15]

The 1950s and 1960s saw an increasing politicization of the struggle. After the Stonewall riots, beginning on New York's Christopher Street on the night of June 27, 1969, the struggle for gay rights became more open, revealing more clearly its synergies with other civil rights groups, such as second-wave feminism in particular. A society centered around white, heterosexual, nuclear families faced increasing scrutiny and attack. Individuals with different living arrangements fought more openly for recognition and change. "Gay power" became an analogue to "black power," and more and more Gay Liberation Fronts formed all over the country, from Chicago to Tallahassee, with local chapters, bars, and book shops.[16]

In this context marriage and the nuclear family as the locus of the republican liberal order were turned on their heads. They became branded as major instruments of a heteronormative oppression of different desire and living arrangements. "Almost everything I was reading at the time led me toward lesbianism," feminist writer and publisher Coletta Reid stated. "In a free society everyone will be gay," Allen Young of the Gay Liberation Movement declared, upending the long-established correlation among freedom, social order, and heterosexuality.[17]

By the end of the 1970s more and more bars, bookshops, and stores, entire streets, and whole neighborhoods, such as the Castro, were gay, and the LGBT movement had scored some memorable legal and political victories. In 1974 Congress passed the first civil rights act on behalf of homosexuals, and that same year the American Psychiatric Association stopped classifying homosexuality as a mental disorder. In 1975 Elaine Nobel was elected to Congress, and two years later Harvey Milk was elected to the San Francisco City Council. By 1979, at least in California, it became illegal to fire people from their job for being homosexual.[18]

In the mid-1980s, Ren recalled, "the second wave of gay rights activism" began, in response to the conservative Reagan Revolution and mainstream Americans touting family values as a way to save America from moral decay. They converged with a newly powerful Christian-conservative movement that derided AIDS as God's punishment for a licentious lifestyle. Antifeminism grew stronger, accusing feminists and lesbians of having plunged men, particularly fathers, into a massive crisis that threatened America to the core. In the 1990s more heterosexual men grew increasingly concerned about their status, facing an ever more powerful feminism and now even spreading a so-called "Gayby-Boom."[19] More lesbian women fought for access to reproductive technologies, and a growing number of men obviously feared that heterosexual fathers had become obsolete.

Becoming Parents, Being Parents

Asked when she first knew she wanted to have children, Ren answered, "I always knew that I would have kids," even though her parents had never pressured her about grandchildren. Both her sisters had male partners but remained childless: "It is kind of funny that I have two sisters, and they are both straight, you know, . . . and they are not going to have kids." In the 1990s she broke off a long-term relationship with a partner fifteen years her senior because she did not share her wish for children. Back then it was very unusual for lesbians to be pregnant: "Of all the lesbians I knew, I was one of the first ones to go ahead and just do it." She knew lesbians with grown children from earlier relationships with men. "And, then, in the last, I would say like ten years, it's become, at least here where we live, very common for lesbians to have babies. A friend of mine wrote a book about getting pregnant when you are a lesbian."[20]

The book by Ren's friend Rachel Pepper is not the only one on the market that has sold well since the early 2000s. Mike and Shum, fathers to five-year-old Teddy, also consulted advice books as they approached fatherhood.[21] Knowledge about becoming and being fathers is also being shared in private groups such as the San Francisco Gay Dads. Lesbians also built networks that have existed since the late 1970s, exchanging information about artificial insemination. As a librarian and mother, Ren serves as a key node of communication in these networks. Furthermore, a growing cohort of lawyers specialize in legal aspects of gay parenthood, and in places like the Bay Area sperm banks and father exchanges focus specifically on a gay clientele. Heidi/Ren and Mike/Shum found each other through a provider located on the other side of the bay.[22]

When Ren expected her first child in 2000, the so-called gayby boom had been growing for some time. She recalled that "we all started to become 34, 35 years old, and then it's like, you gotta figure it out." The terms "lesbian" and "mother" had for decades seemed incompatible; lesbians had been regarded as "anti-mothers" who would topple the family lifestyle. Yet a growing number of queer individuals saw parenthood as part of their life. In the 1990s more gay male couples started families through adoption or surrogate mothers. More lesbians turned to sperm banks and reproductive technologies. "You need to have a level of stability in order to get into the parenting game," Shum pointed out. "A lot of out gay people are kind of now hitting middle age and making families and at least in San Francisco having some prosperity, which will allow them to have kids." For sure, there is some class diversity among gay and lesbian parents.[23] Between 15 and 27 percent of gay men in the United States in 2010 were fathers, and at the millennial turn about a fifth of all lesbian households included children. The statistics vary significantly, depending on how conservative the calculations are. The Census Bureau included data on same-sex partnerships for the first time in 2010. Family configurations in the United States had shifted dramatically at the beginning of the twenty-first century, as the 2000 census showed. Only 7.7 million of the 110 million households in America still conformed to the ideal of the middle-class family with a working father and a stay-at-home mother.[24]

Ren, too, emphasizes how important this generational shift is for the gayby boom. Many among the younger generation of lesbians are well established and have greater access to social resources than earlier generations. For Heidi, children were not initially part of her life plan, in part because of her own unsettled childhood, at times living with her grandparents, without a father, or with several stepfathers, which she described as hard. In the 1990s her then partner brought a child from a previous heterosexual marriage into the relationship, which lasted for six years.[25] To this day, Heidi has stayed in close touch with that daughter. It was during this time that children became part of her life concept.[26] Pregnancy and birth, however, were not among the experiences she was eager to have. Since Heidi and Ren met online, they discussed the desire for children early. There was never any doubt which one of them would go through pregnancy. Ren's older daughter was already fifteen months old at the time, and there existed little doubt that Ren would carry the second child as well.

Ren and Heidi's recollections confirm that the desire for children was a question not of sexual preference but of individual socialization, personal preferences, existing opportunities, and a host of other factors.[27] This is similar with Mike and Shum, who differ in their attitudes toward childbearing. While Mike knew before he came out that he wanted to be a father, Shum grew into it gradually. He was a political activist and had worked for Jimmy Rivaldo, campaign manager for Harvey Milk, yet he did not feel the need to politicize his own attitude toward gay fatherhood. "I don't really have a strong identity of being a gay father," he stated. He thinks much less than Mike about fatherhood and what it means to be a gay father, but he agrees with him: "We think of ourselves as normal." They have never attended a meeting of the San Francisco Gay Dads. Normalization, which in this case means consciously considering one's life as normal, can also be a political strategy. Shum is aware of this, and he regarded this strategy as useful in the fight for the right to same-sex marriage.[28]

Mike and Shum met in college and have been a couple for eighteen years. They have lived together in Europe and in different cities in the United States. Married by now, they never just wanted to donate sperm. Particularly Mike felt strongly about this: "I was really committed, and I wanted to be a father, I wanted to be involved, I wanted to play a part in this child's life—that was essential." It was not just about their own sensibilities. It was also about the desire to not let the child grow up with a lie. The child should know that he or she has a mother and father. Hence they never considered a surrogate mother, independent of the high cost. They thought about adoption, but the complexity of the process and the extremely high cost to gay men, which exceeded even the means of a political consultant and a teacher, deterred them.

Mike and Shum share with Heidi and Ren their disdain for anonymous sperm donors. Ren in particular has strong feelings about this. She regards knowledge of one's parents and family as a birthright, as "this big question" that preoccupies all adoptive children. In coming years, she predicts, this will become an even bigger preoccupation as the many children of the gayby boom embark on a search for their sperm donors and possible half siblings. The movie *The Kids Are All Right* broached the topic in 2010 and became subject of much debate for months. Particularly in the age of the internet and databases as well as the boom in genealogical searches for one's own ancestors, a search for one's family origins can easily lead to a painful experience, Ren thinks: "Why would I really need to put my child through all that [pain], if I don't have to?"[29]

For Ren, the solution initially seemed to persuade a good friend from her college days to serve as a father. Yet as is so often the case when mothers and fathers are acquainted and friends, despite a signed contract Isabella's father found it hard to adjust to his role in this family constellation.[30] Rainbow Flag Health Services offered an alternative for the second pregnancy. First, it referred no anonymous sperm donors so that children could know who their fathers are. Second, donors at Rainbow Flag were looking to play an active role in the life of the child, and the plan said that mothers should integrate them in the family over the course of the first year of the child's life. Third, the institute would release a donor's sperm to no more than four women, so that the family networks remained manageable with a finite number of half siblings. Fourth, the sperm was delivered by certified medical professionals, which meant that mothers and fathers had a clearly defined legal relationship with each other. The father had no legal right to the child, yet could also not be forced to pay child support.[31]

As it turned out, Mike, who was more adamant about becoming a father, produced sperm that was unusable after it had gone through the freezing phase. Shum, on the other hand, who had jumped on the bandwagon of fatherhood thanks to Mike, became the father of three children between February and September 2005, among them Teddy. Another child lives in Oakland, just across the bay, and the third child lives in North Carolina. The mothers flew across the continent in order to use the services of Rainbow Flag. The family networks became even more multifaceted because the mothers in North Carolina decided after two years that they wanted a second child with the same male couple. Mike therefore traveled to North Carolina in order to donate his sperm without having to freeze it first. A side remark by Mike reveals how much fatherhood and family conceptions have changed since the gayby boom. The children in North Carolina, five-year-old daughter Ada and two-year-old Walker, do not have the same biological procreator yet the same fathers, and they deliberately use the plural: "It was important [for the mothers], that it was the same fathers." Even if Mike and Shum differentiate who of them the biological procreator for each child is, they regard themselves as fathers to all five children, including Isabella. In Heidi's and Ren's household, they are also seen as a single unit, as "MikeShum."[32]

Family entanglements and family reactions are diverse. Grandparents, uncles, and aunts exhibit different reactions to the birth of a grandchild, niece, or nephew, depending on how much interest they have for children in general, but also on how well they accept the specific circumstances of these children's conception. Some are enthusiastic, like Ren's parents and Shum's father and second wife, not just because of the joy of becoming grandparents but also because they did not anticipate that their gay child would make them grandparents. Mike's brother, who is a conservative Christian, on the other hand, seems to have difficulty defining his relationship to his nieces and nephews. He thinks of the concept of a "nephew" much like he thinks of the term "marriage" as reserved for a legally sanctioned heterosexual relationship. Some queer families are trying to move beyond labels, such as mother and father, and instead are inventing a new terminology, such as "donor daddy" to express more accurately the new family constellations and the male function in them. Mike's rather conservative parents long struggled with the novelty of the situation. "Because it's that no one they know or have ever known, has been in a situation like this," Mike explains. "My parents are like small-town Texas people. But at the same time, they love all the kids, and even Isabella, who is not, you know, blood related to anybody."

Queer families tend to have many relatives, which means many visitors. Heidi, Ren, Mike, and Shum do not have close relatives nearby. This is, of course, not particular to queer families. Yet the significance of these new family networks is certainly a consequence of the typical gay-lesbian narrative (if there is any), as Shum points out: "Most people in San Francisco and New York and Los Angeles, they don't have fifty relatives within a half-hour drive, so this kind of changes your relationship to your community." Only after recognition of queer life grew was it possible to consolidate and stabilize these new social and family structures. They contribute to what Shum identified as the level of stability necessary to succeed in the "parenting game."

The families' daily routines are typical of the joys and challenges of working parents. Besides two jobs, school, and daycare, the children need to be taken to swim practice and piano and violin lessons, and playdates need to be arranged as well. Heidi walks the dogs in the morning before work and looks after the chickens. Ren is off work on Fridays and does the weekly shopping. Pursuing any hobbies requires utmost personal discipline. While Heidi is a devoted baseball fan, Ren is passionate about surfing and triathlon, requiring an elaborate workout schedule. Mike and Shum help as much as they can, picking the children up from school on occasion, volunteering as chaperones on school trips, taking them to their practice and lessons, or babysitting in the evenings. Parts of their weekends are also reserved for the children. The men have to juggle different families, parenting styles, and rules, depending on which child they are with at any given moment. Having multiple parental units helps ease the burden of parenting and opens new possibilities for all. "We see it as our jobs to help make those mothers' jobs as easy as we can," Mike states. Despite the intense engagements of the fathers, they remain helpers, and the way they have organized their lives currently they could or would not have any of their children live with them. An indication of the difference between fathers and mothers is that the men live in the trendy Mission District while the mothers live in Bernal Heights, knowing that they could reach the more trendy neighborhood if they wanted to.

The position of fathers in queer families is thus at once different from and similar to that of straight fathers. It is fatherhood without the so-called package deal of marriage, house, and job, something many men still think they need to provide.[33] Mike thinks a lot about the break with the package deal of the heterosexual nuclear family, about the newness of his lifestyle as a father, and about the contrast between his role and the role of his own father. He reveals that he also thinks a lot about what makes a good father. "I guess that's the thing that all dads think about," irrespective of whether they are queer or straight, he muses. Shum claims for himself no particular gay-paternal self-consciousness. He thinks of his own position much more in the context of the change toward more flexible gender relations in general, including rising divorce rates and heterosexual patchwork families.[34] He and Heidi, for instance, grew up with various parents and step-parents. "My parents got divorced when I was eight, so I grew up with father and mother living in separate houses. I think half of American kids have that happened, so I just really see our experiences being within that spectrum."

Mike adds that their patchwork family is in many ways easier to handle, precisely because the relationship with their children is not entangled with a (former) romantic relationship between mothers and fathers. "We don't have a lot of extra baggage around our relationships with all these women that don't have to do with that child. . . . In some ways it makes it really easy because there are no complications: we are there because of these kids and not because we used to love each other."

All participants stress that, for now, their living and family arrangement is still a very urban model. Ren and Heidi feel rooted in San Francisco, where Isabella and Teddy go to school in the Castro neighborhood, where teachers might be gay and where there are other children from queer families. "We can't afford a Volvo or a Prius," Ren quips, "but we do lattes, we listen to NPR, we read the *New York Times.* We are the lesbians with the San Francisco values."

Even if their San Francisco values are liberal and anything but heteronormative, all four still feel that children should be brought up by couples, or that at least there should be more than one adult who cares for and looks after them. All four also see parenthood as part of a multilayered gay and lesbian process of institutionalization that includes a reliable and stable relationship. For single parents, they assume, it is more than hard to master all the daily tasks children require. Respect for single parents who shouldered those tasks by themselves is mixed with skepticism of their ability to succeed. Ren, who was willing to be a single parent with Isabella, is most adamant in expressing those concerns. "Since I am a librarian I know all the kids in the school, I see all of them every single week, I teach all of them. . . . [I can tell], it's hard to raise a kid with only one person." Heidi adds, "It's socioeconomics, it doesn't have to do with gays or anything," which has been confirmed by a number of studies in recent decades.[35]

Parents' gender or sexual preference has no impact on the success of a parenting project, as the American Civil Liberties Union points out, "rather, it is influenced most profoundly by a parent's ability to create a loving and nurturing home—an ability that does not depend on whether a parent is gay or straight."[36] In other words, the second, third, or fourth parent does not necessarily have to be a father in the sense of the established tradition.[37] "Even though we have completely assimilated as a nuclear family, I can't say that I believe in the nuclear family," Heidi argues, addressing what on the surface appears to be a paradox. Her household with two parents and two children, she concludes, has banished the ghosts of sexism and patriarchy.

Fathers' Rights Movements

At about the same time as the gayby boom took hold, a heterosexual fathers' rights movement gained momentum. The movement was triggered by the transformations that resulted from the gay rights and women's rights movements, which all aspired to break up the privileged position of heterosexual men in society and to create a more egalitarian society through identity politics. Critics blamed the growing number of unmarried couples, divorces, births out of wedlock, and latchkey children on these changes, thus implicitly—and explicitly—demanding a social order with (white) heterosexual men and fathers at its center. Yet the fatherhood ideal, whose loss is being lamented, is more a reflection of wishful thinking than a realistic view of the past. It represents a romanticized notion of a past patriarchal order that hardly ever existed in this form. By conjuring up this order in times of social uncertainty and transformation, reactionaries clung to biologically conceived notions of stability and the fiction of an ahistorical permanence of the nuclear family. Those who demand a return to the nuclear family order with clear-cut gender divisions inhibit constructively engaging with changes toward an egalitarian and thus more content and productive society.[38]

David Blankenhorn, director of the Institute for American Values and in 1994 co-founder of the National Fatherhood Initiative, declared that since the mid-1960s the absent father had "metastasized" from the African American community into American society as a whole. Blankenhorn saw a "healthy" society threatened by a fatal disease, potentially felling the body politic, unless appropriate measures were taken immediately. While locating the origins of the disease in the black community, Blankenhorn claimed same-sex marriage was the ultimate sign of a society in complete disarray.[39] Metaphors of health and disease have been particularly popular with opponents of gay marriage and queer families. For instance, Tim Daily, fellow at the Family Research Council, which since 1981 has fought for "faith, family, and freedom," diagnosed a polygamous unhealthy lifestyle among same-sex couples, ruining children and America. In conjunction with the AIDS pandemic and how it affected the gay community, a language of health and pathology meant a powerful defamation that became prominent in the public debates of the 1980s and 1990s.[40]

Such commentaries about the threat of fatherlessness and changing family constellations became more and more widespread. Noteworthy is that the conservative fatherhood movement adopted strategies and tactics from the civil rights movement, for instance by issuing calls for action or by propagating a positive self-image of an allegedly marginalized group, namely that of white, heterosexual men. Adding their voices to the chorus were also more moderate commentators and politicians. For instance, in 1999 then Democratic senator Joseph Lieberman saw the increasing absence of fathers as "the single greatest problem plaguing our nation today." Lieberman became Al Gore's vice presidential candidate in 2000. A few years earlier, when Gore served as Bill Clinton's vice president, he himself had initiated a series of national summits on fatherhood. In his remarks at the signing of the Responsible Fatherhood Act, which promised $150 million in federal funds to states in support of programs for responsible fatherhood, Lieberman lamented the absence of fathers and its effects. Bill Clinton in 1995 had also taken up the subject, identifying absent fathers as the "biggest single social policy problem." A year later, Clinton signed the Defense of Marriage Act and the Personal Responsibility and Work Opportunity Reconciliation Act. They transformed social welfare programs away from aid to mothers with dependent children toward aid to families with mothers and fathers. Critics had disparaged the existing policy, in place since the 1930s, claiming that it was encouraging fathers to leave their families rather than reducing poverty and hardship among single mothers. Welfare for single mothers loosened the bonds of fathers to their family, David Popenoe charged. His book *Life without Father* became a manifesto for the fathers' rights movement.[41]

Since the 1980s family politics had been developing into a major political field of Christian conservatives. Ronald Reagan paved the way with his move to position the nuclear family at the heart of his neoliberal political platform. With the creation of the lean state and the growth of conservative values, the calls for traditional families as the foundation of society and as a bulwark against social erosion grew even stronger. Yet the Democratic Party was as eager to support fathers, ever since President Carter had convened his White House Conference on Families in the summer of 1980. Democrats acted with great caution when the call came for the recognition of the diversity of family formations, and they reiterated the great political power of "family values" in the political arena. When Clinton talked about the fundamental importance of family, he usually meant husband, wife, and child(ren). At the same time the conservative family rhetoric often turned out to be hypocritical, by Democrats and Republicans alike.[42]

As public proclamations celebrating family values and advocating for the survival of the nuclear family proliferated in all kinds of media, statistics revealed its demise. The struggle against the recognition of diverse family formations paved the way for the fathers' rights movement in the 1990s. It consisted of a loose coalition of initiatives, groups, and individuals who fought against the perceived marginalization of fathers in family and society. When these groups and individuals talked of the importance of two-parent families for children and society, they undoubtedly referred to heterosexual couples.[43]

The fathers' rights movement included a broad spectrum of voices, even though they were united in their opposition to the broadening of the family concept, as Wade Horn, then president of the National Fatherhood Initiative, explained. David Popenoe asserted that the heterosexual family was the natural mode of living to which humans had been biologically predisposed since the Stone Age.[44] One section within the fathers' rights movement has offered self-help groups, aiding divorced and separated fathers in establishing and maintaining legal and emotional relationships with their children. Many of the participating fathers have valued the conversation and exchange with others who face similar challenges, and some groups have offered conflict mediation. On the other end of the spectrum grew militant groups who saw disenfranchised fathers as suicidal victims of a conspiratorial alliance of feminists, lawyers, judges, and government representatives. David Usher, for instance, of the American Coalition for Fathers and Children, waged a militant campaign against the alleged displacement and enslavement of men in America, visible in the recognition and promotion of same-sex lesbian marriages. He saw the work of hateful lesbian feminists who push men into diaspora and make any healthy maturation of boys impossible.[45]

Others, such as the Mythopoetics, were searching, in a manner of vernacular Freudianism, for a deep connection to their inner manly self in order to release positive male energy.[46] Their goals were similar to those of the Promise Keepers, who filled sports stadiums with their mass gatherings. They promised spiritual renewal through Christian guidance. The reclaiming of male leadership through this method, they argued, was the best antidote to the crisis of family and morality in America. Drawing on similar spiritual motivation, yet more strongly grounded in socioeconomic arguments, was the group that organized the Million Man March for African American men in Washington in October 1995.

Their central message was to urge black men to reassert responsibility for their families.[47]

Other initiatives in the fathers' rights movement came from the afore-mentioned Institute for American Values, led by David Blankenhorn, the National Fatherhood Initiative, and similar groups. These groups have supported research, have powerful public relations strategies, and have lobbied political leaders in order to promote marriage and the family and to reclaim work and responsibility as male domains. However, some men have also established profeminist fathers' organizations that have supported the political goals of the women's movement and have advocated for breaking up patriarchal structures and for setting up a more egalitarian society for men and women.[48]

"Families Come in All Shapes and Sizes"

Some commentators see Dan Quayle, vice president under George H. W. Bush, as trailblazer for the fathers' rights movement. In a speech given on May 19, 1992, before members of the Commonwealth Club of California, he condemned a culture of irresponsible fathers and single mothers. A few weeks earlier riots had shaken Los Angeles after four policemen were acquitted of assault, even though they severely beat Rodney King after a traffic stop. The brutal beating of the black motorist included kicks and more than fifty hits with a baton. Yet in his speech Quale claimed that "the lawless social anarchy which we saw [in the LA riots] is directly related to the breakdown of family structure, personal responsibility and social order in too many areas of our society." He pointed to the so-called urban underclass, in which black women were said to depend on welfare and black men on crime. He saw social welfare programs, the permissive culture of the 1960s, and the loss of Christian values as the root causes of what he perceived as the demise of families and a general lack of personal responsibility. His speech gained notoriety, however, not for his outrageous commentary on the Rodney King case and the obvious racism undergirding it but because his jeremiad against irresponsible fathers and single mothers also included women of the educated white middle class. Quayle complained about the TV character Murphy Brown, the protagonist of a highly popular show with the same name, who decided in her mid-thirties, and at the pinnacle of her career as a TV anchor, to have a child without a man in her life. Quayle chided the TV producers: "It doesn't help matters, when prime time TV has Murphy Brown—a character who supposedly epitomizes today's intelligent, highly paid, professional woman—mocking the importance of fathers, by bearing a child alone, and calling it just another 'lifestyle choice.'"[49]

It seemed that single women, who first pushed men out of the workforce and then reduced them to being sperm donors, or worse helped themselves to male sperm at sperm banks in order to conceive a child, had become in the 1990s a major threat to the male-centered social order of the nuclear family. Quayle elaborated later in his speech that one should be prepared to recognize that two married parents, who work hard and shoulder personal responsibility, were better for a child than a single parent. He probably did not have in mind couples like Heidi and Ren or Mike and Shum. Together, they actually make four parents, all hardworking, married or legally certified in a committed long-term relationship, and very much aware of their parental responsibilities. Quayle instead shared the perspective of the fathers' rights movement, lamenting the gradual disappearance of the father's role, which was said to have changed from patriarchy in the seventeenth century to breadwinner in the nineteenth and to absent father and sperm donor in the twentieth. The movement fought to return classical notions of fatherhood and heterosexual marriage to the center of society.[50] And even if *Time* announced in 1992 that such a nostalgic family model probably existed only in Ronald Reagan's midday nap dreams, it could not ignore the power of the fathers' rights movement.[51]

While advocates of the fathers' movement, many politicians and media lament the end of the father and the family as we knew it, others, such as Heidi, Ren, Mike, and Shum, have created new networks of families and parenting in order to master the challenges of child rearing. Particularly the urban centers have entered the "post–nuclear family" age, even though the nuclear family's position in the center of society has never been as uncontested as reactionary voices want us to believe. These new family configurations are often better suited to the living conditions and concepts of many people in the Western world of the twenty-first century, regardless of whether they are queer or straight. Given the transient nature of modern urban life where families might lack direct access to familial networks, alternatives to the nuclear family rest on different kinship or patchwork networks to create a web of support for child rearing.[52]

In contrast to Vice President Dan Quayle, the producers of *Murphy Brown* were willing and able to think in this new context. In the episode aired on September 21, 1992, the character Murphy Brown reacted to Quayle's critique, in front of a television audience of forty-one million people. The episode had the title "You Say 'Potatoe,' I Say 'Potato,'" alluding to an embarrassing incident in which Quayle, during a visit to an elementary school and with cameras rolling, went to the blackboard to (mis)correct a student's spelling of potato by adding an "e" at the end. Some things might seem hard to imagine, Murphy Brown seemed to be saying, whether in spelling, politics, or family configurations, but "families come in all shapes and sizes."

Conclusion

What is a mother and a father? Obviously, this is a really
complicated thing.
—Mike, San Francisco, October 8, 2010

Mike's question is rhetorical; he knows that there is no clear answer to it.
After all, he sees himself as father of a group of four, or rather five, children, whom he and his partner have conceived or who are step siblings
to their biological children. Genetic kinship is of no major significance in
their lives as fathers. When it comes to his notion of fatherhood, it is more
important to take on responsibilities, to participate in the children's daily
lives whenever possible, to share duties with his partner and the mothers,
and to provide a stable reference point in their children's lives, than to have
participated in the biological conception of these children.

In recent decades there has been a generally growing sense of insecurity about what fatherhood and family mean. For several decades
reactionary voices have been lamenting that life forms and life norms
have become more flexible and diverse since the social and political liberation movements of the 1970s, claiming that with the nuclear family of breadwinning father and homemaking mother with two or three
children, family values have been called into question. Criticism of the
African American community is particularly fierce. In the increasingly
vitriolic debates in the early twenty-first century, they were even vilified
as the historic root cause of a cancer of fatherless families, which was
now "metastasizing" through American society.[1] With the nuclear family and the father as provider and guiding force of his family, the larger
argument goes, the traditional and even "natural" living arrangement
of human beings has gotten lost, and with it the bedrock of American
society and liberalism.[2]

However, American history shows that the nuclear family has never
been the predominant or even "natural" living arrangement and that

there has never been a clear answer to Mike's question of what a father—and a mother—is. For one, the term "nuclear family" did not exist before it was coined by sociologists in the postwar era. For sure since the founding of the nation, a family ideal that matched in large part that of the nuclear family with a caring mother and the father as guiding force had been invoked and described as the bedrock of a liberal republic. Yet already in the Early Republic fears abounded that real life did not match the ideal, and particularly that too few American men would meet the requirement for good fatherhood and thus also for full political participation at a liberal society. At the same time history shows that there were so many different kinds of families, fathers, and men whose personal lives did not match the hegemonic ideal that it does make hardly any sense to speak of a nuclear family being at the center of society and perceive all the other living arrangements as periphery. These non-nuclear-family fathers include men from several religious groups of the early nineteenth century, with the Oneida Community being just one example. They also include the many slaves, Native Americans, and many pioneers on the Overland Trail. Later in the second half of the nineteenth century, migrants flocked to the growing cities, either from the surrounding rural communities or from overseas, and they were often men coming and being without families for an extended period of time at least. All these historic configurations, such as slavery, the westward movement, migration, and urbanization, are considered defining events and powerful forces in US history, and many of its main actors are iconic characters, yet hardly any of them lived a life according to the nuclear family ideal. Networks of kinship and friends dominated the family formation of slaves as well as of many Eastern European immigrants. Men remained bachelors in the American West and in the growing cities. And widows, widowers, and orphans were everywhere as well.

Furthermore, looking back into American history shows that the concept of American society with the father as head of the nuclear family in its center has always been embattled and perceived as endangered. If there is a continuity in the modern history of fatherhood and the nuclear family, it is the ubiquity of the crisis metaphor. When at the turn from the nineteenth century to the twentieth many Americans felt overpowered by modern urban life and developed a sense of crisis, Native American men were invoked as ideal to teach Euro-Americans how to be good fathers, even though nuclear family life has hardly ever been the predominant living arrangement among Native Americans. Only a few years later the Great Depression, with its massive unemployment, was seen as threatening to destroy the father as provider of his family and with him American society. A growing crisis sociology contributed to putting or keeping the nuclear family model at center stage, at least conceptually. In real life men as fathers continued to be perceived as being in crisis. Furthermore, in times of war different concepts of manliness competed with one another, that of the good father and that of the citizen soldier. Among all the father figures in this book, it is the African American father Stan from Watts in the late 1970s who tries harder than any other to meet the challenges of being a provider and protector, in spite of all the disempowering external forces he has to face.

Obviously, giving an answer to Mike's question about what makes a father (and what makes a mother) is complicated today, but it gets even more complicated when looking into history and its messiness. US history is full of different family formations and all kinds of relationships. The middle-class nuclear family with homemaking mother and bread-winning father has never been the living arrangement of a majority of Americans, not even before the 1970s. However, and as the book has shown, even if people were not living according to the dominant model of family life, very often they were judged by others in relation to that model and also measured their sense of self in relation to it. A close look at a variety of sociological surveys, novels, films, autobiographies, letters, diaries, interviews, and other sources has revealed the enormous power that the nuclear family ideal has unfolded, even if sometimes through triggering explicit opposition to it.[3] Many historical actors arranged their lives in different family formations, which were nonetheless shaped by a critical involvement with the nuclear family concept and its formative power. This power is so strong that it is palpable in many chapters of this book, from the revolution to the present.

Thus the many fathers and family formations presented on the previous pages represent the diversity of American history and society, yet they also show the normative power of the nuclear family model and of the provider-protector father as regulatory ideal. The close-ups and life stories in this book reveal how American society granted different opportunities to different people in different living arrangements, for instance depending on their skin color, origin, or occupation, on whom they desired, or on whether they lived in rural or urban environments. Yet they also show how people dealt with the conditions and limitations of their life, how they fought against them and positioned themselves in complex and powerful assemblages. Individuals at once shaped and were shaped by history and society; they adapted to, molded, resisted, and critiqued it. Here, critique means putting oneself in relation to what was initially perceived as true, evident, and even "natural," and showing that there is no timeless essence in history, but that history is "fabricated in a piecemeal fashion from alien forms."[4]

ACKNOWLEDGMENTS

This book has been in the making over a period of fifteen years. Several people and several work and research connections helped bring it to completion. First and foremost, I have to thank the students, doctoral candidates, and colleagues at the University of Erfurt. The North-America Colloquium provides a forum for inspiration and productive criticism. The funding initiative Pro Geisteswissenschaften and the Fritz-Thyssen-Foundation generously supported my project with an Opus Magnum fellowship; Humanities International provided funding for its translation. I am also grateful to the Organization of American Historians for honoring my book with the Willy Paul Adams Award in 2015. Christian Ostermann and the Woodrow Wilson International Center for Scholars in Washington, DC, were wonderful hosts during the summer and fall of 2010. Indispensable for the success of this project was also the help and guidance of many librarians and archivists. Janet Spikes at the Wilson Center and Ryan Bean from the Kautz Family Archives of the YMCA at the University of Minnesota were especially interested, helpful, and knowledgeable.

Of equal importance were the comments of colleagues and friends who engaged with me and my ideas in workshops, conference panels, and lectures in places as far apart as Münster and Melbourne, Warsaw and Washington, DC. I want to especially thank those who read, edited, and critiqued parts of the manuscript at various stages of completion. They are Carolina Dahl, Katharina Dahl, Steve Estes, Norbert Finzsch, James Gilbert, Claudia Kraft, Nora Kreuzenbeck, Barbara Lüthi, Bryant Simon, Olaf Stieglitz, and Viviann Wilmot. Felix Krämer and Irene Martschukat read the manuscript in its entirety—thank you! Tanja Hommen and Clara Platter guided the evolution of this book with competence and patience. Petra Goedde delivered an elegant translation. Of course, all responsibility for any mistakes that made it past the editing into the final version rests with me.

NOTES

INTRODUCTION

1 Foucault, *Security, Territory, and Population*, 126–45.
2 Latour, *Reassembling the Social*, 1–17.
3 Coontz, *American Families*; Cooper, *Family Values*, 7–24.
4 Martschukat and Stieglitz, *Geschichte der Männlichkeiten*.
5 Murdock, *Social Structure*; Parsons and Bales, *Family Socialization*; Heinemann, *Wert der Familie*, 4–5.
6 Coontz, *Way We Never Were*; Hobsbawm and Ranger, *Invention of Tradition*.
7 Butler, "Performative Acts."

CHAPTER 1. FATHERS AND THE NEW REPUBLIC, 1770–1840

1 Howe, *Language and Political Meaning*, 2ff., 76; letter from John Adams to Hezekiah Niles, February 13, 1818, in National Humanities Center, "Making the Revolution"; Rush to Richard Price, May 25, 1786, in Masur, *Rites of Execution*, 64; Wood, *Revolutionary Characters*, 173–202, about Adams's growing skepticism about the republican project's chances of success; McCullough, *John Adams*.
2 Dean, *Governing Societies*.
3 Alcott, *Young Husband*, 234. These deliberations resonate with the ideas by Foucault, *Security, Territory, and Population*; Foucault, *Birth of Biopolitics*.
4 Foucault, *Government of Self and Others*, 5.
5 Smith-Rosenberg, "Dis-covering the Subject," 845.
6 Pincus and Novak, "Political History"; Stollberg-Rilinger, *Was heißt Kulturgeschichte des Politischen?*
7 Howe, *Language and Political Meaning*, 41; Staloff, *Hamilton, Adams, Jefferson*, 191ff.
8 Fliegelman, *Prodigals and Pilgrims*, 3; Wells, *Few Political Reflections*, 33; Yazawa, *From Colonies to Commonwealth*, 95; Howe, *Language and Political Meaning*, 111.
9 Paine, "American Crisis III (1777)," 79. See also Nelson, *National Manhood*, 22, 33ff.; Fliegelman, *Prodigals and Pilgrims*.
10 Lombard, *Making Manhood*, 146–69; Yazawa, *From Colonies to Commonwealth*, 85–110; Wilson, *Ye Heart of a Man*.
11 Henretta, *Evolution of American Society*, 30; Fliegelman, *Prodigals and Pilgrims*, 10.
12 James Wilson, "Address to the Pennsylvania Ratifying Convention," in Bailyn, *Debate on the Constitution*, 1:825; Kann, *Gendering of American Politics*, 98, 121.

13 Burrows and Wallace, "American Revolution," 194, 211ff.; Wilson, "Illusion of Change"; Zagarri, "Rights of Man."
14 Kann, *Gendering of American Politics*, 97; Cott, *Public Vows*, 9–23.
15 Hartog, *Man and Wife*.
16 Mintz, *Prison of Expectations*, 21–40; Pateman, *Sexual Contract*; Kerber, *No Constitutional Right*; Schloesser, *Fair Sex*; Nelson, *National Manhood*, 44–45.
17 Foucault, *Security, Territory, and Population*, 126–45; Howe, *Language and Political Meaning*, 115.
18 Cott, *Public Vows*, 21; on the growing importance of families in relation to the softening of authoritarian structures, see Mintz, *Prison of Expectations*, 28.
19 Rousseau, *Emilius and Sophia*; Rousseau, *Treatise on the Social Compact*; Locke, *Some Thoughts Concerning Education*; Locke, *Two Treatises of Government*; Fliegelman, *Prodigals and Pilgrims*, 4, 12ff., 29–30.
20 Kerber, *Women of the Republic*; Kerber, "Republican Ideology"; Zagarri, "Morals."
21 Ryan, *Empire of the Mother*.
22 Nelson, *National Manhood*, 11ff.
23 James Wilson, "Address to the Pennsylvania Ratifying Convention," in Bailyn, *Debate on the Constitution*, 1:825.
24 Mintz, *Prison of Expectations*, 31ff.; Kann, *Gendering of American Politics*, 51, 83–84; Frank, *Life with Father*, 15, 24; Johansen, *Family Men*, 84, 96; Strickland, "Transcendentalist Father," 22; Alcott, *Young Husband*, 234.
25 Griswold, *Fatherhood in America*, 4, 13.
26 Frank, *Life with Father*, 29; Gillis, *World of Their Own Making*.
27 Alcott, *Young Husband*, 257–58; James, *Young Man's Friend*, 31. For fatherhood as an indicator for maturity, see Kann, *Gendering of American Politics*, 12, 72; Johansen, *Family Men*, 22–24; Frank, *Life with Father*, 25.
28 Dorsey, *Reforming Men and Women*, 50–135; Frank, *Life with Father*, 25; Kimmel, *Manhood in America*, 13–78.
29 James, *Young Man's Friend*; Kirwan, *Happy Home*, 21, 64.
30 Alcott, *Young Husband*, 234; Alcott, *Young Man's Guide*, 32–33, 59; James, *Young Man's Friend*, 18.
31 Cited in Johansen, *Family Men*, 37, 89.
32 Johansen, *Family Men*, 83.
33 Johansen, *Family Men*, 40.
34 Foucault, *History of Sexuality*, 1:94–97; Foucault, "Subject and Power."
35 Frank, *Life with Father*, 33–34, 116.
36 Muzzey, *Christian Parent*, 90ff.; Halttunen, "Humanitarianism."
37 Muzzey, *Christian Parent*, 96ff., 100, 105; Alcott, *Young Husband*, 263; James, *Young Man's Friend*, 18; Kann, *Gendering of American Politics*, 76–77; Mintz, *Prison of Expectations*, 34; Hatton, "'He Murdered Her,'" 115; Gibbs, "Self-Control."
38 Johansen, *Family Men*, 40, 91, 96; Strickland, "Transcendentalist Father," 51.
39 Muzzey, *Christian Parent*, 96; McLoughlin, "Evangelical Childrearing." For Wayland's account, see Johansen, *Family Men*, 95.

40 Muzzey, *Christian Parent*, 101; Alcott, *Young Husband*, 269; Foucault, *Discipline and Punish*; Meranze, *Laboratories of Virtue*; Martschukat, "Horrifying Experience?"

41 Elias, *Civilizing Process*, 103.

42 Rosenblatt, *Bitter, Bitter Tears*; Pollock, *Forgotten Children*; Cole, "Keeping the Peace."

43 Pleck, *Domestic Tyranny*.

44 Kann, *Gendering of American Politics*, 85; Dorsey, *Reforming Men and Women*, 61.

45 Rorabaugh, *Alcoholic Republic*; Frank, *Life with Father*, 29–30; Dorsey, *Reforming Men and Women*, 90–135, 134–35; Alexander, "'We Are Engaged'"; Moroney, "Widows and Orphans."

46 Kirwan, *Happy Home*, 21; Alcott, *Young Man's Guide*, 32–33; James, *Young Man's Friend*, 15.

47 Kann, *Gendering of American Politics*, 79ff.

48 Dorsey, *Reforming Men and Women*, 50–89; Meranze, *Laboratories of Virtue*, 267–68, 272, 280.

49 Foucault, *Discipline and Punish*; Rothman, *Discovery of the Asylum*; Meranze, *Laboratories of Virtue*.

50 According to Cott, *Public Vows*, 21.

51 James, *Young Man's Friend*, 21; see also the *Second Annual Report of the Managers*; Rothman, *Discovery of the Asylum*, 213.

52 *Second Annual Report of the Managers*, 13. Similar views were expressed in the following years in various reports of urban reform societies. See also Mintz, "Regulating the American Family," 394ff.; Meranze, *Laboratories of Virtue*, 280. Similarly, in the early nineteenth century, the establishment of public schools was initially designed to improve the job prospects of children from poor families. Vinovskis, "Family and Schooling," 26–27.

53 In *Ex Parte Crouse* Mary Crouse had challenged the constitutionality of Philadelphia's House of Refuge because it represented a form of imprisonment without a court sentence. Meranze, *Laboratories of Virtue*, 291–92; Mintz, "Regulating the American Family," 395; Coontz, *Way We Never Were*, 128ff.

54 Cited in Peirce, *Half Century*, 56, 286.

55 *Second Annual Report of the Managers*, 11; Rothman, *Discovery of the Asylum*; Meranze, *Laboratories of Virtue*; Teeters, "Early Days," 166ff.; Sutton, *Stubborn Children*; Schlossman, *Love and the American Delinquent*.

56 Cited in Rothman, *Discovery of the Asylum*, 214–15, 235.

57 See appendix to the *Rules and Regulations for the Government of the House of Refuge*, 50ff. See also the *Second Annual Report of the Managers*, 16; *Second Annual Report of the New York Juvenile Asylum*, 7; Peirce, *Half Century*, 77, 81; Pickett, *House of Refuge*, 144.

58 *Second Annual Report of the Managers*, 9ff.

59 *Fourth Annual Report of the New York Juvenile Asylum*, 25; appendix to the *Rules and Regulations for the Government of the House of Refuge*, 55; Meranze, *Laboratories of Virtue*, 286; Pickett, *House of Refuge*, 145.

60 Cited in Peirce, *Half Century*, 89–90.

61 Cited in Peirce, *Half Century*, 91–92.

62 Rothman, *Discovery of the Asylum*, 231; Christianson, *With Liberty for Some*, 119ff.

63 Rothman, *Discovery of the Asylum*, 231–32; Pickett, *House of Refuge*, 144–45, 160–61; Teeters, "Early Days," 172, 183.

64 *Eighteenth Annual Report of the Managers*, 10.

65 Pickett, *House of Refuge*, 160–61.

66 Mintz, "Regulating the American Family," 396; Schlossman, *Love and the American Delinquent*, 33ff.

CHAPTER 2. CHALLENGING LOVE, MARRIAGE, AND THE NUCLEAR FAMILY, 1820–1870

1 Noyes, "The Family and Its Foil," *Oneida Circular* 3, no. 149 (November 16, 1854): 594; Noyes, "The Home-Spoilers," in Barren and Miller, *Home Talks*, 1:313.

2 Coontz, *Marriage*, 161–76.

3 N[oyes], "Family and Home," *Oneida Circular* 7, no. 31 (August 28, 1858): 122.

4 Noyes, December 21, 1852, in Syracuse University Library, Department of Special Collections, Oneida Community Collection, Box 70: Writings 1843–1885, Folder: 1852 D 21 "Our Victories."

5 Noyes in Cooley, *Summary Exposition*, 64.

6 "Our Home," *Oneida Circular* 3, no. 138 (October 21, 1854): 550.

7 "Statement of Principles" (November 3, 1846), Syracuse University Library, Oneida Community Collection, Box 11, Folder: 1846 Ag 18; Noyes, *My Father's House*, 80; Coontz, *Marriage*, 148; Hartog, *Man and Wife*, 155.

8 [Noyes,] "Man and His Home—Prospects," *Oneida Circular* 4, no. 21 (June, 14, 1855): 83.

9 Dubber, *Police Power*; Nelson, *National Manhood*; Wayland-Smith, *Oneida*.

10 Mintz and Kellogg, *Domestic Revolutions*, 43–45; Coontz, *Marriage*, 161–76; Gillis, *World of Their Own Making*.

11 Cott, *Public Vows*, 10ff., 52ff., 64ff.; Hartog, *Man and Wife*.

12 Griswold, *Fatherhood in America*, 5; Coontz, *Marriage*, 154ff.

13 Welter, "Cult of True Womanhood"; Cott, *Bonds of Womanhood*, preface to the 2nd ed., xvii; Nelson, *National Manhood*; Pateman, *Sexual Contract*; Mills, *Racial Contract*.

14 Kerber, "Separate Spheres"; Kerber et al., "Forum."

15 Cott, *Bonds*, 199; Kerber, *Women of the Republic*; Kerber, "Republican Ideology"; Zagarri, "Morals."

16 Ryan, *Empire of the Mother*; Ryan, *Cradle of the Middle Class*, 232; Demos, "Changing Faces of Fatherhood," 50; Demos, "Images of the American Family."

17 Frank, *Life with Father*; Johansen, *Family Men*.

18 His father served as a representative in Vermont between 1808 and 1810 and in 1812; and between 1815 and 1817 he was a Federalist representative in Congress. Thomas, *Man Who Would Be Perfect*, 118.

19 See Battan, "You Cannot Fix," for more on the "free lovers." Noyes's quote in Noyes, "Bible Communism—Pamphlet Published February 1849," cited in Noyes, *Putney Community*, 117, also 190–91; for Noyes's criticism, see *Oneida Circular*, March 21, 1870.

20 Foster, *Religion and Sexuality*, 77; Kern, "Ideology and Reality," 182; Olin, "Oneida Community," 290; Folts, "Fanatic and the Prophetess," 360ff.

21 Noyes in the Daily Journal 1863–1864, in Syracuse University Library, Oneida Community Collection, Box 11; see also "scrapbooks," Boxes 12 and 68.

22 Barkun, *Crucible of the Millennium*, 2–3; Foster, *Religion and Sexuality*, 11; Isaac and Altman, "Interpersonal Processes"; Morone, *Hellfire Nation*, 123–31.

23 Foster, *Religion and Sexuality*, 78; Sutton, *Communal Utopias*, 67–68; Kern, *Ordered Love*; Johnson, "Charles G. Finney."

24 Dorsey, *Reforming Men and Women*, 50–135; Dubber, *Police Power*, 80–90.

25 Thomas, *Man Who Would Be Perfect*, 115ff.; "Mrs. Polly Noyes to a Member of the Church," in Noyes, *Putney Community*, 33; "Petition of the Junior Members of the Noyes Family to Their Father," in Noyes, *Putney Community*, 91–92.

26 Dorsey, *Reforming Men and Women*, 134–35; Kann, *Gendering of American Politics*, 79ff.; Alexander, "'We Are Engaged.'"

27 Thomas, *Man Who Would Be Perfect*, 121; Foster, "Free Love," 172.

28 Olin, "Oneida Community," 287.

29 Noyes, *Putney Community*, 25, 202, statements from 1838 and 1846; Noyes in *Witness*, no. 1 (January 23, 1839): 43, 51; "A Copy of the 'Battle Axe Letter' Written by G.H.N., Putney, January 15, 1837," in Syracuse University Library, Oneida Community Collection, Box 70: Writings 1843–1885; see also his "Advice to Parents," June 2, 1868, about the commune as permanent revival; see also in Box 11, Folder: 1846 Ag 18 the founding declaration, November 3, 1846.

30 Noyes, *My Father's House*, 80, 125, 132.

31 Fish-Kalland, "Oneida Community," 34–35.

32 Noyes, "Improvement of Character," in Barren and Miller, *Home Talks*, 1:139–43; Kern, "Ideology and Reality," 183; Dubber, *Police Power*, 60; Morgan, *Puritan Family*.

33 Noyes, "Childhood Analogous to Heaven," *Spiritual Magazine* 1 (July 15, 1846): 69; Thomas, *Man Who Would Be Perfect*, 126ff.

34 Thomas, *Man Who Would Be Perfect*, 113, 160–61; Foster, *Religion and Sexuality*, 85; Olin, "Oneida Community," 289; Sutton, *Communal Utopias*, 72; Kern, *Ordered Love*, 208.

35 Noyes, "Houses," *Oneida Circular* 2 (December 8, 1852): 26; Thomas, *Man Who Would Be Perfect*, 119.

36 McMillen, *Seneca Falls*; Hartog, *Man and Wife*, 136–66; Cott, *Public Vows*, 64–70; Noyes, "Slavery and Marriage," in *Bible Communism*, 123–28; "Women and Slaves," *Oneida Circular*, December 17, 1853, 23; "Marriage and Slavery—The Bible Argument," *Oneida Circular* 6, no. 47 (December 10, 1857): 185; Thomas, *Liberator*, 228ff.

37 Thomas, *Man Who Would Be Perfect*, 125; Noyes, *Handbook of the Oneida Community*, 27; Wayland-Smith, "Women in Paradise," 3.

38 T.L.P., "Marriage and Divorce," *Oneida Circular* 8, no. 16 (May 12, 1859): 62.

39 Noyes, "Free Love," *Oneida Circular*, February 6, 1865, in Robertson, *Oneida Community*, 281ff.

40 Mandelker, "Religion, Sex, and Utopia," 740–41.

41 Foster, *Religion and Sexuality*, 107; DeMaria, *Communal Love at Oneida*, 204; Noyes, "Becoming as Little Children," *Spiritual Magazine*, December 22, 1849, 339; "Home, Sweet Home," *Oneida Circular* 5 (October 19, 1868): 241; see also *First Annual Report of the Oneida Association*, 16–17; Robertson, *Oneida Community*, 265–93; Cooley, *Summary Exposition*, 4–9.

42 Noyes, "Has the Kingdom of God Come?," *Spiritual Magazine* 2 (July 15, 1847): 65–68; Noyes, *Putney Community*, 235ff.

43 "The Battle-Axe Letter," in *Witness* 1 (January 23, 1839): 43; Syracuse University Library, Oneida Community Collection, Box 70: Writings 1843–1885; Foster, *Religion and Sexuality*, 80–81.

44 Noyes, in Cooley, *Summary Exposition*, 4; "Statement of Principles" (November 3, 1846), Syracuse University Library, Oneida Community Collection, Box 11, Folder: 1846 Ag 18.

45 Noyes, *Handbook of the Oneida Community*, 56.

46 Noyes in Cooley, *Summary Exposition*, 22; Noyes, "Industrial Marriage," *Oneida Circular* 3, no. 45 (March 18, 1854): 179.

47 Noyes, "Industrial Marriage," *Oneida Circular* 3, no. 34 (March 18, 1854): 179; Noyes: "The Utility of Combination," *Spiritual Magazine* 2 (October 1, 1847): 131; "Practical Communism," *Oneida Circular* 1 (June 13, 1852): 121; see also "Our Home," *Oneida Circular* 3 (October 21, 1854): 550.

48 Noyes, "Woman's Slavery to Children," *Spiritual Magazine* 1 (September 15, 1846): 109–10.

49 Noyes, "A Community Journal," *Oneida Circular* 12 (November 5, 1863): 143; Noyes, "The Law of Fellowship," in Barren and Miller, *Home Talks*, 1:205.

50 Sutton, *Communal Utopias*, 76.

51 Noyes, "Industrial Marriage," *Oneida Circular* 3, no. 45 (March 18, 1854): 179.

52 Foster, "Free Love," 167; Foster, *Religion and Sexuality*, 104; "Man and Woman—Their True Relation," *Oneida Circular* 12, no. 2 (March 12, 1863): 6.

53 *First Annual Report of the Oneida Association*, 41, emphasis original; Noyes in Cooley, *Summary Exposition*, 22.

54 Robertson, *Oneida Community*, 272; Nelson, "Dress Reform," 21–25.

55 White, "Designed for Perfection"; Noyes, *My Father's House*, 10; Noyes, "Houses," *Oneida Circular* 2, no. 7 (December 8, 1852): 26.

56 White, "Designed for Perfection."

57 White, "Designed for Perfection," 122–23; "The Upper Sitting Room III," *Oneida Circular*, February 1, 1869, 366.

58 "Advice to Parents" (June 2, 1868), Syracuse University Library, Oneida Community Collection, Box 70: Writings 1843–1885; Kern, *Ordered Love*, 193, 251; DeMaria, *Communal Love at Oneida*, 186; White, "Designed for Perfection," 118.

59 Noyes, "Obedience in Children," *Oneida Circular* 6, no. 14 (April 23, 1857): 54; "Children's Department," *Oneida Circular* 12, no. 36 (November 5, 1863): 143.

60 Noyes, "Government of Children," *Spiritual Magazine* 2 (August 11, 1849): 215–16.

61 Noyes, *My Father's House*, 42.

62 Noyes, *My Father's House*, 104–10, 105.

63 Noyes, *My Father's House*, 70, 80–81.

64 Johansen, *Family Men*, 83–108.

65 Noyes, *My Father's House*, 66; Noyes, *Putney Community*, 214; handwritten manuscript from December 21, 1852, Syracuse University Library, Oneida Community Collection, Box 70: Writings 1843–1885, Folder: 1852 D 21 "Our Victories"; Johansen, *Family Men*, 100ff.

66 "Mutual Criticism," in Noyes, *Putney Community*, 100–112; Nordhoff, *Communistic Societies*; Noyes, *My Father's House*, 13; Foucault, *History of Sexuality*, vol. 1.

67 Noyes, *Putney Community*, 103.

68 Kern, "Ideology and Reality," 184.

69 Zellner, Extraordinary Groups, 61.

70 Noyes, "Positive Virtue," in Barren and Miller, *Home Talks*, 1:122.

71 "A Copy of the 'Battle Axe Letter' Written by G.H.N., Putney, January 15, 1837," in Syracuse University Library, Oneida Community Collection, Box 70: Writings 1843–1885.

72 Noyes in Cooley, *Summary Exposition*, 17–18; Noyes, *Male Continence*, 16; Johansen, *Family Men*, 50ff.; Rotundo, *American Manhood*, 158–59.

73 Noyes, *Male Continence*, 3, 10–11; Kern, *Ordered Love*, 235–36.

74 Noyes, *Male Continence*, 9–10; Foster, *Religion and Sexuality*, 94; Freud, *Three Essays*, claims in the second essay that the diversion of sexual urges away from sexual goals toward new goals—a process that should be called sublimation—would result in cultural achievements.

75 Noyes, *Male Continence*, 20; for more on self-control, suffering, and desire, see handwritten manuscript, December 21, 1852, Syracuse University Library, Oneida Community Collection, Box 70: Writings 1843–1885, Folder: 1852 D 21 "Our Victories."

76 Kern, *Ordered Love*, 240; Kern, "Ideology and Reality," 191.

77 Barker-Benfield, "Spermatic Economy."

78 Sarasin, *Reizbare Maschinen*; Hull, *Sexuality, State and Civil Society*.

79 Frank, *Life with Father*, 46ff.

80 Noyes, *Male Continence*, 18; Noyes in Cooley, *Summary Exposition*, 9.

81 Foster, *Religion and Sexuality*, 98; Kern, *Ordered Love*, 224; Thomas, *Man Who Would Be Perfect*, 100–101.

82 Noyes in the *Oneida Circular*, January 14, 1867, 351; DeMaria, *Communal Love at Oneida*, 154.

83 Fish-Kalland, "Oneida Community," 30–31; Isaac and Altman, "Interpersonal Processes"; Mandelker, "Religion, Sex, and Utopia," 743; Robertson, *Oneida Community*, 268.

84 Kern, *Ordered Love*, 244–45.

85 Noyes, "Family Talk No. 1: Can We Get a Living?," *Oneida Circular* 2, no. 49 (May 4, 1853), 196; Noyes, *My Father's House*, 16.

86 Noyes, *Free Love in Utopia*, xvii–xviii.

87 Kern, *Ordered Love*, 242–43.

88 Cited in Fish-Kalland, "Oneida Community," 46–47.

89 Fish-Kalland, "Oneida Community," 101–2; Smith-Rosenberg, "Female World."

90 Noyes, "The Past, Present, and Future," *Oneida Circular* 1, no. 17 (March 7, 1852): 66.

91 Sutton, *Communal Utopias*, 73.

92 Foster, *Religion and Sexuality*, 102; Kern, *Ordered Love*, 207–8; Zellner, *Extraordinary Groups*, 57.

93 Rice, "Correspondence of the Cincinnati Commercial, Hamilton, Madison County, NY, May 1, 1872," *Oneida Circular*, July 8, 1872; Robertson, *Oneida Community*, 265–66 and 284ff.; Noyes, "Past, Present, and Future," *Oneida Circular* 1, no. 17 (March 7, 1852): 66; Foster, *Religion and Sexuality*, 109ff.

94 Kern, *Ordered Love*, 53–58; Eastman, *Noyesism Unveiled*.

CHAPTER 3. SLAVERY, FAMILY, AND FATHERHOOD, 1830–1860

1 Thomas H. Jones and Daniel Foster, July 15, 1852, in Ripley et al., *Black Abolitionist Papers*, 2:212ff.

2 Jones, *Experience* (1885), in Andrews, *North Carolina Slave Narratives*, 203–79. The publication went through several published editions, in 1854, 1855, 1857, 1858, 1862, 1868, 1871, 1880. I rely here on the 1862 edition, which largely matches the 1854 edition but has a few added passages on Tom Jones's escape and the reunification with his family. The 1885 edition has an added section on his religious experiences and practices and the abolitionist context is de-emphasized.

3 Gilroy, *Black Atlantic*; Kreuzenbeck, *Hoffnung auf Freiheit*; Berlin, *Generations of Captivity*.

4 Lejeune, *Le pacte autobiographique*.

5 Jones, *Experience* (1862), 47, "dependent and suffering," 5. For more on *Slave Narratives*, see Andrews, "Introduction to the Slave Narrative"; Blassingame, "Using the Testimony of Ex-Slaves." For the melding of real and imagined experiences in the narratives, see Dorsey, *Reforming Men and Women*, 187–88; for the representation of slave suffering, see Clark, "Sacred Rights of the Weak."

6 Stowe, *Uncle Tom's Cabin*; Stowe, *Key to Uncle Tom's Cabin*; Dorsey, *Reforming Men and Women*, 192.

7 Jones to Foster, May 5, 1851, in Ripley et al., *Black Abolitionist Papers*, 2:133–34. For both letters from Jones to Foster, see *Liberator*, May 30, 1851, and August, 13, 1852.

8   Finzsch, *Von Benin*, 262ff.; Jones to Foster, July 15, 1852, in Ripley et al., *Black Abolitionist Papers*, 2:212ff.

9   Barnes and Dumond, *Letters of Theodore Dwight Weld*, 1:390, 2:717; Weld, *American Slavery*, 95.

10 Jones to Foster, July 15, 1852, in Ripley et al., *Black Abolitionist Papers*, 2:212ff.; Andrews, "Introduction to the Slave Narrative," 5, 12; Dorsey, *Reforming Men and Women*, 192–93.

11 Jones, *Experience* (1885), 268.

12 See also chapter 11.

13 Foucault, "Subject and Power," 789; Foucault, *Society Must Be Defended*, 237–61.

14 Foner, "Meaning of Freedom," 440; Friend and Glover, "Rethinking Southern Masculinity," vii.

15 Pateman, *Sexual Contract*; Mills, *Racial Contract*.

16 hooks, "Plantation Patriarchy," 3–4.

17 Jones, *Labor of Love*, 9–41.

18 Wendt, "Southern Intellectuals"; Fitzhugh, *Cannibals All!!*, 362; Foby, "Management of Servants."

19 Fitzhugh, *Sociology for the South*, iii. He lamented the suffering, riots, begging, and crime in free societies. Finzsch, *Von Benin*, 272; Friend and Glover, "Rethinking Southern Masculinity," ix; McCurry, *Masters of Small Worlds*.

20 Patterson, *Slavery and Social Death*; Brown, "Social Death."

21 This will be discussed in greater detail in chapter 11.

22 Huggins, "Herbert Gutman"; Harris, "Coming of Age"; Wyatt-Brown, "Mask of Obedience."

23 Blassingame, *Slave Community*; Genovese, *Roll, Jordan, Roll*; Gutman, *Black Family*. For a summary, see Engerman, "Studying the Black Family"; Steckel, "Slavery Period"; Kolchin, *American Slavery*; Stevenson, *Life in Black and White*; Schwartz, *Born in Bondage*; Dunaway, *African-American Family*; West, *Chains of Love*; Hunter, *Bound in Wedlock*.

24 Jones, "Born a Child," 63–64; West, "Surviving Separation."

25 Jones, *Experience* (1862), 31–32; West, "Surviving Separation," 214, 220ff.

26 Jones, *Experience* (1862), 30, emphasis original.

27 Gutman, *Black Family*, 113–14, 185–215; Cody, "Naming, Kinship, and Estate Dispersal."

28 Crow, "Slavery"; Dunaway, *African-American Family*, 270ff.

29 Foner, "Meaning of Freedom," 438, 459.

30 Andrews, *North Carolina Slave Narratives*, 8.

31 Foner, "Meaning of Freedom," 445–49; Roediger, *Wages of Whiteness*.

32 Jones, *Experience* (1885), 255–56.

33 Jones, *Experience*, 244.

34 Jones, *Labor of Love*, 9–41.

35 Williams, *Self-Taught*, 203–215, 206 about North Carolina; Bassett, *Slavery*, 13.

36 Williams, *Self-Taught*; Barrett, "African-American Slave Narratives"; Cornelius, "'We Slipped and Learned to Read'"; Habermas, *Structural Transformation of the Public Sphere*.

37 Douglass, *Narrative of the Life*, 40.

38 Jones, *Experience* (1862), 18ff.

39 Finzsch, *Von Benin*, 203ff.

40 Jones, *Experience* (1862), 26–27.

41 Douglass, *My Bondage*, 246, emphases original.

42 Jones, *Experience* (1862), 27.

43 Andrews, *North Carolina Slave Narratives*, 192.

44 Jones, *Experience* (1862), 5–6, emphases original.

45 Jones, *Experience* (1862), 6, emphases original.

46 Jones, *Experience* (1862), 30, emphasis original.

47 Jones, *Experience* (1862), 32.

48 Coontz, *Marriage*.

49 Jones, *Experience* (1862), 48.

50 Jones to Foster, July 15, 1852, in Ripley et al., *Black Abolitionist Papers*, 2:212ff.; Foucault, *History of Sexuality*, 1:133–59.

51 Jones, *Experience* (1862), 23.

52 hooks, "Plantation Patriarchy," 3–4; hooks, "Reconstructing Black Masculinity"; Jeffrey, "Permeable Boundaries."

CHAPTER 4. DAUGHTERS, FATHERS, AND THE WESTWARD MOVEMENT, 1850–1880

1 Baumler, *Girl from the Gulches*. The book is an edited version of Merriam, *Frontier Woman*, based on master's thesis by Margaret Ronan, "Memoirs of a Frontier Woman" (State University of Montana, 1932). This was the edited version of her mother Mary Sheehan Ronan's memoirs told in 1929. See Smith, "Two Frontiers."

2 Baumler, *Girl from the Gulches*, 88.

3 Turner, "Significance of the Frontier."

4 Slotkin, *Gunfighter Nation*.

5 Jefferson, *Notes on the State of Virginia*; O'Sullivan, "Great Nation"; O'Sullivan, Annexation. For the agrarian myth, see Worster, "Beyond the Agrarian Myth."

6 Faragher, *Women and Men*, 11, 16; West, "Family Life on the Trail."

7 Limerick, *Legacy of Conquest*; Limerick, "What on Earth"; Faragher, "Frontier Trail"; Thompson, "Another Look"; Greenberg, *Manifest Manhood*; Finzsch, "'Extirpate or Remove.'"

8 Pascoe, "Western Women"; Armitage, "Western Women"; Butler, "Through a Lens"; Walsh, "Women's Place"; Schlissel, *Women's Diaries*; Stratton, *Pioneer Women*; Jeffrey, *Frontier Women*.

9 Basso, McCall, and Hagen, *Across the Great Divide*; West, "Longer, Grimmer."

10 Barthes, *Mythologies*; Slotkin, *Gunfighter Nation*, 1–26.

11 The New Western History has for some time demanded to focus the history of the West on families rather than pioneers; West, "Longer, Grimmer," 72–76.

12 Hiner and Hawes, *Growing Up in America*, xx; West, *Growing Up with the Country*; Atkins, "Child's West," 478.

13 Baumler, *Girl from the Gulches*, 88–89.

14 West, *Growing Up with the Country*; Hampsten, *Settlers' Children*.

15 Baumler, *Girl from the Gulches*, 10–11.

16 Baumler, *Girl from the Gulches*, 10ff.

17 Faragher, *Women and Men*, 16–20; Luchetti, *Children of the West*, 113–20.

18 Baumler, *Girl from the Gulches*, 19.

19 Petrik, *No Step Backward*, 3ff.

20 Baumler, *Girl from the Gulches*, 52–70; Madsen, "Montana Trail."

21 Baumler, *Girl from the Gulches*, 79–99.

22 Stewart, "Economic Opportunity or Hardship?," 238.

23 Schlissel, *Women's Diaries*.

24 Faragher, *Women and Men*, 13, 20; Stewart, "Economic Opportunity or Hardship?"; Stewart, "Migration to the Agricultural Frontier."

25 Baumler, *Girl from the Gulches*, 10–11; Frank, *Life with Father*; Harris, "Sex Roles," 45–46; Sanders, *Limiteds, Locals, and Expresses*, 46–47; see also Simons and Parker, *Railroads of Indiana*; Ambrose, *Nothing Like It*, 35.

26 Hofsommer, *Steel Trails of Hawkeyeland*.

27 Baumler, *Girl from the Gulches*, 29–43.

28 Baumler, *Girl from the Gulches*, 69; Prescott, "'Why She Didn't Marry Him,'" 29.

29 Baumler, *Girl from the Gulches*, 37, 43.

30 Baumler, *Girl from the Gulches*, 52ff., 80; Harris, "Sex Roles," 46; Luchetti, *Children of the West*, 123–29.

31 Bierling, *Kleine Geschichte*, 45.

32 Baumler, *Girl from the Gulches*, 86–91.

33 Schlissel, *Women's Diaries*, 83ff.; Walsh, "Women's Place," 244ff.; Faragher, *Women and Men*, 66–87, 110–43.

34 Blackburn and Richards, "Unequal Opportunity on a Mining Frontier."

35 Schlissel, *Women's Diaries*, 76; Prescott, *Gender and Generation*; Peterson del Mar, *What Trouble I Have Seen*; Prescott, "'Why She Didn't Marry Him,'" 28, 35; Petrik, *No Step Backward*; Petrik, "Mothers and Daughters."

36 Baumler, *Girl from the Gulches*, 25, 52, 88.

37 Baumler, *Girl from the Gulches*, 25, 69.

38 Baumler, *Girl from the Gulches*, 13, 34, 81, 91; Prescott, *Gender and Generation*; Mintz, *Huck's Raft*, 146–53.

39 Petrik, *No Step Backward*, 67–68.

40 Petrik, *No Step Backward*, 25ff., 60; almost 50 percent of the female business activity in Helena between 1865 and 1870 was done by prostitutes; Harris, "Sex Roles"; Walsh, "Women's Place," 247; Schlissel, *Women's Diaries*, 95.

41 Baumler, *Girl from the Gulches*, 19, 35ff., 43, 68–69.

42 See also West, *Growing Up with the Country*, 162.

43 Baumler, *Girl from the Gulches*, 12, 58.

44 Baumler, *Girl from the Gulches*, 12, 19, 26–27, 35ff., 43; Luchetti, *Children of the West*, 125–26.

45 Baumler, *Girl from the Gulches*, 12, 19, 22, 58. See also Harris, "Sex Roles."

46 Baumler, *Girl from the Gulches*, 15, 34, 37, 43, 65, 81; Harris, "Sex Roles," 45–46; West, *Growing Up with the Country*; Faragher, *Women and Men*.

47 Baumler, *Girl from the Gulches*, 82–83, 88–89.

48 Baumler, *Girl from the Gulches*, 91; Faragher, *Women and Men*, 91.

49 Baumler, *Girl from the Gulches*, 99, 103ff.

50 His letter from August 23, 1872, is reprinted in Baumler, *Girl from the Gulches*, 111.

51 Slotkin, *Gunfighter Nation*, 1–26.

52 D'Emilio and Freedman, *Intimate Matters*, 134–67; Petrik, *No Step Backward*, 25–58.

CHAPTER 5. BEING A FATHER AND A SOLDIER IN THE CIVIL WAR, 1861–1865

1 Inabinet and Inabinet, *History of Kershaw County*; Berlin, *Generations of Captivity*, 130ff.

2 West, *Texan in Search of a Fight*. West stresses that he did not alter the text for publication; see also Smyrl, "West"; Barr, *Black Texans*; Campbell, *Empire for Slavery*.

3 Foner, "Meaning of Freedom," 441; Bardaglio, *Reconstructing the Household*, 22ff.

4 Of all Confederate soldiers, 36 percent were married; their average age at the time of joining the army was 26.5 years. McPherson, *For Cause and Comrades*, viii, 179.

5 Diary of John Camden West, April 14, 1863, in West, *Texan in Search of a Fight*, 15–16, and "Preface," emphasis original. Simpson, *Hood's Texas Brigade*; Wooster, *Lone Star*; Chicoine: ". . . Willing Never to Go," 576.

6 Faust, *This Republic of Suffering*, 253; Greer, *Counting Civil War Casualties*, 22.

7 Chicoine, ". . . Willing Never to Go," 581–85; McPherson, *Crossroads of Freedom*, 11–12.

8 Hacker, "Census-Based Count."

9 Vinovskis, "Have Social Historians Lost the Civil War?"; Hacker, Hilde, and Jones et al., "Effect of the Civil War"; Faust, *Mothers of Invention*; Clinton and Silber, *Divided Houses* for gender and the Civil War.

10 Snyder, *Citizen-Soldiers and Manly Warriors*.

11 Cullen, "'I's a Man Now.'"

12 Foner, "Meaning of Freedom," 435.

13 West, Diary, April 14, 1863, in West, *Texan in Search of a Fight*, 15.

14 West, Diary, April 28 and May 4, 1863, in West, *Texan in Search of a Fight*, 27, 33.

15 West, Diary, May 16, 1863, in West, *Texan in Search of a Fight*, 45.

16 West, Diary, May 24–June 9, 1863, in West, *Texan in Search of a Fight*, 52–59, 59. See also letters from John C. West and Mary West, May 20, 1863, 61, May 25, 1863, 65, and May 26, 1863, 68; McPherson, *For Cause and Comrades*, 47, 62.

17 McPherson, *Battle Cry of Freedom*, 626–65.

18 Grant, *Personal Memoirs*, 226; McPherson, *Battle Cry of Freedom*, 637.

19 Letters to Master Stark West, July 8, 1863, and Mary West, July 9, 1863, in West, *Texan in Search of a Fight*, 84–88.

20 McPherson, *Battle Cry of Freedom*, 635.

21 McPherson, *Battle Cry of Freedom*, 636, for increased rates of desertion. Letters to Charles West and Mary West, July 27, 1863, in West, *Texan in Search of a Fight*, 89–101.

22 Letter from John to Mary West, August 17, 1863, in West, *Texan in Search of a Fight*, 104–5; on the concept of rejuvenation through battle, see Theweleit, *Male Fantasies*.

23 John to Mary West, September 24, 1863, in West, *Texan in Search of a Fight*, 107; McPherson, *For Cause and Comrades*, 63.

24 Woodward, *Mary Chesnut's Civil War*, 501; McPherson, *Battle Cry of Freedom*, 681.

25 See the letters from October through December 1863, 110–37, and John West to Mrs. James D. Blair, October 31, 1863, in West, *Texan in Search of a Fight*, 125.

26 John to Mary West, November 15, 1863, in West, *Texan in Search of a Fight*, 129.

27 Diary of John Camden West, in West, *Texan in Search of a Fight*, 160.

28 Whites, *Civil War*, 1995; McCurry, *Masters of Small Worlds*.

29 Faust, *Mothers of Invention*, 134, quotes from the diary of Grace Elmore, February 11, 1865.

30 Faust, *Mothers of Invention*, 114–38.

31 Faust, *Mothers of Invention*, 80–92.

32 Whites, *Civil War*, 1995, 41–63; Faust, *Mothers of Invention*, 30–52.

33 John to Mary West, May 20, 1863, and John to Stark West, July 8, 1863, in West, *Texan in Search of a Fight*, 62, 86; Faust, *Mothers of Invention*, 43.

34 Faust, *Mothers of Invention*, 33–45.

35 Whites, *Civil War*, 57–59, 91–95; Wells, "Battle Time"; Faust, *Mothers of Invention*, 32, 92–113.

36 West, Diary, April 18, 1863, in West, *Texan in Search of a Fight*, 19.

37 John to Mary West, December 19, 1863, December 25, 1863, in West, *Texan in Search of a Fight*, 135ff.

38 John to Mary West, June 9, 1863, July 27, 1863, October 9, 1863, January 9, 1864, in West, *Texan in Search of a Fight*, 79–83, 100, 119–121, 131. See also John West to Mrs. Theodore Stark, August 14, 1863, in West, *Texan in Search of a Fight*, 104; John West to Miss Decca Stark, May 23, 1863, in West, *Texan in Search of a Fight*, 79.

39 Faust, *Mothers of Invention*.

40 John to Mary West, May 26, 1863, May 30, 1863, October 9, 1863, November 15, 1863, in West, *Texan in Search of a Fight*, 67–68, 69, 119, 129. See also John West to Little Stark and Mary West, October 9, 1863, in West, *Texan in Search of a Fight*, 117.

41 John to Mary West, May 25, 1863, May 30, 1863 (Jeremiah 49:11), July 27, 1863 ("I have left you . . ."), September 24, 1863, October 9, 1863, November 15, 1863

(Jeremiah 29:11), in West, *Texan in Search of a Fight*, 63, 68, 100, 108, 121, 129; the source refers to Jeremiah 59:11, yet it is more likely a reference to Jeremiah 29:11. See also McPherson, *For Cause and Comrades*, 70; Faust, *Mothers of Invention*, 179–95.

42 Fairclough, *Better Day Coming*.

43 West, *Texan in Search of a Fight*, 3; Michel, "Reconstruction of White Southern Manhood."

44 McMichael, *Sacred Memories*, 1–19, 69; Whites, *Civil War*, 160–98.

CHAPTER 6. BACHELORS IN URBAN AMERICA, 1870–1930

1 John Glover, secretary of the International Committee of the YMCA during a memorial service for Robert McBurney, April 18, 1899, in Doggett, *Life*, 267. See also "Unpublished Manuscript about R.R. McBurney by John F. Moore ca. 1930," 163, in Kautz Family YMCA Archives, University of Minnesota, Robert McBurney Papers, Box 2.

2 Henry Orne, April 19, 1899, "Minutes from Board of Directors Meeting, New York City, April 19, 1899," Robert McBurney Papers, Box 1, and Box 2, "Unpublished Manuscript on R.R. McBurney by John F. Moore ca. 1930," 135; Doggett, *Life*, 268–69.

3 A Ladies' Christian Association was founded only seven years after the YMCA, in 1858. On homosocial and homoerotic relations and male fraternities, see Martschukat and Stieglitz, *Geschichte der Männlichkeiten*, 113–15.

4 Chauncey, *Gay New York*; Boyer, *Urban Masses*.

5 Burke, "Freud and Cultural History." Historians have often relied on Freudian ideas about sexuality for their interpretation, rather than examining them as part of a powerful discourse.

6 Sedgwick, *Epistemology of the Closet*; Chudacoff, *Age of the Bachelor*; Snyder, *Bachelors, Manhood, and the Novel*; Chauncey, *Gay New York*.

7 Kann, *Republic of Men*, 52–78; Lobby, "Republican Bachelorhood."

8 Rotundo, *American Manhood*, 279–80.

9 Chudacoff, *Age of the Bachelor*, 21–44.

10 Chudacoff, *Age of the Bachelor*, 5.

11 Bixby, "Why Is Single Life Becoming More General?," 191–92.

12 Bixby, "Why Is Single Life Becoming More General?," 191.

13 Mumford, *Interzones*; Heap, *Slumming*; Clement, *Love for Sale*.

14 Bixby, "Why Is Single Life Becoming More General?," 190; White, *First Sexual Revolution*.

15 Lutz, *Doing Nothing*, 137ff.

16 Ade, *Single Blessedness*, 17; Jerome, *Reflections of a Bachelor*; Snyder, *Bachelors, Manhood, and the Novel*. The magazine *The Bachelor Book* was published from March to November 1900 in Chicago.

17 Burgess, "Sociological Aspects," 118.

18 Chudacoff, *Age of the Bachelor*, 48ff.

19 Peiss, "'Charity Girls.'"

20 The 1866 *Memorandum* by William E. Dodge is cited in Doggett, *Life*, 75–77.

21 White, *First Sexual Revolution*.

22 Beisel, *Anthony Comstock*; Horowitz, "Victoria Woodhull"; Clement, *Love for Sale*; Fronc, *New York Undercover*.

23 "Statement Made by Anthony Comstock, Oct. 29, 1900, regarding his involvement with Robert R. McBurney and the YMCA's involvement in the New York Society for the Suppression of Vice," Robert McBurney Papers, Box 2; Doggett, *Life*, 107ff.; Kendrick, *Secret Museum*, 125–57.

24 US Bureau of the Census, *Historical Statistics*, Series C, 89–101, 103, Series C, 120–37, 111, Series C, 138–42, 112.

25 Gustav-Wrathall, *Take the Young Stranger*.

26 Doggett, *Life*, 20–21.

27 Pettegrew, "Rescuing Young Men"; for Chicago, see Lupkin, "Temple of Practical Christianity"; Putney, *Muscular Christianity*.

28 "Unpublished Manuscript on R.R. McBurney by John F. Moore ca. 1930," 11–12, Robert McBurney Papers, Box 2.

29 Doggett, *Life*, 24–28; Morse, *Robert R. McBurney*, 5–10.

30 Doggett, *Life*, 51, 58, 59.

31 Doggett, *Life*, 92–95; "Minutes from Board of Directors Meeting, New York City, April 19, 1899," Robert McBurney Papers, Box 1.

32 "Correspondence, with Cephas Brainerd, 1870–1899," Robert McBurney Papers, Box 1.

33 Chudacoff, *Age of the Bachelor*, 81–82.

34 Zeisloft, *New Metropolis*; Snyder, "Paradise of Bachelors"; Lupkin, *Manhood Factories*.

35 Morse, *My Life*, 327.

36 Lupkin, "Manhood Factories," 44ff.

37 "Unpublished Manuscript on R.R. McBurney by John F. Moore ca. 1930," 144, Robert McBurney Papers, Box 2; Morse, *Robert R. McBurney*, 18; Doggett, *Life*, 117.

38 Richard Morse at the memorial service for Robert McBurney, April 19, 1899, in the tower room of the YMCA, in "Minutes from Board of Directors Meeting, New York City, April 19, 1899," Robert McBurney Papers, Box 1; Doggett, *Life*, 259–60.

39 "Unpublished Manuscript on R.R. McBurney by John F. Moore ca. 1930," 25, Robert McBurney Papers, Box 2.

40 "Minutes from Board of Directors Meeting, New York City, April 19, 1899," Robert McBurney Papers, Box 1.

41 Snyder, "Paradise of Bachelors," 265–66; Morse, *Robert R. McBurney*, 30; Doggett, *Life*, 117; Said, *Orientalism*.

42 Foucault, "Subject and Power."

43 Memorial service for McBurney, April 19, 1899, "Minutes from Board of Directors Meeting, New York City, April 19, 1899," Robert McBurney Papers, Box 1; Doggett, *Life*, 259–67.

44 "Unpublished Manuscript on R.R. McBurney by John F. Moore ca. 1930," 141, 145; Robert McBurney Papers, Box 2.
45 "Letters to James McConaughy," Robert McBurney Papers, Box 3; Morse, *My Life*, 196ff.; "Minutes from Board of Directors Meeting, New York City, April 19, 1899," Robert McBurney Papers, Box 1; Doggett, *Life*, 262.
46 Doggett, *Life*, 134.
47 Snyder, "Paradise of Bachelors," 274–75.
48 "Correspondence H. Thane Miller, 1873–1890," Robert McBurney Papers, Box 1.
49 "Letters to James McConaughy," Robert McBurney Papers, Box 3, especially from September 28, 1876, and April 4, 1878.
50 Chauncey, *Gay New York*, 33–45; Heap, *Slumming*.
51 Chauncey, *Gay New York*, 152–58; Gustav-Wrathall, *Take the Young Stranger*, 251.
52 YMCA, *Annual Report*, 15; Cephas Brainerd about the athletic facilities in Kautz Family YMCA Archives, University of Minnesota, Records of the YMCA of the City of New York, Box 371: YMCA Annual Reports, 1853–1902; Doggett, *Life*, 96–97; Putney, *Muscular Christianity*.
53 Cited in Wrathall, "Provenance as Text," 165–78; Letter by John B. Brandt to W.W. Vanarsdale, April 14, 1886, in "Business Correspondence," Kautz Family YMCA Archives, University of Minnesota, Robert Weidensall Papers, Box 27. See also Gustav-Wrathall, *Take the Young Stranger*, 72ff.
54 Sedgwick, *Epistemology of the Closet*. Richard Morse's autobiography was titled *My Life with Young Men*. He did not get married until age forty-two, and only shortly before the Weidensall festivities.
55 Wrathall, "Provenance as Text"; Gustav-Wrathall, *Take the Young Stranger*, 70–90.
56 Gustav-Wrathall, *Take the Young Stranger*, 70–90.
57 Chauncey, *Gay New York*, 331–54; Heap, *Slumming*, 231–76.
58 Gay, *Freud*, 206ff. on Clark, 553ff. for the reception in the United States; Hale, *Freud and the Americans*, 3–23 on Clark, and Hale, *Rise and Crisis*. For the history of sexology in the United States, see Terry, *American Obsession*, and Ned Katz, *Invention of Heterosexuality*.
59 Howard, *Men Like That*.
60 Hale, *Freud and the Americans*, 6; Gay, *Freud*, 553. For self-observation, see Foucault, *History of Sexuality*, vols. 1–2.
61 Katz, *Invention of Heterosexuality*, 14–30, *Dorland's Medical Dictionary*, cited 86. Katz notes the first appearance of the term "heterosexual" in the United States was by Kiernan, "Responsibility," and then in the first US edition of Krafft-Ebing's *Psychopathia Sexualis* in 1893. For a consumerist conceptualization of sexuality, see Stoff, *Ewige Jugend*; Birken, *Consuming Desire*.
62 Freud, *Three Essays*; first published in the United States in 1910.
63 Wile, *Sex Life of the Unmarried Adult*, particularly the essays by Burgess, "Sociological Aspects," and by Groves, "Sex Psychology," 100; Fromm, "Rezension."
64 Burgess, "Sociological Aspects," 153; Dickinson, "Medicine."

65 Henry, *Sex Variants*; Terry, *American Obsession*, 178–267.
66 Foucault, *History of Sexuality*, 1:43.

CHAPTER 7. IMMIGRANT FAMILIES IN URBAN AMERICA, 1880–1920
 1 US Bureau of the Census, *Historical Statistics*, Part I, 105–6.
 2 Diner, *Lower East Side Memories*, 35ff.; Sternlicht, *Tenement Saga*, 7.
 3 YIVO-Archives, Institute of Jewish Research, New York, RG 102: American-Jewish Autobiographies 1942–1970s, Box 13, Folder 155: Minnie Goldstein. Some autobiographies have been published; see Goldstein, "Success or Failure?," 18–34, for a long excerpt from Goldstein's text in English. The original is in Yiddish.
 4 Ellis Island Oral History Project, North American Immigrant Letters, Diaries, and Oral Histories.
 5 Diner, *Lower East Side Memories*, 15, 20; Sternlicht, *Tenement Saga*, 12, 19.
 6 Diner, *Lower East Side Memories*, 25, 31, about generational tensions; Zaborowska, *How We Found America*, 113–64.
 7 The 1857 report to the New York City Council is cited in Czitrom, "Jacob Riis's New York," 30.
 8 "Murder of the Home" in Riis, *Making of an American*, chap. 10, abs. 22; "moral contagion" in Riis, *How the Other Half Lives*, introduction, para. 4; for the slum as cancer, see Riis, *Peril and the Preservation of the Home*, 35.
 9 Wiebe, *Search for Order*, 164–76; Lears, *Rebirth of a Nation*.
10 For "most useful citizen," see New York Public Library, Jacob Riis Papers, Box No. 7: Printed Matter, Folder: Clippings II: Death of Jacob A. Riis; for a connection to Strong, see letters by Roosevelt, December 4, 1894, and January 3, 1895, and May 2, 23, 1900, and November 7, 1901, April 16, 1902, in Library of Congress, Manuscript Division, Jacob A. Riis Papers, Box 4: General Correspondence, 1870–1918. See also "How Jacob Riis Became Roosevelt's Ideal American Citizen," *New York Herald*, September, 13, 1903.
11 Degler, *In Search of Human Nature*; Tucker, *Science and Politics*; Lüthi, *Invading Bodies*, 63, 225–35; Roediger, *Working toward Whiteness*, 16–20; Kosak, *Cultures of Opposition*, 88, describes that the inhabitants of the Lower East Side were often labeled "Russian Hebrews," even though they had come from Lithuania, Poland, Hungary, Romania, or Galicia.
12 Goldstein, *Price of Whiteness*, 35–50; Lüthi, *Invading Bodies*, 208–9; Jacobson, *Whiteness of a Different Color*, 8–9, 39–52; Roediger, *Working toward Whiteness*, 57–130; Brodkin, *How Jews Became White Folks*; Gilman, *Difference and Pathology*, 22–25; Daniels, *Guarding the Golden Door*; Tuerk, "Jacob Riis," 189–90; "Lowest" in Riis, *How the Other Half Lives*, chap. 12; "material" in Riis, *Battle with the Slum*, 192–93; YIVO-Institute, RG 102, no. 155 Minnie Goldstein.
13 "Topics of the Time," 313–14; on the reception of *How the Other Half Lives*, see, e.g., A. F. Schauffler from the New York City Mission in a letter to Riis, December 5, 1890, in Library of Congress, Riis Papers, Box 4: General Correspondence, 1870–1918; Yochelson and Czitrom, *Rediscovering Jacob Riis*; Pascal, *Jacob Riis*.

14 Czitrom, "Jacob Riis's New York," 3–13; Riis, *How the Other Half Lives*, chap. 15.

15 Lyman Abbott of the *Christian Union*, in Library of Congress, Riis Papers, Box
10: Scrapbooks 1881–1900; see also Box 12, letter to Riis, May 10, 1888, and *Asbury
Park Spray*, July 21, 1892, and the many reviews of Riis's *How the Other Half Lives*,
e.g., *New York Tribune* ("The Seamy Side," November 25, 1890); *New York Press*
("In the World of Literature," November 23, 1890). Riis Papers, Box 12: Scrapbooks 1881–1900, about Riis's first lecture on the subject. In 1879 *Harper's Weekly*
published a series on "Tenement Life in New York City" with pictures of tenement
houses. Czitrom, "Jacob Riis's New York," 50, 86, about the slide shows. Yochelson, "Jacob A. Riis"; Hales, *Silver Cities*, 179; Stange, *Symbols of Ideal Life*; Bate,
"Fotografien und der koloniale Blick"; Edwards, "Andere ordnen." About Riis as
tour guide, see Gandal, *Virtues of the Vicious*, 61–73; Mumford, *Interzones*, 133–38;
Heap, *Slumming*, 21. For the picturesque, see Bramen, *Uses of Variety*.

16 Riis, "Tenement House Blight," 770; "The Seamy Side," *New York Tribune*, November 25, 1890.

17 Riis, "Tenement: Curing Its Blight," 25; see also Riis, "Tenement: The Real Problem." "As a city's homes are, so is that city," Riis stressed over and over; e.g., lecture
at the Fort Pitt Hotel in Pittsburgh, December 8, 1911, New York Public Library,
Riis Papers, Box 6, Folder: Lecture Notes 1911.

18 Riis, *Peril and the Preservation of the Home*, 23–24.

19 Riis, "Tenement House Blight," 761; Riis, *How the Other Half Lives*, chap. 4; see
Kosak, *Cultures of Opposition*, 84; McCabe, *Lights and Shadows*, chap. 60. This
guide book promised readers and visitors "full and graphic accounts of its splen-
dor and wretchedness; its high and low life; its marble palaces and dark dens; its
attractions and dangers; its rings and frauds; its leading men and politicians; its
adventurers; its charities; its mysteries, and its crimes."

20 Cited in Czitrom, "Jacob Riis's New York," 41; Trachtenberg, *Incorporation of
America*, 126ff.

21 Czitrom, "Jacob Riis's New York," 25–44; beginning in 1879 the Board of Health
sent fifty physicians into the tenement houses every summer. Semiannual inspec-
tions occurred starting in 1887. See Bayles, *Tenement House Problem*, 32ff., in New
York Public Library, Riis Papers, Box 6, Folder: Miscellaneous Printed Matter.

22 Riis, *How the Other Half Lives*, chaps. 1–3, 10, 24.

23 Riis, *How the Other Half Lives*, chaps. 4–6, here mostly with reference to the Italian neighborhood the Bend; Riis, *Peril and the Preservation of the Home*, 35; Lüthi,
Invading Bodies, 12, 93, 133–95; Cowan and Cowan, *Our Parents' Lives*, 42ff., 58.

24 Riis, *How the Other Half Lives*, chap. 13.

25 Riis, *How the Other Half Lives*, chaps. 7, 8, 10; Riis, "Tenement House Blight," 767.

26 Riis, *How the Other Half Lives*, chap. 4; Craig, "Poor in Great Cities," 125. On "the central subject of all social questions," see: "Poor in Great Cities: Introduction," 399–400.

27 See Cahan, "Russian Jew," on the Jewish potential; Goldstein, *Price of Whiteness*,
35–51.

28 Polonsky, *Shtetl*; Bartal, *Jews of Eastern Europe.*
29 Lüthi, *Invading Bodies*, 204; Sternlicht, *Tenement Saga*, 8ff.; Kosak, *Cultures of Opposition*, 2, 37–60, 92–99; Goldstein, *Price of Whiteness.*
30 Riis, *Peril and the Preservation of the Home*, 27; Riis, *How the Other Half Lives*, chap. 20; Gladden, "Present-Day Papers," 251.
31 Riis, *How the Other Half Lives*, chap. 21.
32 Riis, *How the Other Half Lives*, chap. 11; Kosak, *Cultures of Opposition*, 66–67.
33 Riis, *How the Other Half Lives*, chap. 10; Kosak, *Cultures of Opposition*, 60, 64.
34 Wheatley, "Jews in New York," 326–27; Riis, *How the Other Half Lives*, chap. 11.
35 Riis, *Children of the Poor*; Riis, "Tenement: Curing Its Blight," 27; Riis, "Tenement House Blight," 770; Mintz, *Huck's Raft*, 133–212.
36 Riis, *How the Other Half Lives*, chap. 15; Ramsey, "Wrestling with Modernity."
37 Riis, *How the Other Half Lives*, chap. 15; Riis, *Children of the Poor*, chap. 8; Mintz, *Huck's Raft*, 155, 174.
38 Riis, "Battle with the Slum," 627.
39 See Gratton and Moen, "Immigration, Culture, and Child Labor," on how common child labor was in rural areas and before industrialization.
40 Hindman, *Child Labor*; Mintz, *Huck's Raft*, 173ff.
41 Riis, *How the Other Half Lives*, chap. 12.
42 Riis, *Children of the Poor*, chap. 6.
43 Ellis Island Oral History Project, North American Immigrant Letters, Diaries, and Oral Histories, no. 017: Interview of Dr. Robert L. Leslie by Dana Gumb, August 14, 1985. See Riis, *Peril and the Preservation of the Home*, 104, on alcohol.
44 Scott, "Fantasy Echo."
45 Ellis Island Oral History Project, no. 1159: Interview of Jennie Groer by Janet Levine, August 2, 2000, and no. 139: Interview of Esther Sheinman by Paul E. Sigrist Jr., April 25, 1992.
46 Ellis Island Oral History Project, no. 045: Interview of Julia Levine Greenberg by Paul E. Sigrist Jr., May 9, 1991. See YIVO-Institute, RG 102, no. 34 M. Shapiro, about him being part of a transatlantic network; see also no. 39 Abe Pachter and no. 68 B. Pugach; see also Kosak, *Cultures of Opposition*, 38.
47 Goldstein, "Success or Failure?," 24, 28. See also Ellis Island Oral History Project, no. 057: Interview of Alec Bodanis by Nancy Dallett, November 15, 1989; no. 045: Interview of Julia Levine Greenberg by Paul E. Sigrist Jr., May 9, 1991; no. 188: Interview of Sadie Guttman Kaplan by Paul E. Sigrist, July 2, 1992; no. 062: Interview of Dora Heller Rich by Paul E. Sigrist Jr., August 9, 1991; no. 184: Interview of Gertrude Cooper Klemens by Janet Levine, June 25, 1992; Sternlicht, *Tenement Saga*, 21.
48 Cowan and Cowan, *Our Parents' Lives*, 48–49; YIVO-Institute, RG 102, no. 87 Shin Tess and no. 130 M. Rosenblatt.
49 Goldstein, *Price of Whiteness*, 76, 95–96.
50 Goldstein, "Success or Failure?," 29.

51 See several interviews of the Ellis Island Oral History Project, as well as YIVO-Institute, RG 102: no. 5 Jacob Sholtz, no. 8 Klara Varbalov, no. 21 M. Havelin, no. 33 George N. Herzel, and several others.

52 Goldstein, "Success or Failure?," 23ff.

53 Eisen, "One Hundred Years."

54 Goldstein, "Success or Failure?," 18–19; Ellis Island Oral History Project, no. 003: Interview of Clara Larsen by Nancy Dallett, January 17, 1985; no. 188: Interview of Sadie Guttman Kaplan by Paul E. Sigrist, July 2, 1992; no. 062: Interview of Dora Heller Rich by Paul E. Sigrist Jr., August 9, 1991. See also Kosak, *Cultures of Opposition*, 17, 32–33; Freeze, Hyman, and Polonsky, *Jewish Women*.

55 Ellis Island Oral History Project, no. 173: Interview of Morris Abrams by Dana Gumb, May 28, 1986.

56 Riis, *Peril and the Preservation of the Home*, 172.

57 Goldstein, "Success or Failure?," 21, 31. Several Interviews in the Ellis Island Oral History Project speak about fathers as providers; no. 057: Interview of Frank Shelibovsky by Margo Nash, March 28, 1974; no. 034: Interview of Anna Tenzer by Carlo Scissura, March 27, 1991; Cowan and Cowan, *Our Parents' Lives*, 40.

58 YIVO-Institute, RG 102: no. 36 M. Zeidman, no. 50 Bessie Moskowitz.

59 Goldstein, "Success or Failure?," 28.

60 Ellis Island Oral History Project, no. 116: Interview of Irving Chait by Debby Dane, January 10, 1986; no. 152: Interview of Ida Ozeroff by Paul E. Sigrist Jr., May 9, 1992; no. 139: Interview of Esther Sheinman by Paul E. Sigrist Jr., April 25, 1992; no. 138: Interview of William Rogers by Paul E. Sigrist Jr., April 25, 1992.

61 YIVO-Institute, RG 102, no. 155 Minnie Goldstein; Ellis Island Oral History Project, no. 003: Interview of Clara Larsen by Nancy Dallett, January 17, 1985; no. 057: Interview of Frank Shelibovsky by Margo Nash, March 28, 1974; no. 1159: Interview of Jennie Groer by Janet Levine, August 2, 2000; no. 045: Interview of Julia Levine Greenberg by Paul E. Sigrist Jr., May 9, 1991; no. 062: Interview of Dora Heller Rich by Paul E. Sigrist Jr., August 9, 1991; no. 124: Interview of Max Grossman by Nancy Dallett, January 16, 1986. See also Sternlicht, *Tenement Saga*, 15.

62 Ellis Island Oral History Project, no. 188: Interview of Sadie Guttman Kaplan by Paul E. Sigrist, July 2, 1992; no. 057: Interview of Frank Shelibovsky by Margo Nash, March 28, 1974. See also YIVO-Institute, RG 102, no. 130 M. Rosenblatt. Cowan and Cowan, *Our Parents' Lives*, 56, 214; Yezierska, *Red Ribbon*, 32, 38–39.

63 Sternlicht, *Tenement Saga*, 16, 24.

64 Roediger, *Working toward Whiteness*, 145–56.

65 Yezierska, *Red Ribbon*, 38–39.

66 Goldstein, "Success or Failure?," 28–29. See also interviews with Clara Larsen, Frank Shelibovsky.

67 Ellis Island Oral History Project, Interviews with M. Abrams, S. G. Kaplan, A. H. Tenzer, J. Groer, and E. Sheinman.

68 Mintz, *Huck's Raft*, 201–2; Cowan and Cowan, *Our Parents' Lives*, 99ff.

69 Brumberg, *Going to America*; Mintz, *Huck's Raft*, 203ff.; Cowan and Cowan, *Our Parents' Lives*, 80, 86.

70 Goldstein, *Price of Whiteness*, 98; Goldstein, "Success or Failure?," 32; YIVO-Archives, RG 102, no. 155 Minnie Goldstein; see also her letter to Shlomo Nobel, July 30, 1952.

71 Bayles, *Tenement House Problem*, 16, in New York Public Library, Riis Papers, Box 6, Folder: Miscellaneous Printed Matter.

72 Riis, *Children of the Poor*, chap. 11.

CHAPTER 8. INDIGENOUS AND MODERN FATHERS, 1890–1950

1 Matilda Rose McLaren, Washington Park Gardens, Springfield, Illinois, "The Indian Way of Life," typescript, in Kautz Family YMCA Archives, University of Minnesota, Biographical Records, Box 66: Foster to Friend, Folder: Friday, Joe; see also Boys Work, Box 56, Folder: History of the Indian Guides, H. S. Keltner, 1946, H. S. Keltner manuscript July 1946: "Origin and History of the Indian Guides Father and Son Movement of the Y.M.C.A."

2 Deloria, *Playing Indian*; Dippie, *Vanishing American*.

3 Slotkin, *Regeneration through Violence*.

4 Bederman, *Manliness and Civilization*, 77–120.

5 Proclamation from the office of the mayor of St. Louis on the occasion of the "Y Indian Guide Week," September 19–25, 1971, in Boys Work, Box 51, Folder: National Y Indian Guide Week Kit 1971.

6 LaRossa, *Modernization of Fatherhood*. Recent scholarship on the history of fatherhood states that fathers in nineteenth-century families were more involved than contemporaries in the early twentieth century had assumed.

7 McLaren, "The Indian Way of Life," in Biographical Records, Box 66: Foster to Friend, Folder: Friday, Joe. See also in the same folder the unpublished manuscript "History of Indian Guides," September 30, 1932, apparently written by William Hefelfinger, the first chief of the first tribe. Edna Warren, "How 'Y' Makes Good Indians," *St. Louis Daily Globe-Democrat*, December 8, 1935, 4E.

8 Jackson, *Crabgrass Frontier*; Biographical Records, Box 66: Foster to Friend, Folder: Friday, Joe, "History of Indian Guides," September 30, 1932. The age spectrum of the sons was initially between six and twelve years, but later narrowed to between six and eight years.

9 Donald Leak, "National Board" of the YMCA, in Boys Work, Box 6, Folder: Y Indian Guide Papers, 1970s, 1980.

10 Slotkin, *Regeneration through Violence*; Slotkin, *Fatal Environment*; Greenberg, *Manifest Manhood*; Finzsch, "'Extirpate or Remove.'"

11 See Whitehead, *They Call Me Father*; Black, "Authoritarian Fatherhood." Rogin, *Fathers and Children*, was criticized for creating an apologist view on Andrew Jackson's political paternalism; see Perry, "Review Essay"; Dippie, *Vanishing American*, 56–78.

12 Dippie, *Vanishing American*, 97–98.

13 Dippie, *Vanishing American*, 106–8; Stremlau, "'To Domesticate and Civilize.'"

14 Child, *Boarding School Seasons*; Adams, *Education for Extinction*; Peacock and Day, "Nations within a Nation," 147–48.

15 Ellis, "From the Battle," 261; see the manual "Project: Indian Lore" from 1934, in Boys Work, Box 52, Folder: Program Manuals, Project and Activities 1934.

16 Said, *Orientalism*; Hames, "Ecologically Noble Savage Debate"; Krech, *Ecological Indian*.

17 Medicine, "American Indian Family."

18 Reed, "Family and Nation," 313–15.

19 Hoxie, "Reconstructing Crow Family Life," 304; Shoemaker, "From Longhouse to Loghouse."

20 Shoemaker, "From Longhouse to Loghouse," 332ff.; Rogers and Taylor, "Northern Ojibwa," 236.

21 Said, *Orientalism*, 111ff.

22 Eastman, *From the Deep Woods*, 168; Eastman, *Essential Charles Eastman*; Martínez, "Out of the Woods"; Martínez, *Dakota Philosopher*; Cooper, "On Autobiography"; YMCA, *YMCA in America*, 6.

23 Kugel, *To Be the Main Leaders*; Peacock and Day, "Nations within a Nation," 141ff.

24 Dawson et al., *American Indians*, 2:346–50; Surtees, "Canadian Indian Policy."

25 Kegg, *Portage Lake*; Pejsa, *Life of Emily Peake*.

26 Slotkin, *Regeneration through Violence*.

27 Joseph Conrad's *Heart of Darkness* from 1899 is a central text for the disorienting and destructive effects of *going native* in European colonialism.

28 Bederman, *Manliness and Civilization*, 170–215; Cronon, "Trouble with Wilderness"; Spence, *Dispossessing the Wilderness*; Deloria, *Playing Indian*.

29 Algeo, "Indian for a Night"; Clark and Nagel, "White Men, Red Masks"; Spence, *Dispossessing the Wilderness*.

30 Dippie, *Vanishing American*, 199–215; Gidley, *Edward S. Curtis*; Martínez, "Out of the Woods."

31 See the trilogy by Slotkin or Smith, *Reimagining Indians*; Huhndorf, *Going Native*; Deloria, *Playing Indian*.

32 Dippie, *Vanishing American*, 207–15.

33 Herman, "God Bless Buffalo Bill"; Kasson, *Buffalo Bill's Wild West*.

34 Gilbert, *Perfect Cities*, 109; Gilbert, *Whose Fair?*, 192; Bederman, *Manliness and Civilization*, 35; Dippie, *Vanishing American*, 205ff.

35 Dippie, *Vanishing American*, 215–21; McGrath, "Endless Trail."

36 Haraway, *Primate Visions*, 26–58; Pool, "Männer im Pelz," 165; Cronon, "Trouble with Wilderness"; Zantop, *Colonial Fantasies*.

37 Lutz, *American Nervousness*; Bederman, *Manliness and Civilization*, 77–120; Beard, *American Nervousness*.

38 Degler, *In Search of Human Nature*, 4–47.

39 Bederman, *Manliness and Civilization*, 77–101.

40 Cupers, "Governing through Nature"; Maynard, "An Ideal Life"; Deloria, *Playing Indian*, 102; Wall, *Nurture of Nature*; Young, *Heading Out*.

41 Cupers, "Governing through Nature," 174.

42 Miller, *Growing Girls*.

43 Cited in Maynard, "An Ideal Life," 22; Rotundo, *American Manhood*, 255–62; Cupers, "Governing through Nature," 189; Macleod, *Building Character*.

44 Macleod, *Building Character*, 130ff.; Cupers, "Governing through Nature," 190; Deloria, *Playing Indian*, 95–111; Van Slyck, *Manufactured Wilderness*, 169–213; Cooper, "On Autobiography," 5–6, 11–15. For more on the competitions within the YMCA programs, see Boys Work, Box 14, Folder: Friendly Indian Material 1925–1930 A; see also Boys Work, Box 51, Folder: Certificates, Cards, Forms, Badges 1940–75.

45 Boys Work, Box 50, Folder: National Executive Committee of Y Indian Guides Minutes, Feb. 1951, February 10/11, 1951, in Chicago.

46 See the note by Keltner in a manuscript, in Boys Work, Box 56, Folder: History of the Indian Guides, H. S. Keltner, 1946.

47 Boys Work, Box 56, Folder: Father & Son Programs 1920–50A, and Folder: Father + Son Programs 1920–50B, and Folder: Father + Son Programs 1921–1924A, and folder: Father + Son Programs 1921–1924D, and folder: Place Cards & Stickers National Father and Son Week, ND.

48 LaRossa, *Modernization of Fatherhood*; Frank, *Life with Father*; Johansen, *Family Men*; for England and Germany, see Tosh, *A Man's Place*; Habermas, *Frauen und Männer*.

49 LaRossa, *Modernization of Fatherhood*, 94–95, 104.

50 LaRossa, *Modernization of Fatherhood*, 39, 56, 96, 104–5, 130–31; Guest, *My Job as a Father*, 7, 34–35.

51 Manuscript H. S. Keltner, July 1946: Origin and History of the Indian Guides Father and Son Movement of the Y.M.C.A., in Boys Work, Box 51, Folder: Historical Summaries 1931–1946.

52 LaRossa, *Modernization of Fatherhood*, 70, 87, 134–39.

53 Boys Work, Box 56, Folder: History of the Indian Guides, H. S. Keltner, 1946, Manuscript: Keltner, July 1946: Origin and History of the Indian Guides Father and Son Movement of the Y.M.C.A.

54 See instructions in letter from February 26, 1951 and March 3, 1951, from Wauwatosa, Wisconsin, in Boys Work, Box 6, Folder: Papers, 1947–1963A.

55 Biographical Records, Box 66: Foster to Friend, Folder: Friday, Joe, History of Indian Guides, unpublished Manuscript W. Hefelfinger, September 30, 1932.

56 Boys Work, Box 56, Folder: History of the Indian Guides, H. S. Keltner, 1946, the Manuscripts by Keltner and Matilda Rose McLaren: The Indian Way of Life; see in Biographical Records, Box 66: Foster to Friend, Folder: Friday, Joe, minutes of Longhouse-Meetings, February 19, 1960 in Washington D.C.; see in Boys Work, Box 50, Folder: National Executive Committee Father and Son Y Indian Guides,

Feb. 1960, and the report of the *National Board YMCAs—Urban Action and Program Division: Task Force on Y-Parent-Child Programs*, by Donald Leak, Chairman, Charles Kujawa, Staff, Dallas, TX, Oct. 31, 1979, in Boys Work, Box 6, Folder: Y Indian Guide Papers, 1970s, 1980—A.

57 Boys Work, Box 56, Folder: Constitutions 1940–1978, ND, and entire box on the national organization of the program.

58 Hess, *The Y Indian Guide Program of the Young Men's Christian Association. A Research Study*, January 1960, in Boys Work, Box 56; see also folder: Letters to "Miss Layton" from students, ca. 1944.

59 Boys Work, Box 14, various folders with "Friendly Indian Material," especially the Flyer "Sioux Falls YMCA-Friendly Indian Clubs" in Folder: Y-Friendly Indian Club Leaders' Manual—Sioux Falls, ca. 1941. See also O'Leary, *To Die For*.

60 McLaren, The Indian Way of Life, typed manuscript, in Biographical Records, Box 66: Foster to Friend, Folder: Friday, Joe; unpublished manuscript by Hefelfinger (September 30, 1932) and brochure on the perspective of a boy in Boys Work, Box 6, Folder: Papers 1947–1963C.

61 "Fathers and Sons: Some Educators Look at the Y Indian Guides Movement," in Boys Work, Box 6, Folder: Papers, 1947–1963A.

62 Boys Work, Box 52, Folder: Papers, ND, letter Andrew A. Santanen, Boys' Work Secretary, YMCA Springfield, Illinois: Why Indian Guides?, ca. 1939/40.

63 Boys Work, Box 56, Folder: History of the Indian Guides, H. S. Keltner, 1946; see also Biographical Records, Box 66: Foster to Friend—Folder: Friday, Joe, History of Indian Guides, Hefelfinger manuscript.

64 See the YMCA commissioned study by Hess, *The Y Indian Guide Program*, 1961, 24–27, in Boys Work, Box 56; Boys Work, Box 50, Folder: National Executive Committee: Y Indian Guides, February 1950, minutes of meeting February 11–12, 1950.

65 "How to conduct a Y Indian Guide meeting," Franklin Bens, Birmingham Federation, Boys Work, Box 6, Folder: Papers, 1947–1963B. See also Boys Work, Box 56, Folder: Certificates, Cards, Forms, Badges 1940–75.

66 See instructional manuals in various folders in Boys Work, Box 52.

67 Biographical Records, Box 66: Foster to Friend, Folder: Friday, Joe, Manuscript Hefelfinger (1932); On *Broken Arrow*, see Boys Work, Box 50, Folder: National Executive Committee: Y Indian Guides, Feb. 1950, Minutes, Longhouse, February 11–12, 1950; Slotkin, *Gunfighter Nation*; *Broken Arrow* (dir. Delmar Daves, Twentieth Century Fox, 1950).

68 Biographical Records, Box 66: Foster to Friend, Folder: Friday, Joe, Manuscript Hefelfinger (1932).

69 Boys Work, Box 56, Folder: History of the Indian Guides, H. S. Keltner, 1946, Manuscript H. S. Keltner, July 1946: Origin and History of the Indian Guides Father and Son Movement of the Y.M.C.A.

70 Boys Work, Box 56, Folder: History of the Indian Guides, H. S. Keltner, 1946, manuscript H. S. Keltner and interview with Keltner in the *St. Louis Daily Globe Democrat*, December 8, 1935.

71 Boys Work, Box 6, Folder: Joe Friday Letter & Publisher Letter 1940, 1970, letter Abel J. Gregg to Joe Friday, cc. Mr. L. F. Smith, February 1, 1940, rejecting his continued financial support.

72 Memo January 28, 1944, in Boys Work, Box 6, Folder: Y Indian Guide Papers 1940s; see also letters by Abel J. Gregg (National Boys' Work Secretary) to Lansing F. Smith in New York, February 1, 1940, and from Gregg to Harold Keltner, May 29, 1940, in Boys Work, Box 6, Folder: Y Indian Guide Papers 1940s.

73 "The Beavers Visit Joe Friday," *Long House News* 11, no. 5 (March–April 1947); see also Bulletin, April 1956 in Biographical Records, Box 66: Foster to Friend, Folder: Friday, Joe; and Boys Work, Box 50, Folder: National Executive Committee of Y Indian Guides Minutes, February 18, 1955, and Folder: National Executive Committee of Y Indian Guides Minutes, February 17, 1956.

74 Martínez, *Dakota Philosopher*, S., 77–78.

75 Stoler, *Race and the Education of Desire.*

76 Cooper, "On Autobiography," 5; Zamir, "Native Agency."

77 Spivak, "Can the Subaltern Speak?"

78 Child, *Boarding School Seasons.*

79 Boys Work, Box 6, Folder: Joe Friday letter & publisher letter 1940, 1970, letter Abel J. Gregg to Joe Friday, cc. Mr. L. F. Smith, February 1, 1940; memo from January 28, 1944, Folder: Y Indian Guide Papers 1940s; see in the same folder the letter from February 1, 1940, Abel J. Gregg (National Boys' Work Secretary) to Lansing F. Smith in New York, and letter from Joe Friday, January 24, 1940, in which he outlines his wide-ranging activities; and letter from Abel J. Gregg to Harold Keltner, May 29, 1940.

80 W. H. Finch, *Father & Son Y Indian Guides Cartoon Pamphlet*, Klamath Falls, Oregon, 1956, in Boys Work, Box 56, Folder: Manuals 1929–1935A.

81 Slotkin, *Gunfighter Nation*, 303–12.

82 Memo and appendices by John A. Ledlie to Mr. J. Edward Sprengel, December 14, 1950, in Boys Work, Box 52, Folder: Papers 1950–59.

83 National Long House, Father and Son Y Indian Guide Program: 1972–73 Manual of Practice, ed. by Charles C. Kujawa. Revised April 1, 1972, in Boys Work, Box 6, Folder: Manual of Practice 1972; Folder: Father & Son Y Indian Guide Manual 1973, Charles C. Kujawa for National Board of YMCAs, ed. *The Father and Son Y Indian Guide Manual*, New York: Association Press, 1973; Folder: Y Indian Guide Papers, 1970s, 1980—A, an account by the *National Board YMCA—Urban Action and Program Division: Task Force on Y-Parent-Child Programs*, Donald Leak, Chairman, Charles Kujawa, Staff, Dallas, TX, October 31, 1979.

CHAPTER 9. UNEMPLOYED FATHERS IN THE 1930S

1 The transcripts of the interviews have not been archived. I am relying on the published dissertation.

2 Komarovsky, *Unemployed Man*, 74.

3 Coontz, *Marriage*, 154–57; Griswold, *Fatherhood in America*, 144; Kessler-Harris, "In the Nation's Image"; Kimmel, *Manhood in America*, 20.

4 Barnard College Archives, New York, Mirra Komarovsky Collection, Box 1: Mirra Komarovsky: Recorded and transcribed by Anne W. Lowenthal, 19 June 1997, and 17 July 1997.

5 Komarovsky, "Functional Analysis"; Komarovsky, "Cultural Contradictions"; Komarovsky, "Concept of Social Role"; see her very early critique of "biological determinism" in her master's thesis: "Invention, a Step in Progress," in Mirra Komarovsky Collection, Box 4, Folder 29, "My First Mentor: William F. Ogburn." On Komarovsky, see Tarrant, "When Sex Became Gender"; Tarrant, *When Sex Became Gender*, 107–32; Kampen, "Mirra Komarovsky."

6 Jahoda, Lazarsfeld, and Zeisel, *Marienthal*, here the appendix by Zeisel, "Toward a History of Sociography," 99–126.

7 Habermas, *Legitimation Crisis*, 1, emphasis original; Koselleck, "Krise."

8 Koselleck, "Krise," 643.

9 Lazarsfeld, "Episode in the History of Social Research," esp. 289.

10 Mirra Komarovsky Collection, Box 4, Folder 2: Excerpts from "Blue Collar Marriage"; Box 1: Mirra Komarovsky: Recorded and transcribed by Anne W. Lowenthal, June 19, 1997, and July 17, 1997; Reinharz, "Mirra Komarovsky."

11 Komarovsky, *Unemployed Man*, 4. Komarovsky specifies the city of her study as industrial and as "N—" in the vicinity of New York City. Her cooperation with Lazarsfeld also suggests that it is Newark. For a similar study on the uncertainties of male college students during the women's movement, see Komarovsky, *Dilemmas of Masculinity*.

12 Cavan, "Unemployment," esp. 139; Cavan and Ranck, *Family and the Depression*.

13 Nathan, "Estimates of Unemployment"; Nixon and Samuelson, "Estimates of Unemployment."

14 Roosevelt's nomination speech at the Democratic convention, July 2, 1932, in *Public Papers*, 657.

15 Hopkins in the *New York Times*, March 10, 1935, 7, cited in Griswold, *Fatherhood in America*, 155.

16 Tuttle, *How Newark Became Newark*, 103–6; Cunningham, *Newark*, 264–82; Stellhorn, "Depression and Decline."

17 Bakke, *Unemployed Worker*, 25.

18 Habermas, *Legitimation Crisis*, 1.

19 Angell, *Family Encounters the Depression*; Morgan et al., *Family Meets the Depression*.

20 Komarovsky, *Unemployed Man*, 111.

21 Komarovsky, *Unemployed Man*, 42, for the quote. On 24, she points out that the low proportion might be a result of the selection process. The focus on intact families on relief excludes those who were separated or were dependent on a wage-earning woman. In addition, most survey participants had been married between fifteen and twenty years and thus were relatively stable in their relationship.

22 Cavan, "Unemployment," 140.

23 Komarovsky, *Unemployed Man*, 101.

24 Komarovsky, *Unemployed Man*, 27. The median income in 1935–36 was $1,160; about half of the families earned between $500 and $1,500 annually. Another 18.2 percent made less than $500, among the many African American families; see Bolin, "Economics of Middle-Income Family Life," 62–63; Monroe, "Levels of Living."

25 Monroe, "Levels of Living," 670; Bolin, "Economics of Middle-Income Family Life," 64, 67.

26 In Jahoda, Lazarsfeld, and Zeisel, *Marienthal*.

27 Sielke, "Crisis?"

28 Komarovsky, *Unemployed Man*, 31.

29 Komarovsky, *Unemployed Man*, 133. See similar statements about unemployment and impotence in LaRossa, *Modernization of Fatherhood*, 13.

30 Coontz, *Marriage*, 219.

31 Bakke, *Citizens without Work*, 155–76; Bakke, *Unemployed Worker*.

32 Bakke, *Citizens without Work*; Almond and Lasswell, "Aggressive Behavior."

33 Komarovsky, *Unemployed Man*, 41, 75–78. "Dire poverty was easier to bear than the husband's loss of status to some previously subordinate member." Cavan, "Unemployment," 140.

34 Komarovsky, *Unemployed Man*, 32–38.

35 Habermas, *Legitimation Crisis*, 3; Koselleck, "Krise."

36 Kessler-Harris, *Out to Work*, 253–57; Kessler-Harris, "Gender Ideology"; McElvaine, *Down and Out*.

37 See Kessler-Harris, "Gender Ideology," and Hobbs, "Rethinking Antifeminism"; Kessler-Harris, *Out to Work*, 258; Kessler-Harris, *Woman's Wage*, 57–80; Cott, *Public Vows*, 168ff.

38 Mink, *Wages of Motherhood*, 123–50.

39 Howard, *WPA and Federal Relief Policy*, 279, cited in Rose, "Gender, Race, and the Welfare State," 324.

40 Kessler-Harris, *Out to Work*, 262ff.; Stieglitz, *"100 Percent American Boys"*; Moran, *Governing Bodies*, 38–63.

41 Griswold, *Fatherhood in America*, 155–56 on Hopkins.

42 Komarovsky, *Unemployed Man*, 64. For gender coding of welfare, see Gordon, *Women, the State, and Welfare*; Rose, "Gender, Race, and the Welfare State."

43 Bolin, "Economics of Middle-Income Family Life," esp. 61, 70; US Bureau of the Census, *Historical Statistics*, pt. 1, 131, 133.

44 Cott, *Public Vows*, 167; Cott, *Grounding of Modern Feminism*, 162ff., 204ff.

45 Cousins, "Will Women Lose Their Jobs?"

46 Gilbert, *Cycle of Outrage*; Mackert, *Jugenddelinquenz*.

47 Cited in "Should Married Women Work?," 16, 62.

48 Pruette, *Women Workers*, 155; Kessler-Harris, *Out to Work*, 258.

49 Hunter, "Making a Way," 240; Mumford, *Newark*, 22.

50 Sitkoff, *New Deal for Blacks*; Brueggemann, "Racial Considerations."
51 Clawson, "Poor People, Black Faces"; Kessler-Harris, "In the Nation's Image."
52 Mumford, *Newark*, 13–31; Price, "Afro-American Community"; Jackson and Jackson, "Black Experience in Newark," 46–50; Tuttle, *How Newark Became Newark*, 103ff.
53 Hunter, "Making a Way."
54 Habermas, *Legitimation Crisis*, 9–13.
55 Frazier, *Negro Family*; Myrdal, *American Dilemma*, 997.
56 Habermas, *Legitimation Crisis*, 7.
57 Koselleck, "Krise," 627.
58 Hall, "Question of Cultural Identity," 275; Mercer, "Welcome to the Jungle," 43.
59 Exception is LaFollette, *Study of the Problems*.
60 Pleck, "Theory of Male Sex-Role Identity."
61 Martschukat and Stieglitz, *Geschichte der Männlichkeiten*, 64–73.
62 See the transcript of a radio interview by Susan Stanberg with Komarovsky for NPR, June 7, 1982, in Barnard College Archives, New York, Biographical Files, Mirra Komarovsky, Folder 5; Komarovsky, *Women in the Modern World*; Komarovsky, "Functional Analysis."

CHAPTER 10. FATHERHOOD IN WORLD WAR II AND THE COLD WAR, 1940–1960

1 Wilson, *Ye Heart of a Man*, 4; Riesman, *Lonely Crowd*; Gilbert, *Men in the Middle*, 34–61.
2 Coontz, *Way We Never Were*, 24; Parsons and Bales, *Family Socialization*.
3 Wilson, *Ye Heart of a Man*, 15.
4 Jackson, *Crabgrass Frontier*.
5 Kimmel, *Gendered Society*, 117.
6 Wood, *Lolita in Peyton Place*, 17–29.
7 "The Man in the Gray Flannel Suit," *Look*, May 1, 1956, 104ff.
8 Wilson, *Ye Heart of a Man*, 68.
9 Westbrook, "Fighting for the American Family"; Leff, "Politics of Sacrifice"; Cott, *Public Vows*, 180–99; May, *Homeward Bound*, 49–79.
10 Lears, *Fables of Abundance*, 236–37; Fox, *Madison Avenue Goes to War*; Duis, "No Time for Privacy," 23.
11 Westbrook, "Fighting for the American Family," 202–6; Rockwell, *Norman Rockwell*, 338ff.; Griswold, *Fatherhood in America*, 164.
12 Wylie, *Generation of Vipers*; Lindner, *Rebel without a Cause*; Tuttle, "*Daddy's Gone to War*"; Hale, *Freud and the Americans*, 290–91.
13 May, "Rosie the Riveter Gets Married," 128; Filene, *Him/Her/Self*, 158–90.
14 US Congress, Senate, Subcommittee of the Committee on Education and Labor, *Hearings on Wartime Health and Education: Juvenile Delinquency, Parts 1, 4*, 78th Congress, 1944; US Congress, Senate, Subcommittee on Military Affairs, *Hearings on Married Men Exemption: Drafting of Fathers*, 78 Cong., 1st session, 1943; Griswold, *Fatherhood in America*, 168ff.

15 US Congress, Senate, Subcommittee on Military Affairs, 32; Tuttle, *"Daddy's Gone to War,"* 30ff.

16 US Congress, Senate, Subcommittee of the Committee on Education and Labor, 310; Griswold, *Fatherhood in America*, 170.

17 Malkin, *Marriage, Morals, and War*; Modell and Steffey, "Waging War."

18 Bennett, *When Dreams Came True*, 88; Mettler, *Soldiers to Citizens*.

19 Silverman, "Historical Trauma and Male Subjectivity"; Michel, "Danger on the Home Front."

20 Canaday, "Building a Straight State."

21 May, *Homeward Bound*, xii–xvi.

22 Bennett, *When Dreams Came True*, 201.

23 Coontz, *Way We Never Were*, 31–32; Hartmann, *Home Front and Beyond*, 24.

24 Meyerowitz, *Not June Cleaver*. Ralph LaRossa argues for the recognition of the greater diversity of father figures in the 1950s; LaRossa, *Modernization of Fatherhood*.

25 Wilson, *Ye Heart of a Man*, 1, 5; Weiss, *To Have and to Hold*, 86ff.; Weiss, "Drop-In Catering Job."

26 Coontz, *Way We Never Were*, 25.

27 Griswold, *Fatherhood in America*, 185–218; Ehrenreich, *Hearts of Men*, 14–28; Overstreet, *Mature Mind*; Ruitenbeek, "Men Alone," 80.

28 Zelditch, "Role Differentiation," 339.

29 Johnson, *Lavender Scare*; Gilbert, *Men in the Middle*; Cuordileone, "'Politics in an Age of Anxiety'"; Cuordileone, *Manhood and American Political Culture*; Canaday, *Straight State*.

30 Wilson, *Ye Heart of a Man*, 3.

31 May, Homeward Bound, ix; Canaday, *Straight State*.

32 To be considered middle class one had to have an annual income between three and ten thousand dollars. Of those who counted as middle class, 85 percent earned more than five thousand. Tom Rath's income was seven thousand and he dreamed of earning ten thousand. Coontz, *Way We Never Were*, 76ff.; Mettler, *Soldiers to Citizens*.

33 Jackson, *Crabgrass Frontier*; Hayden, *Building Suburbia*; Onkst, "First a Negro"; Coates, "Case for Reparations"; Sugrue, *Origins of the Urban Crisis Race*.

34 Friedan, *Feminine Mystique*.

35 Wilson, *Ye Heart of a Man*, 11–14.

36 Wilson, *Ye Heart of a Man*, 183.

37 Riesman, *Lonely Crowd*; Gilbert, *Men in the Middle*; Posner, *Public Intellectuals*.

38 Mills, *White Collar*, xii.

39 Ehrenreich, *Hearts of Men*, 33ff.

40 Cohan, *Masked Men*, 68–78; Bruzzi, *Bringing Up Daddy*, 40–50; Wilson, *Ye Heart of a Man*, 187.

41 "The Man in the Gray Flannel Suit," *Look*, May 1, 1956, 104–6; "Man in a Gray Flannel Trap," *Life*, April 9, 1956, 111–14; Louis Coxe, "Recent Fiction," *Yale Review* 45 (1955): 157.

42 Jack Moffitt, Review of "The Man in the Gray Flannel Suit," *Hollywood Reporter*, March 30, 1956.

43 Whyte, *Organization Man*, 146, 278; Louis Lyndon, "Uncertain Hero," *Woman's Home Companion*, November 1956, 41–43, 107.

44 George B. Leonard Jr., "The American Male: Why Is He Afraid to Be Different?," *Look*, February 18, 1958, 95; Lindner, *Must You Conform?*

45 Philip Wylie, "The Abdicating Male . . . and How the Gray Flannel Mind Exploits Him through His Women," *Playboy*, November 1956, 29; Philip Wylie, "The Womanization of America," *Playboy*, September 1958. See also the Playboy Panel on "The Womanization of America," *Playboy*, June 1962, with Norman Mailer and others. Osgerby, *Playboys in Paradise*, esp. 121–48; Gilbert, *Men in the Middle*, 189–214; Krämer, "Playboy Tells His Story."

46 "Playboy's Penthouse Apartment," Part I, *Playboy*, September 1956, 53–60, and Part II, October 1956, 65–70; Cohan, *Masked Men*, 271ff.

47 Ehrenreich, *Hearts of Men*, 42–51, 43.

48 Adams, *Best War Ever*; Brokaw, *Greatest Generation*; Rose, *Myth and the Greatest Generation*; Kimmel, *Manhood in America*, 224ff.

49 Rosenberg, "'Foreign Affairs'"; Silverman, *Male Subjectivity at the Margins*, 52–121.

50 "A Word to Our Readers," 3.

51 Mailer, *White Negro*; Petigny, "Norman Mailer."

52 Lindner, *Rebel without a Cause*; Hale, *Nation*.

53 Kinsey et al., Sexual Behavior in the Human Male; Kinsey et al. Sexual Behavior in the Human Female; Gilbert, *Men in the Middle*, 81–105; Marcus, Making Gay History, 19–70; Meyerowitz, *How Sex Changed*.

54 Norma Mailer, "Superman Comes to the Supermarket," *Esquire*, November 1960, www.esquire.com; Schlesinger, "Decline of Greatness," 46.

55 Dean, *Imperial Brotherhood*.

CHAPTER 11. FAMILIES, FATHERS, AND THE BLACK COMMUNITY, 1950–2010

1 Wicker, *Report of the National Advisory Commission*; Finzsch, "'National Advisory Commission'"; Martschukat, "'You Be a Man.'"

2 Strieker, *Why America Lost the War on Poverty*; Bauman, *Race and the War on Poverty*.

3 Citations according to the script in Klotman, *Screenplays of the African-American Experience*, 97–118, 101.

4 Estes, *I Am a Man*, 131–51.

5 Burnett in Cox, "Slaughterhouse Blues," 29–30.

6 For geographic and social mobility in the movie, see James, "Toward a Geo-cinematic Hermeneutics."

7 bell hooks in conversation with Charles Burnett, in hooks, *Reel to Real*, 196, 233.

8 Arthur Jaffa in conversation with bell hooks, in hooks, *Reel to Real*, 232. Gene is barely audible over the soundtrack of the music. It is also not in the script by

Klotman, *Screenplays of the African-American Experience*, 109ff. Massood, "Aesthetic Appropriate to Conditions," 32–36.

9 Harris, *African-American Screenwriters Now*, 20; hooks, *Reel to Real*, 198.

10 Massood, "Aesthetic Appropriate to Conditions," 36; Lev, *American Films of the 70s*, 140; Alexander, *Why We Make Movies*, 183–95.

11 Merritt, "Charles Burnett," 109; Bell, "Blues People," 30–32; Lev, *American Films of the 70s*, 127–32; Leab, *From Sambo to Superspade*.

12 Diawara, "Black American Cinema," 7; Masilela, "Los Angeles School," 107–17; Guerrero, *Framing Blackness*.

13 Widener, "Writing Watts."

14 James H. Billington, in Library of Congress, "Michael Jackson, the Muppets and Early Cinema Tapped for Preservation in 2009 Library of Congress National Film Registry," December 30, 2009, www.loc.gov; National Film Registry, www.loc.gov; Brill, *Crowds*; Jaffa in hooks, *Reel to Real*, 231; Klotman, *Screenplays of the African-American Experience*, 97.

15 Widener, "Writing Watts," 670.

16 Marable, "Black Male," 26; Fischer, *Suspect Relations*, 159–90; Roediger, *Wages of Whiteness*, 57, emphasis original.

17 Hodes, *White Women, Black Men*; Michel, "Reconstruction of White Southern Manhood."

18 Brundage, *Lynching in the New South*; Waldrep, *Many Faces*.

19 Hale, *Making Whiteness*; Allen, *Without Sanctuary*; Wood, *Lynching and Spectacle*.

20 Wells, "Southern Horrors," esp. 59; Apel, *Imagery of Lynching*; Waldrep, *African Americans Confront Lynching*.

21 Franklin, "Ensuring Inequality," 153. In *Killer of Sheep* Stan is upset when his son calls his mother "mot dear," which denotes southern provincialism. At the same time, in moments of big disappointment Stan's wife longs for her southern past.

22 Wright, *Native Son*, 15; Fanon, "Fact of Blackness"; Kinnamon, "How 'Native Son' Was Born"; Sielke, *Reading Rape*, 103–16; Green, *Fatherless Child*, 43–74; Erb, *Tracking King Kong*.

23 Frazier, *Negro Family*, 325, and Anthony M. Platt's introduction to the book, xxvi.

24 Mailer, *White Negro*; Petigny, "Norman Mailer."

25 Cleaver, *Soul on Ice*, 33, 122–37.

26 Cleaver, *Soul on Ice*, 242; Frazier, *Negro Family*, pt. 4, 271–90.

27 hooks, *We Real Cool*; Wallace, *Black Macho*, 35.

28 Finzsch, *Von Benin*, 490–531; Joseph, *Dark Days, Bright Nights*.

29 For the diversity in the black power movement, see Joseph, *Waiting 'til the Midnight Hour*; Joseph, *Dark Days, Bright Nights*.

30 Austin, *Up against the Wall*; Garrow, "Picking Up the Books."

31 The transfer of the provider concept onto the community matches with the collectivist-Marxist political concepts of the Panthers. Alkebulan, *Survival Pending Revolution*; Morgan, "Media Culture"; Matthews, "'No One Ever Asks'";

LeBlanc-Ernest, "'Most Qualified Person'"; Cleaver, "On Meeting the Needs";
Estes, *I Am a Man*, 158; Brown, *Taste of Power*.

32 Johnson, "Commencement Address."

33 Rainwater, Moynihan, and Yancey, *Moynihan Report*; Estes, *I Am a Man*, 107–29;
Finzsch, "Gouvernementalität"; Chappell, *War on Welfare*.

34 Frazier, *Negro Family*, 125; for a summary of the debate, see Bell et al., "Beyond the
Culture of Poverty."

35 Finzsch, *Von Benin*, 496–97, 516–17.

36 Estes, *I Am a Man*, 112; Giddings, *When and Where I Enter*.

37 Sugrue, "Poverty in the Era of Welfare Reform"; Sugrue, "Structures of Urban Poverty."

38 Estes, *I Am a Man*, 117; Finzsch, "Gouvernementalität"; Horne, *Fire This Time*,
185–243; Ryan, *Blaming the Victim*; Gutman, *Black Family*; Blassingame, *Slave
Community*; White, *Ar'n't I a Woman?*

39 Elkins, *Slavery*; Clark, *Dark Ghetto*; Myrdal, *American Dilemma*.

40 Frazier, *Negro Family*, introduction by Platt, xiv; Du Bois, *Negro American Family*, 18–26; letter from E. Franklin Frazier to W. E. B. Du Bois, August 2, 1939, in
Aptheker, *Correspondence of W. E. B. Du Bois*, 2:193–94.

41 "The American Underclass," *Time*, August 29, 1977; Krämer, *Moral Leaders*.

42 Bauman, *Race and the War on Poverty*, 10–30; Finzsch, "National Advisory Commission"; Finzsch, "Gouvernementalität."

43 Sugrue, "Poverty in the Era of Welfare Reform," 329; hooks, *We Real Cool*, xii; Butter and Schinko, "Introduction."

44 Klotman, *Screenplays of the African-American Experience*, 106.

45 Sugrue, "Poverty in the Era of Welfare Reform," 327.

46 Klotman, *Screenplays*, 106.

47 Overbeck, "'Enemy Within,'" shows how the stereotype expanded in the 1980s.

48 Klotman, *Screenplays of the African-American Experience*, 104–5.

49 Klotman, *Screenplays of the African-American Experience*, 101.

50 Estes, *I Am a Man*, 131–51.

51 hooks, *We Real Cool*, xiv; Wallace, *Black Macho*.

52 Manohla Dargis, "Whereabouts in Watts? Where Poetry Meets Chaos," *New
York Times*, March 30, 2007; Ann Hornaday, "Killer of Sheep," *Washington Post*,
June 1, 2007.

53 Klawans, "That's the Way," 34.

54 The year 1996 saw 55 pregnancies per 1,000 women between the ages of fifteen
and nineteen in the United States, or 85.5/1,000 including abortions. For comparison, in Germany the figures were 13 or 18/1,000.

55 For assessments from both sides of the political spectrum see Gilder, *Wealth and
Poverty*; Murray, *Losing Ground*; Smith, *Family Values;* Kimmel, *Gendered Society*.

56 Rowe, "Marriage and Fathering." Almost all critical comments refer to the census,
as also does Obama in *Audacity of Hope*, 392.

57 Taylor, *Black Fathers*, 9, for citation. For "healthy models of masculinity," see Harris, "To Be Men First."

58 Neal, *New Black Man*.

59 African American Fathers Project, *Turning the Corner*.

60 Rowe, "Marriage and Fathering," 18; Cosby, *Fatherhood*; Cosby and Poussaint, *Come on, People*.

61 Felicia R. Lee, "To Blacks, Precious Is 'Demeaned' or 'Angelic,'" *New York Times*, November 20, 2009; Armond White, "Pride & Precious," *New York Press*, November 4, 2009, www.nypress.com; Sapphire, *Push*.

62 Hymowitz, "Dads in the 'Hood"; Barack Obama, "2004 Democratic National Convention Keynote Address," American Rhetoric, www.americanrhetoric.com.

63 Obama, *Audacity of Hope*, 383–415.

64 Dyson, "Obama's Rebuke"; Howe, "Obama Has Angered Millions of Blacks."

65 Muhammad, "Post Racial Racism."

66 Kay Hymowitz, "An Enduring Crisis for the Black Family," *Washington Post*, December 6, 2008, A15, www.washingtonpost.com.

67 Fuller, *Cosby Show*; Chan, "Bill Cosby."

68 Obama, *Audacity of Hope*, 389–90, 409.

69 Bell, "Blues People," 30; Cox, "Slaughterhouse Blues," 29–30; Klotman, *Screenplays of the African-American Experience*, 99.

CHAPTER 12. QUEER PARENTS AND FATHERHOOD MOVEMENTS, 1970–2010

1 Interview by the author with Heidi and Ren in their house in Bernal Heights, San Francisco, October 7, 2010; all future quotes from Heidi, Ren, and their daughter Isabella as well as biographical information are based on this interview.

2 Chauncey, *Why Marriage?*; Snyder, *Gay Marriage and Democracy*; Rivers, *Radical Relations*; Slater, *Lesbian Family*.

3 In 2008 they chose not to use the small window between June 16 and November 5, when gay marriage was legally permitted, before it finally became a constitutional right through *Obergefell v. Hodges*, 576 US ___ (2015).

4 The right to serve openly in the military was granted in December 2010, after seventeen years of a policy of "don't ask, don't tell." Estes, *Ask and Tell*.

5 Adam, Defense; Chauncey, *Why Marriage?*

6 Stacey, "What Comes after Patriarchy?"; Meade and Haag, "Persistent Patriarchy"; Gavanas, *Fatherhood Politics*; the article by Silverstein and Auerbach, "Deconstructing the Essential Father," generated much discussion.

7 *Bowers v. Hardwick*, 478 US 186 (1986); Ghaziani, *Dividends of Dissent*; Stryker and Van Buskirk, *Gay by the Bay*, 4, 113ff., 121; Sedgwick, *Epistemology of the Closet*, 1–63; Haimes and Weiner, "'Everybody's Got a Dad . . .'"; Kranz and Daniluk, "Living Outside of the Box."

8 Howard, *Men Like That*; Thompson, "Queer Capital"; Boyd, *Wide Open Town*; Kennedy and Davis, *Boots of Leather*; Chauncey, *Gay New York*; Stein, *City of Sisterly and Brotherly Loves*.

9 Boyd, *Wide Open Town*.

10 D'Emilio and Freedman, *Intimate Matters*, 289.

11 Rupp, *Desired Past*, 135; Hampf, "'Dykes' or 'Whores'"; Hampf, *Release a Man for Combat*.

12 Canaday, *Straight State*.

13 Stieglitz, *Undercover*; Johnson, *Lavender Scare*; Cuordileone, *Manhood and American Political Culture*; Canaday, *Straight State*; May, *Homeward Bound*.

14 D'Emilio and Freedman, *Intimate Matters*, 285ff.; Gilbert, *Men in the Middle*, 81–105, 164–88; Meyerowitz, *How Sex Changed*; Corber, *Homosexuality in Cold War America*.

15 Rupp, *Desired Past*, 145–50; Boyd, *Wide Open Town*, 68–101.

16 Rupp, *Desired Past*, 166–76.

17 Rupp, *Desired Past*, 183–84; Love, *Feminists Who Changed America*, 379–80; Echols, *Daring to Be Bad*, 221–25; D'Emilio and Freedman, *Intimate Matters*, 308–18. On marriage and enslavement, see Hole and Levine, *Rebirth of Feminism*, 144; Young, "Out of the Closets," 29.

18 Rupp, *Desired Past*, 179–80.

19 Faludi, *Backlash*.

20 Pepper, *Ultimate Guide to Pregnancy for Lesbians*.

21 Priwer and Phillips, *Gay Parenting*; Savage, *Kid*.

22 Haimes and Weiner, "'Everybody's Got a Dad . . . ,'" 478–79.

23 Gates and Romero, "Parenting by Gay Men and Lesbians."

24 Interview by the author with Mike and Shum in their house in San Francisco, October 8, 2010; Wagner, "Homosexuality and Family Formation"; Mezey, *New Choices*, 4, 25, 30; Lewin, *Gay Fatherhood*, 19; Brody, "Greater Acceptance," 87–91; Johnson et al., *Gay Baby Boom*; Romero et al., "Census Snapshot." See also US Bureau of the Census/Williams Institute, "Census Fact Sheet."

25 Mezey, *New Choices*, 27.

26 Mezey, *New Choices*, 77–78.

27 Mezey, *New Choices*, 144–45.

28 Lewin, *Gay Fatherhood*.

29 A widely shared reason against anonymous sperm donors as Kranz and Daniluk, "Living Outside of the Box," 12ff., show, even though many women finally decide against a known sperm donor for legal as well as personal reasons.

30 Priwer and Phillips, *Gay Parenting*, 62ff.; Haimes and Weiner, "'Everybody's Got a Dad . . . ,'" 480–493, about the often complex legal and personal relationship between mothers and sperm donors.

31 See www.gayspermbank.com.

32 One motive for using the same sperm donor is to promote a sense of a common family heritage; Haimes and Weiner, "'Everybody's Got a Dad . . . ,'" 491; Kranz and Daniluk, "Living Outside of the Box," 19.

33 Townsend, *Package Deal*.

34 Mezey, *New Choices*, 4.

35 Silverstein and Auerbach, "Deconstructing the Essential Father"; Perlesz, "'Fathers' Cannot Easily Be De-gendered"; Bos et al., "USA Longitudinal Lesbian

Family Study," based on five preliminary studies, conducted between 1996 and 2006. Tasker and Golombok, *Growing Up in a Lesbian Family*.

36 American Civil Liberties Union, "Gay Parenting"; Cooper, Cates, and Stacey, "Gay Parenting."

37 Hequembourg, *Lesbian Motherhood*.

38 Krämer, "Playboy Tells His Story"; Traister, "Academic Viagra"; Wickberg, "Heterosexual White Male."

39 Blankenhorn, *Fatherless America*; Koch, "Fatherhood Movement," 488.

40 Dailey, "Gay Parenting," 29–40; Kurtz, "Gay Marriage"; Benne and McDermott, "Gay Marriage."

41 Koch, "Fatherhood Movement," 488ff.; Clinton is cited in Haas and Wisensale, *Families and Social Policy*, 117–18; Popenoe, *Life without Father*; Popenoe, *Families without Fathers*. For changes in welfare, see Chappell, *War on Welfare*.

42 Ribuffo, "Family Policy."

43 Gavanas, *Fatherhood Politics*; Messner, *Politics of Masculinities*; Collier, "Coming Together?"

44 Gavanas, *Fatherhood Politics*, 21; Popenoe, *Life without Father*, 194.

45 Usher, "Gay Marriage"; Baskerville, *Taken into Custody*; Gavanas, *Fatherhood Politics*, 10–11.

46 Bly, *Iron John*.

47 Messner, *Politics of Masculinities*, 32; Kimmel, "Struggle for Men's Souls," 592ff.; Gavanas, *Fatherhood Politics*, 13–14; Gillis, "Marginalization of Fatherhood," 235; Finzsch, "Masculinities."

48 Crowley, "Organizational Responses."

49 Quayle, "Address to the Commonwealth Club"; "Did You Say 'Movement'?," 5–6; Gavanas, *Fatherhood Politics*, 41; Kimmel, *Gendered Society*, 111. Quayle received support from the Institute for American Values; see Whitehead, "Dan Quayle Was Right."

50 Popenoe, *Life without Father*, 6.

51 Dechert, "Family Man," 272.

52 Gillis, "Marginalization of Fatherhood," 235.

CONCLUSION

1 Blankenhorn, *Fatherless America*; Koch, "Fatherhood Movement," 488.

2 Cooper, *Family Values*.

3 Butler, *Giving an Account*, 19.

4 Foucault, "Nietzsche, Genealogy, History," 78; Foucault, "What Is Critique?"

BIBLIOGRAPHY

PRIMARY SOURCES

Archives
Barnard College Archives, New York, Biographical Files.
Barnard College Archives, New York, Mirra Komarovsky Collection.
Ellis Island Oral History Project, North American Immigrant Letters, Diaries, and
   Oral Histories, July 1, 2012. http://solomon.imld.alexanderstreet.com.
Kautz Family YMCA Archives, University of Minnesota, Biographical Records, Box 66.
Kautz Family YMCA Archives, University of Minnesota, Boys Work, Boxes 6, 14, 50,
   51, 52, 56.
Kautz Family YMCA Archives, University of Minnesota, Records of the YMCA of the
   City of New York, Box 371.
Kautz Family YMCA Archives, University of Minnesota, Robert McBurney Papers,
   Boxes 1–3.
Kautz Family YMCA Archives, University of Minnesota, Robert Weidensall Papers, Box 27.
Kautz Family YMCA Archives, University of Minnesota, YMCA of Greater New York
   Papers, Box 60.
Library of Congress, Manuscript Division, Jacob A. Riis Papers, Boxes 4, 10, 12.
Museum of the City of New York, Collections, http://collections.mcny.org/, September
   17, 2012.
New York Public Library, Jacob Riis Papers, Boxes 6, 7.
Syracuse University Library, Department of Special Collections, Oneida Community
   Collection, Boxes 11, 12, 68, 70.
YIVO-Archives, Institute of Jewish Research, New York, RG 102, American-Jewish
   Autobiographies 1942–1970s.

Interviews
Interview with Heidi and Ren in their house in Bernal Heights, San Francisco, by
   Jürgen Martschukat, October 7, 2010, 8–10 PM.
Interview with Mike and Shum in their house in the Mission, San Francisco, by Jürgen
   Martschukat, October 8, 2010, 6–8 PM.

Periodicals
Bachelor Book, March–November 1900.

Chicago Daily Tribune, 1893.
Collier's Magazine, 1955.
Esquire, 1960.
Hollywood Reporter, 1956.
Life, 1956.
Long House News, 1947.
Look, 1956, 1958.
New York Herald, 1903.
New York Press, 1890, 2009.
New York Times, 1966, 2003, 2007, 2009, 2010.
New York Tribune, 1890.
Oneida Circular, 1852–72.
Playboy, 1956, 1958, 1962.
Spiritual Magazine, 1846–49.
St. Louis Daily Globe-Democrat, 1935.
Time, 1954, 1977, 2008.
Washington Post, 2007, 2008.
Witness, 1839.
Woman's Home Companion, 1956.

Visual Material
The Birth of a Nation (D. W. Griffith, USA, 1915).
Broken Arrow (Delmar Daves, USA, 1950).
The Kids Are All Right (Lisa Cholodenko, USA, 2010).
Killer of Sheep (Charles Burnett, USA, 1977/2007).
The Man in the Gray Flannel Suit (Nunnally Johnson, USA, 1956).
Precious (Lee Daniels, USA, 2009).
Rebels without a Cause (Nicholas Ray, USA, 1955).
Stagecoach (John Ford, USA, 1939).
The Wild One (Laszlo Benedek, USA, 1953).

Published Sources
Ade, George. *Single Blessedness and Other Observations*. Garden City, NY: Doubleday, 1922.
African American Fathers Project. *Turning the Corner on Father Absence in Black America*. Atlanta, GA: Morehouse Research Institute and the Institute for American Values, 1999.
Alcott, William A. *The Young Husband; or, Duties of Man in the Marriage Relation*. 1838. New York: Arno Press, 1972.
———. *The Young Man's Guide*. 1844. Boston: T.R. Marvin, 1849.
Almond, Gabriel, and Harold D. Lasswell. "Aggressive Behavior by Clients toward Public Relief Administrators: A Configurative Analysis." *American Political Science Review* 28, no. 4 (1934): 643–55.

American Civil Liberties Union. "Gay Parenting Does Not Place Children at Risk." In *Gay and Lesbian Families*, edited by Kate Burns, 41–45. Detroit, MI: Greenhaven Press, 2005.

"The American Underclass." *Time*, August 29, 1977. www.time.com.

Andrews, William L., ed. *North Carolina Slave Narratives: The Lives of Moses Roper, Lunsford Lane, Moses Grandy, & Thomas H. Jones*. Chapel Hill: University of North Carolina Press, 2005.

Angell, Robert C. *The Family Encounters the Depression*. New York: Charles Scribner's Sons, 1936.

Aptheker, Herbert, ed. *The Correspondence of W. E. B. Du Bois, Vol. II: Selections 1934–1944*. Amherst: University of Massachusetts Press, 1976.

Bakke, E. Wight. *Citizens without Work: A Study of the Effects of Unemployment upon the Workers' Social Relations and Practices*. New Haven, CT: Yale University Press, 1940.

———. *The Unemployed Worker: A Study of the Task of Making a Living without a Job*. New Haven, CT: Yale University Press, 1940.

Barnes, Gilbert H., and Dwight L. Dumond, eds. *Letters of Theodore Dwight Weld, Angelina Grimké Weld and Sarah Grimké, 1822–1844*. New York: Appleton-Century, 1934.

Barren, Alfred, and George Noyes Miller, eds. *Home Talks by John H. Noyes*. Vol. 1. Oneida, NY: Oneida Community, 1875.

Bassett, John Spencer. *Slavery in the State of North Carolina*. Baltimore: Johns Hopkins University Press, 1899.

Baumler, Ellen, ed. *Girl from the Gulches: The Story of Mary Ronan, as Told to Margaret Ronan*. Helena, MT: Montana Historical Society Press, 2003.

Bayles, James C. *The Tenement House Problem in New York: For the Information of the Commission on Legislation Affecting Tenement and Lodging Houses, Provided for in Chapter 84, Laws of 1887, December 14, 1887*. New York: W.P. Mitchell, 1887.

Beard, George M. *American Nervousness: Its Causes and Consequences*. New York: G.P. Putnam's Sons, 1881.

Bible Communism: A Compilation from the Annual Reports and Other Publications of the Oneida Association and Its Branches, Presenting, in Connection with Their History, a Summary View of Their Religious and Social Theories. Brooklyn, NY: Office of the Circular, 1853.

Bixby, J. "Why Is Single Life Becoming More General?" *Nation*, March 5, 1868, 191–92.

Blankenhorn, David. *Fatherless America: Confronting Our Most Urgent Social Problem*. New York: Basic Books, 1995.

Bly, Robert. *Iron John: A Book about Men*. New York: Vintage, 1990.

Bowers v. Hardwick, 478 US 186 (1986).

Brown, Elaine. *A Taste of Power: A Black Woman's Story*. New York: Pantheon Books, 1992.

Burgess, Ernest W. "Sociological Aspects of the Sex Life of the Unmarried Adult." In *The Sex Life of the Unmarried Adult: An Inquiry into and an Interpretation of Current Sex Practices*, edited by Ira S. Wile, 116–54. New York: Vanguard Press, 1934.

Cahan, Abraham. "The Russian Jew in America." *Atlantic Monthly* 82, no. 489 (1898): 128–39.

Cavan, Ruth S. "Unemployment: Crisis of the Common Man." *Marriage and Family Living* 21, no. 2 (1959): 139–46.

Cavan, Ruth S., and Katherine Howland Ranck. *The Family and the Depression*. Chicago: University of Chicago Press, 1938.

Clark, Kenneth D. *Dark Ghetto: Dilemmas of Social Power*. New York: Harper & Row, 1965.

Cleaver, Eldridge. "On Meeting the Needs of the People" (1969). In *Target Zero: A Life in Writing*, edited by Kathleen Cleaver, 212–17. New York: Palgrave Macmillan, 2006.

———. *Soul on Ice*. 1968. New York: Delta Book, 1999.

Cooley, Benjamin F., ed. *Summary Exposition of the Social Theory of the Dissenters, Called Perfectionists, Which Theory Is Called by Them the Bible Argument, Showing the Relation of the Sexes in the Kingdom of Heaven on Earth, Until Which Some of Them Profess to Have Attained, Especially Those in the Oneida Association, in the State of New York*. Worcester, MA, 1850.

Cosby, Bill. *Fatherhood*. Introduction and afterword by Alvin F. Poussaint. Garden City, NY: Doubleday, 1986.

Cosby, Bill, and Alvin F. Poussaint. *Come on, People: On the Path from Victims to Victors*. Nashville: Thomas Nelson, 2007.

Cousins, Norman. "Will Women Lose Their Jobs?" *Current History and Forum* 51, no. 1 (1939): 14–15, 17–18, 63.

Craig, Oscar. "Poor in Great Cities, IX: The Prevention of Pauperism." *Scribner's Magazine* 14, no. 1 (1893): 121–29.

"Defense of Marriage Act." *Congressional Record* 142, no. 102 (July 11, 1996): 7441–47.

Dickinson, Robert L. "Medicine: Medical Reflections upon Some Life Histories." In *The Sex Life of the Unmarried Adult: An Inquiry into and an Interpretation of Current Sex Practices*, edited by Ira S. Wile, 186–211. New York: Vanguard Press, 1934.

Doggett, Laurence L. *Life of Robert R. McBurney*. Cleveland, OH: F.M. Barton, 1902.

Douglass, Frederick. *My Bondage and My Freedom*. 1855. New York: Dover, 1969.

———. *Narrative of the Life of Frederick Douglass, an American Slave, Written by Himself*. 1845. New York: Anchor Books, 1989.

Du Bois, W. E. B. *The Negro American Family*. 1909. Cambridge, MA: MIT Press, 1970.

Dyson, Michael E. "Obama's Rebuke of Absentee Black Fathers." *Time*, June 19, 2008. www.time.com.

Eastman, Charles A. *The Essential Charles Eastman (Ohiyesa). Light on the Indian World*. Rev. ed. Bloomington, IN: World Wisdom Books, 2007.

———. *From the Deep Woods to Civilization: Chapters in the Autobiography of an Indian*. 1916. Lincoln, NE: Bison Books, 1977.

Eastman, Hubbard. *Noyesism Unveiled: A History of the Sect Self-Styled Perfectionists. With a Summary View of Their Leading Doctrines*. Brattleboro, VT, 1849.

Eighteenth Annual Report of the Managers of the Society for the Reformation of Juvenile Delinquents to the Legislature of the State, and the Corporation of the City of New York. New York: Press of Mahlon Day, 1843.

Elkins, Stanley. *Slavery: A Problem in American Institutional and Intellectual Life.* Chicago: University of Chicago Press, 1959.

Fanon, Frantz. "The Fact of Blackness" (1952). *ChickenBones: A Journal.* www.nathanielturner.com.

First Annual Report of the Oneida Association. Exhibiting Its History, Principles, and Transactions to Jan. 1, 1849. Oneida, NY: Leonart, 1849.

Fitzhugh, George. *Cannibals All!! or, Slaves without Masters.* Bedford, MA: Applewood, 1857.

———. *Sociology for the South; or The Failure of Free Society.* Richmond, VA: A. Morris, 1854.

Foby, F. "Management of Servants." *Southern Cultivator* 11 (August 1853): 226–28.

Fourth Annual Report of the New York Juvenile Asylum to the Legislature of the State, and to the Common Council of the City of New York. New York: William H. White, 1856.

Frazier, E. Franklin. *The Negro Family in the United States.* 1939. Notre Dame, IN: University of Notre Dame Press, 2009.

Friedan, Betty. *The Feminine Mystique.* New York: Norton, 1963.

Fromm, Erich. "Rezension von Ira S. Wile, ed., The Sex Life of the Unmarried Adult, New York: Vanguard Press 1934." *Zeitschrift für Sozialforschung* 4 (1935): 114–15.

Gladden, Washington. "Present-Day Papers: The Problem of Poverty." *The Century: A Popular Quarterly* 45, no. 2 (1892): 245–57.

Goldstein, Minnie. "Success or Failure?" In *My Future Is in America: Autobiographies of Eastern European Jewish Immigrants*, edited by Jocelyn Cohen et al., 18–34. New York: New York University Press, 2008.

Grant, Ulysses S. *The Personal Memoirs of U.S. Grant.* 1885–86. London: Cosimo, 2007.

Groves, Ernest R. "Sex Psychology of the Unmarried Adult." In *The Sex Life of the Unmarried Adult: An Inquiry into and an Interpretation of Current Sex Practices*, edited by Ira S. Wile, 97–115. New York: Vanguard Press 1934.

Guest, Edgar A. *My Job as a Father, and What My Father Did for Me.* Chicago: Reilly & Lee, 1923.

Harris, Loren S. "To Be Men First, Then Fathers: Realizing Progressive Black Masculinities: An Introduction." In *BAF. Be a Father to Your Child. Real Talk from Black Men on Family, Love, and Fatherhood*, edited by April S. Silver, 3–10. Berkeley, CA: Soft Skull Press, 2008.

Henry, George W. *Sex Variants: A Study of Homosexual Patterns.* 2 vols. New York: Paul B. Hoeber, 1941.

Horn, Wade F. "Did You Say 'Movement'?" In *The Fatherhood Movement: A Call to Action*, edited by David Blankenhorn et al., 1–16. Lanham, MD: Lexington Books, 1999.

Howard, Donald S. *The WPA and Federal Relief Policy*. 1943. New York: DaCapo Press, 1975.

Howe, Darcus. "Obama Has Angered Millions of Blacks." *New Statesman*, July 31, 2008. www.newstatesman.com.

Hymowitz, Kay S. "Dads in the 'Hood." *City Journal*, Autumn 2004. www.city-journal. org.

Jahoda, Marie, Paul F. Lazarsfeld, and Hans Zeisel. *Marienthal: The Sociography of an Unemployed Community*. 1933. New York: Routledge, 1971.

James, John A. *The Young Man's Friend and Guide through Life to Immortality*. New York: R. Carter, 1857.

Jefferson, Thomas. *Notes on the State of Virginia*. 1787. http://xroads.virginia.edu.

Jerome, Howard K. *The Reflections of a Bachelor*. New York: A.L. Chattert, 1911.

Johnson, Lyndon B. "Commencement Address at Howard University. 'To Fulfill These Rights.'" June 4, 1965. http://cdn.constitutionreader.com.

Jones, Thomas H. "The Experience of Rev. Thomas H. Jones" (1885). In *North Carolina Slave Narratives: The Lives of Moses Roper, Lunsford Lane, Moses Grandy, & Thomas H. Jones*, edited by William L. Andrews, 189–202. Chapel Hill: University of North Carolina Press, 2005.

———. *The Experience of Thomas H. Jones, Who Was a Slave for Forty-Three Years. Written by a Friend*. Boston: Bazin & Chandler, 1862.

Kegg, Maude. *Portage Lake: Memories of an Ojibwe Childhood*. Edmonton: University of Alberta Press, 1991.

Kiernan, James G. "Responsibility in Sexual Perversion." *Chicago Medical Recorder* 3 (1892): 185–210.

Kinsey, Alfred C., Wardell B. Pomeroy, and Clyde E. Martin. *Sexual Behavior in the Human Male*. 1948. Bloomington: Indiana University Press, 1998.

Kinsey, Alfred C., Wardell B. Pomeroy, Clyde E. Martin, and Paul H. Gebhard. *Sexual Behavior in the Human Female*. 1953. Bloomington: Indiana University Press, 1998.

Kirwan, Nicholas M. *The Happy Home*. New York: Harper, 1858.

Klawans, Stuart. "That's the Way of the World." *Nation*, April 9, 2007, 34.

Klotman, Phyllis Rauch. *Screenplays of the African-American Experience*. Bloomington: Indiana University Press, 1991.

Komarovsky, Mirra. "The Concept of Social Role Revisited." *Gender & Society* 6 (1992): 301–13.

———. "Cultural Contradictions and Sex Roles." *American Journal of Sociology* 78 (1946): 184–89.

———. *Dilemmas of Masculinity: A Study of College Youth*. 1976. Walnut Creek, CA: Altamira Press, 2004.

———. "Functional Analysis of Sex Roles." *American Sociological Review* 15 (1950): 508–16.

———. *The Unemployed Man and His Family*. New York: Dryden Press, 1940.

———. *Women in the Modern World: Their Education and Their Dilemmas*. Boston: Little, Brown, 1953.

Krafft-Ebing, Richard von. *Psychopathia Sexualis: With Especial Reference to Contrary Sexual Instinct. A Medico-Legal Study*. Philadelphia: F.A. Davis, 1893.

LaFollette, Cecile Tipton. *A Study of the Problems of 652 Gainfully Employed Married Women Homemakers*. New York: Teachers College, Columbia University, 1934.

Lindner, Robert. *Must You Conform?* New York: Rinehart, 1955.

———. *Rebel without a Cause: The Story of a Criminal Psychopath*. New York: Grove Press, 1944.

Locke, John. *Some Thoughts Concerning Education*. London: Churchill, 1693.

———. *Two Treatises of Government*. London: Churchill, 1690.

Mailer, Norman. *The White Negro: Superficial Reflections on the Hipster*. San Francisco: City Lights Books, 1957.

Malkin, Richard. *Marriage, Morals, and War*. New York: Arden Book, 1943.

McCabe, James D., Jr. *Lights and Shadows of New York Life; or, The Sights and Sensations of the Great City*. Philadelphia: National, 1872.

Merriam, H. G., ed. *Frontier Woman: The Story of Mary Ronan as Told to Margaret Ronan*. Missoula: University of Montana, 1973.

Mills, C. Wright. *White Collar*. New York: Oxford University Press, 1951.

Monroe, Day. "Levels of Living of the Nation's Families." *Journal of Home Economics* 29, no. 10 (December 1937): 665–70.

Morgan, Winona Louise, et al. *The Family Meets the Depression: A Study of a Group of Highly Selected Families*. Minneapolis: University of Minnesota Press, 1939.

Morse, Richard C. *My Life with Young Men: Fifty Years in the Young Men's Christian Association*. New York: Association Press, 1918.

———, ed. *Robert R. McBurney: A Memorial, 1837–1898*. New York: Young Men's Christian Association, 1899.

Moynihan, Daniel P. *The Negro Family: The Case for National Action*. Washington, DC: Government Printing Office, 1965.

Muhammad, Dedrick. "Post Racial Racism in the Post." *Common Dreams*, December 11, 2008. www.commondreams.org.

Muzzey, Artemas B. *The Christian Parent*. Boston: W. Crosby & H.B. Nichols, 1850.

Myrdal, Gunnar. *An American Dilemma: The Negro Problem and Modern Democracy*. 1944. New York: Harper & Row, 1962.

Nathan, Robert R. "Estimates of Unemployment in the United States, 1929–1935." *International Labour Review* 33 (1936): 49–73, 80–81.

Neal, Mark A. *New Black Man*. New York: Routledge, 2005.

Nixon, Russel A., and Paul A. Samuelson. "Estimates of Unemployment in the United States." *Review of Economic Statistics* 21–22 (1939–40): 101–11.

Nordhoff, Charles. *The Communistic Societies of the United States: From Personal Observations*. New York: Harper & Brothers, 1875.

Noyes, George W. *Free Love in Utopia: John Humphrey Noyes and the Origin of the Oneida Community*. Urbana: University of Illinois Press, 2001.

———, ed. *The Putney Community*. Oneida, NY, 1931.

Noyes, John H. *Handbook of the Oneida Community: Containing a Brief Sketch of Its Present Condition, Eternal Economy and Leading Principles.* No. 2. Oneida, NY: Oneida Community, 1871.

——. *Hand-Book of the Oneida Community with a Sketch of Its Founder and an Outline of Its Constitution and Doctrines.* Wallingford, CT: Office of the Circular, Wallingford Community, 1867.

——. *Male Continence.* Oneida, NY: Office of the Oneida Circular, 1872.

Noyes, Pierrepont. *My Father's House: An Oneida Boyhood.* New York: Farrar & Rinehart, 1937.

Obama, Barack. *The Audacity of Hope: Thoughts on Reclaiming the American Dream.* New York: Vintage, 2006.

Obergefell v. Hodges, 576 US ___ (2015).

O'Sullivan, John L. "Annexation." *United States Democratic Review* 17 (1845): 5–10.

——. "The Great Nation of Futurity." *United States Democratic Review* 6, no. 23 (1839): 426–30.

Overstreet, Harry Allen. *The Mature Mind.* New York: Norton, 1950.

Peirce, Bradford Kinney. *A Half Century with Juvenile Delinquents; or, The New York House of Refuge and Its Times.* New York: D. Appleton, 1869.

Pepper, Rachel. *The Ultimate Guide to Pregnancy for Lesbians: How to Stay Sane and Care for Yourself from Preconception through Birth.* San Francisco: Cleis Press, 1999.

"The Poor in Great Cities: Introduction." *Scribner's Magazine* 11, no. 4 (1892): 399–400.

Popenoe, David. *Families without Fathers.* Somerset, NJ: Transaction, 2009.

——. *Life without Father: Compelling New Evidence That Fatherhood and Marriage Are Indispensable for the Good of Children and Society.* New York: Free Press, 1996.

Priwer, Shana, and Cynthia Phillips. *Gay Parenting: Complete Guide for Same-Sex Families.* Far Hills, NJ: New Horizon Press, 2006.

Pruette, Lorine L. *Women Workers through the Depression.* New York: Macmillan, 1934.

Public Papers and Addresses of Franklin D. Roosevelt. Vol. 1: The Genesis of the New Deal, 1928–1932. Vol. 4: The Court Disapproves, 1935. New York: Government Printing Office, 1941.

Quayle, Dan. "Address to the Commonwealth Club of California. On Family Values." May 19, 1992. www.vicepresidentdanquayle.com.

Rainwater, Lee, Danial Patrick Moynihan, and William L. Yancey. *The Moynihan Report and the Politics of Controversy: A Transaction Social Science and Public Policy Report. Including the Full Text of the Negro Family: The Case for National Action by Daniel Patrick Moynihan.* Cambridge, MA: MIT Press, 1967.

Riesman, David. *The Lonely Crowd: A Study of the Changing American Character.* 1950. New Haven, CT: Yale University Press, 2001.

Riis, Jacob A. "The Battle with the Slum." *Atlantic Monthly* 83, no. 499 (1899): 626–34.

——. *The Battle with the Slum.* New York: Macmillan, 1902.

——. *The Children of the Poor.* 1892. New York: Charles Scribner's Sons, 1908.

——. *How the Other Half Lives: Studies among the Tenements of New York.* 1890. New York: Scribner, 1901.

——. *The Making of an American.* New York: Macmillan, 1901.

———. *The Peril and the Preservation of the Home: Being the William L. Bull Lectures for the Year 1903*. Philadelphia: George W. Jacobs, 1903.

———. "The Tenement: Curing Its Blight." *Atlantic Monthly* 84, no. 501 (1899): 18–28.

———. "The Tenement House Blight." *Atlantic Monthly* 83, no. 500 (1899): 760–71.

———. "The Tenement: The Real Problem of Civilization." *Forum* (1898): 83–94.

Ripley, C. Peter, et al., eds. *The Black Abolitionist Papers. Vol. 2: Canada, 1830–1865*. Chapel Hill: University of North Carolina Press, 1986.

Robertson, Constance Noyes. *Oneida Community: An Autobiography, 1851–1876*. Syracuse, NY: Syracuse University Press, 1970.

Rockwell, Norman. *Norman Rockwell: My Adventures as an Illustrator*. Garden City, NY: Doubleday, 1960.

Romero, Adam P., et al. "Census Snapshot: The Williams Institute." December 2007. www.law.ucla.edu.

Rousseau, Jean-Jacques. *Emilius and Sophia; or, A New System of Education*. 1762. London: T. Becket and P.A. De Hondt, 1763.

———. *A Treatise on the Social Compact; or, The Principles of Politic Law*. 1762. London: T. Becket and P.A. De Hondt, 1764.

Rowe, Daryl M. "Marriage and Fathering: Raising Our Children within the Context of Family and Community." *Black Scholar* 37, no. 2 (2007): 18–22.

Ruitenbeek, Hendrik M. "Men Alone: The Male Homosexual and the Disintegrated Family." In *The Problem of Homosexuality in Modern Society*, edited by Hendrik M. Ruitenbeek, 80–93. New York: E. P. Dutton, 1963.

Rules and Regulations for the Government of the House of Refuge, Adopted January 2nd, 1827. New York: Press of Mahlon Day, 1827.

Ryan, William. *Blaming the Victim*. London: Orbach & Chambers, 1971.

Sapphire. *Push*. New York: Knopf, 1996.

Second Annual Report of the Managers of the Society for the Reformation of Juvenile Delinquents in the City and State of New York. New York: Press of Mahlon Day, 1827.

Second Annual Report of the New York Juvenile Asylum to the Legislature of the State, and to the Common Council of the City of New York; Jan. 10th, 1853. New York: William H. White, 1854.

"Should Married Women Work?" *Current History and Forum* 51, no. 1 (1939): 16, 62.

Stowe, Harriet B. *The Key to Uncle Tom's Cabin*. Boston: Jewett, 1854.

———. *Uncle Tom's Cabin; or, Life among the Lowly*. Boston: John P. Jewett, 1852.

Taylor, Kristin C. *Black Fathers: A Call for Healing*. New York: Doubleday, 2003.

"Topics of the Time: Citizenship in the Tenements." *The Century: A Popular Quarterly* 55, no. 2 (1897): 313–14.

Turner, Frederick J. "The Significance of the Frontier in American History" (1893). In *The Frontier in American History*. 1920. http://xroads.virginia.edu.

US Bureau of the Census. *Historical Statistics of the United States, Colonial Times to 1970, Part I+II*. Washington, DC: Government Printing Office, 1975.

US Bureau of the Census/Williams Institute. "Census Fact Sheet." 2010. http://2010.census.gov.

US Congress, Senate, Subcommittee of the Committee on Education and Labor. *Hearings on Wartime Health and Education: Juvenile Delinquency, Parts 1, 4.* 78th Congress. 1944.

US Congress, Senate, Subcommittee on Military Affairs. *Hearings on Married Men Exemption: Drafting of Fathers.* 78 Cong., 1st session, 1943.

Wagner, Cynthia C. "Homosexuality and Family Formation: More-Accurate Counting of Same-Sex Parents May Improve Social Services." *Futurist,* May–June 2010, 6–7.

Weld, Theodore D. *American Slavery as It Is: Testimony of a Thousand Witnesses.* New York: American Anti-Slavery Society, 1839.

Wells, Richard. *A Few Political Reflections Submitted to the Consideration of the British Colonies, by a Citizen of Philadelphia.* Philadelphia: John Dunlap, 1774.

West, John C. *A Texan in Search of a Fight.* Waco, TX: Press of J.S. Hill, 1901.

Wheatley, Richard. "The Jews in New York." *Century: A Popular Quarterly* 43, no. 3 (1892): 323–42.

Whitehead, Barbara D. "Dan Quayle Was Right." *Atlantic Monthly,* April 1993, 47–48.

Whyte, William H. *The Organization Man.* New York: Doubleday, 1956.

Wicker, Tom. *Report of the National Advisory Commission on Civil Disorders* [the Kerner Report]. New York: Bantam Books, 1968.

Wile, Ira S., ed. *The Sex Life of the Unmarried Adult: An Inquiry into and an Interpretation of Current Sex Practices.* New York: Vanguard Press, 1934.

Wilson, Sloan. *The Man in the Gray Flannel Suit.* 1955. New York: Penguin, 1983.

"A Word to Our Readers." *Dissent* 1, no. 1 (1954): 3–4.

Wright, Richard. *Native Son.* 1940. New York: Harper Perennial, 2001.

Wylie, Philip. *Generation of Vipers.* New York: Rinehart, 1942.

Yezierska, Anzia. *Red Ribbon on a White Horse.* 1950. New York: Persea Books, 1987.

Young, Allen. "Out of the Closets, into the Street." In *Out of the Closets: Voices of Gay Liberation,* edited by Karla Jay and Allen Young, 6–31. New York: New York University Press, 1972.

Young Men's Christian Association. *Annual Report of the Young Men's Christian Association of the City of New York.* New York: YMCA, 1870.

Zeisloft, E. Idell. *The New Metropolis.* New York: D. Appleton, 1899.

Zelditch, Morris. "Role Differentiation in the Nuclear Family: A Comparative Study." In *Family Socialization and Interaction Process,* edited by Talcott Parsons and Robert E. Bales, 307–51. New York: Free Press, 1955.

SECONDARY SOURCES

Adam, Barry D. "The Defense of Marriage Act and American Exceptionalism. The 'Gay Marriage' Panic in the United States." *Journal of the History of Sexuality* 12, no. 2 (2003): 259–76.

Adams, David W. *Education for Extinction: American Indians and the Boarding School Experience, 1875–1928.* Lawrence: University Press of Kansas, 1995.

Adams, Michael C. C. *The Best War Ever: America and World War II.* Baltimore: Johns Hopkins University Press, 1994.

Alexander, George. *Why We Make Movies: Black Filmmakers Talk about the Magic of Cinema*. New York: Harlem Moon Broadway Books, 2003.

Alexander, Ruth M. "'We Are Engaged as a Band of Sisters': Class and Domesticity in the Washingtonian Temperance Movement, 1840–1850." *Journal of American History* 75, no. 3 (1988): 763–85.

Algeo, Katie. "Indian for a Night: Sleeping with the 'Other' at Wigwam Village Tourist Cabins." *Material Culture* 41, no. 2 (2009): 1–17.

Alkebulan, Paul. *Survival Pending Revolution: The History of the Black Panther Party*. Tuscaloosa: University of Alabama Press, 2007.

Allen, James. *Without Sanctuary: Lynching Photography in America*. Santa Fe, NM: Twin Palms, 2000.

Ambrose, Stephen E. *Nothing Like It in the World: The Men Who Built the Transcontinental Railroad 1863–1869*. 2000. New York: Simon & Schuster, 2005.

Andrews, William L. "An Introduction to the Slave Narrative." In *Documenting the American South*. http://docsouth.unc.edu.

Apel, Dora. *Imagery of Lynching: Black Men, White Women, and the Mob*. New Brunswick, NJ: Rutgers University Press, 2004.

Armitage, Sue. "Western Women: Beginning to Come into Focus." *Montana: The Magazine of Western History* 32, no. 3 (1982): 2–9.

Atkins, Annette. "The Child's West: A Review Essay." *New Mexico Historical Review* 65 (November 4, 1990): 477–90.

Austin, Curtis J. *Up against the Wall: Violence in the Making and Unmaking of the Black Panther Party*. Fayetteville: University of Arkansas Press, 2006.

Bailyn, Bernard, ed. *The Debate on the Constitution: Federalist and Antifederalist Speeches, Articles, and Letters during the Struggle over Ratification*. 2 vols. New York: Library of America, 1993.

Bardaglio, Peter W. *Reconstructing the Household: Families, Sex, and the Law in the Nineteenth-Century South*. Chapel Hill: University of North Carolina Press, 1995.

Barker-Benfield, G. J. "The Spermatic Economy: A Nineteenth Century View of Sexuality." *Feminist Studies* 1, no. 1 (1972): 45–74.

Barkun, Michael. *Crucible of the Millennium: The Burned-Over District of New York in the 1840s*. Syracuse, NY: University of Syracuse Press, 1986.

Barr, Alwyn. *Black Texans: A History of African Americans in Texas, 1528–1995*. Norman: University of Oklahoma Press, 1996.

Barrett, Lindon. "African-American Slave Narratives: Literacy, the Body, Authority." *American Literary History* 7, no. 3 (1995): 415–42.

Bartal, Israel. *The Jews of Eastern Europe 1772–1881*. Philadelphia: University of Pennsylvania Press, 2005.

Barthes, Roland. *Mythologies*. Translated by Annette Lavers. 1957. London: Paladin, 1972.

Baskerville, Stephen. *Taken into Custody: The War against Fathers, Marriage, and the Family*. Nashville: Cumberland House, 2007.

Basso, Matthew, Laura McCall, and Dee Garceau Hagen. *Across the Great Divide: Cultures of Manhood in the American West*. New York: Routledge, 2001.

Bate, David. "Fotografien und der koloniale Blick." In *Diskurse der Fotografie: Fotokritik am Ende des fotografischen Zeitalters*, edited by Herta Wolf, 115–32. Frankfurt: Suhrkamp, 2003.

Battan, Jesse F. "'You Cannot Fix the Scarlett Letter on My Breast!' Women Reading, Writing, and Reshaping the Sexual Culture of Victorian America." *Journal of Social History* 37, no. 3 (2004): 601–24.

Bauman, Robert. *Race and the War on Poverty: From Watts to East L.A.* Norman: University of Oklahoma Press, 2008.

Bederman, Gail. *Manliness and Civilization: A Cultural History of Gender and Race in the United States, 1880–1917.* Chicago: University of Chicago Press, 1995.

Beisel, Nicola. *Anthony Comstock and Family Reproduction in Victorian America.* Princeton, NJ: Princeton University Press, 1997.

Bell, James. "Blues People." *Sight & Sound* 18 (2008): 30–32.

Bell, Monica, Nathan Fosse, Michèle Lamont, and Eva Rosen. "Beyond the Culture of Poverty." In *The Blackwell Encyclopedia of Race, Ethnicity and Nationalism*, edited by John Stone et al., 1–16. Hoboken, NJ: Wiley, 2016.

Benne, Robert, and Gerald McDermott. "Gay Marriage Threatens Families, Children, and Society." In *Gay and Lesbian Families*, edited by Roman Espejo, 11–15. Detroit, MI: Greenhaven Press, 2009.

Bennett, Michael J. *When Dreams Came True: The GI Bill and the Making of Modern America.* Washington, DC: Brassey's, 1996.

Berlin, Ira. *Generations of Captivity: A History of African-American Slaves.* Cambridge, MA: Belknap, 2003.

Bierling, Stephan. *Kleine Geschichte Kaliforniens.* Munich: Beck, 2006.

Birken, Laurence. *Consuming Desire. Sexual Science and the Emergence of a Culture of Abundance, 1871–1914.* Ithaca, NY: Cornell University Press, 1988.

Black, Jason E. "Authoritarian Fatherhood: Andrew Jackson's Early Familial Lectures to America's 'Red Children.'" *Journal of Family History* 30, no. 3 (2005): 247–64.

Blackburn, George M., and Sherman L. Richards. "Unequal Opportunity on a Mining Frontier: The Role of Gender, Race, and Birthplace." *Pacific Historical Review* 62, no. 1 (1993): 19–38.

Blassingame, John. *The Slave Community: Plantation Life in the Antebellum South.* 1972. New York: Oxford University Press, 1979.

——. "Using the Testimony of Ex-Slaves: Approaches and Problems." In *The Slave's Narrative*, edited by Charles T. Davis and Henry Louis Gates Jr., 78–98. Oxford: Oxford University Press, 1985.

Bolin, Winifred D. Wandersee. "The Economics of Middle-Income Family Life: Working Women During the Great Depression." *Journal of American History* 75, no. 1 (1978): 60–74.

Bos, Henny M., Nanette K. Gatrell, Heidi Peyser, and Frank van Balen. "The USA Longitudinal Lesbian Family Study (NLLFS): Homophobia, Psychological Adjustment, and Protective Factors." *Journal of Lesbian Studies* 12, no. 4 (2008): 455–71.

Boyd, Nan A. *Wide Open Town: A History of Queer San Francisco to 1965.* Berkeley: University of California Press, 2003.

Boyer, Paul. *Urban Masses and Moral Order in America, 1820–1920.* Cambridge, MA: Harvard University Press, 1995.

Bramen, Carrie T. *The Uses of Variety: Modern Americanism and the Quest for National Distinctiveness.* Cambridge, MA: Harvard University Press, 2001.

Brill, Lesley. *Crowds, Power, and Transformation in Cinema.* Detroit, MI: Wayne State University Press, 2006.

Brodkin, Karen. *How Jews Became White Folks and What That Says about Race in America.* New Brunswick, NJ: Rutgers University Press, 1998.

Brody, Jane E. "Greater Acceptance and Support Helps Gay Families." In *Gay and Lesbian Families,* edited by Roman Espejo, 87–91. Detroit, MI: Greenhaven Press, 2009.

Brokaw, Tom. *The Greatest Generation.* New York: Random House, 1998.

Brown, Vincent. "Social Death and Political Life in the Study of Slavery." *American Historical Review* 114, no. 3 (2009): 1231–49.

Brueggemann, John. "Racial Considerations and Social Policy in the 1930s." *Social Science History* 26, no. 1 (2002): 139–77.

Brumberg, Stephan F. *Going to America, Going to School: The Jewish Immigrant Public School Encounter in Turn-of-the-Century New York City.* New York: Praeger, 1986.

Brundage, W. Fitzhugh. *Lynching in the New South: Georgia and Virginia, 1880–1930.* Urbana: University of Illinois Press, 1993.

Bruzzi, Stella. *Bringing Up Daddy: Fatherhood and Masculinity in Post-war Hollywood.* London: bfi, 2005.

Burke, Peter. "Freud and Cultural History." *Psychoanalysis and History* 9, no. 1 (2007): 5–15.

Burrows, Edwin G., and Michael Wallace. "The American Revolution: The Ideology and Psychology of National Liberation." *Perspectives in American History* 6 (1972): 167–306.

Butler, Anne M. "Through a Lens Less Turnerian: Women on the Frontier." *Reviews in American History* 17, no. 3 (1989): 417–22.

Butler, Judith, *Giving an Account of Oneself.* New York: Fordham University Press, 2005.

——. "Performative Acts and Gender Constitution: An Essay in Phenomenology and Feminist Theory." In *Writing on the Body: Female Embodiment and Feminist Theory,* edited by Katie Conboy, Nadia Medina, and Sarah Stanbury, 401–17. New York: Columbia University Press, 1997.

Butter, Michael, and Carsten Schinko. "Introduction: Poverty and the Culturalization of Class." *Amerikastudien/American Studies* 55, no. 1 (2010): 5–18.

Campbell, Randolph B. *An Empire for Slavery: The Peculiar Institution in Texas, 1821–1865.* Baton Rouge: Louisiana State University Press, 1989.

Canaday, Margot. "Building a Straight State: Sexuality and Social Citizenship under the 1944 G.I. Bill." *Journal of American History* 90, no. 3 (2003): 935–57.

———. *The Straight State: Sexuality and Citizenship in Twentieth-Century America.* Princeton, NJ: Princeton University Press, 2009.

Chan, Anne. "Bill Cosby. America's Father." In *Black Fathers: An Invisible Presence in America,* edited by Michael E. Connor and Joseph White, 125–43. Mahwah, NJ: Lawrence Erlbaum, 2006.

Chappell, Marisa. *The War on Welfare: Family, Poverty, and Politics in Modern America.* Philadelphia: University of Pennsylvania Press, 2009.

Chauncey, George. *Gay New York: Gender, Urban Culture, and the Making of the Gay Male World, 1890–1940.* New York: Basic Books, 1994.

———. *Why Marriage? The History Shaping Today's Debate.* New York: Basic Books, 2004.

Chicoine, Stephen. "'. . . Willing Never to Go in Another Fight': The Civil War Correspondence of Rufus King Felder of Chappell Hill." *Southwestern Historical Quarterly* 106 (2002/2003): 576–97.

Child, Brenda. *Boarding School Seasons: American Indian Families, 1900–1940.* Lincoln: University of Nebraska Press, 1998.

Christianson, Scott. *With Liberty for Some: 500 Years of Imprisonment in America.* Boston: Northeastern University Press, 1998.

Chudacoff, Howard P. *The Age of the Bachelor: Creating an American Subculture.* Princeton, NJ: Princeton University Press, 1999.

Clark, David A. T., and Joane Nagel. "White Men, Red Masks: Appropriation of 'Indian' Manhood in Imagined Wests." In *Across the Great Divide: Cultures of Manhood in the American West,* edited by Matthew Basso, Laura McCall, and Dee Garceau Hagen, 109–30. New York: Routledge, 2001.

Clark, Elizabeth B. "The Sacred Rights of the Weak: Pain, Sympathy and the Culture of Individual Rights in Antebellum America." *Journal of American History* 82, no. 2 (1995): 463–93.

Clawson, Rosalee A. "Poor People, Black Faces: The Portrayal of Poverty in Economics Textbooks." *Journal of Black Studies* 32, no. 3 (2002): 352–61.

Clement, Elizabeth A. *Love for Sale. Courting, Treating, and Prostitution in New York City, 1900–1945.* Chapel Hill: University of North Carolina Press, 2006.

Clinton, Catherine, and Nina Silber, eds. *Divided Houses: Gender and the Civil War.* New York: Oxford University Press, 1992.

Coates, Ta-Nehisi. "The Case for Reparations." *Atlantic,* June 2014. www.theatlantic. com.

Cody, Cheryll Ann. "Naming, Kinship, and Estate Dispersal: Notes on Slave Family Life on a South Carolina Plantation, 1786 to 1833." *William and Mary Quarterly* 39, no. 1 (1982): 192–211.

Cohan, Steven. *Masked Men: Masculinity and the Movies in the Fifties.* Bloomington: Indiana University Press, 1997.

Cole, Stephanie. "Keeping the Peace. Domestic Assault and Private Prosecution in Antebellum Baltimore." In *Over the Threshold: Intimate Violence in Early America,* edited by Christine Daniels and Michael V. Kennedy, 148–69. New York: Routledge, 1999.

Collier, Richard. "Coming Together? Post-heterosexuality, Masculine Crisis, and the New Men's Movement." *Feminist Legal Studies* 4, no. 1 (2006): 3–48.

Coontz, Stephanie, ed. *American Families: A Multicultural Reader.* New York: Routledge, 2008.

———. *Marriage, a History: How Love Conquered Marriage.* New York: Penguin, 2005.

———. *The Way We Never Were: American Families and the Nostalgia Trap.* 1992. New York: Basic Books, 2000.

Cooper, Leslie, Paul Cates, and Judith Stacey. "Gay Parenting Does Not Place Children at Risk." In *Gay and Lesbian Families*, edited by Roman Espejo, 23–30. Detroit, MI: Greenhaven Press, 2009.

Cooper, Melinda. *Family Values: Between Neoliberalism and the New Social Conservatism.* New York: Zone Books, 2017.

Cooper, Tova. "On Autobiography, Boy Scouts and Citizenship: Revisiting Charles Eastman's 'Deep Woods.'" *Arizona Quarterly* 65, no. 4 (2009): 1–35.

Corber, Robert. *Homosexuality in Cold War America: Resistance and the Crisis of Masculinity.* Durham, NC: Duke University Press, 1997.

Cornelius, Janet. "'We Slipped and Learned to Read': Slave Accounts of the Literacy Process, 1830–1865." *Phylon* 44, no. 3 (1983): 171–86.

Cott, Nancy F. *The Bonds of Womanhood: "Woman's Sphere" in New England, 1780–1835.* 2nd ed. New Haven, CT: Yale University Press, 1997.

———. *The Grounding of Modern Feminism.* New Haven, CT: Yale University Press, 1987.

———. *Public Vows: A History of Marriage and the Nation.* Cambridge, MA: Harvard University Press, 2002.

Cowan, Neil M., and Ruth Cowan. *Our Parents' Lives: Jewish Assimilation and Everyday Life.* New Brunswick, NJ: Rutgers University Press, 1996.

Cox, Alex. "Slaughterhouse Blues: Interview with Charles Burnett." *Sight & Sound* 12, no. 7 (2002): 29–30.

Coxe, Louis. "Recent Fiction." *Yale Review* 45 (1955): 157.

Cronon, William. "The Trouble with Wilderness; or, Getting Back to the Wrong Nature." In *Uncommon Ground: Rethinking the Human Place in Nature*, edited by William Cronon, 69–90. New York: Norton, 1995.

Crow, Jeffrey J. "Slavery." In *Encyclopedia of North Carolina*, edited by William S. Powell. www.ncpedia.org.

Crowley, Jocelyn E. "Organizational Responses to the Fatherhood Crisis: The Case of Fathers' Rights Groups in the United States." *Marriage and Family Review* 39, no. 1/2 (2006): 99–120.

Cullen, Jim. "'I's a Man Now': Gender and African American Men." In *A Question of Manhood. A Reader in U.S. Black Men's History and Masculinity, Vol. 1: Manhood Rights. The Construction of Black Male History and Manhood, 1750–1870*, edited by

Darlene Clark Hine and Ernestine Jenkins, 489–501. Bloomington: Indiana University Press, 1999.

Cunningham, John T. *Newark*. Newark: New Jersey Historical Society, 1966.

Cuordileone, Kyle A. *Manhood and American Political Culture in the Cold War*. New York: Routledge, 2005.

———. "'Politics in an Age of Anxiety': Cold War Political Culture and the Crisis in American Masculinity, 1949–1960." *Journal of American History* 87, no. 2 (2000): 515–45.

Cupers, Kenny. "Governing through Nature: Camps and Youth Movements in Interwar Germany and the United States." *Cultural Geographies* 15 (2008): 173–205.

Czitrom, Daniel. "Jacob Riis's New York." In *Rediscovering Jacob Riis: Exposure Journalism and Photography in Turn-of-the-Century New York,* by Bonnie Yochelson and Daniel Czitrom, 1–120. New York: New Press, 2007.

Dailey, Tim. "Gay Parenting Places Children at Risk." In *Gay and Lesbian Families*, edited by Kate Burns, 29–40. Detroit, MI: Greenhaven Press, 2005.

Daniels, Roger. *Guarding the Golden Door: American Immigration Policy and Immigrants since 1882*. New York: Hill & Wang, 2004.

Dawson, Dawn P., et al., eds. *American Indians*. Vol. 2. Pasadena, CA: Salem Press, 1995.

Dean, Mitchell. *Governing Societies: Political Perspectives on Domestic and International Rule*. Maidenhead, UK: Open University Press, 2007.

Dean, Robert D. *Imperial Brotherhood: Gender and the Making of Cold War Foreign Policy*. Amherst: University of Massachusetts Press, 2001.

Dechert, Andre. "Family Man: The Popular Reception of *Home Improvement*, 1991–1992, and the Debate about Fatherhood." In *Inventing the Modern Family. Family Values and Social Change in the 20th Century United States*, edited by Isabel Heinemann, 265–88. Frankfurt: Campus, 2012.

Degler, Carl N. *In Search of Human Nature: The Decline and Revival of Darwinism in American Social Thought*. New York: Oxford University Press, 1991.

Deloria, Philip J. *Playing Indian*. New Haven, CT: Yale University Press, 1998.

DeMaria, Richard. *Communal Love at Oneida: A Perfectionist Vision of Authority, Property, and Sexual Order*. New York: Edwin Mellen, 1978.

D'Emilio, John, and Estelle B. Freedman. *Intimate Matters: A History of Sexuality in America*. 1988. Chicago: University of Chicago Press, 1997.

Demos, John. "The Changing Faces of Fatherhood." In *Father and Child: Developmental and Clinical Perspectives*, edited by Stanley H. Cath, Alan R. Gurwitt, and John Munder Ross, 41–67. Boston: Little, Brown, 1982.

———. "Images of the American Family, Then and Now." In *Changing Images of the American Family*, edited by Virginia Tufte and Barbara Myerhoff, 43–60. New Haven, CT: Yale University Press, 1979.

Diawara, Manthia. "Black American Cinema: The New Realism." In *Black American Cinema*, edited by Manthia Diawara, 3–25. New York: Routledge, 1993.

Diner, Hasia R. *Lower East Side Memories: A Jewish Place in America*. Princeton, NJ: Princeton University Press, 2000.

Dippie, Brian W. *The Vanishing American: White Attitudes and U.S. Indian Policy*. Lawrence: University Press of Kansas, 1982.

Dorsey, Bruce. *Reforming Men and Women: Gender in the Antebellum City*. Ithaca, NY: Cornell University Press, 2002.

Dubber, Markus D. *The Police Power: Patriarchy and the Foundations of American Government*. New York: Columbia University Press, 2005.

Duis, Perry R. "No Time for Privacy: World War II and Chicago's Families." In *The War in American Culture: Society and Consciousness during World War II*, edited by Lewis A. Erenberg and Susan E. Hirsch, 17–45. Chicago: University of Chicago Press, 1996.

Dunaway, Wilma A. *The African-American Family in Slavery and Emancipation*. New York: Cambridge University Press, 2003.

Echols, Alice. *Daring to Be Bad: Radical Feminism in America, 1967–1975*. Minneapolis: University of Minnesota Press, 1989.

Edwards, Elizabeth. "Andere ordnen: Fotografien, Anthropologien und Taxonomien." In *Diskurse der Fotografie. Fotokritik am Ende des fotografischen Zeitalters*, edited by Herta Wolf, 335–55. Frankfurt: Suhrkamp, 2003.

Ehrenreich, Barbara. *The Hearts of Men: American Dreams and the Flight from Commitment*. Garden City, NY: Pluto Press, 1983.

Eisen, George. "One Hundred Years of 'Muscular Judaism': Sport in Jewish History and Culture." *Journal of Sport History* 26, no. 2 (1999): 225–39.

Elias, Norbert. *The Civilizing Process: Sociogenetic and Psychogenetic Investigations*. Translated by Edmund Jephcott. Rev. ed. Oxford: Blackwell, 2000.

Ellis, Howard C. "From the Battle in the Classroom to the Battle for the Classroom." *American Indian Quarterly* 11, no. 3 (1987): 255–64.

Engerman, Stanley L. "Studying the Black Family: Review Essay." *Journal of Family History* 3 (1978): 78–101.

Erb, Cynthia. *Tracking King Kong: A Hollywood Icon in World Culture*. Detroit, MI: Wayne State University Press, 1998.

Estes, Steve. *Ask and Tell: Gay and Lesbian Veterans Speak Out*. Chapel Hill: University of North Carolina Press, 2007.

———. *I Am a Man: Race, Manhood, and the Civil Rights Movement*. Chapel Hill: University of North Carolina Press, 2005.

Fairclough, Adam. *Better Day Coming: Blacks and Equality, 1890–2000*. New York: Penguin, 2001.

Faludi, Susan, *Backlash: The Undeclared War against American Women*. New York: Crown, 1991.

Faragher, John M. "The Frontier Trail: Rethinking Turner and Reimagining the American West." *American Historical Review* 98, no. 1 (1993): 106–17.

———. *Women and Men on the Overland Trail*. 1979. New Haven, CT: Yale University Press, 2001.

Faust, Drew Gilpin. *Mothers of Invention: Women of the Slaveholding South in the American Civil War*. Chapel Hill: University of North Carolina Press, 1996.

——. *This Republic of Suffering: Death and the American Civil War*. New York: Vintage, 2008.

Filene, Peter. *Him/Her/Self: Sex Roles in Modern America*. Baltimore: Johns Hopkins University Press, 1986.

Finzsch, Norbert. "Die 'National Advisory Commission on Civil Disorders' und der Diskurs um Gewalt in den USA, 1968." *Amerikastudien/American Studies* 49, no. 3 (2004): 329–48.

——. "'Extirpate or Remove That Vermine': Genocide, Biological Warfare, and Settler Imperialism in the Eighteenth and Early Nineteenth Century." *Journal of Genocide Research* 10, no. 2 (2008): 215–32.

——. "Gouvernementalität, der Moynihan-Report und die Welfare Queen im Cadillac." In *Geschichte schreiben mit Foucault*, edited by Jürgen Martschukat, 257–82. Frankfurt: Campus, 2002.

——. "Masculinities: The Million Man March." *Gender Forum* 32 (2011). www.genderforum.org.

——. *Von Benin nach Baltimore: Die Geschichte der African Americans*. Hamburg: Hamburger Edition, 1999.

Fischer, Kirsten. *Suspect Relations: Sex, Race, and Resistance in Colonial North Carolina*. Ithaca, NY: Cornell University Press, 2002.

Fish-Kalland, Yvonne J. "The Oneida Community: A Study of Women and Utopia." PhD diss., State University of New York at Albany, 2007.

Fliegelman, Jay. *Prodigals and Pilgrims: The American Revolution against Patriarchal Authority 1750–1800*. Cambridge: Cambridge University Press, 1982.

Folts, James D. "Fanatic and the Prophetess: Religious Perfectionism in Western New York, 1835–1839." *New York History* 72, no. 4 (1991): 356–87.

Foner, Eric. "The Meaning of Freedom in the Age of Emancipation." *Journal of American History* 81, no. 2 (1994): 435–60.

Foster, Lawrence. "Free Love and Feminism: John Humphrey Noyes and the Oneida Community." *Journal of the Early Republic* 1, no. 2 (1981): 165–83.

——. *Religion and Sexuality: Three American Communal Experiments of the Nineteenth Century*. Oxford: Oxford University Press, 1981.

Foucault, Michel. *The Birth of Biopolitics: Lectures at the Collège de France, 1978–79*. Edited by Michel Senellart. Translated by Graham Burchell. New York: Palgrave Macmillan, 2008.

——. *Discipline and Punish: The Birth of the Prison*. 1975. New York: Pantheon, 1977.

——. *The Government of Self and Others: Lectures at the Collège de France 1982–1983*. Translated by Graham Burchell. New York: Palgrave Macmillan, 2010.

——. *The History of Sexuality, Vol. 1: An Introduction*. New York: Random House, 1978.

——. *The History of Sexuality, Vol. 2: The Use of Pleasure*. New York: Random House, 1985.

——. "Nietzsche, Genealogy, History." In *The Foucault Reader*, edited by Paul Rabinow, 67–100. New York: Pantheon Books, 1984.

——. *Security, Territory, and Population: Lectures at the Collège de France, 1977–78*. Edited by Michel Sennelart. Translated by Graham Burchell. New York: Palgrave Macmillan, 2007.

——. *Society Must Be Defended: Lectures at the Collège de France, 1975–76*. Translated by David Macey. New York: Picador, 2003.

——. "The Subject and Power." *Critical Inquiry* 8, no. 4 (Summer 1982): 777–95.

——. "What Is Critique?" In *The Politics of Truth*, 41–82. Los Angeles: Semiotext(e), 1997.

Fox, Frank W. *Madison Avenue Goes to War: The Strange Military Career of American Advertising 1941–1945*. Provo, UT: Brigham Young University Press, 1975.

Frank, Stephen. *Life with Father: Parenthood and Masculinity in the Nineteenth-Century American North*. Baltimore: Johns Hopkins University Press, 1998.

Franklin, Donna L. "Ensuring Inequality: The Structural Transformation of the African-American Family. World War II and Its Aftermath." In *American Families: A Multicultural Reader*, edited by Stephanie Coontz, 153–69. New York: Routledge, 2008.

Freeze, Chaeran, Paula Hyman, and Antony Polonsky, eds. *Jewish Women in Eastern Europe*. Oxford: Littman Library of Jewish Civilization, 2005.

Freud, Sigmund. *Three Essays on the Theory of Sexuality*. Translated by James Strachey. 1905. New York: Basic Books 1962.

Friend, Craig T., and Lorri Glover. "Rethinking Southern Masculinity: An Introduction." In *Southern Manhood: Perspectives on Masculinity in the Old South*, edited by Friend and Glover, vii–xviii. Athens: University of Georgia Press, 2004.

Fronc, Jennifer. *New York Undercover: Private Surveillance in the Progressive Era*. Chicago: University of Chicago Press, 2009.

Fuller, Linda K. *The Cosby Show: Audiences, Impact, Implications*. Westport, CT: Greenwood, 1992.

Gandal, Keith. *The Virtues of the Vicious: Jacob Riis, Stephen Crane, and the Spectacle of the Slum*. New York: Oxford University Press, 1997.

Garrow, David J. "Picking Up the Books: The New Historiography of the Black Panther Party." *Reviews in American History* 35 (2007): 650–70.

Gates, Gary J., and Adam P. Romero. "Parenting by Gay Men and Lesbians: Beyond the Current Research." In *Marriage and Family: Perspectives and Complexities*, edited by H. Elizabeth Peters and Claire M. Kamp Dush, 227–43. New York: Columbia University Press, 2009.

Gavanas, Anna. *Fatherhood Politics in the United States: Masculinity, Sexuality, Race, and Marriage*. Urbana: University of Illinois Press, 2004.

Gay, Peter. *Freud: A Life for Our Times*. London: J.M. Dent, 1988.

Genovese, Eugene D. *Roll, Jordan, Roll: The World the Slaves Made*. New York: Vintage, 1974.

Ghaziani, Amin. *The Dividends of Dissent: How Conflict and Culture Work in Lesbian and Gay Marches on Washington*. Chicago: University of Chicago Press, 2008.

Gibbs, Philip A. "Self-Control and Male Sexuality in the Advice Literature of Nineteenth-Century America, 1830–1860." *Journal of American Culture* 9 (1986): 37–41.

Giddings, Paula. *When and Where I Enter: The Impact of Black Women on Race and Sex in America*. New York: Bantam Books, 1985.

Gidley, Mick. *Edward S. Curtis and the North American Indian, Incorporated*. Cambridge: Cambridge University Press, 1998.

Gilbert, James. *A Cycle of Outrage: America's Reaction to the Juvenile Delinquent in the 1950s*. New York: Oxford University Press, 1986.

———. *Men in the Middle: Searching for Masculinities in the 1950s*. Chicago: University of Chicago Press, 2005.

———. *Perfect Cities: Chicago's Utopias of 1893*. Chicago: University of Chicago Press, 1991.

———. *Whose Fair? Experience, Memory, and the History of the Great St. Louis Exposition*. Chicago: University of Chicago Press, 2009.

Gilder, George. *Wealth and Poverty*. New York: Basic Books, 1981.

Gillis, John R. "Marginalization of Fatherhood in Western Countries." *Childhood* 7 (2000): 225–38.

———. *A World of Their Own Making: Myth, Ritual, and the Quest for Family Values*. Cambridge, MA: Harvard University Press, 1996.

Gilman, Sander L. *Difference and Pathology: Stereotypes of Sexuality, Race, and Madness*. Ithaca, NY: Cornell University Press, 1985.

Gilroy, Paul. *The Black Atlantic: Modernity and Double Consciousness*. Cambridge, MA: Harvard University Press, 1993.

Goldstein, Eric L. *The Price of Whiteness: Jews, Race, and American Identity*. Princeton, NJ: Princeton University Press, 2006.

Gordon, Linda, ed. *Women, the State, and Welfare*. Madison: University of Wisconsin Press, 1990.

Gratton, Brian, and Jon Moen. "Immigration, Culture, and Child Labor in the United States, 1880–1920." *Journal of Interdisciplinary History* 34, no. 3 (2004): 355–91.

Green, Tara T. *A Fatherless Child: Autobiographical Perspectives on African American Men*. Columbia: University of Missouri Press, 2009.

Greenberg, Amy S. *Manifest Manhood and the Antebellum American Empire*. Cambridge: Cambridge University Press, 2005.

Greer, Darroch. *Counting Civil War Casualties, Week-by-Week, for the Abraham Lincoln Presidential Library and Museum*. Burbank, CA: BRC Imagination Arts, 2005.

Griswold, Robert L. *Fatherhood in America: A History*. New York: Basic Books, 1993.

Guerrero, Ed. *Framing Blackness: The African American Image in Film*. Philadelphia: Temple University Press, 1993.

Gustav-Wrathall, John D. *Take the Young Stranger by the Hand: Same-Sex Relations and the YMCA*. Chicago: University of Chicago Press, 1998.

Gutman, Herbert G. *The Black Family in Slavery and Freedom, 1750–1925*. New York: Pantheon Books, 1976.

Haas, Linda, and Steven K. Wisensale. *Families and Social Policy: National and International Perspectives*. New York: Routledge, 2006.

Habermas, Jürgen. *Legitimation Crisis*. 1973. Boston: Beacon, 1975.

———. *The Structural Transformation of the Public Sphere: An Inquiry into a Category of Bourgeois Society*. Translated by Thomas Burger. Cambridge, MA: MIT Press, 1989.

Habermas, Rebekka. *Frauen und Männer des Bürgertums: Eine Familiengeschichte (1750–1850)*. Göttingen: Vandenhoeck & Ruprecht, 2000.

Hacker, J. David. "A Census-Based Count of the Civil War Dead." *Civil War History* 57, no. 4 (2011): 307–48.

Hacker, J. David, Libra Hilde, and James Holland Jones. "The Effect of the Civil War on Southern Marriage Patterns." *Journal of Southern History* 76, no. 1 (2010): 39–70.

Haimes, Erica, and Kate Weiner. "'Everybody's Got a Dad . . .': Issues for Lesbian Families in the Management of Donor Insemination." *Sociology of Health and Illness* 22, no. 4 (2000): 477–99.

Hale, Grace E. *Making Whiteness. The Culture of Segregation in the South, 1890–1940*. New York: Random, 1998.

———. *A Nation of Outsiders: How the White Middle Class Fell in Love with Rebellion in Postwar America*. New York: Oxford University Press, 2011.

Hale, Nathan G., Jr. *Freud and the Americans: The Beginnings of Psychoanalysis in the United States, 1876–1917*. New York: Oxford University Press, 1995.

———. *The Rise and Crisis of Psychoanalysis in the United States: Freud and the Americans, 1917–1985*. New York: Oxford University Press, 1995.

Hales, Peter. *Silver Cities. The Photography of American Urbanization, 1839–1915*. Philadelphia: Temple University Press, 1989.

Hall, Stuart. "The Question of Cultural Identity." In *Modernity and Its Futures*, edited by Stuart Hall, David Held, and Tony McGrew, 273–326. Cambridge: Polity, 1992.

Halttunen, Karen. "Humanitarianism and the Pornography of Pain in Anglo-American Culture." *American Historical Review* 100 (1995): 303–34.

Hames, Raymond. "The Ecologically Noble Savage Debate." *Annual Review of Anthropology* 36 (2007): 177–90.

Hampf, M. Michaela. "'Dykes' or 'Whores': Sexuality and the Women's Army Corps in the United States during World War II." *Women's Studies International Forum* 27 (2004): 13–30.

———. *Release a Man for Combat: The Women's Army Corps during World War II*. Cologne: Böhlau, 2010.

Hampsten, Elizabeth. *Settlers' Children: Growing Up on the Great Plains*. Norman: University of Oklahoma Press, 1991.

Haraway, Donna J. *Primate Visions: Gender, Race, and Nature in the World of Modern Science*. New York: Routledge, 1989.

Harris, Erich Leon. *African-American Screenwriters Now: Conversations with Hollywood's Black Pack*. Los Angeles: Silman-James Press, 1996.

Harris, Katherine. "Sex Roles and Work Patterns among Homesteading Families in Northeastern Colorado, 1873–1920." *Frontiers: A Journal of Women Studies* 7, no. 3 (1984): 43–49.

Harris, Robert L., Jr. "Coming of Age: The Transformation of Afro-American Historiography." *Journal of Negro History* 57 (1982): 107–21.

Hartmann, Susan. *The Home Front and Beyond: American Women in the 1940s*. Boston: Twayne, 1982.

Hartog, Hendrik. *Man and Wife in America: A History*. 2000. Cambridge, MA: Harvard University Press, 2002.

Hatton, Ed. "'He Murdered Her Because He Loved Her': Passion, Masculinity, and Intimate Homicide in Antebellum America." In *Over the Threshold: Intimate Violence in Early America*, edited by Christine Daniels and Michael V. Kennedy, 111–34. New York: Routledge, 1999.

Hayden, Dolores. *Building Suburbia: Green Fields and Urban Growth, 1820–2000*. New York: Vintage, 2003.

Heap, Chad C. *Slumming: Sexual and Racial Encounters in American Nightlife*. Chicago: University of Chicago Press, 2009.

Heinemann, Isabel. *Wert der Familie. Ehescheidung, Frauenarbeit und Reproduktion in den USA des 20. Jahrhunderts*. Berlin: DeGruyter-Oldenbourg, 2018.

Henretta, James A. *The Evolution of American Society, 1700–1815: An Interdisciplinary Analysis*. Lexington, MA: DC Heath, 1973.

Hequembourg, Amy. *Lesbian Motherhood: Stories of Becoming*. Binghamton, NY: Harrington Park Press, 2007.

Herman, Daniel J. "God Bless Buffalo Bill." *Reviews in American History* 29, no. 2 (2001): 228–37.

Hindman, Hugh D. *Child Labor: An American History*. Armonk, NY: M.E. Sharpe, 2002.

Hiner, N. Ray, and Joseph M. Hawes, eds. *Growing Up in America: Children in Historical Perspective*. Urbana: University of Illinois Press, 1985.

Hobbs, Margaret. "Rethinking Antifeminism in the 1930s: Gender Crisis or Workplace Justice? A Response to Alice Kessler-Harris." *Gender & History* 5, no. 1 (1993): 4–15.

Hobsbawm, Eric, and Terence Ranger. *The Invention of Tradition*. Cambridge: Cambridge University Press, 1983.

Hodes, Martha. *White Women, Black Men: Illicit Sex in the Nineteenth-Century South*. New Haven, CT: Yale University Press, 1997.

Hofsommer, Don L. *Steel Trails of Hawkeyeland: Iowa's Railroad Experience*. Bloomington: Indiana University Press, 2005.

Hole, Judith, and Ellen Levine. *Rebirth of Feminism*. New York: Quadrangle Books, 1971.

hooks, bell. "Plantation Patriarchy." In *We Real Cool: Black Men and Masculinity*, 1–14. New York: Routledge, 2004.

———. "Reconstructing Black Masculinity." In *Black Looks: Race and Representation*, 87–113. Boston: South End, 1992.

———. *Reel to Real*. 1996. New York: Routledge, 2009.

———. *We Real Cool: Black Men and Masculinity*. New York: Routledge, 2004.

Horne, Gerald. *Fire This Time: The Watts Uprising and the 1960s*. Charlottesville: University Press of Virginia, 1995.

Horowitz, Helen L. "Victoria Woodhull, Anthony Comstock, and Conflict over Sex in the United States in the 1870s." *Journal of American History* 87, no. 2 (2000): 403–34.

Howard, John. *Men Like That: A Southern Queer History*. Chicago: University of Chicago Press, 1999.

Howe, John. *Language and Political Meaning in Revolutionary America*. Amherst: University of Massachusetts Press, 2004.

Hoxie, Frederick E. "Reconstructing Crow Family Life during the Reservation Era." *American Indian Quarterly* 15, no. 3 (1991): 287–309.

Huggins, Nathan L. "Herbert Gutman and Afro-American History." *Labor History* 29, no. 3 (1988): 323–35.

Huhndorf, Shari M. *Going Native: Indians in the American Cultural Imagination*. Ithaca, NY: Cornell University Press, 2001.

Hull, Isabel V. *Sexuality, State and Civil Society in Germany, 1700–1815*. Ithaca, NY: Cornell University Press, 1996.

Hunter, Andrea G. "Making a Way: Strategies of Southern Urban African-American Families, 1900 and 1936." *Journal of Family History* 18, no. 3 (1993): 231–48.

Hunter, Tera W. *Bound in Wedlock: Slave and Free Black Marriages in the Nineteenth Century*, Cambridge, MA: Belknap, 2017.

Inabinet, Joan A., and L. Glen Inabinet. *A History of Kershaw County, South Carolina*. Columbia: University of South Carolina Press, 2011.

Isaac, James, and Irwin Altman. "Interpersonal Processes in Nineteenth Century Utopian Communities: Shakers and Oneida Perfectionists." *Utopian Studies* 9, no. 1 (1998): 26–49.

Jackson, Kenneth T. *Crabgrass Frontier: The Suburbanization of the United States*. New York: Oxford University Press, 1985.

Jackson, Kenneth T., and Barbara B. Jackson. "The Black Experience in Newark: The Growth of the Ghetto, 1870–1970." In *New Jersey since 1860*, edited by William C. Wright, 36–59. Trenton, NJ: New Jersey Historical Commission, 1972.

Jacobson, Matthew Frye. *Whiteness of a Different Color: European Immigrants and the Alchemy of Race*. Cambridge, MA: Harvard University Press, 1998.

James, David E. "Toward a Geo-cinematic Hermeneutics: Representations of Los Angeles in Non-industrial Cinema. 'Killer of Sheep' and 'Water and Power.'" *Wide Angle* 20, no. 3 (1998): 23–53.

Jeffrey, Julie Roy. *Frontier Women: "Civilizing" the West? 1840–1880*. 1979. New York: Hill & Wang, 1998.

———. "Permeable Boundaries: Abolitionist Women and Separate Spheres." *Journal of the Early Republic* 21, no. 1 (2001): 79–93.

Johansen, Shawn. *Family Men: Middle-Class Fatherhood in Early Industrializing America*. New York: Routledge, 2001.

Johnson, David K. *The Lavender Scare: The Cold War Persecution of Gays and Lesbians in the Federal Government*. Chicago: University of Chicago Press, 2004.

Johnson, James E. "Charles G. Finney and a Theology of Revivalism." *Church History* 38, no. 3 (1969): 338–58.

Johnson, Suzanne M., et al. *The Gay Baby Boom: The Psychology of Gay Parenthood*. New York: New York University Press, 2002.

Jones, Jacqueline. *Labor of Love, Labor of Sorrow: Black Women, Work, and the Family from Slavery to the Present*. 1985. New York: Basic Books, 2010.

Jones, Norrece T., Jr. "Born a Child of Freedom, yet a Slave. 'The Threat of Sale: The Black Family as a Mechanism of Control.'" In *American Families: A Multicultural Reader*, edited by Stephanie Coontz, 59–80. New York: Routledge, 2008.

Joseph, Peniel E. *Dark Days, Bright Nights: From Black Power to Barack Obama*. New York: Basic Books, 2010.

———. *Waiting 'til the Midnight Hour: A Narrative History of Black Power in America*. New York: Henry Holt, 2007.

Kampen, Natalie B. "Mirra Komarovsky: Another Appreciation." *WSQ: Women's Studies Quarterly* 33 (2005): 356–64.

Kann, Mark E. *The Gendering of American Politics: Founding Mothers, Founding Fathers, and Political Patriarchy*. Westport, CT: Praeger, 1999.

———. *A Republic of Men: The American Founders, Gendered Language, and Patriarchal Politics*. New York: New York University Press, 1998.

Kasson, Joy S. *Buffalo Bill's Wild West: Celebrity, Memory, and Popular History*. New York: Hill & Wang, 2000.

Katz, Jonathan Ned. *The Invention of Heterosexuality*. New York: Dutton, 1995.

Kendrick, Walter. *The Secret Museum: Pornography in Modern Culture*. 1987. Berkeley: University of California Press, 1996.

Kennedy, Elizabeth L., and Madeline D. Davis. *Boots of Leather, Slippers of Gold: The History of a Lesbian Community*. New York: Routledge, 1993.

Kerber, Linda K. *No Constitutional Right to Be Ladies: Women and the Obligations of Citizenship*. New York: Hill & Wang, 1998.

———. "The Republican Ideology of the Revolutionary Generation." *American Quarterly* 37, no. 4 (1985): 474–95.

———. "Separate Spheres, Female Worlds, Woman's Place: The Rhetoric of Women's History." *Journal of American History* 75, no. 1 (1988): 9–39.

———. *Women of the Republic: Intellect and Ideology in Revolutionary America*. Chapel Hill: University of North Carolina Press, 1980.

Kerber, Linda K., Nancy F. Cott, Robert Gross, Lynn Hunt, Carroll Smith-Rosenberg, and Christine M. Stansell. "Forum: Beyond Roles, Beyond Spheres: Thinking about Gender in the Early Republic." *William and Mary Quarterly* 46, no. 3 (1989): 565–85.

Kern, Louis J. "Ideology and Reality: Sexuality and Women's Status in the Oneida Community." *Radical History Review* 20 (1979): 180–204.

———. *An Ordered Love: Sex Roles and Sexuality in Victorian Utopias: The Shakers, the Mormons, and the Oneida Community*. Chapel Hill: University of North Carolina Press, 1981.

Kessler-Harris, Alice. "Gender Ideology in Historical Reconstruction: A Case Study from the 1930s." *Gender & History* 1, no. 1 (1989): 31–49.

———. "In the Nation's Image: The Gendered Limits of Social Citizenship in the Depression Era." *Journal of American History* 86, no. 3 (1999): 1251–79.

———. *Out to Work: A History of Wage-Earning Women in the United States*. 1983. New York: Oxford University Press, 2003.

———. *A Woman's Wage: Historical Meanings and Social Consequences.* Lexington: University Press of Kentucky, 1990.

Kimmel, Michael. *The Gendered Society.* New York: Oxford University Press, 2000.

———. *Manhood in America: A Cultural History.* New York: Free Press, 1996.

———. "The Struggle for Men's Souls." In *Men's Lives*, edited by Michael Kimmel and Michael A. Messner, 592–94. Boston: Allyn & Bacon, 1998.

Kinnamon, Keneth. "How 'Native Son' Was Born." In *Richard Wright: Critical Perspectives Past and Present*, edited by Henry L. Gates Jr. and K. A. Appiah, 110–31. New York: Amistad, 1993.

Koch, Kathy. "Fatherhood Movement: Can It Reduce the Number of Fatherless Children?" *CQ Researcher* 10, no. 21 (2000): 473–96.

Kolchin, Peter. *American Slavery, 1619–1877.* New York: Hill & Wang, 1993.

Kosak, Hadassa. *Cultures of Opposition. Jewish Immigrant Workers, New York City, 1881–1905.* Albany: State University of New York Press, 2000.

Koselleck, Reinhart. "Krise." In *Geschichtliche Grundbegriffe: Historisches Lexikon zur politisch-sozialen Sprache in Deutschland 3: H-M*, 617–50. Stuttgart: Klett-Cotta, 1982.

Krämer, Felix. *Moral Leaders: Medien, Gender und Glaube in den USA der 1970er und 1980er Jahre.* Bielefeld: transcript, 2015.

———. "Playboy Tells His Story: Geschichte eines Krisenszenarios um die hegemoniale US-Männlichkeit der 1970er Jahre." *Feministische Studien* 27, no. 1 (2009): 83–96.

Kranz, Karen C., and Judith C. Daniluk. "Living Outside of the Box: Lesbian Couples with Children Conceived through the Use of Anonymous Donor Insemination." *Journal of Feminist Family Therapy* 18, no. 1/2 (2006): 1–33.

Krech, Shepard, III. *The Ecological Indian: Myth and History.* New York: Norton, 1999.

Kreuzenbeck, Nora. *Hoffnung auf Freiheit: Über die Migration von African Americans nach Haiti, 1850–1865.* Bielefeld: transcript, 2014.

Kugel, Rebecca. *To Be the Main Leaders of Our People: A History of Minnesota Ojibwe Politics, 1825–1898.* East Lansing: Michigan State University Press, 1998.

Kurtz, Stanley. "Gay Marriage Threatens Families." In *Gay and Lesbian Families*, edited by Kate Burns, 11–25. Detroit, MI: Greenhaven Press, 2005.

LaRossa, Ralph. *The Modernization of Fatherhood: A Social and Political History.* Chicago: University of Chicago Press, 1997.

Latour, Bruno. *Reassembling the Social: An Introduction to Actor-Network-Theory.* Oxford: Oxford University Press 2005.

Lazarsfeld, Paul F. "An Episode in the History of Social Research: A Memoir." In *The Intellectual Migration: Europe and America, 1930–1960*, edited by Donald Fleming and Bernard Bailyn, 270–337. Cambridge, MA: Harvard University Press, 1969.

Leab, Daniel J. *From Sambo to Superspade: The Black Experience in Motion Pictures.* Boston: Houghton Mifflin, 1975.

Lears, T. Jackson. *Fables of Abundance: A Cultural History of Advertising in America.* New York 1994.

———. *Rebirth of a Nation: The Making of Modern America, 1877–1920.* New York: Harper Perennial, 2010.

LeBlanc-Ernest, Angela D. "'The Most Qualified Person to Handle the Job': Black Panther Party Women, 1966–1982." In *Black Panther Party Reconsidered*, edited by Charles E. Jones, 305–34. Baltimore: Black Classic Press, 1998.

Leff, Mark. "The Politics of Sacrifice on the American Home Front in World War II." *Journal of American History* 77 (1991): 1296–318.

Lejeune, Philippe. *Le pacte autobiographique*. Paris: Ed. du Seuil, 1975.

Lev, Peter. *American Films of the 70s: Conflicting Visions*. Austin: University of Texas Press, 2000.

Lewin, Ellen. *Gay Fatherhood: Narratives of Family and Citizenship in America*. Chicago: University of Chicago Press, 2009.

Limerick, Patricia N. *The Legacy of Conquest: The Unbroken Past of the American West*. New York: Norton, 1988.

———. "What on Earth Is the New Western History?" *Montana: The Magazine of Western History* 40, no. 3 (1990): 61–64.

Lobby, Christopher. "Republican Bachelorhood: Sex and Citizenship in the Early United States." *Historical Reflections* 33, no. 1 (2007): 89–100.

Lombard, Anne. *Making Manhood: Growing Up Male in Colonial New England*. Cambridge, MA: Harvard University Press, 2003.

Love, Barbara J. *Feminists Who Changed America, 1963–1975*. Urbana: University of Illinois Press, 2006.

Luchetti, Cathy. *Children of the West: Family Life on the Frontier*. New York: Norton, 2001.

Lupkin, Paula. "Manhood Factories: Architecture, Business, and the Evolving Role of the YMCA, 1865–1925." In *Men and Women Adrift: The YMCA and YWCA in the City*, edited by Nina Mjagkij and Margaret Spratt, 40–64. New York: New York University Press, 1997.

———. *Manhood Factories: YMCA Architecture and the Making of Modern Urban Culture*. Minneapolis: University of Minnesota Press, 2010.

———. "A Temple of Practical Christianity." *Chicago History* 24, no. 3 (1995): 22–41.

Lüthi, Barbara. *Invading Bodies: Medizin und Immigration in die USA*. Frankfurt: Campus, 2009.

Lutz, Tom. *American Nervousness, 1903: An Anecdotal History*. Ithaca, NY: Cornell University Press, 1993.

———. *Doing Nothing: A History of Loafers, Loungers, Slackers, and Bums in America*. New York: Farrar, Straus and Giroux, 2006.

Lyndon, Louis. "Uncertain Hero." *Woman's Home Companion*, November 1956, 41–43, 107.

Mackert, Nina. *Jugenddelinquenz: Die Produktivität eines Problems in den USA der späten 1940er bis 1960er Jahre*. Konstanz: UVK, 2014.

Macleod, David. *Building Character in the American Boy: The Boy Scout, YMCA and Their Forerunners 1870–1920*. Madison: University of Wisconsin Press, 1983.

Madsen, Brigham D. "The Montana Trail: Salt Lake City-Corinne to Fort Benton." *Overland Journal* 13, no. 1 (1995): 19–34.

Mandelker, Ira L. "Religion, Sex, and Utopia in Nineteenth-Century America." *Social Research* 49, no. 3 (1982): 730–51.

Marable, Manning. "The Black Male: Searching Beyond Stereotypes." In *Men's Lives*, edited by Michael Kimmel and Michael A. Messner, 26–32. Boston: Allyn & Bacon, 1995.

Marcus, Eric. *Making Gay History: The Half-Century Fight for Lesbian and Gay Equal Rights*. 1992. New York: HarperCollins, 2002.

Martínez, David. *Dakota Philosopher: Charles Eastman and American Indian Thought*. St. Paul: Minnesota Historical Society Press, 2009.

———. "Out of the Woods and into the Museum: Charles A. Eastman's 1910 Collecting Expedition across Ojibwe Country." *American Indian Culture and Research Journal* 32, no. 4 (2008): 67–84.

Martschukat, Jürgen. "A Horrifying Experience? Public Executions and the Emotional Spectator in the New Republic." In *Emotions in American History: An International Assessment*, edited by Jessica Gienow-Hecht, 181–200. New York: Berghahn, 2010.

———. "'You Be a Man if You Can, Stan': Family Life and Fatherhood in Charles Burnett's 'Killer of Sheep' (1977)." In *Inventing the Modern American Family: Family Values and Social Change in 20th Century United States*, edited by Isabel Heinemann, 223–43. Frankfurt: Campus, 2012.

Martschukat, Jürgen, and Olaf Stieglitz. *Geschichte der Männlichkeiten*. Frankfurt: Campus, 2008.

Masilela, Ntongel. "The Los Angeles School of Black Filmmakers." In *Black American Cinema*, edited by Ntongel Masilela, 107–17. New York: Routledge, 1993.

Massood, Paula J. "An Aesthetic Appropriate to Conditions: Killer of Sheep, (Neo)realism, and the Documentary Impulse." *Wide Angle* 21, no. 4 (1999): 20–41.

Masur, Louis P. *Rites of Execution: Capital Punishment and the Transformation of American Culture, 1776–1865*. Oxford: Oxford University Press, 1989.

Matthews, Tracye. "'No One Ever Asks, What a Man's Role in the Revolution Is': Gender and the Politics of the Black Panther Party, 1966–1971." In *Black Panther Party Reconsidered*, edited by Charles E. Jones, 267–304. Baltimore: Black Classic Press, 1998.

May, Elaine Tyler. *Homeward Bound: American Families in the Cold War Era*. 1988. New York: Basic Books, 1999.

———. "Rosie the Riveter Gets Married." In *The War in American Culture: Society and Consciousness during World War II*, edited by Lewis A. Erenberg and Susan E. Hirsch, 128–43. Chicago: University of Chicago Press, 1996.

Maynard, W. Barksdale. "'An Ideal Life in the Woods for Boys': Architecture and Culture in the Earliest Summer Camps." *Winterthur Portfolio* 34, no. 1 (1999): 3–29.

McCullough, David. *John Adams*. New York: Simon & Schuster, 2001.

McCurry, Stephanie. *Masters of Small Worlds: Yeoman Households, Gender Relations, and the Political Culture of the Antebellum South Carolina Low Country*. Oxford: Oxford University Press, 1995.

McElvaine, Robert S., ed. *Down and Out in the Great Depression: Letters from the Forgotten Man*. Chapel Hill: University of North Carolina Press, 1983.

McGrath, Robert L. "The Endless Trail of the End of the Trail." *Journal of the West* 40, no. 4 (2001): 8–15.

McLoughlin, William G. "Evangelical Childrearing in the Age of Jackson: Francis Wayland's Views on When and How to Subdue the Willfulness of Children." *Journal of Social History* 40, no. 4 (1975): 20–34.

McMichael, Kelly. *Sacred Memories: The Civil War Monument Movement in Texas.* Denton: Texas State Historical Association, 2009.

McMillen, Sally G. *Seneca Falls and the Origins of the Woman's Rights Movement.* Oxford: Oxford University Press, 2008.

McPherson, James M. *Battle Cry of Freedom: The Civil War Era.* New York: Oxford University Press, 1988.

———. *Crossroads of Freedom: Antietam.* Oxford: Oxford University Press, 2002.

———. *For Cause and Comrades: Why Men Fought in the Civil War.* New York: Oxford University Press, 1997.

Meade, Teresa, and Pamela Haag. "Persistent Patriarchy: Ghost or Reality?" *Radical History Review* 71 (1998): 91–95.

Medicine, Bea. "American Indian Family: Cultural Change and Adaptive Strategies." *Journal of Ethnic Studies* 8, no. 4 (1981): 13–23.

Meranze, Michael. *Laboratories of Virtue: Punishment, Revolution, and Authority in Philadelphia, 1760–1835.* Chapel Hill: University of North Carolina Press, 1996.

Mercer, Kobena. "Welcome to the Jungle: Identity and Diversity in Postmodern Politics." In *Identity: Culture, Community, Difference*, edited by Jonathan Rutherford, 43–71. London: Lawrence and Wishart, 1990.

Merritt, Bishetta D. "Charles Burnett: Creator of African American Culture on Film." *Journal of Black Studies* 39, no. 1 (2008): 109–28.

Messner, Michael. *Politics of Masculinities: Men in Movements.* Thousand Oaks, CA: SAGE, 1997.

Mettler, Suzanne. *Soldiers to Citizens: The G.I. Bill and the Making of the Greatest Generation.* Oxford: Oxford University Press, 2005.

Meyerowitz, Joanne. *How Sex Changed: A History of Transsexuality in the United States.* Cambridge, MA: Harvard University Press, 2002.

———, ed. *Not June Cleaver: Women and Gender in Postwar America, 1945–1960.* Philadelphia: Temple University Press, 1994.

Mezey, Nancy J. *New Choices, New Families: How Lesbians Decide about Motherhood.* Baltimore: Johns Hopkins University Press, 2008.

Michel, Sonya. "Danger on the Home Front: Motherhood, Sexuality, and Disabled Veterans in American Postwar Films." *Journal of the History of Sexuality* 3, no. 1 (1992): 109–28.

———. "The Reconstruction of White Southern Manhood." In *Different Restorations: Reconstruction and Wiederaufbau in the United States and Germany: 1865–1945–1989*, edited by Norbert Finzsch and Jürgen Martschukat, 140–64. Providence, RI: Berghahn, 1996.

Miller, Susan A. *Growing Girls: The Natural Origins of Girls' Organizations in America.* New Brunswick, NJ: Rutgers University Press, 2007.

Mills, Charles W. *The Racial Contract.* Ithaca, NY: Cornell University Press, 1997.

Mink, Gwendolyn. *The Wages of Motherhood: Inequality in the Welfare State, 1917–1942.* Ithaca, NY: Cornell University Press, 1995.

Mintz, Steven. *Huck's Raft: A History of American Childhood.* Cambridge, MA: Belknap, 2006.

———. *A Prison of Expectations: The Family in Victorian Culture.* New York: New York University Press, 1983.

———. "Regulating the American Family." *Journal of Family History* 14, no. 4 (1989): 387–404.

Mintz, Steven, and Susan Kellogg. *Domestic Revolutions: A Social History of American Family Life.* New York: Free Press, 1988.

Modell, John, and Duane Steffey. "Waging War and Marriage: Military Service and Family Formation, 1940–1950." *Journal of Family History* 13, no. 2 (1988): 195–218.

Moran, Rachel L. *Governing Bodies: American Politics and the Shaping of the Modern Physique.* Philadelphia: University of Pennsylvania Press, 2018.

Morgan, Edward P. "Media Culture and the Public Memory of the Black Panther Party." In *In Search of the Black Panther Party: New Perspectives on a Revolutionary Movement,* edited by Jama Lazerow and Yohuru Williams, 324–74. Durham, NC: Duke University Press, 2006.

———. *The Puritan Family: Religion and Domestic Relations in Seventeenth-Century New England.* New York: Harper & Row, 1966.

Morone, James A. *Hellfire Nation: The Politics of Sin in American History.* New Haven, CT: Yale University Press, 2003.

Moroney, Siobhan. "Widows and Orphans: Women's Education Beyond the Domestic Ideal." *Journal of Family History* 25, no. 1 (2000): 26–38.

Mumford, Kevin. *Interzones: Black/White Sex Districts in Chicago and New York in the Early Twentieth Century.* New York: Columbia University Press, 1997.

———. *Newark: A History of Race, Rights, and Riots in America.* New York: New York University Press, 2007.

Murdock, George P. *Social Structure.* New York: Macmillan, 1949.

Murray, Charles. *Losing Ground: American Social Policy, 1950–1980.* New York: Basic Books, 1984.

National Humanities Center. "Making the Revolution." http://nationalhumanitiescenter.org.

Nelson, Dana D. *National Manhood: Capitalist Citizenship and Imagined Fraternity of White Men.* Durham, NC: Duke University Press, 1998.

Nelson, Jennifer L. "Dress Reform and the Bloomer." *Journal of American & Comparative Cultures* 23, no. 1 (2000): 21–25.

O'Leary, Cecilia E. *To Die For: The Paradox of American Patriotism.* Princeton, NJ: Princeton University Press, 1999.

Olin, Spencer C., Jr. "The Oneida Community and the Instability of Charismatic Authority." *Journal of American History* 67, No. 2 (1980): 285–300.

Onkst, David H. "'First a Negro . . . Incidentally a Veteran': Black World War Two Veterans and the G.I. Bill of Rights in the Deep South, 1944–1948." *Journal of Social History* 31, no. 3 (1998): 517–70.

Osgerby, Bill. *Playboys in Paradise: Masculinity, Youth, and Leisure-Style in Modern America.* Oxford: Berg, 2001.

Overbeck, Anne. "'The Enemy Within': African American Motherhood and the 'Crack Baby Crisis.'" In *Inventing the Modern Family: Family Values and Social Change in the 20th Century United States*, edited by Isabel Heinemann, 155–76. Frankfurt: Campus, 2012.

Paine, Thomas. "The American Crisis III" (1777). In *The Complete Writings of Thomas Paine*, vol. 1, edited by Philip S. Foner, 79. New York: Citadel Press, 1945.

Parsons, Talcott, and Robert E. Bales, eds. *Family Socialization and Interaction Process.* New York: Free Press, 1955.

Pascal, Janet B. *Jacob Riis: Reporter and Reformer.* New York: Oxford University Press, 2005.

Pascoe, Peggy. "Western Women at the Cultural Crossroads." In *Trails: Toward a New Western History*, edited by Patricia N. Limerick, Clyde A. Miner II, and Charles E. Rankin, 40–58. Lawrence: University Press of Kansas, 1991.

Pateman, Carole. *The Sexual Contract.* Stanford, CA: Stanford University Press, 1988.

Patterson, Orlando. *Slavery and Social Death: A Comparative Study.* Cambridge, MA: Harvard University Press, 1982.

Peacock, Thomas D., and Donald R. Day. "Nations within a Nation: The Dakota and Ojibwe of Minnesota." *Daedalus* 129, no. 3 (2000): 137–59.

Peiss, Kathy. "'Charity Girls' and City Pleasures: Historical Notes on Working Class Sexuality, 1880–1920." In *Passion and Power: Sexuality in History*, edited by Kathy Peiss and Christina Simmons, 57–69. Philadelphia: Temple University Press, 1989.

Pejsa, Jane. *The Life of Emily Peake: One Dedicated Ojibwe.* Minneapolis: Nodin Press, 2003.

Perlesz, Amaryll. "'Fathers' Cannot Easily Be De-gendered: Response to Silverstein and Auerbach." *Journal of Feminist Family Therapy* 18, no. 4 (2006): 93–97.

Perry, Lewis. "Review Essay: Fathers and Children." *History and Theory* 16, no. 2 (1977): 174–95.

Peterson del Mar, David. *What Trouble I Have Seen: A History of Violence against Wives.* Cambridge, MA: Harvard University Press, 1998.

Petigny, Alan. "Norman Mailer, 'The White Negro,' and New Conceptions of the Self in Postwar America." *Mailer Review*, 2007. http://findarticles.com.

Petrik, Paula. "Mothers and Daughters of Eldorado: The Fisk Family of Helena, Montana, 1867–1902." *Montana: The Magazine of Western History* 32, no. 3 (1982): 50–63.

———. *No Step Backward: Women and Family on the Rocky Mountain Mining Frontier, Helena, Montana, 1865–1900.* Helena: Montana Historical Society Press, 1987.

Pettegrew, Justin H. "Rescuing Young Men from the 'Ruin of the City': Religion, Masculinity, and the Founding of the Chicago YMCA, 1853–1858." *Journal of Illinois History* 10 (2007): 191–212.

Pickett, Robert S. *House of Refuge: Origins of Juvenile Reform in New York State, 1815–1857.* Syracuse, NY: Syracuse University Press, 1969.

Pincus, Steven, and William Novak. "Political History after the Cultural Turn." *Perspectives on History: The Newsmagazine of the AHA*, May 2011. www.historians.org.

Pleck, Elizabeth. *Domestic Tyranny: The Making of American Social Policy against Family Violence from Colonial Times to the Present.* Oxford: Oxford University Press, 1987.

Pleck, Joseph H. "The Theory of Male Sex-Role Identity: Its Rise and Fall, 1936 to the Present." In *The Making of Masculinities: The New Men's Studies*, edited by Harry Brod, 21–38. Boston: Allen & Unwin, 1987.

Pollock, Linda A. *Forgotten Children: Parent-Child Relations from 1500–1900.* Cambridge: Cambridge University Press, 1983.

Polonsky, Antony. *The Shtetl: Myth and Reality.* Oxford: Oxford University Press, 2004.

Poole, Ralph J. "Männer im Pelz. Entblößungen und Verhüllungen des natürlichen Körper um 1900." In *Väter, Soldaten, Liebhaber: Männer und Männlichkeiten in der nordamerikanischen Geschichte. Ein Reader*, edited by Jürgen Martschukat and Olaf Stieglitz, 159–82. Bielefeld: transcript, 2007.

Posner, Richard A. *Public Intellectuals: A Study in Decline.* Cambridge, MA: Harvard University Press, 2001.

Prescott, Cynthia Culver. *Gender and Generation on the Far Western Frontier.* Tucson: University of Arizona Press, 2007.

———. "'Why She Didn't Marry Him': Love, Power, and Marital Choice on the Far Western Frontier." *Western Historical Quarterly* 38, no. 1 (2007): 25–45.

Price, Clement A. "The Afro-American Community of Newark, 1917–1947: A Social History." PhD diss., Rutgers University, 1976.

Putney, Clifford. *Muscular Christianity: Manhood and Sports in Protestant America, 1880–1920.* Cambridge, MA: Harvard University Press, 2001.

Ramsey, Paul J. "Wrestling with Modernity: Philanthropy and the Children's Aid Society in Progressive-Era New York City." *New York History* 88, no. 2 (2007): 153–74.

Reed, Julie L. "Family and Nation: Cherokee Orphan Care, 1835–1903." *American Indian Quarterly* 34, no. 3 (2010): 312–43.

Reinharz, Shulamit. "Mirra Komarovsky." In *Women in Sociology: A Bio-bibliographical Sourcebook*, edited by Mary Jo Degan, 239–48. New York: Greenwood, 1991.

Ribuffo, Leo P. "Family Policy Past as Prologue: Jimmy Carter, the White House Conference on Families, and the Mobilization of the New Christian Right." *Review of Policy Research* 23, no. 2 (2006): 311–37.

Rivers, Daniel W. *Radical Relations: Lesbian Mothers, Gay Fathers, and Their Children in the United States since World War II.* Chapel Hill: University of North Carolina Press, 2013.

Roediger, David R. *The Wages of Whiteness: Race and the Making of the American Working Class.* 1991. New York: Verso, 2007.

———. *Working toward Whiteness: How America's Immigrant's Became White. The Strange Journey from Ellis Island to the Suburbs.* New York: Basic Books, 2005.

Rogers, Edward S., and J. Garth Taylor. "Northern Ojibwa." In *Handbook of North American Indians, Vol. 6: Subarctic,* edited by June Helm, 231–43. Washington, DC: Smithsonian Institution, 1981.

Rogin, Michael P. *Fathers and Children: Andrew Jackson and the Subjugation of the American Indian.* New York: Knopf, 1975.

Rorabaugh, William J. *The Alcoholic Republic: An American Tradition.* Oxford: Oxford University Press, 1979.

Rose, Kenneth D. *Myth and the Greatest Generation: A Social History of Americans in World War II.* New York: Routledge, 2007.

Rose, Nancy E. "Gender, Race, and the Welfare State: Government Work Programs from the 1930s to the Present." *Feminist Studies* 19, no. 2 (1993): 319–42.

Rosenberg, Emily S. "'Foreign Affairs' after World War II: Connecting Sexual and International Politics." *Diplomatic History* 18, no. 1 (1994): 59–70.

Rosenblatt, Paul C. *Bitter, Bitter Tears: Nineteenth-Century Diarists and Twentieth-Century Grief Theories.* Minneapolis: University of Minnesota Press, 1983.

Rothman, David. *The Discovery of the Asylum: Social Order and Disorder in the New Republic.* Boston: Brown, 1971.

Rotundo, Anthony. *American Manhood: Transformations of Masculinity from the Revolution to the Modern Era.* New York: Basic Books, 1993.

Rupp, Leila. *A Desired Past: A Short History of Same-Sex Love in America.* Chicago: University of Chicago Press, 1999.

Ryan, Mary P. *Cradle of the Middle Class: The Family in Oneida County, New York, 1790–1865.* Cambridge: Cambridge University Press, 1981.

———. *The Empire of the Mother: American Writing about Domesticity, 1830–1860.* New York: Haworth Press, 1982.

Said, Edward. *Orientalism.* New York: Pantheon, 1978.

Sanders, Craig. *Limiteds, Locals, and Expresses in Indiana, 1838–1971.* Bloomington: Indiana University Press, 2003.

Sarasin, Philipp. *Reizbare Maschinen: Eine Geschichte des Körpers, 1765–1914.* Frankfurt: Suhrkamp, 2001.

Savage, Dan. *The Kid: What Happened after My Boyfriend and I Decided to Get Pregnant: An Adoption Story.* New York: Plume, 1999.

Schlesinger, Arthur M. "The Decline of Greatness" (1958). In *The Politics of Hope and the Bitter Heritage: American Liberalism in the 1960s,* edited by Arthur M. Schlesinger, 37–49. Princeton, NJ: Princeton University Press, 2008.

Schlissel, Lillian. *Women's Diaries of the Westward Journey.* 1982. New York: Schocken Books, 1992.

Schloesser, Pauline. *The Fair Sex: White Women and Racial Patriarchy in the Early American Republic.* New York: New York University Press, 2002.

Schlossman, Steven L. *Love and the American Delinquent: The Theory and Practice of "Progressive" Juvenile Justice, 1825–1920.* Chicago: University of Chicago Press, 1977.

Schwartz, Marie Jenkins. *Born in Bondage: Growing Up Enslaved in the Antebellum South.* Cambridge, MA: Harvard University Press, 2000.

Scott, Joan W. "Fantasy Echo: History and the Construction of Identity." *Critical Inquiry* 27, No. 2 (2001): 284–304.

Sedgwick, Eve Kosofsky. *Epistemology of the Closet.* 1990. Berkeley: University of California Press, 2008.

Shoemaker, Nancy. "From Longhouse to Loghouse: Household Structure among the Senecas in 1900." *American Indian Quarterly* 15, no. 3 (1991): 329–38.

Sielke, Sabine. "Crisis? What Crisis? Männlichkeit, Körper, Transdisziplinarität." In *Väter, Soldaten, Liebhaber: Männer und Männlichkeiten in der Geschichte Nordamerikas: Ein Reader,* edited by Jürgen Martschukat and Olaf Stieglitz, 43–61. Bielefeld: transcript, 2007.

———. *Reading Rape: The Rhetoric of Sexual Violence in American Literature and Culture, 1790–1990.* Princeton, NJ: Princeton University Press, 2002.

Silverman, Kaja. "Historical Trauma and Male Subjectivity." In *Psychoanalysis and Cinema,* edited by E. Ann Kaplan, 110–27. New York: Routledge, 1990.

Silverman, Kaja. *Male Subjectivity at the Margins.* New York: Routledge, 1992.

Silverstein, Louise B., and Carl F. Auerbach. "Deconstructing the Essential Father." *American Psychologist* 54, no. 6 (1999): 397–407.

Simons, Richard S., and Francis H. Parker. *Railroads of Indiana.* Bloomington: Indiana University Press, 1997.

Simpson, Harold B. *Hood's Texas Brigade: A Compendium.* Hillsboro, TX: Hill Jr. College Press, 1977.

Sitkoff, Harvard. *A New Deal for Blacks.* New York: Oxford University Press, 1978.

Slater, Suzanne. *The Lesbian Family Life Cycle.* New York: Free Press, 1995.

Slotkin, Richard. *The Fatal Environment: The Myth of the Frontier in the Age of Industrialization 1800–1890.* New York: Atheneum, 1985.

———. *Gunfighter Nation: The Myth of the Frontier in Twentieth-Century America.* New York: Harper Perennial, 1993.

———. *Regeneration through Violence: The Mythology of the American Frontier, 1600–1860.* Middletown, CT.: Wesleyan University Press, 1973.

Smith, Annick. "The Two Frontiers of Mary Ronan." *Montana: The Magazine of Western History* 39, no. 1 (1989): 28–33.

Smith, George P., II. *Family Values and the New Society: Dilemmas of the 21st Century.* Westport, CT: Praeger, 1998.

Smith, Sherry L. *Reimagining Indians: Native Americans through Anglo Eyes, 1880–1940.* New York: Oxford University Press, 2000.

Smith-Rosenberg, Carroll. "Dis-covering the Subject of the 'Great Constitutional Discussion,' 1786–1789." *Journal of American History* 79, no. 3 (1992): 841–73.

———. "The Female World of Love and Ritual: Relations between Women in Nineteenth-Century America." *Signs* 1, no. 1 (1975): 1–29.

Smyrl, Vivian E. "West. John Camden, Jr." In *Handbook of Texas Online*. www.tshaon-line.org.

Snyder, Katherine. *Bachelors, Manhood, and the Novel, 1850–1925*. Cambridge: Cambridge University Press, 1999.

———. "A Paradise of Bachelors: Remodeling Domesticity and Masculinity in the Turn-of-the-Century New York Bachelor Apartment." *Prospects* 23 (1998): 247–84.

Snyder, R. Claire. *Citizen-Soldiers and Manly Warriors: Military Service and Gender in the Civic Republican Tradition*. Lanham, MD: Rowman & Littlefield, 1999.

———. *Gay Marriage and Democracy: Equality for All*. Lanham, MD: Rowman & Littlefield, 2006.

Spence, Mark D. *Dispossessing the Wilderness: Indian Removal and the Making of the National Parks*. New York: Oxford University Press, 1999.

Spivak, Gayatri C. "Can the Subaltern Speak?" (1988). In *Colonial Discourse and Postcolonial Theory*, edited by Patrick Williams and Laura Chrisman, 66–111. New York: Columbia University Press, 1994.

Stacey, Judith. "What Comes after Patriarchy? Comparative Reflections on Gender and Power in a 'Post-patriarchal' Age." *Radical History Review* 71 (1998): 63–70.

Staloff, Darren. *Hamilton, Adams, Jefferson: The Politics of Enlightenment and the American Founding*. New York: Hill & Wang, 2005.

Stange, Maren. *Symbols of Ideal Life: Social Documentary Photography in America, 1890–1915*. Cambridge: Cambridge University Press, 1989.

Steckel, Richard H. "The Slavery Period and Its Influences on Family Change in the United States." In *Family Systems and Cultural Change*, edited by Elza Berquó and Peter Xenos, 144–58. Oxford: Clarendon, 1992.

Stein, Marc. *City of Sisterly and Brotherly Loves: Lesbian and Gay Philadelphia, 1945–1972*. Chicago: University of Chicago Press, 2000.

Stellhorn, Paul A. "Depression and Decline. Newark, N.J.: 1929–1941." PhD diss., Rutgers University, 1983.

Sternlicht, Sanford. *The Tenement Saga: The Lower East Side and Early Jewish American Writers*. Madison: University of Wisconsin Press, 2004.

Stevenson, Brenda E. *Life in Black and White: Family and Community in the Slave South*. New York: Oxford University Press, 1996.

Stewart, James I. "Economic Opportunity or Hardship? The Causes of Geographic Mobility on the Agricultural Frontier, 1860–1880." *Journal of Economic History* 69, no. 1 (2009): 238–68.

———. "Migration to the Agricultural Frontier and Wealth Accumulation, 1860–1870." *Explorations in Economic History* 43, no. 4 (2006): 547–77.

Stieglitz, Olaf. *"100 Percent American Boys": Disziplinierungsdiskurse und Ideologie im Civilian Conservation Corps, 1933–1942*. Stuttgart: Franz Steiner Verlag, 1999.

———. *Undercover: Die Kultur der Denunziation in den USA*. Frankfurt: Campus, 2013.

Stoff, Heiko. *Ewige Jugend. Konzepte der Verjüngung vom späten 19. Jahrhundert bis ins Dritte Reich*. Cologne: Böhlau, 2004.

Stoler, Ann Laura. *Race and the Education of Desire: Foucault's "History of Sexuality" and the Colonial Order of Things*. Durham, NC: Duke University Press, 1995.

Stollberg-Rilinger, Barbara, ed. *Was heißt Kulturgeschichte des Politischen?* Berlin: Duncker & Humblot, 2005.

Stratton, Joanna L. *Pioneer Women: Voices from the Kansas Frontier*. New York: Simon & Schuster, 1981.

Stremlau, Rose. "'To Domesticate and Civilize Wild Indians': Allotment and the Campaign to Reform Indian Families, 1875–1887." *Journal of Family History* 30, no. 3 (2005): 265–86.

Strickland, Charles. "A Transcendentalist Father: The Child-Rearing Practices of Bronson Alcott." *Perspectives in American History* 3 (1969): 5–73.

Strieker, Frank. *Why America Lost the War on Poverty—and How to Win It*. Chapel Hill: University of North Carolina Press, 2007.

Stryker, Susan, and Jim Van Buskirk. *Gay by the Bay: A History of Queer Culture in the San Francisco Bay Area*. San Francisco: Chronicle Books, 1996.

Sugrue, Thomas J. *The Origins of the Urban Crisis Race and Inequality in Postwar Detroit*. Princeton, NJ: Princeton University Press, 1996.

———. "Poverty in the Era of Welfare Reform: The 'Underclass' Family in Myth and Reality." In *American Families: A Multicultural Reader*, edited by Stephanie Coontz, 325–37. New York: Routledge, 2008.

———. "The Structures of Urban Poverty: The Reorganization of Space and Work in Three Periods of American History." In *The "Underclass" Debate: Views from History*, edited by Michael B. Katz, 85–117. Princeton, NJ: Princeton University Press, 1993.

Surtees, Robert J. "Canadian Indian Policy." In *Handbook of North American Indians, Vol. 4: History of Indian-White Relations*, edited by Wilcomb E. Washburn, 81–95. Washington, DC: Smithsonian Institution, 1988.

Sutton, John R. *Stubborn Children: Controlling Delinquency in the United States, 1640–1981*. Berkeley: University of California Press, 1988.

Sutton, Robert P. *Communal Utopias and the American Experience: Religious Communities, 1732–2000*. Westport, CT: Praeger, 2003.

Tarrant, Shira. *When Sex Became Gender*. New York: Routledge, 2006.

———. "When Sex Became Gender: Mirra Komarovsky's Feminism of the 1950s." *Women's Studies Quarterly* 33, nos. 3–4 (2005): 334–55.

Tasker, Fiona L., and Susan Golombok. *Growing Up in a Lesbian Family*. New York: Guilford, 1997.

Teeters, Negley. "The Early Days of the Philadelphia House of Refuge." *Pennsylvania History* 27 (1960): 165–87.

Terry, Jennifer. *An American Obsession: Science, Medicine, and Homosexuality in Modern Society*. Chicago: University of Chicago Press, 1999.

Theweleit, Klaus. *Male Fantasies*. Translated by Chris Turner et al. 1977. Minneapolis: University of Minnesota Press, 1987.

Thomas, John L. *The Liberator: William Lloyd Garrison: A Biography.* Boston: Little, Brown, 1963.

Thomas, Robert D. *The Man Who Would Be Perfect. John Humphrey Noyes and the Utopian Impulse.* Philadelphia: University of Pennsylvania Press, 1977.

Thompson, Gerald. "Another Look at Frontier/Western Historiography." In *Trails: Toward a New Western History,* edited by Patricia N. Limerick, Clyde A. Miner II, and Charles E. Rankin, 89–96. Lawrence: University Press of Kansas, 1991.

Thompson, Scott A. "A Queer Capital under Construction." *GLQ: A Journal of Lesbian and Gay Studies* 10, no. 4 (2004): 640–42.

Tosh, John. *A Man's Place: Masculinity and the Middle-Class Home in Victorian England.* New Haven, CT: Yale University Press, 1999.

Townsend, Nicholas W. *The Package Deal: Marriage, Work, and Fatherhood in Men's Lives.* Philadelphia: Temple University Press, 2002.

Trachtenberg, Alan. *The Incorporation of America: Culture and Society in the Gilded Age.* New York: Hill & Wang, 1982.

Traister, Bryce. "Academic Viagra: The Rise of American Masculinity Studies." *American Quarterly* 52, no. 2 (2000): 274–304.

Tucker, William H. *The Science and Politics of Racial Research.* Urbana: University of Illinois Press, 1994.

Tuerk, Richard. "Jacob Riis and the Jews." *New York Historical Society Quarterly* 63, no. 3 (1979): 179–202.

Tuttle, Brad R. *How Newark Became Newark: The Rise, Fall, and Rebirth of an American City.* New Brunswick, NJ: Rutgers University Press, 2009.

Tuttle, William M., Jr. *"Daddy's Gone to War": The Second World War in the Lives of Children.* New York: Oxford University Press, 1993.

Usher, David R. "Gay Marriage in California Harms Society." In *Gay and Lesbian Families,* edited by Roman Espejo, 73–79. Detroit, MI: Greenhaven Press, 2009.

Van Slyck, Abigail A. *A Manufactured Wilderness: Summer Camps and the Shaping of American Youth, 1890–1960.* Minneapolis: University of Minnesota Press, 2006.

Vinovskis, Maris A. "Family and Schooling in Colonial and Nineteenth-Century America." *Journal of Family History* 12, no. 1 (1987): 19–37.

———. "Have Social Historians Lost the Civil War? Some Preliminary Demographic Speculations." *Journal of American History* 76, no. 1 (1989): 34–58.

Waldrep, Christopher. *African Americans Confront Lynching: Strategies of Resistance from the Civil War to the Civil Rights Era.* Lanham, MD: Rowman & Littlefield, 2009.

———. *The Many Faces of Judge Lynch: Extralegal Violence in America.* New York: Palgrave, 2002.

Wall, Sharon. *The Nurture of Nature: Childhood, Antimodernism, and Ontario Summer Camps, 1920–55.* Vancouver: UBC Press, 2009.

Wallace, Michele. *Black Macho and the Myth of the Superwoman.* 1979. London: Verso, 1999.

Walsh, Margaret. "Women's Place on the American Frontier." *Journal of American Studies* 29, no. 2 (1995): 241–55.

Wayland-Smith, Ellen. *Oneida: From Free Love Utopia to the Well-Set Table*. New York: Picador, 2016.

Wayland-Smith, Giles. "Women in Paradise: Gender Roles in the Oneida Community." *Oneida Community Journal* 24, no. 1 (2010): 2–7.

Weiss, Jessica. "A Drop-In Catering Job: Middle-Class Women and Fatherhood, 1950–1980." *Journal of Family History* 24, no. 3 (1999): 374–90.

———. *To Have and to Hold: Marriage, the Baby Boom, and Social Change*. Chicago: University of Chicago Press, 2000.

Wells, Cheryl A. "Battle Time: Gender, Modernity, and Confederate Hospitals." *Journal of Social History* 35, no. 2 (2001): 409–18.

Wells, Ida B. "Southern Horrors: Lynch Law in All Its Phases" (1892). In *Southern Horrors and Other Writings: The Anti-lynching Campaign of Ida B. Wells, 1892–1900*, edited by Jacqueline Jones Royster, 49–72. Boston: Bedford, 1997.

Welter, Barbara. "The Cult of True Womanhood, 1820–1860." *American Quarterly* 18 (1966): 151–74.

Wendt, Simon. "Southern Intellectuals and the Defense of Slavery: The Proslavery Thought of George Fitzhugh and Henry Hughes." *Southern Historian* 23 (2002): 56–70.

West, Elliot. "Family Life on the Trail of the West." *History Today* 42 (1992): 33–39.

———. *Growing Up with the Country: Childhood on the Far Western Frontier*. Albuquerque: University of New Mexico Press, 1989.

———. "A Longer, Grimmer, but More Interesting Story." *Montana: The Magazine of Western History* 40, no. 3 (1990): 72–76.

West, Emily. *Chains of Love: Slave Couples in Antebellum South Carolina*. Urbana: University of Illinois Press, 2004.

———. "Surviving Separation: Cross-Plantation Marriages and the Slave Trade in Antebellum South Carolina." *Journal of Family History* 24, no. 2 (1999): 212–31.

Westbrook, Robert. "Fighting for the American Family: Private Interests and Political Obligations in World War II." In *The Power of Culture: Critical Essays in American History*, edited by Richard Wightman Fox and T. J. Jackson Lears, 195–221. Chicago: University of Chicago Press, 1993.

White, Deborah Gray. *Ar'n't I a Woman? Female Slaves in the Plantation South*. New York: Norton, 1985.

White, Janet R. "Designed for Perfection: Intersections between Architecture and Social Program at the Oneida Community." *Utopian Studies* 7, no. 2 (1996): 113–38.

White, Kevin. *The First Sexual Revolution: The Emergence of Male Heterosexuality in Modern America*. New York: New York University Press, 1993.

Whitehead, Margaret, ed. *They Call Me Father: Memoirs of Father Nicolas Coccola*. Vancouver: UBC Press, 1988.

Whites, LeeAnn. *The Civil War as a Crisis in Gender: Augusta, Georgia, 1860–1890*. Athens: University of Georgia Press, 1995.

Wickberg, Daniel. "Heterosexual White Male: Some Recent Inversions in American Cultural History." *Journal of American History* 92, no. 1 (2005): 136–59.

Widener, Daniel. "Writing Watts: Budd Schulberg, Black Poetry, and the Cultural War on Poverty." *Journal of Urban History* 34, no. 4 (2008): 665–87.

Wiebe, Robert H. *The Search for Order, 1877–1920.* New York: Hill & Wang, 1967.

Williams, Heather A. *Self-Taught: African American Education in Slavery and Freedom.* Chapel Hill: University of North Carolina Press, 2005.

Wilson, Joan Hoff. "The Illusion of Change: Women in the American Revolution." In *The American Revolution: Explorations in the History of American Radicalism,* edited by Alfred Young, 383–446. DeKalb: Northern Illinois University Press, 1976.

Wilson, Lisa. *Ye Heart of a Man: The Domestic Life of Men in Colonial New England.* New Haven, CT: Yale University Press, 1999.

Wood, Amy. *Lynching and Spectacle: Witnessing Racial Violence in America, 1890–1940.* Chapel Hill: University of North Carolina Press, 2009.

Wood, Gordon S. *Revolutionary Characters: What Made the Founders Different.* New York: Penguin, 2006.

Wood, Ruth P. *Lolita in Peyton Place: Highbrow, Middlebrow, and Lowbrow Novels of the 1950s.* New York: Garland, 1995.

Woodward, C. Vann. *Mary Chesnut's Civil War.* New Haven, CT: Yale University Press, 1993.

Wooster, Ralph A., ed. *Lone Star Blue and Gray: Essays on Texas in the Civil War.* Austin: Texas State Historical Association, 1995.

Worster, Donald. "Beyond the Agrarian Myth." In *Trails: Toward a New Western History,* edited by Patricia N. Limerick, Clyde A. Miner II, and Charles E. Rankin, 3–25. Lawrence: University Press of Kansas, 1991.

Wrathall, John D. "Provenance as Text: Reading the Silences around Sexuality in Manuscript Collections." *Journal of American History* 79, no. 1 (1992): 165–78.

Wyatt-Brown, Bertram. "The Mask of Obedience: Male Slave Psychology in the Old South." *American Historical Review* 93, no. 5 (1988): 1228–52.

Yazawa, Melvin. *From Colonies to Commonwealth: Familial Ideology and the Beginnings of the American Republic.* Baltimore: Johns Hopkins University Press, 1985.

Yochelson, Bonnie. "Jacob A. Riis, Photographer 'After a Fashion.'" In *Rediscovering Jacob Riis: Exposure Journalism and Photography in Turn-of-the-Century New York,* edited by Bonnie Yochelson and Daniel Czitrom, 121–227. New York: New Press, 2007.

Yochelson, Bonnie, and Daniel Czitrom. *Rediscovering Jacob Riis: Exposure Journalism and Photography in Turn-of-the-Century New York.* New York: New Press, 2007.

Young, Terence, *Heading Out: A History of American Camping.* Ithaca, NY: Cornell University Press, 2017.

Young Men's Christian Association. *YMCA in America, 1851–2001: A History of Accomplishments over 150 Years.* Chicago: YMCA of the USA, 2000.

Zaborowska, Magdalena J. *How We Found America: Reading Gender through East European Immigrant Narratives.* Chapel Hill: University of North Carolina Press, 1995.

Zagarri, Rosemarie. "Morals, Manners, and the Republican Mother." *American Quarterly* 44, no. 2 (1992): 192–215.

———. "The Rights of Man and Woman in Post-revolutionary America." *William and Mary Quarterly* 55, no. 2 (1998): 203–30.

Zamir, Shamoon. "Native Agency and the Making of 'The North American Indian.'" *American Indian Quarterly* 31, no. 4 (2007): 613–53.

Zantop, Susanne. *Colonial Fantasies: Conquest, Family, and Nation in Precolonial Germany, 1770–1870*. Durham, NC: Duke University Press, 1997.

Zellner, William. *Extraordinary Groups: An Examination of Unconventional Lifestyles.* 7th ed. New York: Worth, 2001.

INDEX

abolitionist movement (slavery), 45–49, 53–54, 57, 62

absent fathers: African American, 209–10; in Early Republic, 29; fathers' rights movement on, 237; during frontier movement, 68, 70, 71, 80; theories on impacts of, 142, 164, 185–86, 207, 211, 220; during World War II, 185–86

Adams, John, 7, 9, 12

advice manuals, 188; Early Republic, 12, 13–14, 15, 18; for queer parents, 230

African American fathers: absent, 209–10; Black Panthers role as, 209; Civil War aftermath and, 93; Cosby portrait of, 219–20; father-son relationships for, 45, 49, 214–15, 223; financial support role and struggles for, 5, 179, 181, 200–202, 216–18, 219, 245; Komarovsky study exclusion of, 178; Million Man March on betterment of, 219–20, 239–40; Moynihan Report on, 209–12; Obama on, 221–23; under slavery, 4, 46–47, 49, 51, 56–58, 61–62; unemployed, of 1930s, 179, 181; wives role and relation with, 210, 212, 215–16. *See also* Jones, Thomas H.; *Killer of Sheep*

African Americans: as Civil War soldiers, 84; families under slavery, 49–53, 244; gender roles and relations, 210, 212, 215–16; Great Depression for, 177–80, 181; Great Migration impact for, 206; in Indian Guides, 164; lynchings of, 205–6; manhood and poverty relation for, 200–203, 208, 216–17; manhood and slavery relation for, 47, 49, 50, 51, 56, 57, 61, 204–5, 210–11, 222; marriage statistics for, 219; middle-class pursuit of, 213–14; *Native Son* portrait of, 206–7; 1980s family discourse and census on, 218–19; nuclear family portrait for, 213–15, 216; patriarchal structures in portraits of, 207–8; poverty of 1970s for, 200–203, 208, 212–13; scientific racism on, 121; slave kinship contrast with nuclear family, 51–52, 244; sovereign power struggle for, 208–9; stereotypes, challenging, 204, 212, 216, 218, 223; stereotypes of, 203, 204–7, 209, 210, 212–13, 215, 216, 218, 220, 223; women, stereotypes of, 210, 212, 215; World War II veterans, discrimination against, 191. *See also* slavery

agrarian myth, 65, 66

AIDS/HIV, 226, 229

alcohol consumption, 18–20, 30–31, 170

Alcott, William, 7–8, 13, 16

American Civil War. *See* Civil War

American Dilemma (Myrdal), 179–80, 211

American expansion. *See* frontier movement

American Indians. *See* Native Americans

American Revolution: father model opposing patriarchal tyranny in, 9–10; principles behind, 1, 7–8, 49–50; self-government paradigm with, 7–8; slavery in opposition to principles of, 49–50, 61. *See also* Early Republic

Anglo-Saxon exceptionalism, 66, 123, 167, 169

The Audacity of Hope (Obama), 221, 222–23

bachelorhood: Early Republic, 96–97; 1950s, 188–89, 194–95

bachelorhood, urban (1870–1930), 4; aesthetic of, 105–6; commentators on phenomenon of, 97–99, 115–16; 1890 statistics of, 98; family ideal threat from, 95–96; father figures in, 94, 99, 102, 104–5, 106–7; female companionship/prostitutes of, 97–99, 108; homosocial and homoerotic elements of, 95, 107–11, 115–16; immigration relation to, 95, 96–97; living quarters for, 103–5, *105*; loneliness of, 107; sexual and social sciences on, 95, 113–17; sexualized connotations about, 106; societal treatment of, 94; YMCA role in, 95, 99, 104–12. *See also* McBurney, Robert R.

back-to-nature movement: in boys' education, 150–52, 160; for father-son relationships, 143, 152, 158–60, 164; manhood and masculinity in, 150; in modernity response, 142, 143, 148–49, 150–54; rise of, 146–52; Roosevelt, T., role in, 148–49, 150; YMCA engagement with, 143, 151–52, 158–60, 164

Bakke, E. Wight, 169, 172

Beatniks, 197, 228

The Birth of a Nation (film), 203, 205, 220

Bixby, J., 97–98

The Black Atlantic (Gilroy), 46

Black Macho and the Myth of the Superwoman (Wallace), 208

Black Panthers, 208–9

Blankenhorn, David, 237, 240

Bohemian lifestyle, 98, 195

Bowers v. Hardwick (1986), 226

Bowne, Jacob T., 106

Boy Scouts of America, 147, 151–52

Brainerd, Cephas, 99, 102, 104

Brandt, John C., 109–11

breadwinning. *See* financial support

Broken Arrow (film), 159

Brown, Elaine, 209

Burgess, Ernest W., 98, 115–16

Burnett, Charles, 200–204, 206, 208, 217. *See also Killer of Sheep*

California. *See* frontier movement (1850–1880); San Francisco; Watts, Los Angeles

Canadian indigenous people. *See* Ojibwe Indians

Carlisle Indian Industrial School, 145

Cavan, Ruth S., 167, 170

CCC. *See* Civilian Conservation Corps

Chaplan, Sadie, 136

Chauncey, George, 95, 109

Chief Caribou. *See* Friday, Joe

childhood education: back-to-nature movement in boys, 150–52, 160; Early Republic fathers' role in, 14, 15–16, 18–19; gendered approach to, 142; modern fathers' role in, 153–54; in Oneida Community, 32, 37–38; reform movements on, 19–21

child labor, 127, 129–30, 135–36

child rearing: Early Republic views on, 12, 28; in Oneida Community, 36–37; for queer parents, 224–25, 229–30, 231, 233, 234–35, 241–42

children: fatherhood and genetic relation to, 243; frontier, 64–65, 67, 69–78, 80; Riis on slum, 128–30, 140; urban immigrant, 127, 128–30, 135–36

The Children of the Poor (Riis), 128

Chinese immigrants, 73

Christian conservative movement, 229, 233–34, 238

Christianity: agrarian myth and, 65; Civil War father faith in, 91–92; family values movement and, 218, 239,

masculinity. *See* manhood and masculinity

McBurney, Robert R., *101*; aesthetic of, 105–6; emigration from Ireland of, 94, 99–100; living quarters at YMCA, 104–6, *105*; male intimacy and companionship for, 107–8, 110, 116–17; moral crusade of, 99; paternal role at YMCA of, 94, 99, 102, 104–5, 106–7; social mobility of, 102–3; YMCA introduction for, 100–101

McConaughy, James, 108

middle class: African American pursuit of, 213–14; family ideal relation to model of, 11–12, 51, 62; frontier life striving for, 76, 77; unemployed fathers of 1930s, 167–68, 169; violence in Early Republic, 17–18

military service, 13; gender and racial identity in, 83–84, 227; homosexuality conflicts with, 225, 227; manhood and, 84, 182; women in, 227. *See also* Civil War fathers; World War II veteran fathers

Milk, Harvey, 229, 231

Miller, H. Thane, 107–8

Million Man March (1995), 219–20, 239–40

Mills, Charles W., 28

modern fathers: childhood education role of, 153–54; crisis, approach to, 141–42, 154, 164, 244–45; father-son relationships for, 142–43, 145, 152–55, 158–60, 164; Freud theories and, 142, 154

modernity, 142–43, 145, 148–54, 164

Morse, Richard, 104, 107

mothers: Early Republic role of, 12, 28; fathers' rights movement on single, 224, 240–41; Indian Guides involvement of, 154–55, 159; in Oneida Community, 36–37

Moynihan, Daniel Patrick, 209–12

Murphy Brown (television show), 224, 240–41, 242

"mutual criticism," 38–39

Muzzey, Artemas, 15–16, 17

Myrdal, Gunnar, 179–80, 211

National Association for the Advancement of Colored People (NAACP), 206

National Fatherhood Initiative, 237, 239, 240

Native American fathers, 4, 141–43, 146, 147, 160, 244

Native Americans: assimilation of, 142, 144–45; consumption of, culture, 149–50; destruction of, 163–64; *End of the Trail* sculpture illustration of, 149–50, 163–64; frontier movement impact on, 65; land legislation impacting, 144–45; nuclear family contrasted with kinship of, 146, 244; paternalism in treatment of, 143–44, 151, 157; reeducation policy with, 145; romance and myth around, 142–43, 146, 147, 148–50, 151, 159–60, 162, 164; stereotypes of, 146; tourism impact for, 149–50. *See also* Crow Indians; Father and Son Indian Guides, YMCA's; Ojibwe Indians

Native Son (Wright), 206–7

Neal, Mark Anthony, 219

The Negro Family (Moynihan), 209–12

The Negro Family in the United States (Frazier), 179

New Deal programs and policies, 167, 168, 174–77, 179, 218

New Republic. *See* Early Republic

New York City: bachelorhood in, 94–112, *105*; Irish immigrant wave in mid-1800s, 94, 99–100; Jewish immigrants in, 4, 118–19, 120, 121–22, 130; YMCA in, 94, 99, 100–102, *103*, 104–12, *105*

New York House of Refuge, 21, 22

impact for, 186–87, 190, 191, 227; Kennedy portrait of, 198–99; manhood crisis for, 182, 183–84, 189, 192–93, 198–99, 245; *The Man in the Gray Flannel Suit* portrait of, 4, 182–84, 187, 188–89, 191–96; "other-directed" concerns about, 192–93; "playboy" persona contrast to, 194–95; sovereign power loss of, 193–94

WPA. *See* Works Progress Administration

Wright, Richard, 206–7

Yezierska, Anzia and Bernard, 118, 137

YIVO Institute for Jewish Research, 119, 137

YMCA. *See* Young Men's Christian Association

Young, Allen, 229

Young Men's Christian Association (YMCA), 4; on bachelor "danger zones," 99; bachelorhood role of, 95, 99, 104–12; back-to-nature movement role of, 143, 151–52, 158–60, 164; criticism and controversy with, 109–11; Eastman work for, 147, 152; function and goals of, 94–95, 100–101, 109; homosocial and homosexual relations in, 95, 107–12; McBurney introduction to, 100–101; McBurney living quarters at, 104–6, *105*; McBurney paternal role at, 94, 99, 102, 104–5, 106–7; moral campaign of, 99; New York City, 94, 99, 100–102, *103*, 104–12, *105*. *See also* Father and Son Indian Guides

Zeisel, Hans, 166

ABOUT THE AUTHOR

Jürgen Martschukat is Professor of North American History in the Department of History at Erfurt University. He is the author and editor of numerous books, among them most recently *Das Zeitalter der Fitness* (The Age of Fitness, 2019) and *Geschichte der Männlichkeiten* (An Introduction to the History of Masculinities, second revised edition, 2018).

Petra Goedde is Director of Temple University's Center for the Humanities (CHAT) and Associate Professor of History at Temple University. She is the author of *GIs and Germans: Culture, Gender, and Foreign Relations, 1945–1949* (2003), co-editor of *The Human Rights Revolution: An International History* (2012), and co-editor of *The Oxford Handbook of the Cold War* (2013).